# PUTTING IT ALL TOGETHER

## The Directed Reading Lesson in the Secondary Content Classroom

**GLORIA A. NEUBERT**

*Towson University*

**ELIZABETH A. WILKINS**

*Northern Illinois University*

PEARSON

Boston ■ New York ■ San Francisco
Mexico City ■ Montreal ■ Toronto ■ London ■ Madrid ■ Munich ■ Paris
Hong Kong ■ Singapore ■ Tokyo ■ Cape Town ■ Sydney

**Series Editor:** *Aurora Martínez Ramos*
**Editorial Assistant:** *Erin Beatty*
**Senior Marketing Manager:** *Elizabeth Fogarty*
**Editorial-Production Service:** *Omegatype Typography, Inc.*
**Manufacturing Buyer:** *Andrew Turso*
**Composition and Prepress Buyer:** *Linda Cox*
**Cover Administrator:** *Joel Gendron*
**Electronic Composition:** *Omegatype Typography, Inc.*

**Library of Congress Cataloging-in-Publication Data**

CIP data not available at time of publication.
ISBN 0-205-34384-8

Printed in the United States of America

10  9  8  7  6  5  4  3  2  1        08  07  06  05  04  03

*To Dr. James B. Binko, who has inspired the educational community with his spirit, wisdom, and teaching excellence.*

# CONTENTS

# SAMPLE LESSON PLANS

# ACKNOWLEDGMENTS

The authors wish to acknowledge the outstanding editorial support of Lauren DiPaula and Erin Murphy and the technological support of David Binko. Additionally, this text would not be a reality without the lessons and activities contributed by the following educators: Curt Alford, Carolyn Bendyna, Melissa Brothers, Aaron Copeland, Ann Dolan, Kelly Dison Guthrie, Emmy Furbish, Nancy Gibson, Cynthia Hendrick, Justin Hill, Christine Jankowski, Katie Karcher, Susan Miller, Bethany Petr, Laurie Pham, Kevin Phelps, Deborah Rambo, Matthew Redmond, Amanda Reuter-Lancaster, Heather Semies, Erin Stevens, Kelly Throne, Tracy Thrush, Al Tsamoutalis, Betsy Turner, Tina Wasowicz, Lauren Wilensky, and Cathie Yeagle. We are also grateful for the ideas and resources shared by science majors Eric Benjamin, M. Allison Fischer, John M. Fitz, Julie Gosewisch, and Vicki Hipszer, which helped us compose the lesson on biodiversity.

We would also like to thank the following reviewers: Margaret L. Janz, Jackson University; Kathy Lennox, Mattacheese Middle School; Michael Moore, Georgia Southern University; Christine Oxenford, Earle B. Wood Middle School; and Roxanne Reedyk, Riverview Alternative High School.

Special thanks for their optimism and support go to Carol Starr, Montgomery County Public Schools; Mark Stout, Howard County Public Schools; and David Prudente, Baltimore County Public Schools. Finally, Gloria Neubert is indebted to Joseph and Nathan Binko for helping her maintain balance while completing this project.

# CHAPTER ONE

# IF YOU ARE READING THIS BOOK, YOU ARE EXCEPTIONAL

Reading is easy if you already know how to do it.

—*Edgar Dale, Professor of Educational Communications*

If you are reading this text, you are probably a veteran teacher or teacher candidate. You have chosen secondary education—middle/junior or high school teaching—because you enjoy the subject you teach or will teach. You most likely have taken a host of college courses and workshops in your subject matter. As an expert in content knowledge, you are able to read with relative ease the material—textbooks, journal and newspaper articles, Internet resources, and pamphlets—related to your subject. And that is why you are exceptional. You are the "exception," not the "rule."

Your students, however, are the "rule." They may come to you with an appreciation for your expert area, but they themselves are not experts. Because they are not experts, they cannot read the same scope of material (topics and formats) in your discipline. You will need to help them become better readers to help them understand, and excel in, your discipline.

## BUT I DIDN'T BECOME A TEACHER TO TEACH READING

That is exactly the disposition of this book. You are a *content* teacher, not a *reading* teacher. Your primary responsibility is to teach your students the knowledge and processes of your content area: math, science, social studies, consumer/family science, music, health, English, art, foreign language, physical education, and so on. However, secondary teachers who include reading strategies in their lessons significantly increase their students' chances of mastering content.

Over the past two decades, the authors of this text have worked with secondary teachers who, like you, are experts in their content areas. They realize the importance of their students' using reading as a learning tool for mastering the knowledge and processes of their subjects. We have shaped our Reading in the Content Areas workshops and courses to begin directly in the planning stage of a teacher's day—writing lesson plans, following the format of a Directed Reading Lesson in the secondary content areas. This lesson plan format is a step-by-step outline for a teacher-facilitated, learner-centered lesson that uses reading as the primary source of content knowledge. Individual reading-to-learn strategies are then introduced as we dissect each of the steps of the Directed Reading Lesson. We have chosen this approach rather than exposing teachers to a myriad of reading strategies in isolation and then leaving them to decide how to infuse them appropriately into their lesson plans. Our global-to-analytic approach results in a content-driven lesson plan with reading-to-learn strategies embedded, ready to be executed in the content classroom.

The Directed Reading Lesson for secondary content areas has its roots in the Directed Reading Activity (DRA) used in elementary schools since the early 1900s. Emmett Betts (1946) in his seminal work *Foundations of Reading Instruction* outlined the steps of the DRA and justified each part of the activity with "basic principles of learning which have been experimentally appraised and time tested" (p. 490). The format of the Directed Reading Lesson plan presented in this text has been adapted to focus on secondary content learning and more recently proven reading-to-learn strategies, while still maintaining the enduring "basic principles of learning."

We are gratified by the unsolicited, anecdotal reports from secondary teachers of standard, gifted, English as a Second Language (ESL), and special needs students, as well as administrators, all of whom have witnessed student success in mastering content as a result of learning guided through a Directed Reading Lesson approach. Statements like the following are representative:

*I've taught meiosis before—for several years—with varying degrees of success, but never have I experienced the level of learning and enthusiasm my students had this year when I used the Directed Reading Lesson format!*

—High School Science Teacher

*The Directed Reading Lesson approach to reading greatly improved my students' success. For so many years, I felt helpless when my students resisted learning my content area because they couldn't read. The Directed Reading Lesson provided me with a structure to motivate students to learn about my content area. Now I know how to build their background knowledge before they start reading and how to model and guide their thinking while they read.*

—Middle School English Teacher

*All students were able to summarize the story well as a result of my DRL approach. Even my autistic student's summary showed much more coherence and understanding of the reading.*

—High School Teacher of Developmentally Disabled Students

*I really believe in the Directed Reading Lesson. It pulls together all the pieces of effective reading instruction into one model. Our school believes in it so much that we have included it as one of our school improvement plan tasks. We have only three tasks and the DRL is one of them!*

—Middle School Staff Development Teacher

*Through a skillfully crafted Directed Reading Lesson, you extended your students' understanding of "The Star Spangled Banner." Your students were engaged in active learning; the graphic organizer provided direction without encumbering your students' reading of the selection; the background information provided from the Fort McHenry website not only extended your students' understanding of the poem, but also grounded the piece in its historical context; the critical re-reading of the poem challenged them to analyze why their National Anthem affects them every time they hear it. This lesson was clearly a part of a series of lessons designed to appropriately address the indicators of the United States History curriculum.*

—Social Studies Department Chair's Observation Report of a First-Year Teacher's Lesson

*Instruction on the Directed Reading Lesson allows my teachers to go back into their classes on Monday, continue teaching their discipline material, and begin or enhance their inclusion of good reading practices. Additionally, the Directed Reading Lesson reinforces so many aspects of good teaching!*

—High School Principal

*Teachers who follow the steps in the Directed Reading Lesson find that students access information about their content area in depth and retain and apply that information. Most importantly, they understand what reading involves and why they need to approach reading assignments intentionally and strategically. . . . The use of the Directed Reading Lesson has improved student learning more than any other professional development topic in my twenty-eight years with this school system.*

—Middle School Coordinator of Instruction

*We are particularly interested in teacher candidates who are able to articulate ideas about the integration of reading strategies as a component of social studies instruction. We have discovered that students from your program are the best prepared for such interview questions. Without fail, they possess a deep understanding of the nuances of such instruction and how it is applied to social studies. These candidates allude to sophisticated pre-reading strategies, the challenges of expository text structure, all within the model of a Directed Reading Lesson informed by recent research on teaching and learning.*

—Social Studies Curriculum Coordinator

Recently, we have also begun to collect quantitative evidence from teachers who are using the Directed Reading Lesson. At one workshop we conducted on the Directed Reading Lesson, eighteen English, ESL, and special needs teachers from three different school systems collected data on 274 students in grades 6–12, including standard, honors, ESL, learning-disabled, and emotionally disturbed students. During the next three weeks (actually twelve school days), these teachers taught their regular curriculum and employed their regular curriculum materials, including both narrative and expository readings, ranging from the second grade reading level to advanced materials, such as literary criticism of *The Scarlet Letter.*

For the first reading, the teachers employed the "assign" method: read the chapter and answer the questions. For many, this was normal operating procedure. For the subsequent readings, they taught using the Directed Reading Lesson procedure. After each reading and before the entire class discussion, students wrote a summary of what they learned from the reading. The summaries were scored using a 4-point rubric developed by the State Department of Education for state assessment purposes.

Results revealed that without the Directed Reading Lesson, student summaries averaged a score of 1.8. With the first Directed Reading Lesson, the average score improved to 2.6, and by the second application of the Directed Reading procedure, summary scores were averaging 3.0.

The primary goal of this book is to teach you to use the Directed Reading Lesson format so that your students can learn the knowledge and processes of your content with text. We begin by examining the process you do so well—reading.

## WHAT IS READING?

Let's examine what you must do when you read. Go back and reread the first two pages of this book. Can you discern what your brain is doing?

Probably not; it happens so naturally for you. You read on automatic pilot (proving again how "exceptional" you are as a reader).

Reading is one of the most difficult assignments you will ever request of your brain. The following is a physiological description, based on magnetic resonance imaging research, of what your brain does to comprehend just one word:

The word [graphics] (for example, *dog*) is first recorded in the visual cortex [in the back of the brain], then decoded by a structure on the left [back] side of the brain called the *angular gyrus,* which separates it into its basic sounds, or phonemes (e.g., the letters d-o-g are pronounced "duh, awh, guh"). This process activates Brocas' area [front, left side of the brain] so that the word can be identified. The brain's vocabulary store and reasoning and concept formation abilities, along with activity in Wernicke's area [middle, left side of the brain], combine to provide meaning producing the thought of a furry animal that barks. All this occurs in a fraction of a second. . . . Keep in mind that although the process outlined . . . appears linear and singular, it is really bidirectional and parallel, with many phonemes being processed at the same time. (Sousa, 2001, p. 183)

All of this to comprehend the graphic and semantic features of *one* printed word! And this is only to process two of at least five cueing systems we use to make meaning of textual material. How complex the reading process is, yet for those of us who do it well, how very easy it seems. But then, we—the teachers—are most likely the exceptions. Most of our students are the rule.

When secondary content teachers use the term *reading,* they typically mean *comprehension,* understanding what one reads—making meaning from print—in order to learn content information. To accomplish this end, your brain must activate at least five different cueing systems: graphic, semantic, syntactic, experiential background, and text structure. These cueing systems are sources of information your brain engages in recursively to make meaning of textual material.

## Graphics

The print on the page is the *graphic* cueing system. This is the printed representation of speech sounds or spoken words. The print you are looking at now is an example of a graphic cueing system—an alphabetic one you must be able to decode to derive meaning from this text. A graphic cueing system can also be a pictorial device that displays some meaning, for example, a bar graph showing the relationship between harvest quantities and rainfall amounts, or a flowchart that demonstrates the steps to the enactment of a bill into a law.

Without the ability to decode, you have little chance of arriving at meaning. For example, answer the following question:

⚐□ℳ◆　◆≈ℳ　◆◆■　□⺐◆ℳ　⺐■　◆≈ℳ　ℳ♋◆◆　□□　⺐■
◆≈ℳ　◆ℳ◆◆⬱

Unless you have been schooled in decoding Wingdings, a script available with some word processing programs, you no doubt cannot answer the question. You have no idea what the question is because you have no command of the graphic cueing system. But now try to derive meaning from the same question in a familiar graphic system:

Does the sun rise in the East or in the West?

Easy?

"Substantial facility in the accurate and automatic decoding of words" is necessary for comprehension (Duke & Pearson, 2002, p. 208). Students who have not developed at least minimum fluency with decoding of script by the time they are in secondary schools need assistance over and above what you, the content teacher, can do to help them use reading-to-learn strategies. Usually readers with such disabilities require intensive, remedial reading instruction with an educator, usually a reading specialist, who is trained in learning-to-read techniques.

## Semantics

Now try answering this question:

Have the authors of this text used any malapropisms in this chapter?

No doubt, you can decode this sentence. Whether you can answer this question, however, depends on whether you know the meanings of the words, especially *malapropisms*. Thus, another cueing system readers must employ to make meaning of print material is *semantic* knowledge, the vocabulary of the reading selection, the meaning of words.

**REFLECT**

Students in your classes must deal with three different categories of vocabulary words: general, nonspecific, and technical. Below are three examples of each category. Can you differentiate among the types?

| **General** | **Nonspecific** | **Technical** |
|-------------|-----------------|---------------|
| affluent | race | binomial |
| youth | court | plate tectonics |
| clean | radical | simile |

*General* vocabulary refers to words whose definitions remain constant and appear in the reading material of all the disciplines. Because of their relative stability and frequency of occurrence, general vocabulary words are the easiest for students to learn and use in comprehending reading.

*Nonspecific* vocabulary refers to words that change meaning, often from discipline to discipline. For example, students can learn the dimensions of, and positions on, a tennis *court* in physical education, learn the judicial ramifications of appearing in *court* when studying social studies, and then read about a gentleman *courting* a lady in a piece of romantic poetry. Because of the variability of definitions of nonspecific vocabulary, these words can cause memory interference for readers, which requires careful discernment during the reading process.

*Technical* vocabulary refers to words that have only one definition and are usually unique to a particular content area. They are often labels for concepts that have much information associated with them in that discipline. Because of students' limited exposure to these words and the complexity of meanings associated with them, technical vocabulary words can make reading difficult.

## Syntax

Look at the following list of words. Read each one aloud to prove you can decode the graphics. Then ask yourself if you know the meaning of each word. If you do not, look the unknown words up in the dictionary or ask someone to explain the meaning of the words to you, so we assume that you can employ the first two reading cueing systems already discussed—graphic and semantic—before going on to the next activity.

| | | | |
|---|---|---|---|
| a | cones | function | on |
| as | daily | graph | shows |
| below | data | line | snow |
| best | fit | maximum | sold |
| collected | for | number | temperature |
| | | of | the |

Now read the following sentence, which is composed only of the words above, and explain the sentence in your own words.

The graph below shows a line of best fit for data collected on the number of snow cones sold as a function of the maximum daily temperatures.

This sentence is taken from the Maryland High School Assessment Prototype (Maryland State Department of Education, 1998–1999) and is representative of reading required of students taking Algebra I in secondary school. No doubt, you found it easier to understand the meanings of the isolated vocabulary words than to comprehend the words when they were strung together in a sentence. Why is that?

Read the next sentence, taken from a ninth grade English reading test (Maryland State Department of Education, 1998–1999), and determine what your brain has to do to construct initial meaning from this sentence:

> With a last kiss for her husband, John, Ramsey and her three women passengers (two sisters-in-law and one family friend) began a historic journey of four thousand miles from New York City to San Francisco, making her the first woman to drive an automobile across the United States.

In both the algebra and the English example, you are wrestling with the third cueing system—*syntax.* Syntax is the order of words in sentences, clauses, and phrases. A reader's intuitive knowledge of patterns of language derived from listening and speaking helps determine meaning. Thus in the English example, we know that Ramsey's husband's name is John by the placement of *John,* next to *husband.* But in the algebra sentence, putting the words *line, of, best,* and *fit* together into the concept *line of best fit* forces us to determine a meaning, including—but beyond—the meaning of the four isolated words.

The complexity of the syntax, that is, the number and placement of embedded clauses and phrases, can also make meaning more complicated. The reader must take each concept and relate it in a syntactically prescribed way to the other concepts. So, in the English sentence, we must connect the following thought units:

> With a last kiss
> for her [*who is "her?"*] husband, John,
> Ramsey [*"her" above*] and her [*Ramsey's*] three women passengers
> (two sisters-in-law and one family friend)
> began a historic journey
> of four thousand miles
> from New York City
> to San Francisco
> making her [*Ramsey*] the first woman
> to drive an automobile
> across the United States.

The thinking required to comprehend this one, albeit lengthy, sentence, involves the brain in complex problem solving that connects all the concepts within and among the phrases and clauses and yields valid comprehension.

Long sentences, or sentences with many thought units, are not the only type that complicate comprehension. Short sentences can also contain syntactic structures that cause readers to pause in their understanding. For example:

> Nathan loves skateboarding. This concerns his parents.

Word substitutions (anaphora), such as replacing *skateboarding* with *This* in the sentence above, require readers to understand a syntactic interpretation that requires a backward reference. Additionally, clauses assigned as the subjects of sentences (e.g., *Driving the expressway every day can be exhausting.*), relative clauses (e.g., *The woman who is sitting on the bench is my sister.*), and even appositives (e.g., *Freeman, the director of the show, gave us the tickets.*) can cause comprehension problems.

Fluency with complex syntactic structures requires that students be exposed to such structures through wide and frequent reading. Spoken syntax tends to be more informal, repetitive, and less complex than written sentence structures and therefore can be a supplement to, but not a substitute for, helping students become better comprehenders of written material. One only becomes a better reader by reading.

## Experiential Background

We come now to the fourth cueing system readers must activate for comprehension— *experiential background.* Read the following passage (Gutkoska in Stover, Neubert, Lawlor, 1993, p. 71), which is written on a fourth grade level in terms of vocabulary and syntactic complexity. Your purpose-for-reading is to determine:

1.  In what kind of activity are the young men engaged?
2.  What was the final team score?

> **STATE CHAMPIONS**
> John Martin knew that the entire contest rested on his shoulders. With the score 19–18 in favor of State High, John realized that his match with Bill Favor would determine the state championship. With the speed and cunning of a fox, Bill Favor from Alton High managed a take down and near fall in the first few seconds of the match. Through two and one-half periods the score remained the same, but finally in the closing seconds of the final period, John managed a reversal. The students from State High were thrilled and screamed with delight. Shortly later the bell sounded. The contest had come to the end. At last, the championship had been decided.

If you are having difficulty answering the two purpose-for-reading questions, do not feel singled-out. Although they can decode the passage, know the meaning of the words, and are not struggling with syntax that is too complex, many of the participants in our classes and workshops cannot answer the questions. It is not their graphic, semantic, or syntactic systems that are inadequate for comprehending this reading, but their *topical experiential backgrounds.* These are educators and future educators who have either not been to a wrestling match or who have watched a match but have not attended to its scoring system. If you were able to answer the two purpose-for-reading questions, in all likelihood you have had direct or vicarious experience with the sport of wrestling and its scoring system.

Everything we read requires us to bring some background to that reading. That is why no two people ever comprehend a piece in exactly the same way. Their experiential backgrounds are different; therefore, each person filters the information differently. And just as inadequate backgrounds hinder comprehension, enriched backgrounds facilitate comprehension. For example, we once taught a seventh grade boy who could barely read content material on a fourth grade level but could read a highly technical Toyota engine manual with ease because he had worked with his father in the family-owned motor repair business since he was very little. His comprehension of this engine manual was facilitated by his life experiences.

## Text Structure

The fifth cueing system readers use for comprehension is *text structure.* A text structure is the major thought pattern required for the reading, such as comparison and/or contrast, cause and effect, chronological order/sequence, or problem and solution. For example, a reading in a health class may require the understanding of the causes and effects of stress on the body, and a reading in a math class may be based on the text structure of sequence, the steps in solving word problems using algebraic models.

Text structures may also be operationally defined as the organization of a particular genre of writing, for example, the format of a recipe (ingredients, steps in preparation, nutritional information) or of a scientific journal article (background, design of the study, results, conclusions, implications, further research).

## SO WHY REQUIRE READING IN THE CONTENT CLASSROOM?

If reading is such a complex process, why use it in the secondary classroom as a learning medium? Why not put the books on the shelf and show videos and films? Or just lecture to the students? According to Samuel Johnson, "People have . . . got a strange opinion that everything should be taught by lectures. Now, I cannot see that lectures can do so much as reading the books from which the lectures are taken." Research has revealed that "lecture continues to be the most prevalent teaching mode in secondary and higher education, despite overwhelming evidence that it produces the lowest degree of retention for most learners" (Sousa, 2001, p. 95). Just because students have been told the content information is no guarantee that the students understand the content information.

Our experience convinces us that students in secondary school can learn more effectively by reading than by listening and viewing. When students read, they actively construct meaning for themselves. To process and learn new content knowledge, students must be able to connect the new learning with information already in their backgrounds, information stored in memory. They must search through, activate, retrieve, and apply this prior knowledge. While reading, students are able to control time for these private, thoughtful connections.

Reading is a recursive process, not a linear one. Readers who are comprehending and learning do not move from left to right on each line of the page and from top to bottom of the page in a linear, time-consistent fashion. Good readers move back and forth on the line and page, depending on whether they must return to some previous information to understand. They move back and forth, utilizing graphic, semantic, syntactic, background, and structure cues. They move back and forth when they make connections among various points in the reading. Often they pause, without even noticing, and reflect on what they have just read. This pause, replay, recursive process is not possible in a lecture or viewing experience.

Also, the ability to read is a lifetime gift. We give this gift by insisting that our students learn how to comprehend and learn from a variety of reading material. Scot Lehigh (1999) of the *Boston Globe* said it so well:

> [R]eading is one of life's most accessible pleasures. . . . Reading, after all, is not just the portal to imagination and understanding. It is also . . . the way we move beyond workaday concerns to establish an enduring life of the mind that makes us something more than what we own or how we make our living. (p. F10)

Long after our students have forgotten the contributions of the Mesopotamian culture, which vitamin the skin is able to produce when exposed to sunlight, or how Shakespeare employed verbal irony, the ability to read will sustain them through a lifetime of academic and personal endeavors.

Developing this lifetime skill of reading is not easy, however. At times, you may need to tell your students that reading is a demanding mental process, one that requires focus and a huge dose of diligence on their part. If one wants to do it well, one has to practice, and that takes patience, persistence, and self-discipline. Henry David Thoreau said, "To read well . . . is a noble exercise . . . one that will task the reader more than any exercise which the customs of the day esteem. It requires training such as the athletes underwent." Students should not expect that any type of learning, especially content knowledge and reading, can come without labor, some discomfort, some disequilibrium. But the rewards of this hard work are intrinsically and extrinsically rewarding.

Effort is particularly necessary due to the nature of the textbooks that most secondary school systems adopt today. The vocabulary, syntax, experiential background, and text structures required to understand the information and processes of the content areas place high demands on the reader.

**REFLECT**

We have worked with many schools to help faculty members more completely understand their learners and the nature of the texts provided by their school systems. What can you conclude from the following data we have gathered?

- In a typical comprehensive high school, the ninth grade student population (*n* = 250–470) can have a reading achievement range from level 3 to level 17 (based on the Nelson-Denny Reading Test, given 2000).
- Even in high schools where a high proportion of the student body goes on to four-year colleges, and 50 percent of the ninth grade students read above grade level, still 25 percent or more of the ninth grade students often read below grade level (based on the Nelson-Denny Reading Test, given 2000).
- In a standard, heterogeneous ninth grade content class (e.g., a social studies/government class with twenty-five students) the comprehension scores can range from the 5th to the 93rd percentile (based on the Nelson-Denny Reading Test, given 2000).
- In an honors or advanced ninth grade content class, the comprehension scores can range from the 45th to the 99th percentile (based on the Nelson-Denny Reading Test, given 2000).
- In a standard ninth grade content class, it is not unusual for one-half or more of the students to find the assigned textbook to be at a frustration reading level (based on data from the *Degrees of Reading Power* test, 2000, and cloze procedures). A frustration reading level is the level at which the reader comprehends less than 50 percent of the information contained therein. A frustration level will thwart the learning of content. For example, see Table 1.1, Class Reading Profile Based on Cloze Procedure for

**TABLE 1.1　Class Reading Profile Based on Cloze Procedure for Assigned Textbook (Earth Science Standard Class)**

| NAME | RESPONSES CORRECT (%) | TEXT |
|------|------------------------|------|
| Anthony | 20 | frustration level |
| Ara | 36 | frustration level |
| Arone | 36 | frustration level |
| Ashley | 80 | independent level |
| Chris | 68 | independent level |
| Danielle | 40 | instructional level |
| Dan | 42 | instructional level |
| David | 46 | instructional level |
| Erika | 48 | instructional level |
| Heather | 38 | frustration level |
| Hammie | 66 | independent level |
| Jamie | 70 | independent level |
| Jason | 42 | instructional level |
| Jawana | 28 | frustration level |
| Jimmy | 28 | frustration level |
| Joe | 22 | frustration level |
| Lloyd | 44 | instructional level |
| Nicole | 40 | instructional level |
| Nikki | 42 | instructional level |
| Ryan | 36 | frustration level |
| Sarah | 38 | frustration level |

Assigned Textbook. Of the twenty-one students in this earth science ninth grade class, nine students will find the assigned text to be at a frustration reading level for them. (The cloze procedure is explained in Appendix B.)

■ In an honors or advanced ninth grade content class, it is not unusual for some students to find the assigned textbook at a frustration reading level for them, nor for over half the class to find the reading material at an instructional level (based on data from *Degrees of Reading Power* test, 2000, and cloze procedures). An instructional level is the level at which the reader comprehends 75 percent or more. This level of reading is ideal for classroom use because it is challenging, but not frustrating. It provides for optimal growth in reading because of its syntactic and semantic complexities. Instructional-level reading material requires teacher-guided instruction and support. Instructional-level reading is sometimes referred to as being in the *zone of proximal development* (ZPD). ZPD, a term attributed to social-constructivist Lev Vygotsky (1978), is the time in a student's learning that he or she can accomplish some learning task, if guided by an adult or a more capable peer. This guidance or support is called *scaffolding*. This scaffolding helps the learner eventually reach independence in performing the task.

■ In most ninth grade classes (standard or advanced), only a few (typically one to four) students can read the assigned textbook independently, that is, with better than 90 percent comprehension and without teacher-guided instruction and support (based on data from *Degrees of Reading Power* test, 2000, and cloze procedures). For example, see Table 1.1. Only four students in this class can read the assigned textbook independently.

**REFLECT**

So, what do you conclude from this data? Our experience leads us to the following tenets for reading in the content areas:

**1.** *Secondary students should read textbooks to learn content knowledge.* The textbooks that have been purchased by the school systems typically mirror the system's content curricula. By reading these materials, students have the best chance to achieve the content goals of the school system and the content standards of learned societies, which usually guide the establishment of state curricula (e.g., National Council for the Social Studies; American Alliance of Health, Physical Education, Recreation and Dance; National Council of Teachers of Mathematics; National Art Education Association).

**2.** *A multitext approach should be used in the content areas.* With the wide range of student reading achievement levels typical in secondary classrooms, expecting the same textbook to be appropriate for all students is unrealistic. We refer to this metaphorically as the "bowling ball" disposition to textbook selection: using one bowling ball to topple all ten pins. The problem with this disposition is that the bowling lane (reading range) is so wide that one bowling ball (text) cannot begin to touch enough pins (students). Teachers must learn to employ multitext approaches in their classrooms.

Look again at Table 1.1, the results of the cloze procedure on the textbook bought by the school system for an earth-science class. Of the twenty-one students in the class, four students can read this text independently, that is, with better than 90 percent comprehension and without teacher-guided instruction and support. Eight students can read it instructionally and thus will require teacher-guided instruction and support. Nine students will find the textbook frustrating and will attain less than 50 percent comprehension of the content explained therein without teacher-guided instruction and adaptations. This class would profit from the availability of other reading materials to challenge the four students on an independent level, and still other reading materials that would not frustrate the nine students.

Frustration and boredom are emotional reactions to reading in the classroom, but they are also physiological reactions. Students who must cope consistently with curriculum that is well beyond their level of readiness (i.e., frustration-level reading material) experience stress and a chemical imbalance in the brain resulting from overproduction of neurotransmitters that impede learning. A consistent diet of a redundant curriculum (i.e., comparable to independent-level reading material) also results in the brain not releasing an appropriate level of neurochemicals, which causes apathy (Tomlinson & Kalbfleisch, 1998). Additionally, the students who can handle the reading independently, if denied the challenge of processing instructional-level reading material, are not given the opportunity to continue to improve their semantic and syntactic competence.

Teachers should also consider using additional reading material for students who are still not fluent in the use of decoding skills. These students will gain fluency only if they read extensively and with materials at their independent reading levels. Too often the system-provided textbook is at the frustration level for these students.

Teachers must lobby for and employ multitext approaches in their classrooms. Teachers should have available to them textbooks that cover the curricular content, but in different editions at different readability levels. Some middle schools, for example, have purchased sets (40–50 copies) of three different texts, instead of purchasing 120–150 copies of the same textbook. The books cover the same essential information—history, geography, culture, religion, and so on—but each is written on a different readability level, that is, a different level of difficulty in terms of semantics and syntax. In this way, a social studies teacher teaching a unit on Japan can assign different texts to students based on their instructional reading range.

With this type of multitext approach, all students read for the same purpose regardless of the reading material assigned to them, then share information from various sources during discussion. For example, when the students investigate the government of Japan, they all read to discover the makeup of its government body, the "Diet." Sometimes, the various texts will be redundant and reinforce the information in each. At other times, varying facts and perspectives surface from different texts. The teacher can then challenge students to engage their critical thinking skills to judge the validity of various or conflicting information or to reconcile discrepancies by integrating the information from various texts (Perfetti, Britt, & Georgi, 1995; Stahl, Hynd, Britton, McNish, & Bosquet, 1996).

Secondary English classes can employ a multitext approach by having the teacher select two to five novels of varying reading level difficulty but which all demonstrate the same writing style or theme. For example, the high school teacher for a unit on naturalism might select *Maggie: Girl of the Streets* by Stephen Crane for the bright but learning disabled students in the classes because it is short. He might select *The Grapes of Wrath* by John Steinbeck for the better readers and *Fallen Angels,* a young adult novel by Walter Dean Myers, for the less able readers in the class. After each group reads and discusses the literal level of its novel and shares the novel's story line, the entire class can discuss common characteristics that demonstrate the technique of naturalism.

Another strategy is to give the students reading options within a theme. For example, Rebecca Joseph, a city middle school English teacher teaching a thematic unit entitled "There's No Place Like Home," gives the students the options of reading *Dear Mr. Henshaw* (Cleary, 1983), *The Great Gilly Hopkins* (Paterson, 1979), *Journey* (MacLachlan, 1991), *Missing May* (Rylant, 1993), *Monkey Island* (Fox, 1991), or *Somewhere in the Darkness* (Myers, 1992). She introduces the novels by giving a brief "book-talk" on each, then allows students a significant part of the class period to begin reading or to skim each. By the end of the period, each student completes a form listing his or her first, second, and third choices. The teacher then strategically assigns each student to a novel, based on student interest and reading level. The novels are read in literature groups, but the entire class discussions focus on a class definition of *home* (Strover, 1996).

Teachers can also provide students with accessible reading material by conceptualizing *reading materials* as broader than texts purchased by the school system on the curricular topics. Reading materials for content learning should include articles from the Web, newspaper articles, pamphlets, journal and magazine articles, books from the library, computer software, and other sources. For example, a health teacher in a high school, who taught classes of students whose instructional reading levels ranged from two to college level, taught a reading lesson on the topic of Hepatitis A, B, and C using the following materials:

- The assigned textbook for those students who could read this text instructionally
- An article on hepatitis from a recent *Better Homes and Gardens* magazine for the students for whom the text was at frustration level
- A web article about recent clinical research findings for the students for whom the text was at independent level

When they read, they shared the same purpose-for-reading: to learn the causes, symptoms, and prescriptions for hepatitis A, B, and C. In addition to allowing all members of the class to read from an accessible reading selection, this multitext approach provided opportunities for all students to make significant contributions and apply critical thinking to the various facts and viewpoints gleaned from the different sources.

The Web can be helpful when implementing a multitext approach. For example, a business education teacher used a reading taken from a government website when teaching a lesson on federal student loans. This selection was substituted for a chapter found in the text because it was easier reading for this class of students and more current in the information it provided. An art teacher also used a website as the source for reading material because information about the photographer being studied was not available in the system-purchased text.

**3.** *Content teachers should not use the read-the-chapter-and-answer-the-questions-at-the-end-of-the-chapter approach to reading.* The read-the-chapter-and-answer-the-questions-at-the-end-of-the-chapter approach to reading is assigning, not teaching. Unless the assigned textbook is on an independent reading level for all students in a content classroom, the teacher must ready the students for reading. The students must be brought up to the level of the reading by specific, teacher-led instruction. Then the students must be guided explicitly in purposeful, strategic silent reading. Following their silent reading, they must be involved in conversational debriefings that allow their content understandings to be confirmed, reinforced, and extended. This requires active teaching on the part of the content teacher and cognitive engagement on the part of the students.

**4.** *All content teachers must teach their students how to manipulate to their advantage the cueing systems required for comprehension of reading material in their content area.* Content teachers are the experts in their disciplines. It is they who know the technical vocabulary, have repeated practice with the syntax of their content, are most familiar with the background knowledge assumed in a reading, and recognize the text structures of their discipline. It is the content teacher who is best able to "integrate reading and subject matter learning in seamless fashion, using language and literacy to scaffold students' learning" (Vacca, 2002, p. 184). This is not a job for the English teacher or reading teacher. To be done authentically, the content teacher—the expert—must do it. Science teachers are the best enablers of students enrolled in science. Art teachers are the best enablers of students enrolled in art class. Foreign language teachers are the best enablers of students taking a foreign language. Fill in your discipline in this repeated sentence.

## SUMMARY

You, the teacher, are the most important variable for your students in achieving the goals of your content area. Using instructional-level reading material (independent level for inadequate decoders) and including appropriate reading strategies as a regular part of your lesson plans, you can optimize the chances that your students become successful in acquiring the knowledge and learning the processes of your content area. You are teaching them to learn with text. In addition, you are helping your students become better readers—a learning tool for life—by expanding their vocabularies, improving their competence with mature syntax, and developing their fluency.

# CHAPTER TWO

# CONTENT + READING = THE DIRECTED READING LESSON

Stacy is a tenth grade student who has struggled most of her life. Her mother died when Stacy was very young and she and her father have a volatile relationship, at best. During her lifetime, Stacy has been in numerous foster homes. She has been in drug rehab on several occasions and attends school under the supervision of a juvenile officer. When Stacy returned from a recent suspension, she showed me an alarm strapped to her leg and informed me that she is currently under house arrest.

In addition to the issues above, Stacy has ADD. She has great difficulty focusing, staying on task, and comprehending and recalling information. In the classroom, she is either in constant motion or fighting to stay awake. This is her second year in my child-care completer program.

On the day I began my first-ever Directed Reading Lesson with a reading selection, Chapter 1 of *Mary by Myself,* I immediately noticed that Stacy was calm—in fact, I had her undivided attention. She managed to stay focused for the entire 78-minute period as we moved through each part of the Directed Reading Lesson. I was pleased and intrigued.

The following day when the class was seated and settled, I asked who could remind us what topic we had investigated the day before. Almost before I had finished my sentence, Stacy blurted out "SIDS—Sudden Infant Death Syndrome" and much detail from our lesson. I was pleased and shocked. Stacy often blurted out in class, but never answers. I smiled, praised Stacy, and watched as several of her classmates looked at her in disbelief.

Later in the period, I had an opportunity to ask Stacy how she remembered SIDS and so much about it. She flashed a big smile and quickly replied, "It was all that reading and discussion, Mrs. Riley. You never taught us that way before."

I now search for reading for every topic. It may take a while to restructure the majority of my lessons, but I believe that it will make a difference for all my students. It certainly did for Stacy!

—*High School Consumer and Family Science Teacher*

The Directed Reading Lesson plan is an outline for a teacher-guided, learner-centered lesson that uses reading as the primary source for content knowledge. We have structured this text to follow a MODEL-ANALYZE-APPLY approach to teacher training, so that you can discover the parts of the Directed Reading Lesson inductively. In this chapter, you will be instructed to read four Directed Reading Lesson plans. We will refer to these MODELS in subsequent chapters as we ANALYZE each part of the Directed Reading Lesson. At the conclusion of the analysis of each part, you will be guided by a series of questions to APPLY your learning in order to design your own content Directed Reading Lesson plan. In order for you to engage fully in the ANALYSIS of the lesson plans, you will be prompted throughout the text to answer questions and to examine particular parts of specific lesson plan models. The "Reflect" icon will appear in the margin as your signal.

# REFLECT

Arrows (with the page number of the lesson plan referred to) will appear in the margins to cue you to pause, locate, and analyze a model as directed in the body of the text.

Let's begin! You will now read four Directed Reading Lesson plans that secondary content teachers have developed. Although the four lesson plans are different in content and topics, they all follow the same procedure—the steps of the Directed Reading Lesson. Each lesson is written in a scripted manner, so that, as you read, you can "watch" these lessons unfold in a classroom.

The first three plans are included in this chapter. The first is a science lesson that has students read *to be informed;* the second is an English lesson that has students read *for literary experience;* the third plan is an art lesson that has students read *to perform a task.* We have selected these three lesson plans as our anchoring examples so that you experience the Directed Reading Lesson with different content disciplines and with the three generic purposes-for-reading (*to be informed, for literary experience,* and *to perform a task*). In this way, we can demonstrate the universality of the Directed Reading Lesson format.

The fourth lesson plan you read will be one in your content area and selected from the appendix of this text. The appendix includes twenty-two Directed Reading Lessons written by inservice teachers or preservice interns teaching in the following content areas: art, business education, consumer and family science, English (including ESL), French, health, mathematics, music, physical education, science, social studies, Spanish, and special education. Most of these lessons are first attempts at a Directed Reading Lesson. Although very good examples, they should not be viewed critically as exemplars. If you teach gifted or advanced placement students, you may also choose to read the social studies lesson, "The Development of the Supreme Court's Power." Special education teachers may want to read the lesson, "Aquatic Safety," a physical education reading lesson written for special needs students, in addition to the lesson "Reading a Menu."

Each Directed Reading Lesson begins with the following contextualizing information: Class Description, Unit Title, Unit Goals, Topic of the Lesson, Lesson Objectives, Assessment, Macrostructure Reading Skills, and Materials. The Procedure follows in each lesson plan. This is a script of how the lesson will be executed following the parts of the Directed Reading Lesson format.

Although called *lessons,* these plans are not necessarily single-day lessons. Depending on whether the school is on a 50-minute, 90-minute, or modular schedule, these lessons will vary in the number of days required to complete them. Therefore, we employ the term *lesson* to refer to a complete Directed Reading procedure, that is, the preparation for, silent reading of, and debriefing on a content area reading that is at an instructional or frustration level for the students.

Read the four Directed Reading Lessons (three in this chapter and one you select for your content from Appendix A) to be informed. List the parts of the Directed Reading Lesson and beside each part explain its rationale or purpose. Specifically, your purpose-for-reading the four lesson plans is to complete the chart shown in Figure 2.1. Complete one chart for all four plans. Some of the answers are included on the chart as models of the type of responses you should include.

**FIGURE 2.1   The Directed Reading Lesson**

| PARTS | RATIONALE/PURPOSE |
|---|---|
| 1. Readiness | 1. |
|   a. Motivation |   a. To focus attention; to help students "connect" to the topic |
|   b. |   b. |
|   c. |   c. |
|   d. |   d. |
| 2. Silent Reading | 2. |
| 3. | 3. |
| 4. | 4. |
| 5. | 5. |

The subsequent chapters in this text will refer you back to this chart as each phase and part of the Directed Reading Lesson is examined.

## SCIENCE LESSON
### Directed Reading Lesson

**Class Description:** Middle school, grade 7; general science course. Students are of heterogeneous ability levels—below, average, and above average. We have already studied tornadoes and dust storms in our unit on natural disasters and this lesson will introduce the disaster of "cities on fire."

**Unit:** Natural Disasters

**Topic:** Cities on Fire

**Unit Goals:** At the conclusion of the unit, students will be able to:

1. Identify the *causes* of specified natural disasters
2. Identify the positive and negative *effects* of natural disasters
3. Identify *preventive strategies or solutions* for natural disasters

**Lesson Objectives:** Students will:

1. Write definitions for the following terms: *grid plan, tinder,* and *rushes*
2. Describe at least three causes for citywide fires
3. Classify each of the causes as either a result of the physical environment or a result of planning or technology limitations
4. Propose solutions to each of the problems (causes) identified
5. Argue, in a paragraph, whether they believe Baltimore is in danger of catching on fire

**Performance Assessment**

| Objective | Performance Assessment |
|---|---|
| 1. | Observation of vocabulary partner work; review of students' vocabulary notebooks |
| 2. | Completed graphic organizer; class discussion of graphic organizer |
| 3. | Completed graphic organizer; class discussion of graphic organizer |
| 4. | Completed graphic organizer; class discussion of graphic organizer |
| 5. | Paragraphs collected and reviewed |

**Reading Type:** Reading to be informed

**Macrostructure Thinking for Reading:** Cause and effect (other thinking skills employed in lesson: classification, problem and solution)

### Materials

- Reading from Bessie Bradwell's account of the Great Chicago Fire. The Chicago Historical Society and the Trustees of Northwestern University, 1996 (http://fire.at. nwu.edu/fire/witnesses/bradwell.html).
- Text chapter, "Cities on Fire."
- Pictures
     "Fleeing from the Burning City"
          (http://fire.at.nwu.edu/fire/witnesses/pic0597.html).
     "Memories of the Chicago Fire"
          (http://fire.at.nwu.edu/fire/witnesses/pic0178.html).
     "Rushes in Marshland" (www.chias.org/www/diorama/w3.html).
- Transparency, "Grid Plan of Washington, D.C." (www.mapquest.com).
- Dry wood, soaked wood, porcelain crucible and lid, Bunsen burner, thatched paper sample
- "Cities on Fire" graphic organizer
- Row House in Charles Village, Baltimore City, homework handout

## Procedure

### 1. Readiness

*a. Motivation:* "Look at the bulletin board, entitled 'Natural Disasters,' on the right hand side of the room. It will remind you of the two types of natural disasters we have studied thus far in this unit. What are those two types of natural disasters?"

*Expected student responses:* tornadoes and sandstorms

"Today, we begin our study of a third type. What I am about to show you happened in Chicago [point to Chicago on the world map on the wall] in the late 1800s. [Show students the picture, "Memories of the Chicago Fire."] This is a painting by Julie Lemos. What type of natural disaster is it showing? [*fire*] Yes, in fact a city on fire. This is Ms. Lemos' depiction of the Great Chicago Fire of 1870. Imagine what is happening in this painting, as I read you a passage written by a girl named Bessie Bradwell. She was thirteen years old when the fire occurred, very close in age to you, and this is how she described her experience."

We had retired when we were awakened by the fire. I was thirteen years old at the time. Arising I concluded to save my best clothes by putting them on. My mother, Myra Bradwell, slipped on a wrapper and proceeded to pack a trunk with our most precious possessions. . . . With her birdcage tightly clasped in her arms and the poor little bird gasping for breath in the smoke, she went down to the Lake at the floor of Washington St. with my brother. When she saw the city was doomed, my father, Judge Bradwell's first thought was to save the rare old law books which he had been collecting for years and which, if they were burned, he could never replace. . . .

On the street it was confusion worse confounded with people crowding you on all sides. It was like a snowstorm only the flakes were red instead of white. On one side I was jostled by a man shrieking, "Oh the poor prisoners, they will be burned alive, locked up in their cells." . . . Never shall I forget the sight as I looked back on the burning city. On the bridge, a man hurrying along, said, "This is the end of Chicago." . . . My coat had been on fire two or three times. People would run up to me and smother the flames with their hands. Then we hurried on, the fire madly pursuing us. . . . The Lakefront was covered with dry goods that had been taken out of the stores and placed in the park. My father concluded that the fire would sweep all over the park and that the only way to save the trunk was to bury it. He went to a neighbor's house and got a shovel and proceeded to dig a hole in the park to bury the trunk. . . . My mother told me many thrilling tales of the sights she saw there on the Lakefront. The church of the Rev. Mr. Patterson caught fire first from the tower and swept down. A bystander said, "Oh what a pity, the church is going." . . . As the fire burned all inflammable goods up to the Lake front, my family were obliged to go down to the very edge of the Lake and bathe their faces to keep from burning up.

"It is hard to imagine the horror of experiencing something like this, but a man named Waud actually had the composure to make sketches during this fire. This is one of those drawings [show picture, "Fleeing from the Burning City"]. What do you see here?"

**b. *Tapping and Developing Background of Experience:*** "Has anyone ever been in a fire, or had a fire affect someone you know?"

*Students share experiences.*

"How do we deal with fires today?"

*Expected student responses:* fire department called, use of hoses and hydrants, special suits for fire fighters

"Yes, they have special equipment that allows them to extinguish the fires before they spread very far."

"Have you heard on the news anything about the huge wildfires that have occurred in California, Wyoming, or Oregon [point to these states on the wall map] that sweep through the forests? These wildfires are too big for the fire department to fight effectively with their regular ground equipment. Can you imagine what would happen if such a large fire happened in a city? That's exactly what happened in the city of Chicago in 1870 that you just saw and heard about. There was another major city fire in 1666 in London [point to London on the world map]. Today, we will read about both of these cities on fire as we explore our third topic in this unit on natural disasters."

*Transition:* "Before we begin reading, there are a few new vocabulary words we need to learn so you can work through the reading to find out more about these fires. Move to your vocabulary pairs and take out your science vocabulary notebooks now."

**c. *Concept Development:*** "The first new concept is *grid plan* [show the words printed on the chalkboard]. Now look at this transparency. It shows a map of part of the city of Washington, D.C. Take note of how the streets are arranged. This map is also a grid plan. Discuss with your partner a draft definition for grid plan."

*Expected definition:* a city map with streets arranged in criss-crossed lines

Call on one vocabulary pair to give its draft definition. Instruct the other pairs to listen to determine whether they agree. Ask for any revisions, and agree on a class definition. Students copy the concept, definition, and drawing into their science vocabulary notebooks.

"The next word is *tinder* [show the word printed on the chalkboard]. To help you determine the definition of this word, I am going to do a lab demonstration for you."

*Demonstration:* Use one piece of wood that is extremely dry and brittle (a representation of *tinder*) and one that has been soaked in water overnight. After letting the class examine the pieces of wood, take small chunks of them and place them in two separate porcelain crucibles and apply a burner flame to them. The *tinder* piece will burst into flame; the wet one will not. Ask the students to describe what happened with each piece of wood. Place the lid of the crucible on it to extinguish the fire. This demonstration is done under a fume hood to avoid setting off smoke detectors.

"The piece of wood that burst into flames is an example of *tinder.* The piece that did not burst into flames is *not tinder.* With your vocabulary partner, draft a definition of *tinder.* After students have had time to discuss and draft a definition, call on one vocabulary pair to give its draft definition. Instruct the other pairs to listen to determine whether they agree.

Ask for any revisions, and agree on a class definition. Students copy the word and definition into their science vocabulary notebooks.

   *Expected definition:* a very dry piece of wood that catches fire easily

   "Next we will examine the word *rushes*. Who here has ever woken up late for school? And what happens? Your mother or father or guardian [point to *rushes*] you to get dressed. What does the use of *rushes* mean when this happens? [*to hurry*] The definition we need of *rushes* for our upcoming reading today is different from the use of *rushes,* meaning to hurry, you may have used. Close your eyes and visualize this scene":

> You are going on a car trip to Ocean City. You are riding down the road and the driver pulls off into a parking lot. Sand has blown over onto the pavement. You get out of the car in your shorts and t-shirt and stroll over to the water's edge. This is not the ocean side of Ocean City, but the bay side, where the water is still and there is a good chance that as you walk along the edge, your feet will sink into marsh, the waterlogged soil. You decide to sit down and watch the animals and birds around this part of bay. You see some birds pausing on the tall stems of the *rushes* and cattails that grow in this marsh.

   "Now open your eyes and with your partner, draft a definition of *rushes.*" Call on a vocabulary pair to tell their draft definition. Instruct the other pairs to listen to determine whether they agree. If students need more prompting, show them the picture of the marsh and point to the *rushes*. Ask for any revisions, and agree on a class definition. Students copy the word and definition into their science vocabulary notebooks.

   *Expected definition:* tall grasses that grow in and around the edges of bodies of water

*Transition:* "Now that we have an understanding of some new key vocabulary, we are ready to comprehend the reading, "Cities on Fire.""

**d. Purpose-for-Reading:** "Today you will be reading to be informed. You will use the thinking skill of cause and effect to determine the factors that caused citywide fires to occur in London, England, in 1666 and in Chicago in 1870. I am giving each of you a graphic organizer. [Place transparency of this graphic organizer (Figure 2.2) on the overhead projector and point out the following parts.] Notice the title of the column on the left: Factors That Allowed Such Large Fires to Occur. The first section under this column is for you to record the factors that caused the London fire, and below it is a place for you to record the factors that caused the Chicago fire to occur. You will be reading the chapter entitled 'Cities on Fire' in your textbook. Open to the table of contents in the front of the text and locate the page on which this chapter begins."

**2. Silent Reading:** Students read the chapter silently and complete their graphic organizers. I circulate to assist students who might be having difficulty with the graphic organizer, clueing them to sections they may need to reread to locate correct answers. After fifteen minutes, I interrupt the students and ask them if they have used their new vocabulary words in the responses on their graphic organizers.

**3. Discussion:** Place transparency of blank graphic organizer on overhead projector. Ask for student responses and record on the graphic organizer. Ask students for elaboration, as necessary. Instruct students to add any information or revise their own graphic organizers, if needed. Point out the new vocabulary words learned as students contribute responses using these terms.

   *Expected student responses are on the graphic organizer.*

*Transition Activity:* "Before we look back at the reading again, let's look over the list we just created. Which of these factors resulted from the physical environment, that is, nature, and which of these resulted from lack of good planning by people living there or lack of technology available at the time? Take each factor and categorize it as either an N (caused by nature) or T (caused by planning or technology). Work with your vocabulary partner on this activity."

**FIGURE 2.2** **"Cities on Fire" Graphic Organizer**

| CAUSE AND EFFECT | PROBLEM AND SOLUTION |
|---|---|
| *Factors That Caused Large Fires to Occur* | *Solutions to Remove This Factor* |
| London Fire, 1666 | |
| ■ *Houses entirely wood (T)\** | ■ *Build with brick, stone, or steel* |
| ■ *Roofs made from rushes (T)* | ■ *Use modern roofing material* |
| ■ *No public water (T)* | ■ *Use pipes and fire hydrants* |
| ■ *No real fire departments (T)* | ■ *Fire departments with modern trucks and equipment* |
| ■ *No rain that summer (N)* | |
| ■ *Everything tinder dry (N)* | |
| ■ *Windy days (N)* | |
| ■ *Houses close together on a grid plan (T)* | ■ *Space buildings and plan city better* |
| Chicago Fire, 1870 | |
| ■ *Houses of wood (T)* | ■ *Build with modern materials* |
| ■ *Sun scorched (N)* | |
| ■ *Wind (N)* | |
| ■ *No fire department (T)* | ■ *Have fire departments with modern trucks and equipment* |

*Italics on graphic organizer are expected student responses.

*Expected student responses are on the graphic organizer.*

"Which of these types of factors, physical/nature or planning/technology, could the designers of cities change or control to avoid future city fires?"

*Expected student response:* One cannot control nature, but one can control the planning/technology factors.

**4. Rereading:** "Skim over the part of the reading entitled 'After the Disaster' and the last paragraph of 'Chicago Burns Down' to get some ideas of what was actually done to improve conditions and rebuild these cities. Then using the thinking skill of problem and solution, write in the right-hand column of your graphic organizer possible solutions that could be used today to solve the planning/technology problems listed on the left-hand side of the chart. Discuss this with your partner, then we will debrief as an entire class."

*Expected student responses on the graphic organizer.*

**5. Follow-up (Reinforcement):** Hand out homework entitled "Row Houses in Charles Village, Baltimore City." "For homework tonight, you will apply the different causes of fires to a new situation. Baltimore City is known for its row houses. Who has seen these houses? What does it mean when we use the term *row house*? [*joined houses, sometimes twenty to a block*] The newer ones in the suburbs are sometimes called *town houses*, because they are styled after the ones in town, in the city. I have put a picture of some row houses on your homework ditto. Read along with me while I read the directions on your homework handout":

Look at this photograph of row houses in downtown Baltimore. Based on the causes of citywide fires we discussed in class, do you think there is danger of a major city fire happening in Baltimore? Write an answer to this question using at least four factors we discussed in class that have contributed to large city fires in the past. Be sure to edit your work.

Lesson plan by Bethany Petr, April 1999.

# ENGLISH LESSON
## Directed Reading Lesson

**Class Description:** High school, grade 9; heterogeneous, standard class (below average and average in achievement); reading achievement range of levels 5–10; an inclusion class with five students who are learning disabled for reading

**Unit:** Thematic, Characters in Conflict

**Topic:** "The Scarlet Ibis," Symbolism in Titles

**Unit Goals:** At the conclusion of the unit, students will be able to:

1. Recognize and explain the author's effective use of *symbolism* as part of character development
2. Identify the type(s) of conflict evident in a narrative

**Lesson Objectives:** Students will:

1. Define and use new vocabulary from the short story: *infallible, caul*
2. Explain the narrative elements of the short story "The Scarlet Ibis"
3. Explain the conflict as one of opposing tendencies or feelings within a single character
4. Explain the literal and symbolic meaning of the short story's title
5. Recognize and explain the use of symbolism found in other print material

### Performance Assessment

| *Objective* | *Assessment* |
| --- | --- |
| 1. | Observation of vocabulary partner work, review of students' vocabulary notebooks |
| 2. | Story maps completed, class discussion of story map |
| 3. | Class discussion of types of conflict |
| 4. | Class discussion of the symbolism of the short story's title |
| 5. | Locating and explaining symbolism found in the student's independent reading; collected and reviewed |

**Reading Type:** Reading for literary experience (appreciation and analysis)

**Macrostructure Thinking Skill for Reading:** Narrative components: setting, character, problem/conflict, significant events, solution

### Materials

- Overhead transparency of a map of the world
- Students' vocabulary notebooks
- Short story "The Scarlet Ibis," by James Hurst
- Film clip from *The Other Sister*
- Transparency of scarlet ibis (bird)
- Background information on the scarlet ibis from www.xmission.com/~hoglezoo/birds/ibis.htm
- Picture of an Amish woman wearing a caul
- Story map
- Picture of the McDonald's golden arches

## Procedure

### I. Readiness

*a. Motivation:* "We continue today with our unit, Characters in Conflict. As we have seen in this unit, conflict for characters can take many forms. Who can recall the two different types of conflict we have experienced so far in this unit?"

*Expected student responses:* (1) conflict between individuals; and (2) conflict of a character against circumstances interfering with his or her achieving a goal

"I am going to show you a clip from the movie *The Other Sister.* The movie is about a *mentally* challenged girl who has been released from a school for special needs students. In the scene you will watch, this girl is in conflict. Identify the issue over which the conflict has arisen, and classify it as either conflict type 1 or type 2."

Class watches five-minute clip. Teacher leads discussion of the conflict between the mother and girl over the issue of whether the girl is able to handle the challenge and independence of marriage. Conflict has shades of type 1 and 2 in it.

**b. *Tapping and Developing Background of Experience:*** "Today, the short story we will read involves a character who has a *physical* disability. And like the girl in the video segment, one of the characters must struggle to be independent. Now we all have "physical disabilities" of one type or another. Some of us wear glasses to see correctly; some people have diabetes and have to take insulin shots. Some of us have allergies or asthma. What other kind of disabilities are there?"

*Student responses will be varied based on their life experiences. More disabling disabilities will, no doubt, be mentioned, for example, paralysis, blindness, and mental limitations.*

"People with more complicated or life-threatening mental and physical disabilities struggle every day. Sometimes what we might consider a simple task can cause them pain and frustration. And just like the mother in the video, family members of those with disabilities also struggle. How was the mother in the video feeling?"

"Take out your journals and for the next five minutes, let's write about how it might feel if we had a brother or sister who has a severe physical or mental disability living at home with us."

"The short story you will read today was probably set in the early part of the 1900s in North Carolina [point to on transparency of world map] where the author, James Hurst, grew up. But the title of the story is "The Scarlet Ibis," the name of a bird that lives in northern South America, from Venezuela to eastern Brazil [point to on transparency] but can come as far north as Florida. You probably have seen this bird before but do not recognize it by this name. Here is what it looks like [show transparency of scarlet ibis—flamingo]. What name do you know it as? How would you describe its appearance?"

*Expected student responses:* flamingo, bright pink feathers, long, skinny legs, long beak, looks top-heavy considering size of body and legs

"As you read, keep in mind that the scarlet ibis usually travels in flocks and finds its food by rooting around in mud at the bottom of river banks or larger bodies of water. It eats small shellfish, fish, frogs, and even small snakes from the water."

**c. *Concept Development:*** "Before we begin reading, there are a few vocabulary words that will be new to you in the reading, so we will learn them now so you can use them in the reading for better comprehension. Turn to the vocabulary section in your English notebooks and change seats so you are seated next to your vocabulary partner." (Vocabulary partners are changed each quarter. Stronger students are paired with weaker students. Sometimes a strong student is paired with another strong student for challenge.)

"The first word is *infallibility.* What does the prefix *in-* mean? [*not*] Keep that in mind and read the following sentences on the transparency, and then with your vocabulary partner draft a definition of *infallibility.*"

1. His IQ was over 160. No matter what type of math problem he tried to solve, he got it correct! It was as if he were *infallible.*
2. Roman Catholics believe that when the Pope speaks on matters of faith, he speaks *infallibly.*

Call on a vocabulary pair to give their draft definition. Ask the class to listen to decide whether they agree. Revise the definitions based on class consensus.

*Expected class definition:* not making errors, cannot be wrong or incorrect

"In your vocabulary notebooks, record the word *infallibility,* the definition we agreed on that I wrote on the chalkboard, and the two sentences from the transparency."

"The next word is *caul.* Have any of you visited a Mennonite or Amish area, or seen pictures of Mennonite or Amish women? [Show picture of Amish woman wearing a caul.] What do they usually wear on their heads or hair? [*little caps*] Sometimes they are referred to as *cauls.* How would you define this type of *caul*? [*a covering for the head or hair*] That's correct. This word, *caul,* originated, however, because occasionally—although it is rare—a baby is born with a part of the fetal sack or membrane still covering its head. The physician or midwife simply removes it, but folklore says that babies born with a *caul* have special powers. With your vocabulary partner, let's draft a definition that will fit both of these uses of *caul.*"

*Expected class definition:* something covering all or part of the head; at birth, a thin covering over the baby's head that is removed immediately after birth

Call on a vocabulary pair to give their draft definition. Ask the class to listen to decide whether they agree. Revise the definitions based on class consensus.

"In your vocabulary notebooks, record the word *caul,* the definition we agreed on that I wrote on the chalkboard, and a note about Amish women's cauls and birth cauls."

**d.  Purpose-for-Reading:**  "Today you will be reading the short story entitled 'The Scarlet Ibis' by James Hurst for literary experience. As you read, try to see this story as a movie in your mind. Picture the characters, especially Doodles, the young boy with the disability. Either while you read or after you read, complete the story map for narratives." Distribute story map handout (Figures 2.3 and 2.4) and review the components of a narrative with the class: setting, characters, conflict, significant events, and solution or outcome.

**2.  Silent Reading:**  Students read the short story, independently and silently, and complete the story map graphic organizer. Teacher circulates and assists students having difficulty. "Remember that good readers often must do some rereading if they do not understand what they just read."

**3.  Discussion:**  [Oral retelling] "Before we begin our discussion of the story, turn to the person sitting next to you, and retell the story to your partner in your own words. Refer to the text or your story map if you need it. Each of you will have a turn."

*Students take turns orally retelling their version of the story.*

[Reader response] "Before we debrief on your story map, I am curious about what you thought of the story. Did you like it? How did you feel about Doodles? What are your feelings toward Brother?"

*Student volunteers share affective responses.*

[Debriefing and consensus on story map] "I put a transparency of the story map on the overhead. Let's discuss your interpretations of this story."

*Students suggest responses for the story map. Teacher fills in agreed-on answers and encourages students to revise their own story maps if appropriate.*

Conflict type is revealed to be type 3: conflict of opposing tendencies or feelings within a single individual or character. Students are asked to skim the passage to find examples of this type of conflict within the Brother.

*Expected student responses:* the love–hate, kindness–anger, pride–embarrassment feelings of Doodles' Brother

**FIGURE 2.3    Story Map Graphic Organizer**

Title: _____ "The Scarlet Ibis" _____    Author: _____ James Hurst _____

**Setting: (when and where):** _1918; late summer; in the South; Old Woman Swamp; Horsehead Landing_

**Characters (use the two new vocabulary words in your descriptions)**

| Name | Identification (Who is this person?) and Description |
|---|---|
| **1.** Doodles (William Armstrong) | _Invalid, shriveled body, big head, buried the scarlet ibis_ |
| **2.** Narrator | _Doodles' Big Brother, 6 years older than Doodles, often ashamed of Doodles, believed in his own infallibility in teaching Doodles, was sometimes mean to Doodles, taught Doodles to walk when Doodles was 6 years old, planned to teach Doodles to run, swim, and climb trees_ |
| **3.** Dad | _Had a coffin built for Doodles when he was very young, expected him to die, built him a go-cart when he could not walk_ |
| **4.** Mom | _Took care of Doodles_ |
| **5.** Aunt Nicey | _Doodles' aunt who believed that he had special powers because he was born with a caul_ |

**Significant Events**

1. _Doodles grins at Brother._
2. _Brother shows Doodles his casket._
3. _Brother teaches Doodles to walk because he is ashamed of him._
4. _Scarlet ibis appears, dies, and is buried by Doodles._
5. _Brother runs away from Doodles in the rain._

**Conflict:** _Within Brother (his feelings about Doodles); love and hate; kindness and meanness; pride and embarassment_

**Conflict Type:** _conflict of feelings within a single character_

**Outcome/Solution:** _Doodles dies._

Italics = Expected student responses

4. **Rereading:** "The title of this short story is significant. In fact, it is _symbolic_. Let's see if we understand the term _symbolic_ and its root word, _symbol_. Look at this picture [show picture of the McDonald's arches]. What actually is this? [_a sign_] But what does it stand for or represent? What do you think of when you see it? [_fast food_] Let's complete this chart for the items listed under 'What is it?' "[show transparency].

| _What is it?_ | _What does it stand for?_ |
|---|---|
| McDonald's sign | _fast food_ |
| Police officer | _authority_ |
| Skeleton and crossed bones | _poison_ |
| Tomb of the Unknown Soldier | _unidentified Americans killed in wars_ |
| Peacock | _pride_ |
| Dove | _peace_ |
| Snake | _evil_ |
| Rose or heart | _love_ |
| American flag | _patriotism; the American people_ |
| Elephant and donkey | _Republicans and Democrats_ |

"Everything on the left-hand side of the chart under "What is it?" is a _symbol_. With your partner, draft a definition of _symbol_."

_Expected definition:_ something that represents something or someone else

**FIGURE 2.4    Graphic Organizer Given to Students with Reading Learning Disability**

Title: _____ "The Scarlet Ibis" _____    **Author:** _____ James Hurst _____

**Setting (when and where):**

**Characters (use the two new vocabulary words in your descriptions)**

Name                            Identification (Who is this person?) and Description
1.
2.
3.
4.
5.

**Significant Events**

1. (p. 2) (*Hint:* what Brother sees)
2. (p. 4) (*Hint:* an act)
3. (p. 6–7) (*Hint:* an act and a realization)
4. (p. 11–12) (*Hint:* an event)
5. (p. 13) (*Hint:* an act)

**Conflict:**

**Conflict Type:**

**Outcome/Solution:**

"Copy that definition along with five examples from our transparencies list into your vocabulary notebooks."

"James Hurst gives his short story a symbolic title, 'The Scarlet Ibis.' There is a scarlet ibis in the story, isn't there? But the scarlet ibis is also symbolic. With your partner, revisit the text and story map, and discuss the symbolism of the scarlet ibis. What does it represent and why? Is the scarlet ibis an appropriate symbol for this story? Why or why not?" Once you have some ideas, we'll discuss this as a class.

*Expected student responses, with additional probing questions, as needed:* The scarlet ibis represents Doodles. Both have similar body shapes, both are weak, neither has control over how he/it got to this family (the bird was blown off course by a storm, Doodles is a result of his birth—read *orally from the text to stress this point),* both fall victim to death. Because of these similarities, the symbol choice is appropriate.

**5. Follow-Up (Reinforcement):** "For homework tonight, find an example of symbolism used in another story or in an advertisement. You may select a symbol from one of the books you have read this year during Reader's Workshop. You may have children's books at home that you read or that your siblings are still reading. Children's books often use symbols. Or you may find an advertisement in the newspaper or a magazine that uses a symbol. Do not use anything from television or the Internet this time. Bring in the reading material that uses the symbol, if available; otherwise, describe it in writing. Then write a description of the symbol (that is, what it actually is), and then explain its symbolic use. You will use your notes to present these to your group members tomorrow."

Ideas for this lesson were contributed by Towson University English interns Albert Tsamoutalis, Tracy Thrush, Katie Karcher, and Aaron Copeland, December 2000.

## ART LESSON
### Directed Reading Lesson

**Class Description:** Fundamentals of Art; entry-level, high school art course; course satisfies the one credit of art required for a state diploma; grades 9 through 12; achievement range in class can be AP/Honors to level V, special education; ESOL students—levels 1–3 (primarily Hispanic)—also take this art course

**Unit:** Native American Art

**Topic:** Native American Round Weaving

**Unit Goals:** At the conclusion of the unit, students will be able to:

1. Identify the contributions to art the different Native American cultures have made
2. Create art in the style developed by the Native Americans

**Lesson Objective:** Students will create art in the style developed by Native Americans; that is, they will make a round weaving on a loom made from wire coat hangers, using a complementary, monochromatic, or analogous color scheme.

**Affective Objective:** Students will appreciate the contributions to the world of art made by Native Americans.

**Performance Assessment**

1. Observation of students as they create their weavings and during gallery walk
2. Completed round weavings, evaluated for weaving techniques and color schemes
3. Follow-up paragraphs, evaluated for titles, explanations, and judgments

**Reading Type:** Reading to perform a task

**Macrostructure Thinking Skill for Reading:** Sequence

**Materials:**

- Mittler and Ragans, *Understanding Art* (Lake Forest, IL: Glencoe, 1992), Lesson 2.
- Websites: www.tribal.collectors.com (site with contemporary pottery and rugs of the Hopi and Navajo Indians), www.mtnloom.com (site with pictures of various types of looms), available for student viewing on computer projector, as copies, or transparencies
- Transparency of Figure 13.8, p. 198 of text

## Procedure

### I. Readiness

*a. Motivation:* As students enter room, they are directed to examine the pictures of Navajo rugs that are displayed on the computer projector from Arizona Tribal Collectors (or pictures from books displayed around room or set out on desks; or transparencies of such art pieces). Ask students in writing (1) to describe the art inherent in these woven rugs, (2) to hypothesize who the artists might be, (3) which design they prefer and why, and (4) how they might be made. Entire class discussion of student predictions follows.

"Today we continue our study of *Native American Art*. What you are looking at are contemporary versions of weavings originally done by Native Americans."

*b. Tapping and Developing Background of Experience:* "Weaving is one of the Native Americans' most important contributions to the art world. Woven materials were originally used for clothing, blankets, and rugs. They were usually highly decorated and expressed the artists' beliefs, customs, or traditions."

"Has anyone here seen a modern or historic Native American weaving?"

"Has anyone traveled to the West or Southwest and seen Native Americans working on this craft?"

*Transition:* "Well, today, each of you will create a round weaving in the tradition of the original Native Americans."

Announce partners for this weaving project. Partners are decided by the teacher prior to this lesson, and pairings are heterogeneous in terms of reading achievement level (for tutorial purposes).

***c. Concept Development:*** "In doing your round weaving, you will read a series of directions. You will be reading to perform a task. There are several vocabulary words, probably new to you, that you will need to understand to successfully create a round weaving."

> **1.** *loom.* Write the word on the chalkboard or have it typed on a transparency. "When you were younger, did any of you make potholders? What did you use to make them? [Show potholder loom, if available.] This is a loom."

"If you read *The Odyssey* in English class, you probably remember Odysseus' wife, Penelope. She spent years waiting for Odysseus to return from his adventures. She passed the time weaving a tapestry, sitting at one of these [show picture/transparency/slide of upright loom from *www.mtn.loom.com* or comparable source]—a loom.

"What is a loom?"

> *Expected student response:* a frame to hold fibers and threads while one is weaving

Teacher writes class definition on the chalkboard or transparency. Students record the word and definition in their art vocabulary notebooks.

"Looms come in all sizes and shapes. Today we will shape coat hangers to make our looms." [Show completed loom made from coat hangers.]

> **2.** *warp* and *weft.* "There are two types of threads used in round weaving: warps and wefts [show words on chalkboard or transparency]. Watch while I demonstrate how to create warps [create six passes and tie off seventh at the center]. How would you describe a warp?"

> *Expected student response:* threads running vertically and attached to the frame

Teacher writes the class definition on the chalkboard or transparency. Students record the word and definition in their art vocabulary notebooks. Students also draw a loom and several warps and label them.

"Now watch as I create wefts [create several wefts, using the basic, tabby weave]. How would you describe a weft?"

> *Expected student response:* threads passed over and under the warp

Teacher writes class definition on the chalkboard or transparency. Students record the word and definition in their art vocabulary notebooks.

"Now open your textbooks to p. 198, and with your assigned partners identify the *loom,* the *warp,* and the *weft* in Figure 13.8." Call on various students to come to the overhead projector and point out the three parts on the transparency of Figure 13.8.

"On p. 198 of your text, read the first paragraph/column, 'What You Will Learn' and 'What You Will Need.' Be prepared to tell us what decision you will need to make to have all the materials you need to begin reading the directions and making your weaving [students read silently]."

> *Expected student response:* the colors of the fibers we want to use

"We learned the terms *complementary, monochromatic,* and *analogous* (Chapter 1) early in the year. Turn to your neighbor and review the terms. Refer to your vocabulary notebooks if you need a reminder or turn to Lesson 1 in your text.

"Native Americans selected colors to convey feelings and beliefs. Consider what feeling certain colors might suggest. Now decide on your color scheme and be prepared to explain if it is complementary, monochromatic, or analogous." Several students are then called on to share their color schemes and labels. *Depending on the nature of the class, this selection process might have to be more teacher directed.*

Instruct students to get remaining materials needed for their round weavings as listed in their textbooks.

*d. Purpose-for-Reading:* "Your purpose-for-reading today is to read directions that you will follow in chronological order to create your own round weaving in the way the Native Americans did. You will use 'What You Will Do' to guide you in making your weaving. Before you begin, let's review some important points about reading to perform a task." *The following should be on a transparency. If this is new to students, lead them through each of the steps.*

- Read through *all* the directions first to get the big picture of what you will be creating.
- Begin with Step 1. Read the directions for the first step, then do what is described one sentence at a time. Try to visualize what the direction is telling you. Use illustrations to guide you when they are provided (e.g., Figure 13.9 for Step 3 and Figure 13.10 for Step 4).
- *Reread* several times if you need to. Directions are terse and usually require several readings.
- When you finish Step 1, *reread* it to be sure you have completed all of it.
- Repeat Step 2, then Step 3, and so on.

"For the first part of this weaving project, do only Steps 1 through 4 and the first sentence of Step 5. After each step, have your partner verify you have completed that step correctly."

**2. Silent Reading:** Students work independently on their round weaving, reading the directions silently. Teacher circulates to affirm results, to remind of strategies for reading to perform a task, to demonstrate a step in the weaving process, when needed, and to answer questions.

**3. Discussion:** "Let's review what you have done so far." Teacher has students tell in their own words the steps they used to create their round weavings thus far. Teacher lists steps on chalkboard and has students orally elaborate on the accomplishment of each step.

*Expected student responses:*

1. Make the frame with two coat hangers.
2. Select the fiber colors.
3. Cover the frame using half-hitch knots.
4. Create a warp, make six passes; stop the 7th in the center, tie all passes.
5. Make a weft using a tabby weave. Do several circuits.

**4. Rereading:** "Look at the weaving samples and reread the first paragraph on p. 198. What were the Native Americans trying to do with various color and weaving techniques?"

*Expected response:* express their mood, feelings, beliefs, customs, and traditions

"I am now going to demonstrate two different warping techniques that you can then use to express your feelings, etc. in your round weaving." Teacher demonstrates dovetailing and interlocking, having students refer to Figure 13.10 in the text.

"Listen while I read aloud all of Step 5 [read Step 5]. Now continue your weaving, using both or one of these warping patterns. Consider the feeling you are trying to express." Circulate around the room.

**5. Follow-Up:** "Give your work a title. In a paragraph, explain how the color scheme and weaving pattern were used to express a feeling or belief. If you were to do this again, what changes would you make? When finished, exchange with someone and have them proofread your work."

Weavings are displayed around the room. A gallery walk provides time for classmates to observe the works and the paragraph explanations.

## SUMMARY

Verify your responses to the purpose-for-reading given for this chapter. The Directed Reading Lesson has five main parts, with the first part, Readiness, having four phases:

1. Readiness
   a. Motivation
   b. Tapping and Developing Background of Experience
   c. Concept Development/Vocabulary
   d. Purpose-for-Reading
2. Silent Reading
3. Discussion
4. Rereading
5. Follow-up

In the next eight chapters, the rationale for each part and phase will be verified and analyzed.

In the Directed Reading Lesson, you, the teacher, are the primary facilitator who coaches students in learning with text by:

- Selecting content reading accessible for learners
- Fostering interest
- Tapping and extending students' experiential backgrounds
- Expanding students' vocabulary knowledge
- Engaging students in constructing meaning by reading purposely and strategically
- Leading students in instructional discussions that foster higher-level thinking
- Holding students accountable for the acquisition of content concepts and principles by monitoring their comprehension through observational and artifact performance assessment

## YOUR TURN

The goal of this text is to have you produce a Directed Reading Lesson plan for your content area, one that you can execute with the students you currently teach. If you are a preservice teacher you might be teaching this lesson during a field experience or during a microteaching experience on campus.

At this point, you should have a global understanding of a Directed Reading Lesson in the content area. In subsequent chapters, you will be directed to use reflective questions to guide you in drafting a Directed Reading Lesson for your students. The following will help you begin your planning:

1. *In writing, describe the class for whom you will plan a Directed Reading Lesson.* Content area? Middle or high school? Grade? Achievement/ability range? Unit? Topic of the Lesson?
2. *Review your unit goals and select the topic for your lesson.* Because the ultimate goal of a Directed Reading Lesson is deep understanding of the topic, we recommend that you base your Directed Reading Lesson on an essential understanding of the unit you are teaching. Also note that these lessons take time because teaching for true understanding takes time, which is too often not allocated (Fournier & Graves, 2002).
3. *Select the material students will read.* We recommend using the text materials your district has purchased since they should parallel your curriculum goals and because you are probably expected to use them. Construct and administer a cloze procedure (explained on pp. 231–232 in Appendix B) on the reading material. Examine the results to determine if this single reading will be accessible to all your students or if you should use a multitext approach for your Directed Reading Lesson.
4. *Write the objectives and the assessments for your lesson.* We assume that you have sufficient background in lesson planning to accomplish this independently.

# CHAPTER THREE

# MOTIVATION

To awaken interest and kindle enthusiasm is the sure way to teach easily and successfully.

—*Tyron Edwards, American theologian and editor*

1. Readiness
   **a. Motivation** ◄◄◄
   b. Tapping and Developing Background of Experience
   c. Concept Development/Vocabulary
   d. Purpose-for-Reading
2. Silent Reading
3. Discussion
4. Rereading
5. Follow-Up

The Directed Reading Lesson begins with Motivation. It is the first step in getting the students ready to comprehend the selected reading material. The purpose of the Motivation phase of Readiness is to help students focus their attention on the content topic for the session, to arouse their curiosity and interest, and to help them connect, that is, relate the topic in some way to their lives.

We teachers sometimes forget that our students in all likelihood left our class yesterday and did not give another thought to the study of isosceles triangles in geometry class, posterization in computer class, present indicative forms in Spanish class, or percussion instruments in music class. We, on the other hand, have been reflecting on that last lesson and drafting and revising our next one. Since we arrived at school, we have been readying our room, the materials, and our own cognitive dispositions for the lesson. So when students enter our classroom, we are already focused on, and interested in, the topic of our lesson. We are cognitively ready for it, but the students are probably not. They might be thinking about the math quiz coming up next period, or the weekend plans they just made with their friends, or how to ask for the car for Friday night, or whom they might vote for in the upcoming school election, or. . . . Chances are good that our students will need us to initiate this motivation:

1. By focusing their attention on the subject and specific topic of today's class
2. By arousing their curiosity and interest
3. By helping them perceive how the topic is connected to their lives

Successful motivations do require that we help students focus because without proper attention, learning is impossible. Sometimes, either arousing curiosity and interest or perceiving the connection of the topic to their lives is sufficient to motivate students for the upcoming learning.

pp. 16, 20, 25

**REFLECT**

In the three anchoring lesson plans you read in Chapter 2, did the teachers include attending to the specific topic, arousing curiosity and interest, and connecting the topic to students' lives in the Motivation phase of their lessons?

The science teacher begins her lesson reminding students of the unit by referring them to the bulletin board on natural disasters (1. attending to the content topic). Then she shows them a painting and reads from a true account of a city fire (2. arousing their curiosity and interest), pointing out that the account was written by a girl who was the same age as they (3. connecting to students' lives).

However, neither the English teacher nor the art teacher relates the topic of the lesson directly to the students' lives. The English teacher depends on the movie clip to arouse student interest. She begins her lesson by first reminding them that they are investigating a unit entitled Characters in Conflict. The art teacher displays pictures of Indian rugs to attract the attention of his students before even reminding them that they will be continuing with the unit on Native American art.

p. 214

Many of the lesson plans in Appendix A use the Motivation phase of the Directed Reading Lesson to connect the lesson topic to the students' lives. Look at the high school social studies lesson, "The Development of the Supreme Court's Power," written for academically gifted students. This teacher connects the topic directly to students' lives by referring to current events—the role of the judicial branch in the election of the president during the Bush–Gore campaign that was occurring at the time. In the lesson for Business English, "The Successful Job Interview," the teacher has little difficulty connecting the topic to the students' immediate lives because the reading deals with the interview process for a full-time job, in which these seniors will be involved within a few months. The special education teacher opens her lesson, "Reading a Menu," by reminding students that they will be "walking to Patrick's Pizzeria for lunch" on Wednesday and that today's lesson will help them to decide what they will order for lunch. The English teacher, introducing the novel *Roll of Thunder, Hear My Cry,* after telling students that this novel deals with injustice, prejudice and unfairness, asks students to recall a time in their own lives that they believe they were treated unfairly. And in the high school introduction to algebra lesson, " Problem-Solving Strategies," the mathematics teacher uses the Motivation phase to establish the importance of algebra in solving problems in everyday life.

p. 153

p. 228

p. 146

p. 177

More and more, students are directly asking teachers to explain *why* they must study a particular subject or topic within a subject. The need is not obvious to them, and they are not intrinsically motivated. The need to learn for a grade—an extrinsic motivator—is becoming less effective as a motivator for many adolescents. We need to provide rationales for students, and the Motivation section of the Directed Reading Lesson is often the appropriate placement for such an explanation.

Professional organizations, such as the National Council of Teachers of Mathematics (NCTM) and the National Council for the Social Studies (NCSS), have written standards that include helping students see connections of subject matter to their personal lives. NCTM's *Principles and Standards for School Mathematics* (2000) includes the following statement:

School mathematics experiences at all levels should include opportunities to learn about mathematics by working on problems arising in contexts outside of mathematics. These connections can be to other subject areas and disciplines as well as to students' daily lives. . . . The opportunity for students to experience mathematics in context is important. Mathematics is used in science, the social studies, medicine and commerce. . . . Data analysis and statistics are useful in helping students clarify issues related to their personal lives. . . . By grades 9–12, students should be able to use their knowledge of data analysis and mathematical modeling to understand societal issues and workplace problems in reasonable depth. (p. 65)

NCSS's *Curriculum Standards for Social Studies* (1994) states:

> Each person experiences life in an individual way, responding to the world from a very personal perspective. People also share common perspectives as members of groups, communities, societies, and nations—that is, as part of a dynamic world community. A well-designed social studies curriculum will help each learner construct a blend of personal, academic, pluralist, and global views of the human condition in the following ways:
>
> - Students should be helped to construct a *personal perspective* that enables them to explore emerging events and persistent or recurring issues, considering implications for self, family, and the whole national and world community. (p. 6)

One way to help students "construct a personal perspective" to a topic of a lesson in any subject area, as well as to arouse curiosity and stimulate interest, is for the teacher to read aloud excerpts from trade books, nontextbook reading material available to the general public, in the Motivation section of the Directed Reading Lesson. (Trade books can also be appropriately used in other parts of the Directed Reading Lesson, e.g., Developing Background of Experience and Concept Development.) For example, in the anchoring lesson plan in Chapter 2, the science teacher reads a real-life account from the memoirs of Bessie Bradwell found in the Chicago Historical Society and available on the Web. This personal account of a large, city fire brings *voice,* that is, the perspective of a real person, to the objective textbook account of the Chicago fire. In the health plan, "Eating Disorders," the teacher reads from Deborah Hautzig's autobiography, *Second Star to the Right* (1999), to introduce the topic of eating disorders from the perspective of a young woman who suffers from this illness. The health plan on AIDS uses a similar approach by reading a story, found on the Web, of Christopher, a young man dying of AIDS. The consumer and family science teacher in the lesson "Sudden Infant Death Syndrome—SIDS" reads the first chapter of *Mary by Myself* (Smith, 1999), a first-person, present-tense account of a young girl's shock and grief over her baby sister's death.

p. 16

p. 161

p. 165

p. 136

Experiencing readings from trade books engages the emotional center of the brain, the limbic system. These emotions can positively affect the learning and retention of content information. These readings are new, different, interesting, and novel, and the brain responds with attention to novelty.

In addition to the value of reading aloud as motivation, reading to students has other benefits:

> [A] meta-analysis of the research on reading aloud to students in grades kindergarten through 12 (Martinez, 1989) showed that reading aloud contributes to gains in reading comprehension, gains in vocabulary scores [semantics], and improved scores on sentence structure and usage tests [syntax] (Lesesne, 1996, p. 246).

The oral reading of excerpts from young adult and adult literature is appropriate in all secondary content areas. For example, an excerpt from *Out of the Dust* by Karen Hesse (1997), a fictional account of a teenage girl's life during the 1930s dust storms in Oklahoma, can be a powerful lead-in or companion to a chapter from the American history text about the last years of the New Deal, or from an earth science text about weathering and soil formation.

A biology teacher initiating the study of arthropods might read aloud to students from the Michener novel *Chesapeake* (1978) the description of the puzzled tribesman Pentaquod struggling with the difference between a soft crab and a hard crab, as a perspective on arthropods with soft and hard exoskeletons. Melanie Flanagan, a Maryland middle school science teacher, reported during one of our workshops that she has read "It's Raining Frogs and Fish," a chapter from *Strange Mysteries from around the World* (1997) by Seymour Simon, about national reports of animal showers as a successful motivator for a lesson on the water cycle.

Physical education teachers will find the field ripe with fiction and nonfiction appropriate for motivating students. For example, *Roughnecks* by Cochran (1997) is an account of one day in the life of a football player who is playing the championship game on home turf with college scouts in the stands, and Dygard's *Outside Shooter* (1979), focusing on basketball, is just one of several sports Dygard has used for his fictional novels. For inspiration, sports celebrity biographies and autobiographies, such as *Althea Gibson* by Biracree (1989) and *For Love of the Game* (1998) by Michael Jordan, can be used.

To motivate and challenge high school students, geometry teachers have read from *Flatland* (Abbott, 1952), a fascinating and challenging fictional account of life in a two-dimensional land, and follow-up novels like *Flatterland: Like Flatland Only More So* (Stewart, 2001), *Sphereland: A Fantasy about Curved Spaces and an Expanding Universe* (Burger, 1965), and *Planiverse: Computer Contact with a Two-Dimensional World* (Dewdney, 1984).

Music teachers find excerpts from Steinbeck's *Grapes of Wrath* (1939) excellent for introducing folk songs by Woody Guthrie, and meter in music can be paralleled with poetic meter using Shel Silverstein's *Falling Up* (1996). Selected readings from biographies of musicians, such as *Blues Singers: Biographies of 50 Legendary Artists of the Early 20th Century* and its follow-up, *More Blues Singers: Biographies of 50 Artists from the Later 20th Century* (Dicaire, 2000, 2001), can attach a persona to the music studied.

Children's literature and picture books (books with text occupying 0 to 25 percent of a page because illustrations are the primary means of communicating meaning) can also be used for motivation. Science teachers have read to their secondary students the perennial childhood favorite *The Very Hungry Caterpillar* (Carle, 1987), a lively and contrastive illustration of metamorphosis, and *Everyone Poops* (Gomi, 1993), a comical, yet quite valid, introduction to the digestive and urinary systems. *The Librarian Who Measured the Earth* (Lasky, 1994) is applicable to both science and mathematics courses. It tells the story of Eratosthenes, the ancient Greek scholar who calculated the circumference of the earth and was off by only two hundred miles from modern calculations. *The Dot and the Line* (Juster, 2001) is a picture book, made into an Emmy award–winning short film, that will interest math students in the concepts of point and line, as well as challenge their vocabulary knowledge. Factorials in math are the subject of picture book *Anno's Mysterious Multiplying Jar* (Anno & Anno, 1983), and *Sir Cumference and the First Round Table* (Neuschwander & Geehan, 1997) is a humorous tale of how the terms *radius, diameter,* and *circumference* were coined.

Social studies teachers teaching world cultures have a large array of vivid picture books available to them. For example, *Sacred River* by Ted Lewin (1995) is a powerful reading to introduce the geography of India with a focus on the Ganges river, and *Volcano* (Lauber, 1986) is a pictorial essay of the eruption of Mount St. Helens. The content topic of World War II, with a focus on the dropping of the bomb on Hiroshima and the internment of Japanese Americans in camps, is emotionally presented in picture books such as *Hiroshima No Pika* (Maruki, 1982) and *Baseball Saved Us* (Mochizuki, 1995). Social issues, as well, can be introduced with children's books. For example, *Fly Away Home* (Bunting, 1991) puts the issue of homelessness in an extraordinarily new light, even for adults.

Foreign language teachers will find that many children's literature books, such as the Ramona Quimby (Cleary), Curious George (Rey), and Harry Potter (Rawlings) series, have been translated from English into foreign languages taught in the schools. Art teachers can introduce readings about specific artistic styles with picture books, such as *Mysteries of Harris Burdick* and *The Z Was Zapped* (Van Allsburg, 1984, 1987) for the topic of surrealism.

Children's literature can be read aloud by the teacher in the English class to introduce literary concepts in a concrete manner. For example, *Terrible Things* (Bunting, 1980) demonstrates allegory, and *Wilfrid Gordon McDonald Partridge* (Fox, 1985) teaches what a memory is, in preparation for secondary students writing their own personal narratives about a childhood memory.

In addition, magazine and journal articles can be used by teachers for Motivation. Magazines, such as *National Geographic* and *Smithsonian,* have articles related to art, health, foreign language, music, science, and social studies curricular topics. There is also a myriad of specialty magazines that can be sources of oral, teacher readings to use as motivation for lessons. Just a few examples are: *Prevention* (health), *Strings* (music), *Hispanic* (Spanish), *American Artist* (art), *Fortune* (business education), *Discover* (science), *Dance Spirit* (dance), *American History Illustrated* (social studies), and *Parents* (family and consumer science).

Finding trade books for specific content topics can be done with relative ease. School librarians or media specialists are a proximate and reliable source of information for finding trade readings that content teachers can use with particular topics. Most have been schooled in their graduate programs in sources for locating trade materials and have search engines at their disposal. Eileen Moore, media specialist in the Baltimore County Public School system, gives us these sites for searches:

> When I want to find trade materials to match curriculum, I often go to Follett's Title-wave. It allows a search by subject, keyword, Dewey, and reading level (to name a few of its functions) and gives reading level and reviews for novels. Anyone can register to use Follett's service. Their web address is www.flr.follett.com. I also have found Kay Vandergrift's sites to be very helpful. The web address for these sites is http://scils/rutgers.edu/special/kay/. Another site is the Information Literacy Projects site [http://www.maslibraries.org/Publications/samplers/list.html] built by teachers and librarians in Maine. These literature-based activities might give teachers ideas as they are trying to integrate literature into their content areas (personal communication, July 20, 2003).

Another search engine, available to librarians through EBSCO Information Services (www.epnet.com) is NoveList, which assists librarians in retrieving trade books for content topics from a list of more than 100,000 fiction titles and more than 56,000 titles with full-text reviews and summaries.

The Horn Book Guide Online (www.hornbookguide.com) allows teachers to search for trade books on specific topics. It provides critical reviews, gives grade level designations, and assigns a 1–6 quality rating for each book. A recent search on the topic of AIDS by a high school health teacher resulted in 61 fiction and nonfiction citations.

The software package DRP Book Link CD-ROM (Touchstone Applied Science Associates, Inc., 2002) also allows the user to search for a list of books on a particular topic (e.g., ecology or Africa). More than 20,000 titles are included, and the user may request that the generated list include annotations of the related titles. For example, a search using the keyword *desert* (nonfiction for a geography middle school unit) yielded an annotated list of more than eighty entries. A search conducted for fiction books for a high school unit on Africa yielded two books, *Song of Be* by Beake (1993) about a fifteen-year-old Namibian girl caught in the conflict between her nomadic tribe and the white culture, and *Things Fall Apart* by Achebe (1959), a novel with a Nigerian male protagonist facing a similar cultural challenge. Both books would serve the high school social studies teacher well in bringing personal voices to the study of the political scene in Africa.

The publications of professional organizations also regularly publish lists of trade materials that can enhance content areas. For example, *Social Education,* the secondary journal of the National Council of Teachers of Social Studies, publishes a special yearly supplement, "Notable Children's Trade Books in the Field of Social Studies," in the April/May issue, arranged according to social studies topic or theme. The National Council of Teachers of English publishes a yearly list of outstanding picture books that can be used in various content areas. This is available online at www.ncte.org. The National Science Teachers Association publishes every March a list of outstanding science trade books for children in their *Science and Children* journal. In their spring 2001 newsletter, the North Carolina Geographic Alliance published a list (Psteboe), arranged by state setting, of historical and current fiction titles appropriate for secondary students. There is at least one title, and typically three to five, for each of the fifty United States.

## SUMMARY

The initial step of the Readiness section of the Directed Reading Lesson is Motivation, the teachers' attempt to hook the students at the beginning of the class. In planning this phase of the Directed Reading Lesson, read the selection students will ultimately process and then ask yourself the following questions:

### Questions for Planning the Motivation Phase of the Directed Reading Lesson

1. How do I help my students focus on the topic of this reading?
2. How do I cultivate their interest in this topic?
3. What can I say and have students do to help them make a personal connection to the topic of this reading and lesson?
4. Is there a trade reading I can read during the Motivation phase to tap the interest of my students and help them connect to the topic of today's lesson?

## YOUR TURN

1. Reread the reading selection you have chosen as the centerpiece of your Directed Reading Lesson, using the questions in the previous section as your purpose-for-reading.
2. Search web and library resources for a trade book to read in the Motivation section. (This will develop your habit of regularly searching for, and being attuned to, such enrichment materials.)
3. If you are using this textbook as part of a course or workshop experience, teach your Motivation activity to another participant. Have your colleague react to his or her experience. Does your colleague:
   - Find the activity interesting?
   - Believe your Motivation will be appropriate and interesting to your students?
   - Have any advice for revision?

# TAPPING AND DEVELOPING BACKGROUND OF EXPERIENCE

*Reading is seeing by proxy.*

—*Herbert Spencer, British philosopher and sociologist*

1. Readiness
   a. Motivation
   b. **Tapping and Developing Background of Experience** ◀ ◀ ◀
   c. Concept Development/Vocabulary
   d. Purpose-for-Reading
2. Silent Reading
3. Discussion
4. Rereading
5. Follow-Up

After the Motivation phase to begin the Directed Reading Lesson, the Readiness step continues with the Tapping and Developing Background of Experience phase. What did you generalize to be the purpose of this phase from your reading of the four model lesson plans?

The purpose of this part of the lesson is to ensure that students have the necessary topical background to comprehend the upcoming content reading. If you recall the wrestling example from Chapter 1, you can understand how important it is for your students to go into the reading with the topical background necessary for understanding the new information they are about to learn.

## TAPPING BACKGROUND OF EXPERIENCE

Tapping background of experience is a process whereby the teacher helps students recall what they already know about a topic. Most veteran teachers are well aware of the importance of tapping students' background in relationship to content previously learned. That is the type of tapping we call *review*. Read the following transcript of a high school journalism teacher as he reviews or taps his students' background on a recently studied topic, news stories (expected student responses are in italics).

Yesterday, we read about news stories. What are the two parts of a conventional news story? [*lead, body*]

What is the major function of the lead? [*to summarize the story*]

What is typically included in the lead? [*who, what, when, where, why, and how*]

What is the major function of the body? [*elaboration of detail*]

Today, we are going to examine leads to determine the various ways leads can be written.

This journalism teacher wants his students to be aware of what leads include and how they differ from the body of the news story, because in the current lesson the students will need to avail themselves of this information when they learn to write various types of leads. He is helping his students mobilize their cognitive structures—specifically, the relevant topical information stored in their long-term memories to which they will connect the new information from today's lesson. They will construct meaning by connecting their previous background knowledge about the function of leads and what information newspaper leads contain to the new information they will encounter in the upcoming reading on the various types of newspaper leads.

Many textbooks build tapping of background into their chapters, often as the first activity. For example, a chapter on inequalities in an algebra text begins by reminding students that they have worked previously with simple equations and inequalities such as $x = 4$ and $x < 4$. Students are then directed to graph the solutions on number lines and to discuss with a partner how the solutions compare to each other. This review of previously learned content is followed with an introduction of another way of comparing an equation and an inequality through adding, subtracting, multiplying, and dividing inequalities by positive and negative integers, because now students have actively engaged the old information and are ready for connections.

Research has shown that the activation of topical background of experience facilitates comprehension (Levin & Pressley, 1981); however, it has also shown that learners are not adept at automatically drawing on their prior knowledge (Anderson et al., 1985). We have experienced this even in our workshops and university courses. If we are feeling the pressure of time, we are tempted to skip the tapping of background phase, telling ourselves that these mature participants can surely make the connections on their own. Yet in spite of the interest and general attentiveness of our learners, their performance is never as complete as we know it should be when we yield to this temptation. Often, we must even pause and do the tapping in the body of the lesson because it becomes clear that the teachers, our learners, have not made the connections on their own.

Sometimes, the tapping of background phase reveals some misinformation the students have about the topic. This provides an opportunity for teachers to correct the students' ideas. It is important to correct this misinformation because students tend to remember best what comes first in a learning episode (Sousa, 2001). Some readers ignore text information that refutes their background knowledge, so we should ensure that students with misinformation tackle this discrepancy. Researchers have concluded that dissatisfaction with incorrect information must be created before the student can alter the misinformation (Guzzetti, Snyder, & Glass, 1992).

pp. 17, 21, 25 Look back at the three Directed Reading Lessons in Chapter 2. Each teacher taps students' background of experience. What topics do they focus on and why? The science teacher has the students share what they know about recent wildfires in the western United States as a way of mobilizing connections to large, out-of-control fires, like those they will read about in the upcoming chapter. The English teacher asks about types of disabilities with which the students might have direct or vicarious life experience, then helps them make an emotional connection by writing how they might feel if they had a sibling with a disability. Thus, they are ready to connect to the disabled Doodles and his brother in the upcoming short story. The art teacher asks students if any of them have traveled to the West or

Southwest and seen Native Americans actually doing weavings. This allows students to share experiences they might have had on the topic of weavings.

In all three lessons, the teachers tap into students' general life experiences, not necessarily their school learning as was the case in the journalism and algebra examples cited earlier in this chapter. The following questions taken from lessons in Appendix A demonstrate how other content teachers also find this approach effective:

*How many of you now have or had had part-time jobs? Did any of you go to an interview for a job? How did you feel? What did you wear? Did you know anything about the company before the interview?* ("The Successful Job Interview," English lesson)

*Has anyone ever been to the Caribbean?* ("Une escale exotique a la Martinique," French lesson)

*Assume that a biographer wants to write about you. What events in your life would you like included in your biography?* ("Nikki-Rosa," English lesson)

*How many of you have been swimming in any of the places shown in these pictures? How did you play with your friends in the water to make sure neither you nor your friend was hurt?* ("Aquatics Safety," physical education/special education lesson)

*Think about a time you have gone out to dinner with your family. The hostess hands you a menu. Your parents tell you to look at the menu to see what you want to eat. What did you do to make the choice?* ("Reading a Menu," special education daily skills lesson)

*Do you know a family that has experienced SIDS?* ("Sudden Infant Death Syndrome (SIDS)," family and consumer science lesson)

*How many of you have family members who served in WWI, WWII, Vietnam, or Desert Storm?* ("Civil War Music: Battle Hymn of the Republic," music lesson)

*How many of you compete in sports or vigorous activity outside of school? How many of you eat a pregame meal? What does it consist of?* ("Healthy Eating for Maximum Performance," physical education lesson)

*Have you ever heard stories about the origins of primitive peoples?* ("Una Leyenda del Caribe," Spanish lesson)

pp. 214–215
pp. 210–211
pp. 203–204

Sometimes, tapping into both previously learned curriculum information and life experiences is appropriate. Look at the high school social studies lesson, "The Development of the Supreme Court's Power." In this lesson, the teacher asks students if they discussed with their family and friends during the Thanksgiving holiday the role of the electoral college in deciding the presidential election outcome. After including the students' life experiences, he proceeds to review, tapping their backgrounds of experience about their previous school learning related to how the Constitution establishes the powers of the three branches of the government and the system of checks and balances. The middle school social studies lesson, "The History of Maryland," taps into previously learned curriculum, namely, why and how the colonies of Virginia and Massachusetts were established, and then taps students' life experiences by having them share a picture of a place they have visited in Maryland in preparation for a reading about the establishment of Maryland as one of the thirteen original colonies. The science lesson, "Relationships in a Habitat," also combines previous learning about biospheres and ecosystems, then segues into a discussion of students' life experiences with communities and habitats.

## DEVELOPING BACKGROUND OF EXPERIENCE

The second essential aspect of the Tapping and Developing Background of Experience phase of the Readiness stage is the developing of students' background knowledge. This is the time in the lesson to provide background knowledge that is needed for adequate comprehension of the upcoming reading but that is not already a part of the students' cognitive structures. It is important that we not forget that our students do not necessarily have the same life or school experiences we do. Therefore, it is essential to ask ourselves during our planning time (1) what background knowledge is needed for optimum comprehension of, and learning from, the upcoming reading, (2) whether our students have this knowledge, and (3) if they do not, how we can best provide it for them during this phase of the Directed Reading Lesson.

p. 130

Look at the business education lesson, "Student Loans for Higher Education." The teacher decided that her students needed to understand how costly higher education is today if they are to appreciate the importance of reading and learning about government loans; therefore, she includes in the developing phase of the lesson an examination of a chart that

p. 165

reports the current cost of best-bargain colleges. The health teacher in the lesson on AIDS also provides background data for the students: the number and rate of increase of cases of AIDS in specific states. She, too, is attempting to provide students with background knowledge that will sensitize them to the importance of learning from the upcoming reading.

Notice that in the lesson plan on AIDS, the teacher shows students a picture of the HIV virus during the developing background phase of the lesson. This teacher is aware that readers create mental images and scenes (Sadoski, 1999) and that good comprehenders rely on these images as they process text. They have a "movie of the mind" as they read. Poor comprehenders and unmotivated readers report that they do not create pictures in their minds; that is, they do not form mental images while reading, and thus reading for them is a frustrating activity (Beers, 1996a; Davey, 1983). "I couldn't see it, so I wouldn't know what was happening" (Beers, 1996a, p. 33). Such frustration and lack of understanding due to lack of sufficient background of experience does not occur only to students. It happens to any reader who does not have the background to conjure the images required for a movie of the mind while reading. Here is an account taken from Neubert's teaching journal:

> *I teach a course in young adult literature and am always searching for books which give a multicultural perspective. A high school teacher recommended to me the Newbery Honor book* Shabanu *by Suzanne Fisher Staples (1989). Set in the Cholistan Desert of Pakistan, the novel tells the story of a Muslim girl from a nomadic family who must struggle with tradition and her independence. I began the book optimistically but found myself working very hard to maintain my attention. So many names, terms, customs, description of attire and places—lungi, hookah, goatskins, toba, desert settlements, Dingarh, Cholistan, Sibi, Ramadan, tunics, Mehrabpur, milk pots, Rajput princes of India, spiced lentils, Rahimyar Khan, camel thorn, mounds of pogh, thorn trees, camels' brass leg bracelets, thatch huts—were foreign to me. I was struggling, trying to weave pieces together of how this place and its people looked. The sole picture of Shabanu on the cover was hardly sufficient. Truthfully, by the end of the first chapter, I simply wanted to abandon the book. Instead, I did some "homework" to develop my background on the geography of Pakistan, its people, and Muslim traditions by visiting Internet sites and perusing some picture books in our library. My second read of the first chapter of this novel was an entirely different experience. This time I saw the setting and the people as I read, and I was able to focus on the conflict being played out.*

pp. 146–148

If this novel were to be used in an English or social studies class as an entire class reading, no doubt students would need to develop their backgrounds just as this adult reader did. For example, look at the English lesson plan that introduces the novel *Roll of Thunder,*

*Hear My Cry* by Taylor (1976). In order for the students to see a movie of the mind while reading and to understand and appreciate the conflicts caused by the social and political climate of the time, the teacher develops students' backgrounds through song lyrics and a gallery of pictures of people, settings, and events in the Depression of the 1930s.

Additional background of experience is developed through engaging students in a "jigsaw" activity, a form of cooperative learning (Aronson, Blaney, Sikes, Steohan, & Snapp, 1978). Students are first assigned to one of four "expert" groups. Strongest readers are assigned to examine pictures and read a selection about sharecropping; "mature students" view pictures and read a selection on the Ku Klux Klan and the Jim Crow laws; "weaker readers" examine pictures and read a selection about the location and physical features of Mississippi in the 1930s. All of these reading selections are from resource books borrowed from the school library. After these expert groups have read the selections and through discussion decided on the major characteristics of their assigned subtopics, the students are reassigned to jigsaw groups. Each jigsaw group is made up of four students, one from each expert group. Each "expert" summarizes his or her reading and explains the information or characteristics. In this way, all students are exposed to significant background information in a relatively brief period of time.

Without sufficient background of experience, readers cannot conjure images, and without images or a movie of the mind, readers have difficulty comprehending and remembering. In addition, creating mental images helps readers make inferences and predict what is going to happen as they read (Gambrell & Jawitz, 1993). Maybe that is why so many students would rather watch a video than read a book—because the images are provided for them in the film version. When we invite students to get ready to learn content from a reading, we must consider what images are needed and whether the students have the background to conjure appropriate images.

Read the following excerpt from the Prologue to Kweisi Mfume's *No Free Ride: From the Mean Streets to the Mainstream* (1997). Your purpose-for-reading questions are (1) Do you predict that the gangbanger and his posse will listen to Mr. Mfume? Why or why not? (2) What images did you see while you read?

**REFLECT**

I met him on a hot August afternoon in 1994. I cannot recall his name, but that is not important. He was no different from many other young black men in this country: poor, bright, and troubled. Not so very long ago, that description would have easily fit me. And perhaps it is this, more than anything else, that drew me to this menacing figure with imposing eyes and a slanted pose who ranged like a hawk over this rough West Baltimore street corner, a place legendary for its uncanny ability to dominate generation after generation of black men. Perhaps it was my own history here, the ghosts of a squandered youth and shattered hope that elicited my empathy for this stranger. Perhaps it was the traces of my own blood that had spilled and dried years ago on that same slab of concrete at the intersection of Robert and Division streets that spurred me to reach out to him.

It is always a difficult thing to gain the trust of a street warrior, and on this day I looked far from trustworthy. I was accompanied by veteran journalist Steve Kroft and his "60 Minutes" news crew. They were trailing me as part of a story they were doing on the growing influence of the Congressional Black Caucus. We had already walked several blocks and filmed in what an outsider might regard as generic urban blight: the buildings boarded up, the laundry hanging above row house stoops, pregnant teenage girls, and old folks peeking out from behind drawn window shades. For me and hundreds of thousands of African Americans across the nation, these were and are the symbols of home.

My visit this day was both deliberate and contrived. We had come to my old neighborhood to capture a look back in time to my roots. The place had changed drastically from the days when I had walked the streets as a young tough. Poverty held the community in a viselike grip. The buildings, those which were still standing, revealed the deep seriousness of the evil plagues of unemployment, drugs, government neglect, and despair that had seized control of the area. Bans of idle, bitter-youth no longer attempted to attend the inferior schools which dotted the community. Here, crime too often was a daily occurrence.

I was chairman of the Congressional Black Caucus and that alone had made me the focus of the story. I suspect that filming me in the midst of this other America was "60 Minutes' " way of underscoring the irony of my ascension. But the media spectacle, the video cameras, the lights, and the bustling technicians clouded me in a shroud of suspicion to those nearby who watched.

In the eyes of this young gang-banger and the others around him I was conspicuously out of my element. Almost catlike, he began to move quickly in the other direction and his posse followed suit. You didn't need a Ph.D. to know what was going on. They thought I was the Man. They probably thought that the camera crew was there to film them dealing drugs or to cast them as an example of the urban problem. The fact that they believed any or all of it upset me.

Moments such as this reminded me that in the eyes of some I have become part of the Establishment that they loathe, a system which stacks statistics and insurmountable odds against them. It's an Establishment of great punishment and little reward, one that many people of color both fear and distrust. On this day, I strangely yearned to set the record straight. To let these young guys know I was not part of any kind of conspiracy that seeks to further bring them down. I was not among the media vultures that thrive and grow fat off the carcasses of poor people crushed under the colossus of urban woes. I was not one of those insincere politicians who make empty promises built on a bunch of false assumptions. I wondered how I could make them realize that I didn't represent that part of the Establishment, that my life, too, is rooted in the same pain and frustration that bonds them together.

"Stay here," I told the camera crew without so much as looking at them. Even in hindsight, I cannot explain the strange mix of emotions that propelled me out into the street that day. As much as I've tried, I can't define the rush of emotion that I felt that sent me running off toward the gang, darting past the row houses of Division Street and around the corner eastward to the opening of the alley. I was not afraid to confront them, though I wasn't fully sure what I would say to them when I did. (pp. 1–3)

When we read this in our teacher workshops and literacy courses and pose those purpose questions, most of the participants who respond "No" (i.e., they do not believe the gang members will listen to Mfume), base their predictions on Mfume's resemblance to members of the Establishment—dressed in suit and tie—which this group of people mistrusts. In other words, they have an image of Kweisi Mfume in their long-term memories and are able to see him approaching the boys. Students who do not know who Mfume is and do not know what he looks like and how he typically dresses respond that the camera crew was with Mfume, and therefore he was not trusted. Once they are reminded that Mfume dismisses the camera crew, they have no factual basis for a prediction. If a secondary teacher were to have students read this for class, the teacher would be wise to show a picture of Mr. Mfume and provide some background on his ascension out of poverty to become chairman of the Congressional Black Caucus as part of developing background of experience prior to reading.

Assessing and developing background of experience is an especially important step in a reading lesson when one works with students of diverse backgrounds, that is, "students who differ from the mainstream in terms of ethnicity, primary language and social class" p. 150 (Au, 2002, p. 392). Look at the ESL/English lesson for ninth grade students, "Nikki-Rosa." The class is about to launch into a unit on biographies that will include reading biographies and eventually writing a brief biography. The teacher begins this initiatory lesson by displaying several biographies and giving a brief talk about each. The teacher is careful to include biographies that will be of interest to fifteen-year-old students, to include selections about notable individuals from the native countries represented by students in the class, and to show pictures of the individuals while they listen to the teacher highlight the major accomplishments of each person featured. In this way, students' cultural backgrounds are affirmed and broadened.

Recently, we were instructing a tenth grade ESL government class, consisting mainly of Hispanic students who had been in the United State less than one year, and who, with their families, had immigrated from primarily rural environments. They now live and attend high school in a suburban setting. The reading for which they were being readied reported on the assistance the federal government gives to large cities to remedy urban problems such as school overcrowding, drug and gun problems, and housing neglect and shortage. Even though the school these students attended was only a ten-minute car or bus ride away from a major city, only two students in the class reported ever being in a city. Surprised by this lack of needed background, we quickly designed a developing background phase for this class that showed the students pictures of cities and conditions they would read about so that when they read they could imagine the environment for the problems and solutions reported in the article.

Sometimes, as we did in the ESL class, a teacher might still misjudge students' background, despite the most thoughtful planning. Veteran educators report that most often, through experience at their schools with their students and parents, as well as experiences with the wider community, they almost intuit what background students in their classes have and what they do not have. But, when in doubt, ask!

We worked with classes of eighth grade students about to embark on a unit entitled "The Writers' Voice." Prior to starting this unit and during our planning of it, we asked the students to write a response to this prompt: "In previous grades, you learned the difference between a character in a story who is a *protagonist* and a character who was an *antagonist*. Explain the difference and give an example of a protagonist and an antagonist from a short story or novel we have read this year in English."

What we learned by skimming these responses was that many of our students were harboring the concept of protagonist as the good person in the story and the antagonist as the bad person. With this knowledge of their backgrounds, we planned an activity to correct their misinformation.

While planning the reading lessons for the novel *Roll of Thunder, Hear My Cry,* the teacher asked her students at the end of one of her classes to write down what they remembered from their seventh grade social studies unit about the following topics: the Ku Klux Klan, the Great Depression, and Jim Crow laws. Their responses indicated a need to substantially refresh their memories prior to reading the novel; therefore, the teacher decided to include the jigsaw activity during the Tapping and Developing Background of Experience phase.

**p. 21**

Look at the English lesson plan model in Chapter 2. How did the teacher develop background of experience for the short story "The Scarlet Ibis"? Why did she choose to develop this specific topic?

**REFLECT**

To accomplish the objectives of this lesson, especially objective 4 dealing with the symbolism of the title, students need to see the scarlet ibis, to know what it looks like, and to be aware of its natural habitat; otherwise, they will not be able to explain the connection between this flamingo and the character Doodles—in appearance and displacement.

It is not only narrative readings that place imaging demands on readers. Imaging while reading expository passages will also facilitate comprehension. In the French lesson, "Une Escale Exotique a la Martinique," the students take a virtual tour of Martinique so that they can see the island as they read to discover the island's climate, industries, government, connection to France, and so on. The middle school math teacher has students examine different types of graphs from mass media in the lesson "Line, Bar and Pie Graphs" so that students can imagine the types of graphs as they read to discern the characteristics of line, bar, and pie graphs. The music teacher, in the lesson "Traditional African Instruments," shows

**p. 157**

**p. 171**

**p. 182**

and demonstrates African instruments in the developing background phase of the lesson so students will be able to conjure images of these instruments as they read about the materials needed to make them. And in the English lesson, "Tales of the Mysterious," students use maps to label locations where sea serpent sitings have occurred, so that they can "see" the area being described in the reading.

p. 142

Access to computer technology provides teachers with almost unlimited resources for developing their own and their students' backgrounds. According to the U.S. National Center for Education Statistics and from *Education Week's Technology Counts 2001* report, by the fall of 2000, 98 percent of public schools in the United States had access to the Internet, with "virtually no differences in school access to the Internet by school characteristics such as poverty level and metropolitan status" (International Reading Association, 2001, p. 13). This allows teachers to take students on virtual tours, experience people and events via video clips, and access written information, thus developing topical background and images for upcoming reading.

Several of the lesson plans in this text use websites to develop student background. For example, the high school French lesson has students visit Martinique on the Web; the high school social studies lesson, "The Development of the Supreme Court's Power," has the students taking a virtual tour of the Supreme Court chambers and seeing pictures of the current justices; and the choral music lesson on the "Battle Hymn of the Republic" includes pictures from the Civil War selected from a website about the North and religion.

Textbook chapters sometimes include photographs and charts to help the reader form an image while reading. Unfortunately, students do not always attend to these automatically; therefore, it becomes the responsibility of the teacher to bring these to the attention of the students prior to reading. For example, we have witnessed science teachers who overview the surface parts of the amoeba and paramecium, using overhead transparencies of textbook pictures, prior to students reading a chapter in their biology textbook on the movement and feeding of these protozoans, to ensure that students have a movie of the mind of these protists in action as they read.

## SUMMARY

The second step of the Readiness section of the Directed Reading Lesson is Tapping and Developing Background of Experience, the teacher's attempt to ensure that students have the necessary topical background to comprehend the upcoming content reading. Whatever background is needed should not be assumed, nor should it be assumed that if students have the background they will automatically recall it. The teacher needs to bring that background to the students' conscious working memories.

Tapping background of experience readies students for the upcoming reading by mobilizing connections for the new learning, validating their topical background knowledge, sensitizing them to the importance of the upcoming information, and continuing to spark their interest and curiosity. Developing background of experience provides the lacking prerequisite topical background, thus adding insurance for comprehension of the upcoming content reading.

This background of experience phase appears to have a positive effect on students' general disposition for learning. One middle school social studies teacher reported, "I have noticed that by tapping their strong experiential backgrounds and adding to it, they feel empowered and validated and more willing to share during the rest of the lesson." Gloria Ladson-Billings in *Dreamkeepers: Successful Teachers of African American Children* (1994) calls this strategy essential to "culturally relevant teaching," that is, "moving between . . . two cultures," the students' cultural background and the dominant culture (p. 18).

The secret to a successful Tapping and Developing Background of Experience phase of the Directed Reading Lesson is the teacher's careful reading and reflection on the background needed to comprehend the upcoming reading and learning. In planning this phase of the Directed Reading Lesson, teachers should read the content material and ask themselves the following questions:

**Questions for Planning the Tapping and Developing Background
of Experience Phase of the Directed Reading Lesson**

1. What topical background information is assumed for comprehension of this reading?
2. What do I see when I read this selection?
3. Do my students have this background from previous lessons or from general life experiences? How will I review this information with them?
4. If they do not have the necessary background, how can I provide it?
5. Will my students be able to form images from this reading? If not, how can I provide them these images prior to reading?

## YOUR TURN

1. Reread the content selection for your lesson. Read first to make a list of the topical background that is assumed for comprehension of this passage. Then read again to make a list of the images you see while you are reading.
2. Once you have made these two lists, you can draft your plans for this part of the Directed Reading Lesson by using questions 3–5 in the previous section.
3. If you are using this textbook as part of a course or workshop experience, share the draft of your background of experience phase with, or teach this phase to, another participant. Have this colleague react to your draft. Does your colleague:
   - Find your tapping interesting and appropriate?
   - Find your development interesting and appropriate?
   - Think your tapping and development of background will be interesting and appropriate for your intended audience of students?
   - Have any advice for revision?

# CHAPTER FIVE

# CONCEPT DEVELOPMENT/ VOCABULARY

But words are things, and a small drop of ink,
Falling like dew, upon a thought, produces
That which makes thousands, perhaps millions, think.

*—George Gordon, Lord Byron, British poet*

1. Readiness
   a. Motivation
   b. Tapping and Developing Background of Experience
   **c. Concept Development/Vocabulary**
   d. Purpose-for-Reading
2. Silent Reading
3. Discussion
4. Rereading
5. Follow-Up

From your reading of the model lessons, what did you discern as the purpose of the Concept Development/Vocabulary phase of Readiness? In our view, the purpose of this phase is to ready the students with an initial understanding of the key concepts they will need to understand the content selection.

A concept is the idea we have of something by understanding its observable characteristics or essential attributes. We label concepts with words. For example, the concept *metamorphosis* has the following essential attributes: (1) a developmental process, (2) common to insects and amphibians, and 3) characterized by an abrupt, hormonally induced and regulated transformation from a larval to an adult form. The concept *verb* has these essential attributes: (1) a part of speech and (2) denotes action or state of being. Sometimes a concept is represented by more than one word, for example, *saturated fat* and *high blood pressure*. Our stock of concepts, represented by oral and written words, is our vocabulary. Educators often use the terms *word, word knowledge,* and *vocabulary* interchangeably.

In middle and high school reading material, the vocabulary in academic and performance subjects is daunting. For example:

**Art**

| | | | |
|---|---|---|---|
| woven | design | rhythm | harmony |
| relief sculpture | pigment | aesthetic view | tempera |
| composition | megaliths | ziggurat | |

**Health**

| | | | |
|---|---|---|---|
| hypoglycemia | epidermis | sebum | receptor |
| capillary | socialization | conditioning | repression |
| sublimation | | | |

**History**

| | | | |
|---|---|---|---|
| contraband | neutrality | embargo | inalienable |
| endowed | economic recession | platform planks | sovereignty |
| devastation | | | |

**Algebra**

| | | | |
|---|---|---|---|
| domain | continuity | range | maximum value |
| line of symmetry | x-intercept/zero(s) | y-intercept | |

**Science**

| | | | |
|---|---|---|---|
| table | glucose | carp | chitin |
| structural molecule | capillary action | potassium | polarity |
| theory | waterspouts | | |

As established in Chapter 1, word knowledge, or semantics, is one of the essential cueing systems for reading comprehension. Studies on the effect vocabulary priming has on comprehension (e.g., McKeown, Beck, Omanson, & Pople, 1985; Ryder & Medo, 1993) have led many educators to believe it is the most important cueing system.

Teaching essential vocabulary can improve students' comprehension of a reading selection (Beck, Perfetti, & McKeown, 1982). This is because the more words we understand, the better are our chances of comprehending. We do not suggest that a reader must know the meaning of every word in a passage; in fact, rarely is this the case. But as the percentage of words the reader understands decreases, so does the reader's overall understanding of the passage.

Because failure to understand even a few key words can seriously impede comprehension and learning in the content classroom, vocabulary instruction belongs in every content area. Words must be selected judiciously and taught directly, prior to reading, by the teacher who is the content specialist. "Hardly any instructional activity can pay such high dividends in relation to time spent as teacher-directed vocabulary instruction" (Blair-Larson & Williams, 1999, pp. 26–27). Research has shown that directly teaching vocabulary significantly increases students' comprehension (Stahl & Fairbanks, 1986). Such increases can go a long way toward moving students from limited to useful learning of content information through reading.

Some school systems have set specific expectations of vocabulary mastery. For example, educators in Montgomery County, Maryland, expect that by middle school students will learn and use 8–10 new words per week in each discipline. Yet in spite of such standards, research (Alvermann & Moore, 1996) and our own experience with teachers leads us to conclude that systematic vocabulary instruction is rare (McKeown & Curtis, 1987) because most content teachers (aside from English, ESL, and foreign language teachers) do not view their role as one who should directly teach vocabulary.

# INCIDENTAL LEARNING OF VOCABULARY

The most efficient way for students to learn new words is to be exposed to a rich language environment. In fact, the most efficient way we learn new words is by surrounding ourselves with people who speak well. Exposure to others using words new to us in a social or professional context allows us to learn through direct experience and thus to incorporate the words into our receptive vocabularies. Eventually we generate these words in our speaking and writing. Unfortunately, we cannot count on all our students having such rich language environments. A 1999 report from the National Institute of Health reported that a child at twelve to eighteen months of age from a family at or below the poverty line hears 600–700 words per hour, a child from a middle-income family hears 1200–1300 words per hour, and a child from an upper-income family hears 2900–3100 words per hour (Montgomery County Public Schools, 2001).

Another incidental way to learn new words efficiently and effectively is by wide reading over time (Nagy, Herman, & Anderson, 1985), through which the reader learns words from context. Unfortunately we cannot rely on our secondary students to do their own independent wide reading. Even youngsters who were voracious readers in elementary school often become dormant readers during their secondary years due to the distractions of adolescent socialization. The National Assessment of Educational Progress looked at long-term reading trends between 1984 and 1996 and found that the percentage of seventeen-year-olds who said they read for fun each day dropped from an already low 31 percent to 23 percent (Lehigh, 1999). Even for those students who do read widely, for a new word to be learned from context while reading, it must be encountered several times (six times being the most frequently recommended number from research) before a reader sufficiently understands it and can recall its meaning (Jenkins, Stein, & Wysocki, 1984). Therefore, even though students can learn new vocabulary without our assistance, direct instruction with discussion of words and their meanings is more effective for acquisition of essential content vocabulary (Duke & Pearson, 2002; Nelson-Herber, 1986).

## INEFFECTIVE PRACTICE

Not all direct instruction methods are effective, however. Classroom practices such as looking up words in a dictionary or glossary, using vocabulary workbooks, and discussing a list of decontextualized words during class more often result in students misunderstanding or not learning the meanings, thus reinforcing negative attitudes about word study.

Dictionary and glossary definitions too often:

- Are vague (e.g., system: a set of elements along with the connections between them that form a whole or work together)
- Include words in the definition often unknown to the student (e.g., ionosphere: the part of the earth's atmosphere beginning at an altitude of about 40 kilometers, extending outward 400 kilometers or more, and containing electrically charged particles)
- Use figurative language (e.g., erode: to eat into)

Dictionary and glossary definitions are written by experts who already know the meaning of the words, which makes it difficult to judge the clarity of the explanation for the learner. Using the "look up the words in the dictionary" approach puts students in a passive mode. The teacher might as well dictate the definitions or give a transcript of the definitions to students because this "look it up" approach makes no provision for the students' active construction of meaning of the concept.

Published vocabulary workbooks, most often employed in English classes, can also put students in the position of passive learners. In some vocabulary workbooks, each chapter contains a list of selected words that are unrelated to the reading students are doing in class. Words are followed by definitions and sentences that students are directed to study. The only difference is that students do not consume time locating the words and definitions. Often no assistance or clues for the active construction of a meaningful definition are provided for students; thus students must memorize or find some way on their own to process the definitions and construct meaning for themselves.

Newer vocabulary workbook series sometimes have students actively engaged by having them examine two or more sentences for each vocabulary word and having them then decide on the meaning of the word from the sentence context before going on to matching and insertion exercises. Although this approach is better than giving the meanings to the learners, it is still limited by the lack of relevance to the content being studied and by the subsequent lack of immediate use and reinforcement of these terms.

The list-of-words-in-isolation, or decontextualized approach includes having the teacher present selected vocabulary words and ask for volunteers to tell what the words mean. For those students who already know the meaning of a word, it is a retrieval process, little more than recalling what they already know. For those who do not know the word, it is passive reception of the meaning from another student. The student telling the meaning serves as the "oral dictionary" for the other students. Again, there is no guarantee that the listening students have constructed meaning of the concept from this approach. For example, a language arts teacher, realizing that understanding the term *duck blind* was crucial to students' understanding of the plot and setting of the upcoming reading, asked the class what *duck blind* meant, thus fulfilling the need to directly teach essential vocabulary. One student in the class, a regular hunter with his father and uncles, explained that it was "a place hunters hide to shoot ducks." Nonmastery of that meaning was evident during the postreading discussion of the story when several students expressed confusion about the "blind ducks."

Having witnessed this decontextualized approach in secondary schools leads us to conclude that too often students attempt to define words for which they do not actually know the meanings. What happens is that the other students in the class are exposed to these invalid definitions and remember them as opposed to the accurate definition that is revealed by the teacher.

To experience how this decontextualized approach feels from the student's perspective, pretend your instructor has determined that you need to understand the following two essential concepts for an upcoming reading in class:

    *predelecter*         *abodent*

She asks you to tell her what these two terms mean. What does each word mean? You do not know!?

When we use this activity in teacher workshops, we ask the teachers how they feel. Invariably, someone says "ignorant" or "stupid." And that is how students feel because they are not given the opportunity to discover what the words mean when we employ the in-isolation approach. We have just made them aware of what we had already decided, they don't know the meaning of the word or words. We decide they need to know specific words, we select words to preteach because we know they do not know the meanings, then we ask them to tell us what they mean.

A variation of this approach is when the teacher gives the students a list of words or words on index cards, then orally recites or shows students a definition of one of the words. Students are to find the word from the list that matches the definition. Like the decontextualized approach, unless the students already know the meaning of the words, they have no chance to identify the correct word. This is a retrieval activity, one based on the assumption that students have already learned the meanings of the words and now are retrieving the meanings from their brains for review and reinforcement. This vocabulary activity is fine for review and reinforcement of word meanings, but first the teacher must assist in initial learning of the meaning of the words. Initial learning requires a way for students to construct the meaning for themselves.

## AN INTERACTIVE APPROACH
## TO VOCABULARY PRIMING

Most secondary school teachers have been trained in, and espouse a commitment to, interactive pedagogy. Thus, their daily plans involve students in searching for meaning of essential concepts, interacting with each other and the teacher in that search, and connecting new learning to what is relevant to them and their experiences (Neubert & Binko, 1992; Stover, Neubert, & Lawlor, 1993). Vocabulary instruction can also actualize this philosophy. The approach to direct vocabulary instruction outlined here is based on the view that essential content vocabulary can and should be taught directly through interactive pedagogy.

## Step 1. Judiciously Select the Essential Content Vocabulary to Prime

During planning, the teacher should select from the upcoming reading material only vocabulary that left unlearned would impede learning of the content material. These words should be primed, that is, taught prior to reading, so that roadblocks to comprehension are removed. When students learn the meanings of words prior to reading material that requires them to use this knowledge, they get immediate practice and reinforcement of word knowledge. If the words taught are essential to accomplishing the learning outcome of the lesson, students will then have to use the words in written responses and oral discussions of the content during and after reading, thus continuing to reinforce understanding and support long-term retention.

You may be tempted to select every word students might not know in the upcoming reading, but the key is to select only those words that:

1. Must be understood to accomplish the learning outcomes for that specific reading
2. Are not clearly explained in context
3. Are not already in the students' generative vocabulary

If this list is lengthy, it might be a signal that the reading is entirely too difficult for the students at this time and that an alternative medium for students to learn the particular content should be considered. The key here is to prime only vocabulary essential to the purpose-for-reading. Few readers know or need to know every word to satisfactorily comprehend a passage. One to five new, essential content vocabulary items—well learned prior to reading and reinforced by use during and after the reading—will have a more positive impact on the comprehension of the content reading than a superficial exposure to a lengthy list of words.

The first step in selecting the words for the Concept Development/Vocabulary phase of the Readiness portion of the Directed Reading Lesson is for the content teacher to write the purpose-for-reading the students will have as their focus when they read the content selection. The teacher must first determine the essential knowledge the students should learn from the reading. How to determine and state the purpose-for-reading is the subject of Chapter 6 of this text.

The next step is to complete the key, that is, the acceptable and expected student responses to the purpose-for-reading. Let's assume that you are a health or consumer science teacher who attended one of our recent reading workshops. You are continuing a unit on diet with your students. The upcoming reading, Chapter 5, is about dietary guidelines developed by the federal government for Americans. In compliance with your curriculum learning outcomes, you set the following purpose-for-reading: "You will be reading Chapter 5 to be informed about dietary guidelines. You will explain in your own words the *effect* the following guidelines have on your body. You will use the graphic organizer shown in Table 5.1 to record your responses."

This key becomes the word bank from which you will select the vocabulary for priming. The words in the key are the pool of essential vocabulary words students must comprehend if they are to be able to explain the rationale for each of the national dietary guidelines and eventually actualize them in their daily diets.

You now begin the elimination process, eliminating words you know are already in your students' receptive vocabularies and words that you believe are adequately explained in context in the reading. When the teachers in our workshop completed this activity, they found three concepts that they needed to prime: *moderate, nutrient density,* and *high blood pressure.* They did not include words that might appear to be difficult, such as *nutrients, carbohydrates, saturated fat,* and *cholesterol,* because these were words that would have been necessary to prime with previous chapters. They might want to review these terms, but initial learning was unnecessary because they would have been previously primed.

**TABLE 5.1   Dietary Guidelines for Americans**

| GUIDELINE (CAUSE) | WHY? (EFFECT ON YOU AND YOUR BODY) |
| --- | --- |
| 1. Eat a variety of foods. | 1. *Variety is more interesting; get nutrients body needs.* |
| 2. Balance the food you eat with physical activity. | 2. *Weighing too much results in greater risk of health problems.* |
| 3. Choose a diet with plenty of grain products, vegetables, and fruits. | 3. *High in carbohydrates; sources of vitamins, minerals, and fiber.* |
| 4. Choose a diet low in fat, saturated fat, and cholesterol. | 4. *Less risk of heart disease, cancer, and weight gain.* |
| 5. Choose a diet moderate in sugars. | 5. *High sugar equals low nutrient density.* |
| 6. Choose a diet moderate in salt and sodium. | 6. *Too much salt can cause high blood pressure.* |

Expected student responses are in italics.

Notice that these health or consumer science teachers chose not only technical concepts such as *nutrient density* and *high blood pressure* but also a general vocabulary word, *moderate,* because it is needed to understand the content information. Content specialists are responsible for teaching students essential general, nonspecific, and technical vocabulary—not only the technical register of their discipline.

## Step 2.  Plan a Contextual Strategy for Each Vocabulary Word

When teachers hear the word *context,* they often think of a sentence that includes the selected vocabulary word. Sentences that provide sufficient context clues for students to determine a valid definition, however, are often difficult for the teacher to write. This is because teachers, like writers of dictionaries and glossaries, are experts who already know the meaning of the vocabulary word, thus the sentence they choose to present to students appears appropriate to them. Too often the sentence does not rule out erroneous definitions because it does not provide students with adequate clues to infer all the essential attributes of the concept. For example, the sentence, "Mary is good-natured, but her sister is *cantankerous,*" was given to students to help them construct a definition of *cantankerous.* Some validly inferred from the sentence context that Mary's sister is grumpy, but others inferred that she is even more pleasant than Mary.

Sometimes presenting more than one sentence context clue for a word allows students to construct a valid definition because additional essential attributes of the concept are revealed, as occurs when these two sentences are presented together for the purpose of constructing a definition of *cantankerous:*

Mary is good-natured, but her sister is *cantankerous.*

James was so *cantankerous* at the party that no one wanted to socialize with him.

Teachers should also keep in mind that only rarely should they use the focus vocabulary word as it appears in the upcoming text. If it has sufficient context for the students to infer meaning while reading, then there is no need to prime this word; if it does not have sufficient context in the reading, it will not have sufficient context clues by itself for inducing meaning during priming activities. Teachers may choose to use the actual sentence from the upcoming reading, but in conjunction with one or more other sentences that actually assist in establishing the meaning.

p. 21

p. 182

Look at the English lesson plan in Chapter 2 and the music lesson, "Traditional Instruments of Africa," in Appendix A. The English teacher displays two sentences to help her students discern the meaning of *infallibility,* and the music lesson plan involves students inducing the meaning of *resonate* from three sentences using various forms of the word.

p. 150
p. 216
Another useful approach is to ask students to apply their knowledge of structural analysis (meanings of roots, prefixes, suffixes, compounds, hyphenated forms) to discover the meaning of a word. The teacher of the ESL class in the lesson "Nikki-Rosa," after helping the students induce the meaning of *biography,* then has them apply the previously learned suffix, *-er,* and define *biographer.* In the lesson "The Development of the Supreme Court's Power," the social studies teacher provides sentence context clues, but also capitalizes on the students' understanding of the prefix, *un-,* to help them define *unconstitutional*
p. 205
and the root *regulate* to teach them *regulatory.* A similar approach is used in the science lesson, "Relationships in a Habitat," with the prefix, *inter-,* to assist the students in inducing the definition of the word *interaction.* Structural analysis in a foreign language class often includes the recognition of cognates. A cognate is a word in a foreign language that shares the same or a similar graphic form and meaning to a word in the learner's native or known
p. 225
language. The Spanish lesson, "Una Leyenda del Caribe," includes a reference to cognates as students are deriving the definitions of the words *oscuridad* and *soportar.*

Teachers often find contextual strategies other than sentence clues more successful for assisting students in constructing meaning for new content vocabulary. These include using concrete representations, guided imagery, and concept attainment as clues.

A concrete representation can be a direct experience, seeing the real artifact, or seeing a picture of the vocabulary word. The brain loves pictures! The adage "a picture is worth a thousand words" certainly applies here. What easier way to learn the word *cataract* in the life science class than to view a model of the eye and see where and how a cataract develops. Or students can learn *cataract* in social studies by viewing the cataracts of Niagara Falls and those in New Guinea on websites located in advance by the teacher. Even abstract vocabulary words can be learned through pictures. For example, the definition of *affluent* can be constructed by students after they examine a series of pictures of affluent people whom they recognize—Bill Gates, Michael Jordan, Oprah Winfrey, Donald Trump, and so on. (To rule out the idea that affluent people must be "famous," the teacher should also include a picture of someone who is affluent, but not in the news.) Mathematics teachers can prime the word *triangle* by having students view triangles from M. C. Escher's drawings, triangles in flags, and triangular building supports through the website The Amazing Picture Machine (www.ncrtec.org/picture./htm). Or the same website can be searched for pictures of rainforests, taigas, and deserts when the scientific term *biome* is taught.

In theory, what is happening is that the brain is connecting the abstract with the concrete, and abstract language is being encoded as mental imagery. "Verbal and nonverbal semantic systems are functionally and anatomically distinct . . . yet they are interconnected" (West, O'Rourke, & Holcomb, 1998). Research studies abound demonstrating that imagery-based techniques for vocabulary study are far superior to techniques that do not involve images (Powell, 1980).

pp. 17, 22, 26

**REFLECT**

Look at each of the anchoring lesson plans in Chapter 2. How does each teacher employ concrete representations to teach vocabulary? The science teacher uses a transparency of Washington, D.C., to teach *grid plan;* the English teacher shows a picture of an Amish woman wearing a caul to lead students to an understanding of a baby born with a *caul;* the art teacher shows a picture of a *loom* and then demonstrates how to *warp* and *weft.*

p. 154
See what examples of concrete representations to teach specific vocabulary words you can find in the lesson plans in Appendix A. For example, in the high school English lesson, "The Successful Job Interview," students watch a video segment without sound to learn
p. 182
the concept *nonverbal messages.* The music teacher in the lesson "Traditional Instruments of Africa" combines real artifacts with a sentence to help students understand the meaning of *gourd.* The family and consumer science teacher displays contrasting pictures and sen-
p. 138
tences to assist students in learning the difference between *prone* and *supine.* The special education teacher in the lesson "Reading a Menu" has students examine pictures on the

p. 228
p. 199

menu to define *strombol, pasta,* and *submarine.* A demonstration with two balloons, one filled with air, the other with helium, is used in the science lesson, "Leftovers," to teach *gravity.*

Guided imagery, or visualization, is another imagery-based, contextual strategy, in which the teacher describes a scene to help students create a picture of the vocabulary word in their minds. A secondary school teacher who wants students to define *mutualism* would instruct them to do the following:

> *Close your eyes and look at a blank screen. I will describe a scene for you and you should see it with your mind's eye.*
>
> *It is a beautiful summer afternoon. You are riding in the front passenger seat of a car with the windows and sunroof open. It is sunny, 90 degrees, and a warm breeze blows through the car from the right. You are riding on a dual highway and going about 35 mph. As you gaze out the right car window, you catch occasional glimpses of the ocean. Often the ocean is blocked from your view by the tall sand dunes, which are so prominent on this part of the ocean beach. On top of the dunes are tall grasses that wave in the strong breeze coming off the ocean. The driver calls your attention to something up ahead on the right on the top of one of the dunes. As you focus on this dune, you realize that there are two horses standing on the dune—two wild horses that frequent this part of the ocean area. Your driver approaches slowly as not to distract the horses and pulls the car to a stop on the side of the road so that you can watch the horses as they graze on the grasses. The black stallion appears to be eating comfortably, but many gnats flying about his head noticeably distract the brown horse. He eats, but continuously interrupts his meal to swish his head, mane, and tail, apparently in an attempt to get rid of the annoying bugs. As you watch, an amazing phenomenon occurs. An egret, a tall white bird, common to this part of the country and ocean, lands on the back of the brown horse and begins to snap and eat the circling gnats. As the egret feasts, the brown horse no longer interrupts his eating and no longer stops to swish his tail and shake his head and mane. Watch the horse and egret. This is an example of mutualism.*

The teacher then continues with guided imagery by describing a second scene involving bees and flowers or ants and acacia trees, ending with labeling this second scene also an example of *mutualism.*

p. 18

If you reexamine the science lesson in Chapter 2, you will see that the teacher also uses guided imagery, in this case to teach rushes, and she shows a picture as a backup for her students.

The third contextual strategy for helping students to construct definitions is concept attainment. Concept attainment is an inductive approach during which the teacher presents examples and nonexamples of the vocabulary word and asks students to process these clues to define the new vocabulary word. For example, in math class, the teacher can assist students in the construction of the meaning of *set,* as a "clearly defined collection of objects," by having students examine the following:

| **Sets** | **Not Sets** |
|---|---|
| 1. The Great Lakes | 1. Large lakes of the world |
| 2. Subjects taken this year by all students in this class | 2. Attractive teachers on this faculty |
| 3. Whole numbers | 3. Good Oriole baseball players |
| 4. Students in this class who own a live hippopotamus | |

p. 158

Look at the Concept Development/Vocabulary phase of the French lesson, "Une Escale Exotique a la Martinique." Notice how the teacher uses concept attainment to teach

p. 172

p. 17

"France d'outremer" by presenting two lists of countries, one that is "France d'outremer" and one that is not. To teach the word *adjacent,* concept attainment is executed through direct experience in the math lesson, "Line, Bar, Pie Graphs," by having two students stand near one another, almost touching, and another two students stand at opposite ends of the room. The first two students are described as *adjacent;* the second pair as *not adjacent.* Now look at the science lesson in Chapter 2. Here the teacher combines concept attainment and lab demonstration (a direct experience type of concrete representation) to teach the meaning of *tinder.* She uses two pieces of wood, identifies one as *tinder* and the other as *not tinder,* then sets both on fire. Students observe that the one labeled *tinder* bursts into flames and the other does not.

Concept attainment is also an effective strategy for teaching students the meaning of closely related or contrasting vocabulary words. For example, in science class, students can define the vocabulary words *herbivore* and *carnivore* after examining the following lists:

| **Carnivores** | **Herbivores** |
| --- | --- |
| Lions | Rabbits |
| Domestic cats | Squirrels |
| Dogs | Grasshoppers |
| Vultures | Bees |

Or in math class, *simple* and *compound interest* can be taught as contrasting concepts: "The following two examples of methods of computing interest on a principal sum illustrate the differences between *simple interest* and *compound interest.* Both examples use a $100 principal and 7% interest. Use the examples in the following charts and differentiate between *simple interest* and *compound interest.*"

**Simple Interest**

| YEAR | PRINCIPAL ($) | INTEREST ($) | ENDING BALANCE ($) |
| --- | --- | --- | --- |
| 1 | 100.00 | 7.00 | 107.00 |
| 2 | 100.00 | 7.00 | 114.00 |
| 3 | 100.00 | 7.00 | 121.00 |
| 4 | 100.00 | 7.00 | 128.00 |
| 5 | 100.00 | 7.00 | 135.00 |
| | Total interest 35.00 | | |

**Compound Interest**

| YEAR | PRINCIPAL ($) | INTEREST ($) | ENDING BALANCE ($) |
| --- | --- | --- | --- |
| 1 | 100.00 | 7.00 | 107.00 |
| 2 | 107.00 | 7.49 | 114.49 |
| 3 | 114.49 | 8.01 | 122.50 |
| 4 | 122.50 | 8.58 | 131.08 |
| 5 | 131.08 | 9.18 | 140.26 |
| | Total interest 40.26 | | |

Contributed by Carolyn Bendyna, June, 2001.

p. 162

Look at how concept attainment is used in the health lesson, "Eating Disorder," to teach the related concepts *normal body image* and *distorted body image.*

When planning any type of contextual strategy, the teacher should be cognizant of the background of the students (see Chapter 4). Students must know the meaning of surrounding vocabulary words if sentence clues are given for new vocabulary, have sufficient background to conjure an image described by their teacher during guided imagery, and be familiar with the examples and nonexamples used in concept development lists.

Teachers must also consider how they can capitalize on students' background of experience to help students connect a new conceptual understanding to their previous backgrounds. For example, the teacher who wants to teach *cataract* as a specific landform might begin by asking if any students have ever been to Niagara Falls or ever seen it on TV or video and then ask them to describe the falls. Notice in the art lesson in Chapter 2 that the teacher begins by asking students if they ever made potholders as youngsters, or if they had read about Penelope weaving in *The Odyssey*.

Another important consideration when planning the contextual strategy is to help students avoid brain interference when they must learn new definitions for nonspecific words. Look back to the science lesson in Chapter 2. The word *rushes* as a distinctive feature of a marsh is the new definition the students are to learn, but the teacher recognizes that most of her students will already know *rushes* as meaning hurrying. She encourages students to recall that meaning, then tells them that they are about to learn a second meaning for the word *rushes*. The French teacher does the same with *la peche* with the lesson "Une Escale Exotique a la Martinique." She asks the class what meaning they know for this word, affirms that definition as valid, and then tells them that it can also mean something else that they will now learn.

## Step 3.  Use the Vocabulary Priming Process during the Concept Development Phase of Readiness

**REFLECT**

To prepare you with a movie of the mind for the explication of this process, we recommend that you now reread the Concept Development/Vocabulary phase of two or more lesson plans in this text. Your purpose-for-reading is to be informed about the steps in the vocabulary priming process. You will list the steps used each time a new word is taught.

The transition between the Tapping and Developing Background of Experience and the Concept Development/Vocabulary phases of Readiness includes a statement by the teacher to the students that there are new vocabulary words, essential to their comprehension of the upcoming reading, that they must now learn. If you revisit the three model lesson plans in Chapter 2, you will notice that each teacher has included such a statement. The first word is then shown visually to students—written on the board, transparency, or PowerPoint slide—and read aloud by the teacher to ensure correct pronunciation. It may then be repeated by the students, if the teacher feels that this step is necessary.

pp. 17, 21, 26

The contextual clues for that word are then revealed. The teacher's directions to the students after a word is presented in context should be "Now draft a definition for X." The term *draft* is deliberately chosen to let students know that this is a beginning idea, that it does not have to be perfect, that it is a hypothesis that will be shared first with a peer, then with the class, possibly shaping the definition along the way. Students should be encouraged to be risk-takers in a safe environment that allows them to practice and appreciate the study of language. They should define new vocabulary in their own words so it is meaningful to them.

Next, the teacher instructs students to collaborate with their vocabulary partner, share their definitions, and revise them (if needed) to reach consensus. The purpose of this sharing is to capitalize on the social nature of learning and to encourage students to use their critical thinking skills to accept or reject their original definitions. "[P]ositive effects result from social interactions during word learning" (Ruddell, 1994, p. 436). Decisions about pairing students as vocabulary partners should be made by the teacher based on specific strengths and needs of individual students, not solely on proximity of seating in the classroom. We recommend pairing a stronger reader with a less able reader for vocabulary study. If students have to relocate for concept development to be seated next to their vocabulary partners, there is the added benefit of this exercise recirculating blood to the brain. This minute of movement results in 15 percent more blood to the brain (Sousa, 2001).

Finally, the teacher calls on a pair of vocabulary partners to share their draft of the meaning of the word. The other students are instructed to listen to see whether they agree or would like to revise the draft. The draft is written on the chalkboard or overhead, accepted by the class, or revised until consensus is reached.

An optional activity at this time is to have a preselected student, the Verifier, read a definition of the word from a dictionary or glossary. For most general vocabulary, this additional step is not needed, but it can be particularly effective for technical content vocabulary because the published definition often both reinforces and extends students' understanding of the word. For example, a social studies teacher primed the word *barter* through guided imagery with her seventh grade students. The students' final definition was "to trade things instead of using money." The teacher had checked the glossary definition in his planning and asked the Verifier for the day to read the published definition at this point in the process: "to trade by exchange of commodities rather than by the use of money." Because the students had constructed the meaning of *barter,* understood the concept, and had written their definition in their own words, they now could understand the glossary definition, especially the word *commodities.*

If the vocabulary word lends itself to physical movement, now would be the time for the students to act out the word. For example, the word *avert* could be acted out by vocabulary partners, one *averting* eyes, the other *averting* an accident with another car. This physical activity of acting out the meaning of the word helps store the meaning in long-term memory (Sousa, 2001).

The final step in the vocabulary priming process is to direct students to record the word and definition in their vocabulary notebooks. Students need a separate vocabulary section in each of their content notebooks. This is a place students can go to review the major concepts of the unit being studied. It provides them an organized location for ready access to the key vocabulary of the unit and course.

What students record for each vocabulary word are (1) the clues or a facsimile of the clues the teacher presented (e.g., sentences for *cantankerous,* a list of names for *affluent,* their own drawing of a waterfall that is a *cataract,* lists of *carnivores* and *herbivores,* and horse–egret, and bee–plant for *mutualism*), (2) the class definition, and possibly (3) the published definition (e.g., for *barter*).

Whenever examples have been given, it is helpful to have students add examples of their own. For example, students might be asked with their partners to add to the lists of *sets, carnivores* and *herbivores,* and *affluent* individuals they know or know of that had been provided by the teacher, or even to use adding to this list as the purpose-for-reading of the upcoming content selection. Can students who are learning the word *cantankerous* write in their vocabulary notebooks about a time in their lives that they felt *cantankerous* and why? This personalizing of the definition helps the students connect the new concepts to their backgrounds, and these new examples are tests of mastery that can serve as an assessment of the instructional process.

Some teachers prefer their students to record information about words primed in a set format in their vocabulary notebooks. There are several published graphic organizers for precisely this purpose (e.g., Frayer, Frederick & Klausmeier, 1969; Schwartz & Raphael, 1985). We recommend one word per page, organized as follows:

Word: _____

Clues to meaning (provided by the teacher):

Class definition:

Published definition:

Examples (in words or pictures):

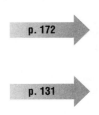

Sometimes the Concept Development/Vocabulary phase includes a review of previously learned and recorded content vocabulary if they will be part of the expected responses to the purpose-for-reading and the teacher believes that the students may not yet be fluent with the retrieval of the meanings of these words. In the "Line, Bar, and Pie Graphs" lesson, the math teacher includes a review of *independent variable* and *dependent variable* after she has executed the initial learning of *constant* and *adjacent* because these two terms were only recently learned and not often generated prior to this lesson. The teacher of the "Student Loans for Higher Education" lesson also has students review several previously primed vocabulary words first by having students discuss what they recall with their vocabulary partners, then by verifying the accuracy of their recall by looking at their notes in their vocabulary notebooks.

## SUMMARY

Vocabulary instruction need not be met with moans from students—or from the teacher. Classroom experience with this vocabulary priming approach has demonstrated that students and teachers can feel motivated and be successful when engaged in direct and participatory vocabulary instruction in the content areas. Students are actively engaged, unraveling the meaning of terms in a collaborative environment. They are using inductive reasoning, critical thinking, and problem solving. They have the opportunity to construct knowledge and build new knowledge for themselves instead of receiving information from the dictionary, another student, or the teacher. Coupled with the reinforcement of encountering the newly learned vocabulary during the subsequent silent reading, and using the words to answer the purpose-for-reading during silent reading, in oral debriefing and discussion of the purpose-for-reading, and possibly in rereading and follow-up activities, this vocabulary priming process and the remaining parts of the Directed Reading Lesson facilitate initial construction of meaning and opportunities for meaningful use of the essential content words. This is classroom time well invested in learning key vocabulary, the building blocks for the major principles students should master in a unit of study, as evidenced in this e-mail from intern Patricia Eldreth during her student teaching semester:

> *I used the vocabulary method I learned in your class with three classes of standard students. I chose three essential terms to prime. For two I wrote sentences; for one [I] showed color pictures of examples and non-examples. I was a bit concerned about the time it took to induce these definitions, but I was determined to give your way a try. The next day I conducted a warm-up for which the students had to define the three concepts. I collected the papers and reviewed their responses that night. I was amazed that 79 out of 80 students were able to define* all *the words correctly. (The 80th student had been absent the day I primed the vocabulary with the students.) (personal communication, November 26, 2002)*

In planning this phase of the Directed Reading Lesson, you should read again the content material you have chosen for your lesson, write the purpose-for-reading, and ask yourself the following questions:

**Questions for Planning the Concept Development/Vocabulary
Phase of the Directed Reading Lesson**

1. What answers are acceptable, and what answers do I expect to the purpose-for-reading? (Complete the key.)
2. What words from the key can I eliminate for priming because they are clearly explained in the context of the reading or because my students already know these words? Are any of these key words ones I have already taught but should review with students prior to reading?

3. Are the remaining words fewer than five (certainly fewer than seven)? If not, should I divide this reading into two readings with a separate vocabulary priming section for each?

4. Determine the contextual strategy for each word I will prime:
   a. Can I use a direct experience, concrete representation, or guided imagery?
   b. Can I use structural analysis?
   c. Can I plan a concept attainment activity?
   d. Will a series of sentences using the word be effective?
   e. How can I personalize the context for the students and connect this meaning to what they already know?
   f. Do students already know a meaning for this nonspecific word? If so, should I surface the known meaning first, then introduce the new meaning?

## YOUR TURN

1. Although Concept Development/Vocabulary is the next phase on the Readiness portion of the Directed Reading Lesson when you *teach* your lesson, you must *plan* the Purpose-for-Reading phase first. The bank of words from which you will select the vocabulary words for priming depends on the purpose-for-reading you give the students. Therefore, proceed to Chapter 6 and plan your Purpose-for-Reading phase, then return to this page to plan Concept Development/Vocabulary.

2. Now that you have your purpose-for-reading, you can complete your key with the answers you expect and find acceptable. The key is the word bank from which you will select the words for priming. Question 2 in the previous section can guide you in selecting the words you will prime with the students.

3. If you have more than seven words, consider dividing this reading into two parts and writing a Directed Reading Lesson for each part. The abundance of words needed to be primed may be an indication that this reading is too difficult for one lesson.

4. Now decide how you will prime each vocabulary word. Question 4 in the previous section will guide you.

5. If you are using this textbook as part of a course or workshop experience, teach the vocabulary words to two colleagues using the contextual strategies you have planned. Substitute nonsense words (e.g., *karub* when really teaching *territory*) for this activity. You will not of course do this with your students, but your colleagues may already know the meaning of the words you chose if you use the actual word. By substituting nonsense words, you put your colleagues in the place of true learners. (By the way, we did this with you in this chapter when we asked you to define *predelecter* and *abodent*. These are words we made up to ensure that you would feel like a student.)

   Be sure to review the vocabulary priming process explained in Step 3 on pp. 53–55 before you begin teaching. After teaching, consider the following:
   ■ From your perspective, how successful were your planned contextual strategies for each word?
   ■ Did you follow the vocabulary priming process for each word, including:
      Showing and pronouncing the word for students
      Revealing the context clues
      Learner pairs drafting a definition
      Reaching class consensus on a definition
      Recording in a vocabulary notebook
   ■ Ask your two colleagues if they felt successful with the contextual strategies you chose. Would they suggest the use of different contextual strategies?

# PURPOSE-FOR-READING

*One should not read to swallow all, but rather see what one has use for.*

—*Henrik Ibsen, Norwegian dramatist*

---

1. Readiness
   a. Motivation
   b. Tapping and Developing Background of Experience
   c. Concept Development/Vocabulary
   **d. Purpose-for-Reading**                    ◀ ◀ ◀
2. Silent Reading
3. Discussion
4. Rereading
5. Follow-Up

---

The final phase of the Readiness step of the Directed Reading Lesson is stating the purpose-for-reading. What is the purpose of this phase?

The purpose of this part of the lesson is to focus the learner on the goal of the reading experience. Having a purpose helps readers determine what is important when reading and gives them parameters for monitoring the successful completion of the reading task.

Although ultimately we hope to teach students to set their own reading goals (as discussed in Chapter 13 on self-regulated learning), we must often tell students the specific purpose-for-reading because we know the content that needs to be learned, and younger and less skilled readers are usually unable to discriminate trivial from important textual information.

Below are the three purposes-for-reading from the lesson plan examples in Chapter 2. Although they are from different content areas, what similar features do you note among them?

*Science: Today you will be reading to be informed. You will use the thinking skill of cause and effect to determine the factors that caused citywide fires to occur in London, England, in 1666 and in Chicago in 1870.*

*English: Today you will be reading the short story entitled "The Scarlet Ibis" by James Hurst for literary experience. . . . Complete the story map for narratives.*

*Art: Your purpose-for-reading today is to read directions that you will follow in chronological order to create your own round weaving in the way the Native Americans historically did.*

The purpose-for-reading should be written so that it includes three features: (1) the main topic of the reading, (2) the generic purpose-for-reading, and (3) the primary thought pattern that will be activated for comprehension.

Each of the purpose-for-reading statements just cited includes a statement of the *topic* of the content reading—"citywide fires" (science lesson), "the short story entitled "The Scarlet Ibis" (English lesson), and "round weaving" (art lesson). The recognition of the topic for the reading activates the reader's relevant cognitive structure and readies it to receive the new knowledge.

The *generic purpose-for-reading* is also stated for the students—either literary experience (the appreciation and analysis of a reading selection, most often a narrative, as in the English example), or to be informed (for exposition, as in the science example), or to perform a task (a specialized form of exposition in which the reader must follow directions, as in the art example). Good readers know intuitively to read differently for these three purposes. For example, do you read a novel (literary experience) the same way you read directions for assembling a new outdoor grill (to perform a task)? Of course not. Labeling the generic type of purpose-for-reading for an upcoming selection helps novice readers discern differences among types of readings they encounter and adjust their reading style accordingly.

The third feature in the purpose-for-reading statement is the primary *thought pattern* students will employ to comprehend the selection. The primary thought patterns are cause and effect, classification/categorization, chronological order/sequence, comparison and/or contrast, description, definition, enumeration/simple listing, pro and/or con, and problem and solution. The thought pattern is the basis of the text structure—the macrostructure of the reading selection, how the text is organized—an important cueing system for comprehension. It is this text structure that serves as the pattern readers follow to discriminate important ideas and to connect ideas. There is a substantial body of research that attests that students' awareness and use of text structure is highly related to better reading comprehension and recall (Armbruster, Anderson, & Ostertag, 1987; Dickson, Simmons, & Kameenui, 1998, Goldman & Rakestraw, 2000; Meyer, Brandt, & Bluth, 1980; Short & Ryan, 1984). Students from sixth grade through college show a developmental trend in using text structure to facilitate their comprehension (McGee, 1982). This improvement over time is likely due to additional exposures to various text structures through the secondary school experience. By labeling the text structure of the upcoming reading in the statement of the purpose-for-reading, teachers put students on track to attending to the properties of specific text structures. This is particularly important for poor readers who are generally insensitive to text structures.

## TEXT STRUCTURE

### Narrative

Text structure is either narrative or expository. A narrative tells a story; an expository selection informs. Narrative text structures are found in novels, short stories, plays, and narrative poems. Although considered the primary text structure of the English and foreign language content area, narrative structures are also frequently found in other content areas. For example, the story of Tecumseh, defender of Native American land, is included in a U.S. history text. Likewise, the biography of Edward Hopper, an American painter who lived from 1882 to 1967 and greatly influenced the style of oil paintings, is reported in the art text, and the story of David Kessler, past head of the Food and Drug Administration, whose efforts for food labeling have influenced the lives of so many Americans, is narrated in a health text.

Narratives require the reader to process a "story grammar," a mental set of the properties of all stories—setting, characters, conflict, significant events, and outcome or solution. (These properties also require the reader to process the plot by applying the thinking skills of chronological order, cause and effect, and problem and solution. Understanding the characters and setting requires the reader to use the thinking skills of enumeration and description.) The story grammar properties form a structure good readers rely on to react emotionally and personally to the story, store information in long-term memory, and assist with recall. Armed with an internalized story grammar, readers can search for a property they have missed, or predict events and behaviors, thus enriching their involvement with the reading and their overall comprehension.

pp. 22–23

Look at the English lesson plan in Chapter 2 that engages readers with the narrative "The Scarlet Ibis." The teacher gives the students a story map graphic organizer to complete during or after reading. The students then use their story maps as memory triggers as they orally retell the short story to a partner in the Discussion part of the Directed Reading Lesson. The story map is a material scaffold (Dickson, Simmons, & Kameenui, 1998) that focuses students' attention on the essential properties of the narrative as they read. Research supports the link between the attention to story grammar and improved comprehension (Fitzgerald & Spiegel, 1983; Pearson & Fielding, 1991). This approach has been shown to be particularly helpful to readers such as those for whom this lesson was designed, low-level readers who appeared not to have yet internalized the properties of narrative text structure. The story map graphic organizer is the visual representation of the text structure. It is designed to hold students accountable for the properties that help them develop understandings of the short story and support their reactions to the story. Look at the Spanish lesson, "Una Leyenda del Caribe." It, too, employs a narrative text, a legend from the Caribbean, and a story map, *map del cuento,* with the story grammar properties translated into *escenario, personajes, problema, suceso* 1, 2, 3, 4, 5, and *solucion,* to assist novice foreign language students in the comprehension of the narrative.

pp. 225–226

Teachers who distribute story maps as companions to reading narratives in secondary classes report:

> *Using the story map greatly increased the students' understanding of the story. If they then wrote their summaries or we used an oral retelling exercise with partners, they had the basic elements. Without the story map, students included many irrelevant details, left out important ones, could not express an affective reaction, or expressed reactions that were not grounded in the realities of the story.*

—High School English Teacher

In recent years, reader response approaches have become quite popular with teachers, especially English teachers. A reader response approach stresses an aesthetic stance, reflecting on a reading—readers' subjective reactions to a reading. In this approach, there is no right or wrong answer, assuming the reaction is rationally defensible. This is the approach that connects students and their lives to the reading. In contrast to the aesthetic stance is the efferent stance, by which a reader carries away information from the reading (Rosenblatt, 1978). This is the "correct answer," objective, text-based approach. This is the stance most often applied to expository readings.

Historically, the aesthetic stance has been neglected in the literary approaches in secondary schools. Our experience in classrooms has convinced us that teachers do not have to suffer from a "theoretical schizophrenia" (Appleman, 2001). It does not have to be an either/or model of instruction, but it can be an inclusion of both the efferent and aesthetic stances. Teachers who choose a reader response approach to narratives do not have to abandon the development of students' sensitivity to the cueing system of text structure. Usually, the properties of the story grammar structure represent the objective, text-based experience of the narrative, "an object to be viewed and held apart, scrutinized with a keen and distant eye." The reader response approach is the subjective experience, "looking within ourselves for meanings and understandings" (Langer, 1995, p. 6).

Langer (1995) refers to these subjective interpretations as

> envisionments, text-worlds in the mind . . . [that] differ from individual to individual . . . [because of] one's personal and cultural experiences, one's relationship to the current experience, what one knows, how one feels, and what one is after. Envisions are

dynamic sets of related ideas, images, questions, disagreements, anticipations, arguments, and hunches that fill the mind during every reading, writing, speaking, or other experience when one gains, expresses, and shares thoughts and understandings." (p. 9)

p. 148

Look at the English lesson plan on *Roll of Thunder, Hear My Cry*. The teacher gives the students several purpose-for-reading questions. They are to complete a "character web," an activity that involves them in objectively identifying the major characters, but also in subjectively noting their own envisionments of the qualities of each character's personality. When students are finished reading, they are asked to attend to text structure by writing a brief summary of the first six chapters, which must include objective reference to setting and conflict, and to significant events as they perceive them.

These objective suppositions about plot, setting, and characters, as well as their relationships, are objective, surface ideas from the text that help students create their envisionments. Students are directed to respond subjectively to the novel by applying the "It Wasn't Fair When . . . " prompt, used earlier in the Motivation of the lesson, to the concept of injustice as they perceive it applied in the novel. In keeping with reader response theory, this teacher begins with the students' personal engagement with the novel, their envisionments. It is "the reader's unmediated, felt response to the text. . . . The author's world is not mediated by the intrusions of others—scholars or teachers" (Milner & Milner, 1999, p. 83). This personal response emanates from the individual student's "personality traits, memories of past events, present needs and preoccupations, a particular mood of the moment" (Rosenblatt, 1938), but it is also integrated and grounded on text-driven, objective responses stemming from the properties of the story grammar.

p. 150

Unless it is narrative poetry, Directed Reading Lessons that have poetry as the primary reading should focus on the reader response approach as the purpose-for-reading. Look at the poetry lesson "Nikki-Rosa." The ESL students are given the purpose-for-reading: "You will be reading for literary experience. Pretend that the girl, Nikki, has written this as a letter to you. Write back to her and react to her letter. Begin your letter with 'Dear Nikki.'" The students will begin with their personal reactions to the poem. These initial envisionments will then be shared with group members for further meaning negotiation and eventually with the entire class. Common interpretations will be noted and ambiguities will be discussed and possibly resolved. All ideas must be grounded in the text, that is, supported from the poem for meaning. At the end of these discussions, the teacher may want to share some critical commentaries and then let students decide if they agree with these professional sources.

p. 158

The reader response approach has little history in content areas other than English, and then typically with readings for literary appreciation. Other content area readings and readings to inform are appropriate for applying this more personal stance in conjunction with the more traditional objective perspective. For example, look at the French lesson plan "Une Escale Exotique a la Martinique." The purpose-for-reading is primarily for the students to be informed about Martinique—its location, climate, industries, government, people, and so forth—and the students do complete a column of a matrix with this detailed information. But notice that after they read, they are instructed by the teacher to first write their reactions to the objective data they collected on their matrix about Martinique: "How do you feel about Martinique as a place to visit on vacation? As a place to live permanently?"

## Expository

The second category of text structure is expository, a text written to inform, explain, show, and tell. The primary purpose of reading expository text is to gain information—a text-based, efferent stance. We want our students to read expository selections so that they comprehend, store, recall, and use the content information.

Readers of expository text look immediately for the "point of reference"—"where the piece is going"—and use it as the framework for building understanding (Langer, 1992, p. 37). This framework is inexplicably linked to the text structure of the particular text. Unlike narratives that have one overarching text structure (story grammar properties), expository readings have a range of structures, dependent on the thought pattern or patterns required for understanding. Research has shown that students have more difficulty comprehending and recalling expository information than they do narrative properties (Zabrucky & Ratner, 1992).

The most common expository text structures employed in secondary textbooks are categorization/classification, cause and effect, chronological order/sequence, comparison and/or contrast, definition, description, enumeration/simple listing, pro and/or con, and problem and solution. Research has revealed that chronological order/sequence text structures are easier for students than enumeration and description text structures, and enumeration and chronological order/sequence are significantly easier than comparison and contrast text structures (Englert & Thomas, 1987). Cause and effect structures have been shown to be troublesome for many readers through college (Horowitz, 1985).

Below are brief definitions of nine text structure types and examples of content topics explained via these frameworks in secondary content textbooks, essays, magazine articles, pamphlets, newspapers, and website passages.

### Text Structure—Definition and Examples from Secondary Content Readings

1. **Cause and effect:** analysis of conditions and outcomes of an event. *Examples:*
   - Factors that affect the rate at which solids and gases dissolve in liquids (science)
   - Effects (direct and indirect) of failing to pay back student loans (business education)
   - Cause and effects of tsunamis (geography)
2. **Classification/categorization:** dividing a group of items into smaller groups that share common characteristics; usually a reading that classifies or categorizes also inherently defines each subgroup by giving characteristics to distinguish each group, and thus compares and/or contrasts the subgroups. *Examples:*
   - The earth's history on the geological time scale as divided into four geologic eras: Precambrian, Paleozoic, Mesozoic, and Cenozoic (science)
   - Types of polygons (geometry)
   - Categories of orchestra instruments (music)
3. **Chronological order/sequence:** ordered steps in a process; stages in development; events according to time. *Examples:*
   - Nutritional requirements at each stage of life (health)
   - Stages of the dissolving process (science)
   - A chronology of the major battles during the American Revolution (history)
4. **Comparison and/or contrast:** explicating similarities (compare) and/or differences (contrast) between or among people, places, processes, objects, events, and so on, usually involving a list of traits as the basis of the comparison and contrast. *Examples:*
   - The similarities and differences between city and rural schools in Mexico (Spanish)
   - The differences in lifestyle between the New England and Southern colonists (history)
   - The similarities and differences between holidays in France and the United States (French)
5. **Description:** concrete details that give the reader a mental picture of the object, person, scene, and so on. *Examples:*
   - The structural composition of an atom (science)
   - The phenomenon of land bridges crossed by Ice Age hunters (history)
   - The motifs seen in pre-Colombian art (art)

6. **Definition (extended):** not a brief dictionary definition, but a more lengthy explanation of characteristics of a concept. *Examples:*
   - Depth of field in taking a photograph (art)
   - What a family is (English essay)
   - The components of a healthy diet (health)

7. **Enumeration/simple listing:** a list of factors that does not require a specific order. *Examples:*
   - The varied roles of the President (social studies)
   - Treatments for Alzheimer's disease (health)
   - Tourist attractions in Paris (French)

8. **Pro and/or con:** a presentation of one or both sides of an issue in an attempt to persuade; sometimes making a judgment about which is best, sometimes presenting errors in arguments in order to prove one side as correct or best. *Examples:*
   - Reasons to fund programs for the homeless (English)
   - Advantages and disadvantages of ocean thermal energy conservation (science)
   - Pros and cons of altering rules in sports based on the utilization of technology (physical education)

9. **Problem and solution:** clarifying the problem, posing solutions and sometimes consequences of solutions; sometimes combined with cause and effect, with the cause or the effect representing the problem. *Examples:*
   - Solutions for the problem of acid rain (science)
   - Solutions for the problem of illiteracy (English)
   - Solutions undertaken historically by the government for the problem of Native Americans displaced from their land by settlers moving west (history)

It is the responsibility of the secondary teacher to read the selected content material and identify the major thought pattern(s) that students should employ to comprehend and learn from the reading. The name of the thought pattern becomes a part of the stated purpose-for-reading question, thus helping to develop students' awareness of the types of text structures.

pp. 18, 27

**REFLECT**

Look back at the two expository lessons in Chapter 2. What are the thought patterns identified and labeled by the teachers in the purpose-for-reading statements?

The science lesson requires cause and effect processing to determine the factors that caused citywide fires to occur in London and Chicago. The art lesson requires chronological order/sequence processing to follow the steps to create a round weaving.

Table 6.1 shows the primary thought patterns that are required in the expository materials read during lessons in Appendix A.

## GRAPHIC ORGANIZERS

In addition to labeling the type of text structure in the purpose-for-reading statement so that students become aware of various patterns, comprehension has been shown to be facilitated by insisting that students actually use the particular text structure in the form of a graphic organizer (e.g., Alvermann, 1986; Bromley, Irwin-DeVitis, & Modlo, 1995; Friend & Bursuck, 1999; Murray & McGlone, 1997; Pearson & Spiro, 1982; Weisberg & Balajthy, 1989). "It is hard to talk about an invisible process [a thinking pattern]; graphic frames create an objective form for a subjective thinking process" (Clarke, 1990, p. 39). At first teachers provide graphic organizers for the students, then students learn to construct their own graphic organizers. This self-regulating skill will be discussed in Chapter 13.

p. 19

Look back at the science Directed Reading Lesson in Chapter 2. This lesson has the students reading for two thought patterns: cause and effect and problem and solution. The teacher gives the students a graphic organizer on which to list the causes of the fires and the corresponding solutions for each of the causes. The teacher adds arrows to suggest the relationship between the solutions and the causes—the solution pointing at the cause it will

**TABLE 6.1    Thought Patterns for Expository Readings in Appendix A**

| CONTENT AREA | THOUGHT PATTERN | LESSON TOPIC |
|---|---|---|
| Art | Simple listing; chronological order | Photomontage |
| Business education | Comparison and contrast<br>Cause and effect | Federal student loans |
| Consumer and family science | Problem and solution | SIDS |
| English | Chronological order<br>Pro and con | Successful job interview<br>Sea serpents' existence |
| French | Description | Martinique |
| Health | Comparison and contrast<br>Cause and effect; problem and solution | Eating disorders<br>AIDS |
| Mathematics | Definition; comparison and contrast<br>Chronological order | Graphs<br>Problem-solving steps |
| Music | Classification<br>Description | Instruments of Africa<br>"Battle Hymn of the Republic" |
| Physical education | Enumeration<br>Cause and effect | Water safety<br>Eating for best performance |
| Science | Classification; comparison and contrast<br>Classification | Asteroids, comets, and meteors<br>Relationships in a habitat |
| Social studies | Chronological order<br>Chronological order; cause and effect | George Calvert<br>Judicial process and review |
| Special education | Simple listing | Ordering lunch from a menu |

thwart. First the students read to find the causes of the fire (the fire is the effect) and fill in the left-hand column. Later in the lesson, they will reread to locate solutions for each of the causes (the problem) and fill in the right-hand column.

A graphic organizer is a type of "mediated scaffolding . . . an external support provided by [the] teacher . . . during initial instruction in the conventions of text presentation and organizational patterns of text structures" (Dickson, Simmons, & Kameenui, 1998, p. 286). It is a visual representation of a thought pattern. It is a visual way to show relationships among key bits of information; it is a visual arrangement of ideas into a pattern. A graphic organizer combines the verbal with the visual pathway to the brain. The abstract language is encoded as a part of a mental image of the relationships. The linguistic elements (words, phrases, paragraphs) are combined with the nonlinguistic elements (circles, boxes, arrows) to show relationships. Graphic organizers provided by the teacher can also compensate for an inconsiderate reading selection—a reading that is not written in a coherent, thought pattern–friendly manner. The graphic organizer will then cue the students as to how to organize the information that is presented so that it can be stored in memory and recalled efficiently.

Guided by the list of text structures on pp. 61–62, look at each graphic organizer included in the lessons in Appendix A that utilize expository readings. Reflect on how the visual arrangement of each graphic organizer cues students to the thought pattern and to the relationships among the ideas from the reading. Did you notice that the flow chart with arrows used in "The Successful Job Interview" lesson indicates the chronological order of steps by using arrows and a sequence going from top to bottom and left to right? The graphic organizer for the music lesson, "Traditional Instruments of Africa," is arranged as a

REFLECT

p. 155

p. 183

p. 141

visual outline with the three major categories—wind, percussion, and string—at the top, and subcategories below. The English lesson, "Tales of the Mysterious," has one side for pro, the ideas of those who believe in the existence of sea serpents, and one side of the graphic organizer for con, the ideas of those who do not believe in sea serpents. These ideas then come together into "My Conclusion and Justification," the reader's decision after considering both sides of the argument.

Use of graphic organizers has the added benefit of fostering accountability on the part of the students. Less able readers often focus on decoding, not meaning, when they read (Baker & Brown, 1984), and some readers do not even realize that they do not understand what they are reading (Garner & Reis, 1981). Having a graphic to fill in focuses readers concretely on meaning. Empty space on a graphic, that is, a section with no response, is a signal to the student and the teacher that something is missing, possibly not understood, and that rereading is in order.

## Considerations and Cautions

pp. 155, 180

**1.** Notice that no two graphic organizers in the sample plans are identical, even if they employ the same thought pattern. For example, the English "Successful Job Interview" lesson plan and the mathematics "Problem-Solving Strategies" lesson plan both rely on the thought pattern, chronological order/sequence. The graphic organizers are both linear to correspond with the thought pattern, yet they are fashioned differently to correspond to the details of the reading. The social studies lesson, "History of Maryland," is also based on chronological order/sequence, but its graphic organizer is set up as a time line to reflect the travels of George Calvert since that is how the reading is organized.

p. 212

pp. 162, 201

Look at the health lesson, "Eating Disorders," and the science lesson, "Leftovers." Both have graphic organizers for the thought pattern of comparison and contrast. Both use a matrix with the items being compared and contrasted across the top and the variables listed down the left side. Sometimes a reading is quite literal in telling the reader what variables will be compared and contrasted; others require the reader to infer such categories. It is the teacher's responsibility to decide which variables the students should attend to while reading and to construct the graphic organizer in accordance with these goals. The general rule here is that teachers must adapt a generic graphic organizer to fit the unique presentation of a particular reading.

**2.** The thought pattern of compare and contrast can take several forms:

p. 221

- **Matrix** (as in the health plan, "Eating Disorders," and the science plan, "Leftovers")
- **T-chart** (see the social studies lesson, "The Development of the Power of the Supreme Court")
- **Semantic feature analysis chart** (see Figure 6.1.)

p. 224

- **Venn diagram** (see the Spanish lesson, "Una Leyenda del Caribe")

All of these visual representations are comparing and contrasting two or more people, processes, places, objects, or events, yet they are not necessarily interchangeable. For example, a Venn diagram works best for comparison and contrast of two items. Visually, it becomes difficult to discern details when circles for a third or more items are layered over the original circles. Venn diagrams also work best for readers who have a strong spatial sense. For readers who prefer a linear alignment, such as a matrix or T-chart, insisting that they complete a Venn diagram could actually obstruct comprehension. Semantic feature analysis charts work only for items whose variables can be described with a "Yes" or "No" form of response, representing that the variable either exists or does not exist for the item.

**3.** Often a reading does not literally tell the reader how items compare or contrast; thus the reader must infer this generalization based on details provided in the reading. In such cases, the teacher is wise to have the students complete a comparison and contrast matrix

**FIGURE 6.1   Graphic Organizer: Semantic Feature Analysis Chart**

*Thought pattern:* Comparison and contrast

*Topics:* Capitalism, socialism, and communism

*Directions:* For each question, place a plus sign (+) in the box if the answer is "determined by the market," and place a minus sign (–) if the answer is "determined by the government" for that particular economic system.

|  | CAPITALISM | SOCIALISM | COMMUNISM |
|---|---|---|---|
| What and how much should be produced? | + | +/– | – |
| How should goods and services be produced? | + | +/– | – |
| Who gets the goods and services that are produced? | + | +/– | – |

Semantic Feature Analysis contributed by Kevin Phelps, December, 2001.

with the details, examine the details recorded on these charts inductively, looking for commonalities and differences, then complete a T-chart or Venn diagram with their generalizations. That is, the matrix format is for data collection; it does not literally yield the comparison and contrast generalizations. Some more capable readers, such as academically gifted students for whom the social studies lesson, "The Development of the Power of the Supreme Court," was designed, may be able to work directly with the T-chart or Venn, but the less capable readers may need the intermediary step. Or if the matrix approach is chosen, the teacher will need to lead the students during the subsequent discussion to discern the comparison and contrast generalizations. Look at the health lesson, pp. 162–163 "Eating Disorders." The students collect data about three types of eating disorders on a matrix, then during the Discussion part of the Directed Reading Lesson, the teacher leads students to examine the data and generate four similarities among the eating disorder types. In any case, the teacher must make a decision as to the competence of the students in the class in relation to the reading when selecting the graphic organizer for initial reading of expository selections that require the use of the comparison and contrast thought pattern.

**4.** Unfortunately, some content readings are "inconsiderate texts" (Herman et al., 1987); that is, they are not written in such a way that the text structure is obvious and the writing coherent and unified. In such cases, the teacher may have to impose a text structure. Ann Dolan, a middle school social studies teacher, reported to us that this was often the case with readings from a text selected by her school system for a year-long course in world cultures. The goal of a lesson early in the school year was to have the students create a time line of significant events beginning with the Stone Age that they could continue throughout the unit. Unfortunately, the text chapter followed a more random thematic sequence (hunting, gathering, farming, etc.), not a chronological sequence. Consequently, the teacher used two graphic organizers in this lesson. The first graphic organizer, completed during Silent Reading, had the students list information and dates according to thematic categories (see Figure 6.2). Then for Rereading, the students were given these instructions:

> *Use the data you collected for your first graphic organizer, and create a time line for Prehistory and the Beginnings of Civilization. Be sure to use equal time intervals, give the time line a title, and include five significant events, beginning with 30,000–3,000 years ago.*

**FIGURE 6.2 Prehistory and the Beginnings of Civilization Graphic Organizer**

*Directions:* Read pages 14–18 in your *Ancient World* book on the topic of Prehistory. Write notes under the headings listed below.

*Section: Prehistory*

| **Heading One: The Stone Age: Hunting and Gathering to Farming** |
| --- |
| Introduction: |
| Fire: |
| Settling New Areas: |
| **Heading Two: The Beginning of Farming** |
| Introduction: |
| Farming in Other Places: |
| Taming Animals: |

*Directions:* Read pages 19–23 in your *Ancient World* book on the topic of Beginnings of Civilization. Write notes under the headings listed below.

*Section: Beginning of Civilization*

| **Heading One: Advantages of Settled Life** |
| --- |
| Introduction: |
| The Population Grows: |
| Early Villages and Towns: |
| **Heading Two: The Growth of Cities** |
| Introduction: |
| Earliest Cities: |
| Governments Form: |
| **Heading Three: The First Civilizations** |
| Introduction: |
| Trade Helps Civilizations Spread: |
| Social Classes Develop: |

Contributed by Ann Dolan, October, 2001.

Thus, the data gathered from the initial reading of the selection and recorded on the first graphic organizer became the data for the second graphic organizer, the one this middle school teacher believed would ultimately better assist students in learning and recalling significant developments during this period of time.

**5.** Graphic organizers for a particular reading may also be used across a unit or course of study. For example, in the French lesson plan, "Une Escale Exotique a la Martinique," the students use the thinking pattern of description and complete a column, "La Martinique," of a matrix, "Un Voyage Autour de Monde aux Pays Francophones." They had a similar column when they read a description of France and when they read a description of Montreal. They will also complete such a column when they read about La Guyane. At the end of the unit, this chart will promote recall when the teacher leads a discussion to assist students in comparing and contrasting countries where French is spoken.

p. 159

**6.** When students complete a graphic organizer, they should include the vocabulary words they learned during the Concept Development/Vocabulary phase of Readiness, because the words selected appeared necessary to answer the purpose-for-reading question. This recognition of the word while reading and the use of the word in written responses are major parts of the reinforcement of the word meaning. Look, for example, at the math lesson, "Line, Bar, and Pie Graphs." The teacher primed the words *constant* and *adjacent,* and they are expected responses on her graphic organizer. Notice that in the story map graphic organizer for the English lesson "The Scarlet Ibis" in Chapter 2, the teacher literally reminds students in writing that they should "use the two new vocabulary words" in their descriptions of the appropriate characters.

p. 173
p. 23

## SUMMARY

The Purpose-for-Reading phase of the Readiness step of the Directed Reading Lesson sends students into the reading with a goal to accomplish. Such a mission is intended to engage them strategically for efficient and effective learning of content.

In planning this phase of the Directed Reading Lesson, you should ask yourself the following questions:

**Questions for Planning the Purpose-for-Reading Phase
of the Directed Reading Lesson**

1. What is the generic purpose of the content reading I am using for my Directed Reading Lesson? (literary appreciation? to be informed? to perform a task?)
2. Is this a narrative or an expository reading?
3. What is the major topic of this reading?
4. What is the text structure (i.e., the major thought pattern) of this reading? Analyze the macrostructure.
5. Should the purpose-for-reading also foster a reader response approach, a more subjective, personal response? (For example: How does this account make you feel? What does this reading remind you of in your own life? What in this reading surprised you?)

   Now, write the purpose-for-reading question. Be sure to include the generic reading purpose, thought pattern, and topic.
6. Do this content reading and its purpose-for-reading lend themselves to using a graphic organizer to facilitate student comprehension and learning? If so, ask yourself the following:
   - How do I design it so that it matches the text structure and the specific presentation in this reading?
   - If the thought pattern is comparison and contrast, would a matrix, T-chart, Venn diagram, or semantic feature analysis chart be most appropriate?

## YOUR TURN

1. Answer questions 1–5 in the previous section. You may need to reread to answer some of these, especially to determine the text structure.

2. Write your purpose-for-reading statement.

3. Now answer question 6 in the previous section.

4. If you are using this text as part of a course or workshop experience, share the draft of your purpose-for-reading question and graphic organizer, if you designed one, with another participant. Have this colleague react to your purpose-for-reading. Does your colleague:

   ■ Find the three features (topic, generic purpose-for-reading, thought pattern) included in your purpose-for-reading statement?

   ■ Think your graphic organizer is appropriate for the type of reading (narrative or expository) and the thought pattern you have identified?

   ■ Think the graphic organizer gives appropriate visual clues to help students see relationships among information?

5. Ask your colleague to read the material you have selected for this Directed Reading Lesson and complete the graphic organizer you created.

   ■ Are your colleague's responses what you expected? That is, does your graphic organizer yield the content knowledge you expected?

   ■ Does your colleague have any questions about, or suggestions for revising, your graphic organizer?

6. Now return to the end of Chapter 5, "Concept Development/Vocabulary," pp. 55–56. There you will be guided in selecting the words for vocabulary priming and for devising contextual strategies for teaching the concepts.

# CHAPTER SEVEN

# SILENT READING

Books had instant replay long before televised sports.

—Bert Williams, African American pantomime artist and comedian

1. Readiness
   a. Motivation
   b. Tapping and Developing Background of Experience
   c. Concept Development/Vocabulary
   d. Purpose-for-Reading
2. **Silent Reading**   ◀◀◀
3. Discussion
4. Rereading
5. Follow-Up

As teachers, we are not typical readers of the content selections. We are expert readers. When we read, we automatically activate our relevant background and set goals for what we want to get from the reading; we use our internalized text structure knowledge and our goal to guide us in selecting, organizing, and reacting to what we read; we understand the vocabulary because of our expert backgrounds; we image what we read; and we intuitively monitor our degree of learning in relationship to our goals. If we are to be successful teachers, we must assist our students in reading as we do. We must stop *assigning* content readings and begin *teaching* content readings. As teachers, we must be sensitive to the fact that our students are reading this material for the first time. A first time reading is unlike any subsequent reading. And a first time reading by students for whom the subject matter, vocabulary, syntax, and text structure may be foreign or obscure needs teachers who will help transform frustration or instructional level readings to independent level readings by incorporating Readiness activities into their content lessons.

By now you have planned all the phases of the Readiness step of the Directed Reading Lesson. Readiness is designed to move your students "up" to the reading. You have accomplished this by:

1. Helping students connect to the topic (Motivation)
2. Tapping and developing their topical background knowledge (Tapping and Developing Background of Experience)
3. Priming the students on key vocabulary (Concept Development/Vocabulary)
4. Providing them a content goal to accomplish in the upcoming reading (Purpose-for-Reading)

This e-mail correspondence from staff development teacher Scott Degasperis is typical of teachers' testimonies of the type of planning for a reading lesson in which you have been engaged:

> *I did my Directed Reading Lesson this week. It went very well! I chose a challenging reading for a seventh grade standard science class. I had some concern that it may be too hard for them, but the structure of the Directed Reading Lesson built in the support the students needed to make it successful. Now I am sharing the format with other teachers. (personal communication, December 12, 2000)*

We now move on to the second part of the Directed Reading Lesson: Silent Reading. The purpose of Silent Reading is for the reader to answer the purpose-for-reading established during the preceding Readiness section.

Teachers should have students read content material silently—not orally. Silent reading is the kind of reading students will do most in real life, and silent reading is faster than oral reading (Betts, 1946). In our workshops, we sensitize educators to the need to use silent reading by conducting the Readiness portion of a reading lesson with the participants as students, then having them take turns and read orally. No matter the composition of the audience (e.g., teachers, administrators, middle school, high school, any content area), the results are always the same. The participants have difficulty answering questions about the purpose-for-reading established, and they voice frustration at not having been able to look back or reread because it was expected that they would follow along.

Those who actually read aloud have little comprehension of the part they read because they wanted to be sure their pronunciation and intonation sounded correct. "The aim of silent reading is to get the thought; the aim of oral reading, to express it" (Betts, 1946, p. 513). Oral readers naturally focus their main attention on decoding—accurate word calling—and have little reading energy left for their own comprehension. Oral reading can also make even capable readers self-conscious and anxious as they "perform" for their peers, causing mispronunciations, substitutions, and omissions. Such labored reading further interferes with the comprehension of the student listeners.

If students are reading aloud for an audience of their peers or listening as a peer (or the teacher) reads to them, they cannot read in a recursive manner, replaying and pausing as good readers do, and taking notes to answer purpose-for-reading questions. But, when students read silently, they are able to use the multiple clueing systems of graphics, semantics/vocabulary, syntax, background, and text structure. They can control their own pace and use self-correcting strategies such as looking back and rereading a sentence, word, or paragraph. They can pause and reflect on what they have just read. They can take notes to answer the purpose-for-reading questions or fill in parts of a graphic organizer as they locate specific responses.

Some secondary students have had little practice with silent reading and have come to rely on the aural feedback to keep them focused as they read orally. These readers need practice in silent reading, and Readiness is designed to motivate and focus them as they actively search for the answers to the purpose-for-reading.

Without some assistance in decoding, remedial readers may have such difficulty with the graphics that their comprehension is significantly limited. For these students, the teacher might need to provide an audiotape of the reading to use with a headset. The teacher will also provide instruction on pausing the tape, so they can still use recursive reading as they focus on comprehending. (Many publishers and nonprofit organizations, such as Recording for the Blind [Broadwater, 2001] now make available texts on tape for students with reading difficulties. Sometimes teachers may find it necessary to make the tape recordings themselves.) Look again at the special education lesson, "Aquatic Safety." The teacher uses a book on tape for the very low level readers and nonreaders in this class.

p. 192 →

Teaching students some strategies, such as the following, will help them become successful, independent readers:

### What to Do When You Can't Read a Word
1. Look at that word again—ending, middle, beginning.
2. Read on, and then come back to the hard word and try again.
3. Stretch out the letters; take the word apart.
4. Think about what would make sense.
5. Think about what would sound right.
6. Substitute a word that makes sense.
7. See if it looks like a word you've seen before.
8. Put word parts together.
9. Skip the word and go on. (Routman, 1998, p. 388)

Oral reading is not always inappropriate in the secondary content classroom, for example, reading a portion of text aloud to support an answer during the upcoming *Discussion* or reading character parts in a play. But students should read orally only after they have had time to read silently for comprehension and to develop confidence in their fluency so as to give a rehearsed recitation.

## METACOGNITIVE MONITORING DURING SILENT READING

What makes expert readers experts is their use of various goal-oriented strategies as they construct meaning and learn with text. Often referred to as *metacognitive strategies* or *executive control processes* (Flavell, 1976; Wagner & Sternberg, 1987), these strategies allow readers to plan, monitor, and regulate comprehension. Expert readers recognize when they sufficiently comprehend and when they do not sufficiently comprehend, and they use metacognitive fix-it strategies to improve comprehension. The following metacognitive strategies used during Silent Reading assist students in learning with the content text:

- **Imaging/movie of the mind:** Trying to picture what is being read; using one's background of experience, as well as pictures, illustrations, or other visuals provided in the reading or by the teacher to visualize what is being read
- **Checking for purpose:** Evaluating if and to what extent the answers to the purpose-for-reading are being found
- **Taking notes/organizing:** Writing answers to the purpose-for-reading, filling in a graphic organizer provided by the teacher, or constructing one's own graphic organizer to organize the information
- **Retelling:** At various points in the reading, checking comprehension by stopping to articulate silently what has been learned or by sharing orally this retelling with a peer who is also reading the content material
- **Rereading/lookbacks:** Looking back to what has already been read—a word, group of words, a sentence, a group of sentences, a paragraph, or several paragraphs—and rereading to understand
- **Inserts/questions:** When rereading and other metacognitive fix-it strategies fail, using the margin or an adhesive note to write a question for clarification during the discussion or write a comment, a reflection, or an impression to use in a discussion
- **Noting key content vocabulary:** Stopping to pay particular attention to understanding words primed by the teacher prior to silent reading and to note any other vocabulary that seems crucial to the topic and purpose-for-reading

The conclusion that metacognition facilitates reading comprehension and increases content learning has been supported by substantial research (e.g., Andrade, 1999; Billingsley & Wildman, 1990; Palinscar & Brown, 1984; Paris, Wasik, & Turner, 1991; Pressley, Gaskins, Wile, Cunicelli, & Sheridan, 1991; Pressley, Johnson, Symons, McGoldrick, & Kurita, 1989; Pressly, Schuder, & Bergman, 1992; Schoenfield, 1987; Weinstein, 1994; Weisberg, 1988). Classroom research has shown that good readers in secondary school do see reading as a recursive process that includes questioning, rereading, and rethinking (Lifford, Byron, Eckblad, & Ziemian, 2000). By grade 8, good comprehenders are able to monitor their reading and spontaneously use the metacognitive strategy of look-backs and rereading (Garner & Reis, 1981).

Some unsuccessful readers focus primarily on decoding. Often, they are simply unaware of needing to make sense of the text (Baker & Brown, 1984). "Comprehension problems among unsuccessful readers with reasonably adequate decoding skills are often related to their failure to participate actively and strategically while engaged in the reading process" (Ryan, Ledger, Short, & Weed, 1982, p. 54). Others appear to monitor their reading and are aware of not understanding but do not know what to do to resolve comprehension obstacles (Garner & Reis, 1981).

Many students believe that looking back and rereading is bad, inappropriate, or an indication that they are stupid. Even preservice teachers and master teachers have confessed to us that they believed they were not good readers because they often had to go back to something previously read and reread to fully comprehend. Graduate student Gail Shaffer said:

> This may be the single most gratifying thing I have learned from you. I've always reread and when I was young and considered a "good reader," I thought it was my dirty little secret that I wouldn't dare reveal to anyone for fear of looking bad because I didn't get it the first time through. (personal communication, June 20, 2002)

It is important that teachers tell students explicitly that these metacognitive strategies are what expert readers do to understand when they read. "Blessing" these strategies is often the first step toward convincing secondary students to try them.

In spite of the facts that (1) secondary students do not naturally employ metacognitive strategies during reading, (2) metacognitive strategies can facilitate comprehension, and (3) metacognition can be taught, research has found that teachers do not typically monitor or encourage the use of such strategies (Fillion & Brause, 1987). The Directed Reading Lesson with its Silent Reading component presents the secondary content teacher with the appropriate opportunity to make students aware of during-reading metacognitive strategies and to encourage their practice.

pp. 18, 22, 27
In the anchoring lesson plan examples in Chapter 2, attention to metacognitive strategies during reading is direct and overt. In both the science lesson and the English lesson, the students have graphic organizers to help them take notes and organize. While the students are reading silently, the science teacher circulates, assisting students who appear to be having difficulty completing their graphic organizers and encouraging them to reread. After several minutes of silent reading time, she interrupts and reminds students to use their new vocabulary—noting key content vocabulary—in their responses to the purpose-for-reading. In the English lesson, just prior to silent reading, the teacher encourages students to use imaging—seeing the story as "a movie in the mind." She cues them to picture the characters, especially the main character, Doodles. During silent reading, she circulates and assists students who appear to be having difficulty completing their graphic organizers. She even says aloud to the entire class, "Remember that good readers often must do some rereading if they do not understand what they just read." The art lesson also has direct instructions from the teacher to use imaging, visualizing for each step in the directions, and to reread each step several times to understand how to do a round weaving.

**REFLECT**
Look at the lesson plans in Appendix A of this text. Identify the during-reading metacognitive strategy or strategies that each teacher includes. For example, the art teacher

p. 128
p. 131
p. 167
p. 200

in the "Photomontage" lesson reminds students that they "may need to read the steps for each photomontage more than once" (rereading). The business education teacher in "Student Loans for Higher Education" tells students that because the reading material has been duplicated for them they should highlight as they read and then transfer the essential information to their graphic organizers (taking notes/organizing). The health teacher in the lesson on AIDS interrupts the students during silent reading and instructs students to retell their partner what they have learned thus far. The science teacher, teaching about the "leftovers" in space, reminds students to "look at the pictures that are included near each of the reading sections," to facilitate their imaging of asteroids, comets, and meteors.

Focusing on too many during-reading metacognitive strategies at one time may overwhelm students. In particular, students should not be interrupted too often during silent reading. Silent reading should be exactly that—reading in a silent environment. Secondary students should be exposed to these various strategies and encouraged to use them over time by different content teachers. Internalization of metacognitive strategies requires regular and repeated exposure and practice. Students need to understand that these strategies are universal, not unique to a particular content or type of reading. They need to practice them with guidance from teachers so that they can be successful.

## SUMMARY

The Silent Reading phase gives students the opportunity to process the reading selection in a recursive manner and successfully accomplish the goal set by the purpose-for-reading. In planning this part of the Directed Reading Lesson, you should select judiciously from the list of During-Reading Monitoring Strategies.

## DURING-READING MONITORING STRATEGIES

### IMAGING/MOVIE OF THE MIND

**TEACHER:** Pause a moment in your reading. What are you seeing as you read? Who will describe to us what you are seeing?

**STUDENT:** What do I see while I am reading? Should I look again at the pictures or other graphics given in the reading or by the teacher?

### CHECKING FOR PURPOSE

**TEACHER:** Are you finding the answers to the purpose-for-reading? Are you having difficulty with any?

**STUDENT:** Am I finding the answers to the purpose-for-reading? Do I need to go back and search for any?

### TAKING NOTES/ORGANIZING

**TEACHER:** Are you making a list of the characters and ideas about them to help you remember who they are? Are you able to fill in the graphic organizer? What ideas are you getting about the structure so that you can create a graphic organizer for the details? Who will tell us one major idea you underlined?

**STUDENT:** Can I draw a graphic organizer to match the structure of this reading? Do I need to start a list of the characters and who each is? Should I underline or highlight?

### RETELLING

**TEACHER:** Let's pause in our reading and tell the person next to us what we have learned thus far in our reading.

**STUDENT:** Can I retell in my own words what I have read thus far? If I cannot do this, what part or parts should I reread?

*(continued)*

## DURING-READING MONITORING STRATEGIES (continued)

### LOOK-BACKS/REREADING

**TEACHER:**   Are you confused about anything you have read? Might it help to look back at what you have already read, then reread and try to clarify that point?

**STUDENT:**   Should I go back and reread all or part of what I don't understand or what I missed, or should I read on to see if that clarifies my understanding?

### INSERTS/QUESTIONS

**TEACHER:**   If you have tried but still do not understand some part of the reading that you believe is important to learning the content information, put a sticky note on that page with your question written on it. We'll try to resolve this when we have a discussion following the silent reading.

**STUDENT:**   I have tried to understand this by looking back and rereading, but I am still confused or have a question. Should I put a sticky on this page with my question on it to alert me to ask about it when we discuss this reading?

### NOTING KEY CONTENT VOCABULARY

**TEACHER:**   Which key vocabulary have you found in your reading thus far? What does _____ mean? Discuss each word with the person next to you.

**STUDENT:**   Which new words represent important ideas related to the topic of this reading? Have I paid particular attention to the words that were primed in class prior to silent reading? Can I explain each in my own words? If not, I should look back and check for the meaning of these new terms in the reading or in my vocabulary notebook.

## Y O U R   T U R N

1.  Decide which during-reading, metacognitive monitoring strategy or strategies you will incorporate into your Directed Reading Lesson. Write these into your plan. Over time, be sure to use a variety of these strategies in your Directed Reading Lessons.

2.  You might want to make a note to yourself that during Silent Reading you will ensure silence in the room (except when you call your students' attention to using a metacognitive strategy) so that students will not be distracted from their focus—constructing meaningful responses to their purpose-for-reading.

3.  If you have readers for whom fluent decoding is still a problem, you should plan a minilesson on the decoding strategies listed on p. 71. A display of this list on a poster board could then be referred to as students read silently.

4.  If you are using this textbook as part of a course or workshop experience, share the draft of *Silent Reading* with another participant. Does your colleague:
    ■  Find your selected metacognitive strategies appropriate in number and placement, that is, prior to students beginning reading or after they have been reading for a time?
    ■  Have any suggestions for revision?

# CHAPTER EIGHT

# DISCUSSION

To live effectively is to live with adequate information.

—*Norbert Wiener, American mathematician and "father of cybernetics"*

1. Readiness
    a. Motivation
    b. Tapping and Developing Background of Experience
    c. Concept Development/Vocabulary
    d. Purpose-for-Reading
2. Silent Reading
3. **Discussion** ◄◄◄
4. Rereading
5. Follow-Up

You have readied your students to read the content material and they have read silently. It is now time for them to share with you and each other their individual responses to the purpose-for-reading and to reach consensus on the answers to these goals established for reading. The third part of the Directed Reading Lesson, Discussion, is:

- A talking-to-learn and listening-to-learn experience for the students
- A time during which the students demonstrate accountability for their achievement during the Silent Reading phase
- An opportunity for teachers to assess the adequacy and accuracy of the content information the students have comprehended
- A time for students to affirm the accuracy of the content information they learned, to adjust any inaccurate understandings they acquired, and to refine their inadequate responses
- An opportunity to use and hear the new vocabulary learned during Readiness

In most cases, the purpose-for-reading has students do thinking that requires understanding of information that is explicitly stated or clearly implied in the reading. The purpose-for-reading is usually a lower-level question that requires readers to recognize and record factual information from text. For example, in the anchoring lesson plans in Chapter 2, the students read to identify factors that caused large fires to occur (science lesson); the setting, characters, and plot of a short story (English lesson); and step-by-step directions for weaving (art lesson). All of this factual information is explicitly stated or clearly implied in the text.

Text-based information in the content is usually *declarative knowledge* or *procedural knowledge*. Declarative knowledge is *knowing that* . . . For example, as a result of the silent reading activity in the science lesson the students *know that* there were eight factors that caused the London Fire of 1666 and four factors that caused the Chicago Fire of 1870. After reading "The Scarlet Ibis," the English students *know that* the setting of the story is on a farm in North Carolina in the 1900s, the characters include Doodles, the boy who has a physical disability, the narrator who is Doodles's older brother, and so on. Procedural knowledge is *knowing how to perform a task.* In the art lesson, as a result of reading, students *know how* to create a round weaving.

Secondary teachers begin with text-based, lower-level questions because understanding text-based information is crucial to "building a coherent representation of text" (Harris & Sipay, 1990, p. 574), that is, crucial to achieving reading comprehension and learning content. This is not to suggest that students do not use higher-level thinking as they read content material for the first time. Certainly competent readers do; in fact, they move recursively between lower- and higher-level processing. Understanding detail is prerequisite to constructing valid generalizations about a content topic. Having the students first discuss the literal details helps to ensure the accuracy and adequacy of information. The first reading is like no subsequent reading; its purpose for content learning is to configure the pattern of the reading (story grammar? comparison and contrast? cause and effect? and so forth) and how the details fit into that pattern.

The purpose of the Discussion phase, then, is to ensure understanding and retention of this foundational, text-based, factual information. The Directed Reading Lesson is designed to deliberately move students into higher-level thinking during the subsequent Rereading and Follow-Up steps, often to learn a generalization related to content-specific unit goals. Therefore, it is appropriate for the teacher to generate a purpose-for-reading that has students reading to construct and record text-based information and to lead a discussion that verifies that information.

An example of this intentional movement from lower- to higher-level thinking about content is seen in the reading of a health chapter on exercise. Students record the causes and effects of cramps, strains, disc ruptures, lower back pain, tendonitis, and hernias, as reported literally in the textbook, during the Silent Reading step. This information is verified during Discussion. Then, during rereading, the teacher leads the students to examine what all these conditions have in common, that is, to use inductive reasoning to generalize the content unit goal: poor muscle tone can result in serious injury and chronic pain.

## THE TEACHER AS DISCUSSION FACILITATOR

During Discussion, the teacher is a facilitator, asking students for their responses and guiding them to complete, valid responses for the purposes set. It is crucial during Discussion that the content teacher assume the role of the discussion facilitator, not the source of answers. The teacher is discussion guide, prober, enabler, devil's advocate, redirector, and disentangler. Debriefing the answers to the purpose-for-reading should not be a simple recitation of responses to promote rote memorization of information; it should be a probing by the teacher to foster student understanding of the reading. Look at how the teachers describe their roles during Discussion in the math lesson, "Problem-Solving Strategies" and in the music lesson, "Civil War Music: 'Battle Hymn of the Republic.'"

p. 178
p. 190

Maintaining a true discussion usually involves the teacher making additional requests for clarification, for example:

Tell us more about that.
What do you mean by . . . ?
What else . . . ?
How does that relate to . . . ?
Why is that important?

Sometimes teachers request students to revisit the text to prove or clarify a point—"Where did you find that in the reading?" or "Would you locate the source for that information and read it aloud to the class?" In this scenario, a student may read orally a short segment of the text as a basis for an answer to the purpose-for-reading. Thus, the teacher has the students appropriately practice oral reading and use the content of what they read aloud as grist for discussion. This approach requires students to think critically about the segment read orally and determine the validity of it as the basis for a response to the purposes set.

The Discussion should be in the form of an instructional conversation. Discussions are *instructional* because they are designed to promote learning with the teacher using eliciting questions, restatements, and pauses to extend student contributions. They are *conversational* because the discussion is characterized by "multiple, interactive, connected turns," with responses building on and extending previous ones (Woolfolk, 1998, p. 355). Only if all questioning of students fails should the teacher become the lecturer, soliloquist, diatribist, informant, deliverer, or "font of all knowledge." Lecturing "continues to be the most prevalent teaching mode in secondary . . . education, despite overwhelming evidence that it produces the lowest degree of retention for most learners" (Sousa, 2001, p. 95). Teaching is more effective when students are the discussants because students construct their own knowledge and use their own language as opposed to passively receiving the knowledge from teachers.

As responses are reviewed during the Discussion phase, students have an additional opportunity to read and speak the vocabulary primed in Readiness. The vocabulary words primed were chosen because they were needed to answer the purpose-for-reading; therefore, they should appear in student responses.

p. 18
The science lesson plan in Chapter 2, "Cities on Fire," is a good example of how to give specific attention in Discussion to vocabulary words primed during the Concept Development/Vocabulary phase of Readiness. The students have read to learn the factors that caused the great fires in London and Chicago. This information is literally stated and explained in the science text chapter. Notice under description of Discussion, the teacher asks for student responses and records the correct responses on the graphic organizer. The implied procedure is that the teacher will record only correct responses. The teacher "ask[s] students for elaboration, as necessary" and "[i]nstructs students to add any information or revise their own graphic organizers, if needed." Notice that the teacher deliberately plans on calling attention to students' use of vocabulary learned during Readiness: "point out the new vocabulary learned as students contribute responses using these terms."

## SMALL GROUPS DURING DISCUSSION

p. 206
You probably noticed that some of the lesson plans include an intermediary step between Silent Reading and Discussion with the entire class. For example, look at the biology lesson, "Relationships in a Habitat." This teacher places students in small groups before the class discussion to discuss the purpose-for-reading. The teacher chooses this intermediary step because (1) her class, a heterogeneous, standard class, has a wide range of reading achievement levels in it; and (2) the initial purpose-for-reading requires students to process a lengthy reading and extrapolate extensive detail. By including small-group discussion, students have additional time to process the content information, to learn more, prior to participating in the entire-class discussion during which consensus will be reached on the validity and adequacy of information. Research supports the notion that students learn more effectively when they have systematic, multiple exposures to detail. In fact, if students are to use the details in a meaningful way, they need to be exposed to the details three or four times (Nuthall, 1999; Nuthall & Alton-Lee, 1995). Additionally, these multiple exposures should not exceed two days' duration (Rovee-Collier, 1995). Thus, the format of the Directed Reading Lesson provides multiple exposures through Silent Reading, Discussion, (small-group and entire-class) and Rereading.

p. 151

Look now at the poetry lesson, "Nikki-Rosa." This teacher uses small-group discussion in conjunction with a reader response approach with a poem. During the students' silent reading of the poem, they read in order to write a letter to the author. This is their "response," their "envisionment," of the meaning they have made from the poem. Then, during the Discussion, students are put into prearranged groups to share these reactions and to look for commonalities in their responses. When a reader response approach is used, this small-group discussion group becomes an "interpretive community," a "gathering of students in which each student's personal responses are elaborated, informed, and enlarged by interactions with others" (Milner & Milner, 1999, p. 99). It is an opportunity for readers to share reactions, broaden perspectives, air new insights, entertain multiple perspectives, resolve disputes, and arrive at meaning together (Milner & Milner).

Small-group work sessions are a form of *collaborative learning.* They are designed to encourage the sharing of student ideas that lead to better understanding of the reading. Small-group discussion is a scaffolding activity (Vygotsky, 1978), providing learner assistance for those students who, in spite of their best efforts, might not be able to comprehend the assigned content reading sufficiently to answer completely or accurately the purpose-for-reading set for silent reading. What students do not learn during the independent silent reading, they will have a chance to learn by talking and listening. Small-group discussion of a reading is learning with guidance and social interaction. And because this social collaboration also increases interest in the content topics (Hootstein, 1995; Zahorik, 1996), it enhances the probability of learning content.

Small-group discussion benefits even the most competent learners. The collaborative exchange among only two to four members gives them more frequent opportunities to test the clarity of their expression of ideas than does an entire-class discussion. Even competent readers will experience conflicting ideas during peer discussion, which requires critical defense of their perspectives, often leading to "cognitive restructuring and growth in understanding" (Alvermann, 2000, p. 137). In fact, it has been shown that giving a good explanation can be even more effective for learning than receiving the explanation (Webb & Palincsar, 1996).

Classroom research across grade levels, cultures, and content areas has consistently concluded that students organized into small groups can support and increase each other's learning and retention (Alvermann et al., 1996; Davidson, 1985; Flood, Lapp, Flood, & Nagle, 1992; Grouws & Cebulla, 2000; Johnson, Johnson, Holubed, & Roy, 1991; Jordan, 1985; Sharan & Sharan, 1992; Slavin, 1995; Sousa, 2001; Tompkins, 1997; Walberg, 1999; Webb,1991; Zemelman, Daniels, & Hyde, 1998). Research has also revealed that secondary students covet the on-task talking time provided by small-group discussion and recognize the facilitative effects of collaborative learning. For example, in one seminal study it was reported that "students in the middle grades . . . were adamant in their belief that 'they had a better understanding of what they read when they listened to their peers discuss a selection' " (Alvermann, 2000, p. 140).

## CONSIDERATIONS WHEN IMPLEMENTING SMALL-GROUP DISCUSSION

It takes preparation on the part of teachers for small-group discussions to work effectively. Teachers need to determine the actual constituency of each small group—which students will work with which students. Because the purpose of small-groups is tutorial (i.e., students review what they have learned independently, affirm or revise their knowledge, and rehearse responses for the entire-class discussion that will follow), students should be grouped heterogeneously according to reading achievement. Using homogeneous groups, especially when students for whom the reading material is at frustration level are put together, will not maximize the learning opportunity inherent in heterogeneous, small groupings. Less able readers learn from more competent readers; more competent readers learn by teaching less able readers.

Teachers also need to determine the size of each group. Small-groups should be two to four students working together. Dyads (two per group) are best when students and teachers have had little experience with small-group activities, or with students who have a history of off-task behavior. Dyad groupings should include one member who is reading the assigned material instructionally and one for whom the reading is at frustration level, or one independent reader and one instructional reader. Triads (three per group) work well when the class has almost an equal number of students for whom the text is on an independent, instructional, or frustration level. Each triad can consist of one student for whom the text is independent level, one for whom it is instructional level, and one for whom it is frustration level. Look at how triad grouping is used in the health lesson, "Eating Disorders." What is the basis for the teacher's grouping constituency?

p. 163

Quads (four per group) can also be used, again including in each group students at different reading levels. We recommend that groups not be larger than four students, because the more students in a group, the fewer chances an individual has to contribute to the discussion. It is easy for a student to withdraw from discussion with a larger number in a group. Research on grouping practices supports the recommendation that "small teams of three to four members seem more effective than larger groups" (Lou et al., 1996, p. 452).

Here is how a teacher might describe his grouping constituency using quads based on reading achievement:

> The class is divided into five groups of four students (quads) and one group of three students (triad). The two independent readers are put into different groups. Four of the five students who read the material at a frustration level are placed in twos into a dyad with one independent and one instructional-level reader. The fifth student at a frustration level will be put into a group of three with two instructional-level readers. I will assist each group as needed.

p. 151

Look at the criteria for the quad constituency used in the ESL lesson plan, "Nikki-Rosa." This teacher has expanded the criteria due to the nature of her learners.

Teachers should also consider student personality when determining group constituency. For example, a good reader who tends to dominate discussions should not be placed in the same group with a reticent, less able reader who might be reluctant to be assertive with a more competent reader who has an extroverted personality.

Finally, teachers must be sure that students have a clear goal for their discussion. At this point in the Directed Reading Lesson, the students' task is to review and reach consensus on the answers to the purpose-for-reading. To achieve this goal, the teacher should appoint a facilitator who is responsible for keeping the conversation on-task and ensuring that all members contribute. All group members are responsible for recording the agreed-on answers so that they can contribute with responses and justification during the entire-class discussion that will follow.

## ORAL RETELLING DURING DISCUSSION

p. 22
p. 212

Sometimes, teachers include a structured activity during the small-group Discussion step of the Directed Reading Lesson. For example, look at the English lesson, "The Scarlet Ibis" in Chapter 2 and the social studies lesson, "History of Maryland," in Appendix A. What specific type of activity have the teachers included in the Discussion step of their lessons?

Oral retelling is "a reflection tool that requires readers to organize information they have gleaned from the text in order to provide a personalized summary. Students engaging in retells must review all they know about a text; select key points that reflect main ideas; consider key events, problem, solution, characters, and setting, then weave the information into a meaningful communication" (Hoyt, 1999, p. 39). This "meaningful communication" occurs when oral retelling is used in the classroom with partners taking turns retelling what they have read to one another. This is an authentic audience judging the adequacy and validity of the oral retelling.

Oral retelling is also effective for students in secondary classes who need to engage in an additional reflection activity to strengthen or deepen their understanding of the content information. For example, we taught a Directed Reading Lesson to a group of eighth grade students in an English class, using Edgar Allan Poe's short story, "The Cask of Amantillado." It was not until we used oral retelling during Discussion that several of the students learned that the antagonist had died by being entombed alive in the catacombs. Without this retelling activity, it is questionable whether these students would have come to an understanding of the conflict's resolution.

Retellings have been shown to improve students' comprehension of specific narratives and of their sense of story grammar (Morrow, 1986). Our experience convinces us that retellings are also effective with expository content readings. Oral retellings can be used immediately after Silent Reading in place of a small-group discussion, during which students simply review the written responses on their graphic organizers, and prior to the entire-class discussion. This is how oral retelling is used in the "Scarlet Ibis" lesson plan in Chapter 2. Or the teacher may choose to use an oral retelling after the entire-class discussion, as in "The History of Maryland" lesson plan. She waits until she has led the students through the discussion of the purpose-for-reading, then engages them in an oral retelling to synthesize the information and reinforce their understanding of the chronological order of the events.

To maximize effectiveness, teachers should carefully structure the use of oral retellings. The following guidelines are key to using oral retellings to improve understanding of content reading:

p. 212 →

- When oral retelling is first introduced, the teacher should explain to students why they are using retellings and then should model a retelling for the students.
- Students need to be reminded to use the thought pattern as the structural basis for their oral retellings. For example, the social studies teacher of the "History of Maryland" lesson plan reminds students, "This reading is written in chronological order. Be sure to do your oral retelling in chronological order. Begin with 1625 when George Calvert retires from the English royal court. Include details of the important events that occurred."
- Teachers should encourage retellers to use their graphic organizers and reading material as support for their retellings. Oral retelling is not a memorization and recall activity, but an opportunity to articulate a coherent, valid, and complete summary of the purpose-for-reading goal. As they retell, students should be assessing their own comprehension, noting gaps, connections, disconnections, and so on; therefore, they may need to pause and reexamine their notes or reading material to add to or revise their oral summaries.
- Listeners also have the responsibility of assessing the oral retellings of their peers. They should be silent during the entire retelling, listening carefully so that they can check off on their own graphic organizers what information the reteller includes. At the conclusion of the retelling, listeners should discuss with the retellers what information they did not hear, or information they heard that they believe is inaccurate.
- The teacher should inconspicuously arrange for the least able reader in the group to give his or her oral retelling last so that he or she can profit from first listening to the retellings of better comprehenders.

Oral retelling can be the first step in the use of a comprehension strategy called *reciprocal teaching*. Extensive research on reciprocal teaching has shown that it can significantly improve comprehension of secondary students in all content areas, (Palincsar & Brown, 1983, 1984, 1985, 1986), especially when teachers directly explain and model each of the steps.

Either with an entire class or small groups (which we prefer), reciprocal teaching involves a student who is the leader or "teacher." We usually appoint the facilitators of each of the small groups to be the "teachers." The following outlines the steps we have used to incorporate reciprocal teaching into the Discussion step of the Directed Reading Lesson.

1. The students appointed to be the "teachers" for this session begin by referring to their graphic organizers and offering an oral summary, a retelling, of what has been read. Other students in the group then add or offer changes to the oral summary presented.
2. The "teachers" ask their group members questions that help to identify the important information in the reading, modeling the types of questions classroom teachers ordinarily ask. The group members respond, locating evidence for their answers as needed. The classroom teacher circulates from group to group to settle confusions or disputes.
3. The "teachers" identify parts of the reading that were difficult or confusing to them and ask group members to clarify. The "teachers" might ask other members of the group to identify aspects of the reading they found difficult or confusing and lead the group to help clarify these parts. Again, the classroom teacher circulates and is available to assist in clarifications that cannot be resolved by the students.
4. The "teacher" asks the group members to predict what will be the topic of the next lesson or segment of the text, or what will happen in the next part of the novel.

## WRITTEN SUMMARIES AFTER DISCUSSION

p. 225

Another way to have students review and reinforce their learning during the *Discussion* step is to have them write a summary after the entire-class discussion has been completed. This procedure is used in the Spanish lesson "Una Leyenda del Caribe." The students are arranged in triads, meet for ten minutes to discuss the story map, participate in a teacher-led debriefing, then write a summary in Spanish, using their story maps as their notes for their drafts. In essence, the Directed Reading Lesson's Readiness through Discussion phases are prewriting steps for the drafting of a summary written in Spanish. This review step is included because the nature of the students and the content requires repetition for appropriate reinforcement; that is, the level III Spanish students practice the use of the language through writing the summary.

Research on students' ability to summarize, either as oral retellings or in written form, has shown the following:

- Summaries written by students improve their comprehension and also help them monitor their own understanding of text (Hare & Borchardt, 1984; King, 1992; O'Donnell & Dansereau, 1992; Wittrock, 1990).
- Summarization instruction improves learning from expository texts (Armbruster, Anderson, & Ostertag, 1987).
- Poor readers do not readily engage in self-directed summarization (Palincsar & Brown, 1983); "better readers at various levels of schooling are more adept than less able readers at selecting textually-important content for their recall and summaries" (Spivey & King, 1998, p. 670).
- The ability to summarize is a developmental process, with students in grades 7 and above most able to become proficient in summarization (Brown & Day, 1983).

When teachers have students use their graphic organizers to guide their oral retellings (oral summaries) or their written summaries as a part of the Discussion step, teachers are providing them an opportunity to improve their learning as well as guided practice in how to summarize. The completed graphic organizers include the text structure and the significant details necessary for adequate summaries. Establishing these parameters helps to avoid the "knowledge-telling" ploy (Brown & Day, 1983) often used by younger and less able students. Knowledge-telling refers to students who state all they know about some part of the answer without including the relevant information for the complete answer. When students are instructed then to summarize, either orally or in writing, they are charged with organiz- ing the information into a coherent summary of the text—"a meaningful communication" (Hoyt, 1999, p. 39). If the student is unable to generate this "meaningful communication," it is a clear indication that the student is not learning sufficiently. Thus, the summary becomes a formative assessment for both the students and the teachers.

## SUMMARY

The Discussion step of the Directed Reading Lesson is an opportunity for students to en- gage in listening, speaking, reading, and writing to interact with classmates and the teacher. "No matter what the subject, the people who read it, write it, and talk it are the ones who learn best (NCTE Language and Learning Across the Curriculum Committee, 2002, p. 1). As students put thought into speech and refine their comprehension through verbal interaction with others, learning and retention of content are reinforced, thinking skills are sharpened, language-processing skills are practiced, and social skills and self- esteem are enhanced. Talking demands that students be active learners and construct knowledge for themselves (Stover, Neubert, & Lawlor, 1993).

In planning the Discussion step of the Directed Reading Lesson, you should ask your- self the following questions:

### Questions for Planning the Discussion Step of the Directed Reading Lesson

1. Are there students in my class for whom this reading is at the frustration level? Is this reading lengthy and does it require significant detail to answer the purpose-for- reading? Do the answers to these questions suggest that my students would profit by a small-group discussion prior to the entire-class debriefing?
2. If I plan to use small groups, should I use dyads, triads, or quads, in light of the num- ber of students for whom this reading is at the independent, instructional, or frustra- tion level?
3. In consideration of students' personalities and reading levels, whom should I group together for this discussion activity?
4. Should I appoint a facilitator who leads the group in a general review of the purpose- for-reading, and/or should I have the students engage in oral retellings? Should I teach, model, and initiate reciprocal teaching with the small groups?
5. Would this group of students profit by writing a summary after we have an entire- class debriefing of the purpose-for-reading?
6. Do I know the content sufficiently to engage the students in an *instructional conver- sation,* rather than a *recitation,* during the entire-class debriefing?
7. Will I (or a student scribe) record the valid and complete responses on the chalk- board? Overhead? PowerPoint?

## YOUR TURN

1. Answer questions 1–7 in the previous section.
2. If you are using this text as part of a course or workshop experience, share the draft of your Discussion plan with another participant. You should be able to defend your rationale for the following:
   - Using or not using small-group discussion prior to the entire-class debriefing
   - Choosing dyad, triad, or quad groupings
   - Grouping based on student personalities
   - Choosing a general review during small-group discussion, an oral retelling, or re- ciprocal teaching
   - Using or not using a written summary by students

# CHAPTER NINE

# REREADING

Either you think—or else others have to think for you and take power from you.
—*F. Scott Fitzgerald, American novelist*

---

1. Readiness
   a. Motivation
   b. Tapping and Developing Background of Experience
   c. Concept Development/Vocabulary
   d. Purpose-for-Reading
2. Silent Reading
3. Discussion
4. **Rereading**                                        ◀◀◀
5. Follow-Up

---

The fourth part of the Directed Reading Lesson is Rereading. When you read the anchoring lesson plans in Chapter 2, what did you determine to be the purpose of this step? Rereading is designed to have students attend to the reading for new purposes, that is, purposes differ-ent from that given in Readiness. Because research has shown that comprehension improves across reading trials (Barnett & Seefeldt, 1989), the teacher often directs the stu-dents to reread the entire selection for the new purposes. Sometimes, students only need to reread a select portion of the text or skim the entire text or graphic organizer to satisfy the new purpose(s). An exception to this would be if the reading material is a play. With a play, the entire work might be read aloud to convey the creative effect. The initial silent reading of the play serves as the rehearsal for this oral reading.

The purpose of Rereading is to have students extend their understanding of the con-tent. Students use what they have learned from their initial reading (Purpose-for-Reading, Silent Reading, Discussion), and now extend their thinking beyond that information.

## HIGHER-LEVEL QUESTIONING

Up to this point in the Directed Reading Lesson, the purpose-for-reading questions to be answered during Silent Reading and then reviewed in Discussion have generally required text-based responses, explicitly stated or clearly implied in the reading. Once this founda-tion has been validated during Discussion, students should be led to use this knowledge as grist for higher-level thinking. Higher-level questions require students to use the textual information, but then go beyond the text to answer. Higher-level questions "require the mental manipulation of information to create an acceptable response" (Hamaker, 1986). Answers to higher-level questions should require students to support their responses with details and facts.

Various types of higher-level questions can be used during Rereading. The lesson plans in this text primarily use the following types: concept formation, generalizations, critical thinking, and creative thinking.

## Concept Formation

Concept formation is a form of inductive reasoning (Neubert & Binko, 1992); it is a thinking process for "organizing information about an entity and associating that information with a label (word)" (Marzano et al., 1988, p. 146). A concept is a "big idea" (Dixon, Carnine, & Kameenui, 1992) that can be applied in various situations within or across content areas.

pp. 23–24

Look at the English lesson in Chapter 2, "The Scarlet Ibis." The teacher has the students engage in concept formation in the Rereading section. The students induce the meaning of the concept *symbolic*. They then revisit the short story and their story maps and apply this knowledge by explaining the story's symbolic title. The students' ability to apply the concept is based on their understanding of the facts of the story from their initial reading and their use of higher-level thinking.

When reading for literary experience, as in the English lesson, Rereading is the appropriate time for the investigation of literary analysis techniques, or concepts, such as symbolism, irony, imagery, motif, point-of-view, theme, and couplet. During the initial reading and discussion of the literature, the teacher should ensure declarative knowledge; during the Rereading the teacher should review or teach inductively the literary concept, then have students apply that literary concept to the literature just read.

## Generalizing

Generalizing is inferring general statements from facts or examples; it is stating "characteristics about classes or categories of persons, places, living and nonliving things, and events" (Marzano, Pickering, & Pollack, 2001, p. 134). Like concept formation, generalization is a form of inductive reasoning. When students generalize a "big idea" statement in a content area, it is often a unit goal or a principle that will be applied in the unit or throughout the course. Generalizations are easier to recall than all the supporting facts; therefore, the generalizations can be retrieved more readily and used in future learning.

pp. 184–185

For examples of generalizing, look at the Rereading step of some of the lesson plans. In the music lesson, "Traditional Instruments of Africa," the teacher has the students reread declarative knowledge about specific African instruments and leads them to induce the generalizations that in order to produce sound, something vibrates or makes a pitch, something echoes or resonates, and something gives each instrument a unique sound. These generalizations will help students toward the future accomplishment of Unit Goal 4—"apply acquired knowledge to create and demonstrate musically artistic products"—when they create their own African instruments. In the high school music lesson, "Civil War Music: 'Battle Hymn of the Republic,'" the teacher has students reread the lyrics and then generalize the purpose of the song they will be called on to remember when they begin to perform it.

p. 190

p. 151

During the Rereading step in the English lesson, "Nikki-Rosa," students use their declarative knowledge to generalize the "essential criteria for good biographies," which are an accurate description of the events in the person's life and an accurate description of the person's feelings toward the events. This big idea will be used later to accomplish the major goal of this unit. Notice that these are learners for whom English is not their native language. Too often English language learners are "subject to instruction oriented toward lower level skills rather than higher level thinking" (Au, 2002, p. 401). This is avoided if the Directed Reading Lesson format is correctly executed.

pp. 175–176
p. 180

Both math lesson plans have students generalize in the Rereading step. In "Line, Bar, and Pie Graphs," the teacher has students reexamine the factual details from the reading, examples, and graphic organizer to generalize when it is appropriate to use each of the graph types. In "Problem-Solving Strategies," the teacher guides the students to reexamine each of the five steps used to solve the problems, determine commonalities, and write a general rule—a generalization for steps in problem solving. In both cases, the math students will need to recall and apply this knowledge throughout the math course.

## Critical Thinking

Critical thinking is a reflective thinking process "that is focused on deciding what to believe or do" (Ennis, 1985a, p. 54). It is the basis of decision-making and problem solving. Critical thinking is looking at information and reaching a sound conclusion (Marzano et al., 1988). It is making judgments about what one reads (fact or opinion? biased or objective? authentic? credible? assumptive? relevant? realistic? important? appropriate? valid? reliable? logical? complete? worthy?) and using factual information to support the judgments. Critical thinking requires a questioning attitude, a healthy skepticism, and suspended judgment.

p. 192

Look at the physical education lesson, "Aquatic Safety." Each special needs student works with a partner who has read a different book on water safety from the one she or he has read. Partners use critical thinking to reach consensus on the questions: "What do you think is the most dangerous thing about swimming? Why?" and "If you and a friend were going swimming outside, what safety rule is the most important one to remind your friend of? Why?" Notice that students are required to explain why they made their decisions by citing factual information from their reading.

p. 163
p. 160

In the health lesson "Eating Disorders," the teacher instructs the students to review the facts from their reading and graphic organizers and decide which eating disorder is the most dangerous. She also requires them to cite evidence from the reading to support their opinions. During Rereading in the French lesson, "Une Escale Exotique a la Martinique," students must decide whether the author's portrayal of the people of Martinque is realistic and give reasons for their choice. As with "Eating Disorders," the students must use the factual information from the initial reading to make their critical thinking decision and cite this information in supporting their decision.

p. 144

The middle school English lesson "Tales of the Mysterious," also involves students in thinking critically. After collecting evidence from the expository article about the existence or nonexistence of sea serpents, the students are challenged to make their own decision about the credibility of the evidence.

## Creative Thinking

Creative thinking is an inventive thinking process. It is "using known information or material to generate the possible" (Presseisen, 1985, p. 45). It is the "application of data in varying unique combinations and, indeed, the collection of unusual data or data not commonly used, to produce . . . a new synthesis; it requires comprehension and recall of considerable experience and data" (Beyer, 1987, p. 36). It requires thinking up alternatives (Scriven, 1976) and thinking outside the box. Creative thinking involves encouraging "students to see similarities in events and entities not commonly linked" (Marzano et al., 1988, p. 27).

p. 213

Look at the social studies lesson "The History of Maryland." During Rereading, the teacher encourages creative thinking; she has the students use their initial reading and discussion knowledge to role-play George Calvert and write the King a letter asking for a charter in the new land. Students are "using known information" about Calvert's travels to create something new (to "generate the possible") a letter from Calvert to the King.

p. 201

In the science lesson "Leftovers," students are given a futuristic scenario about a problem an astronomer faces in the year 2050. They must use the knowledge they learned from the reading about asteroids, comets, and meteors to propose a creative solution to the problem.

pp. 19, 27

pp. 167–169

pp. 133–134

The science lesson and the art lesson in Chapter 2 both encourage students' creative thinking during Rereading. Can you explain how each uses creative thinking?

If students are to reach their potential using higher-level thought processes, they must practice (Cawelti, 1999). Higher-level thinking can be difficult for students; therefore, teachers should consider using small-group discussion during the Rereading step. Just as small groups can be used in the Discussion to help students learn with guidance and social interaction, they can be used for the same purpose during Rereading. The choice to include small-group discussion as a part of Rereading is seen in the health lesson "AIDS." Due to the nature of the questions and the complexity of the thinking required, this teacher has judged that small-group discussion during this Rereading would facilitate achievement.

Another example of the use of small-group discussion during Rereading can be found in the business education lesson "Student Loans for Higher Education." Because of the complex problem-solving activities requiring knowledge previously learned about financial aid, information acquired in this lesson on student loans, and math work, the teacher has students work in quads to process the Rereading assignment.

All reading material in secondary content areas lends itself to both lower- and higher-level processing. All students, regardless of school ability level, are capable of higher-level thinking (Marzano et al., 1988). Therefore, every Directed Reading Lesson can include the foundational, lower-level, text-based questions as well as the higher-level questions that extend content learning. This provides students with authentic practice in higher-level thinking, a cognitive skill needed more than ever in everyday life. According to recent U.S. Department of Labor studies (Gonyea, 2002) problem-solving skills (use of higher-level thinking skills) are at the top of employers' wish lists for skills in employees.

## READING STANCES

Another way to view the kinds of thinking students do when they read is to look at questions that tap into the various reading stances. Adapted from Judith Langer's (1995) reader response theory, reading stances are ways readers recursively interact with the reading material as they develop their interpretations. They are "different vantage points or perspectives from which good readers gain ideas and build well-rounded, thoughtful understanding of a text" (Paulis, 1998, p. IV-5). Reading stances are used by teachers to guide their questioning in order to enhance student comprehension of text (Maryland State Department of Education, 2001). The four reading stances are global, interpretive, critical, and personal.

### Global Stance

The global stance is the "big picture" view of the reading. It is comparable to the astronauts' view of the earth as they orbit: They see the outline of land and sea but cannot tell whether the trees are leafless or in full bloom. It is like telling someone whether the movie you just saw was a comedy or a mystery. It is readers' ability to give one-paragraph summaries of what they read.

The following are examples of global stance questions for the three generic reading purposes—to have a literary experience, to be informed, and to perform a task. Note that some of the questions under each stance might be appropriate for more than one generic reading purpose. For example, the first example given, "summarize the reading in 2–5 sentences" is an appropriate global question for each of the three generic purposes, but it is listed only under Reading for Literary Experience.

**Reading for Literary Experience**
- Summarize the reading in 2–5 sentences.
- Describe the mood of this selection.
- Describe the picture you have in your mind of this story.

### Reading to Be Informed
- Explain the most important point of this reading.
- Explain what someone could learn from reading this.
- Explain the author's message.

### Reading to Perform a Task
- Explain who would use this information.
- Explain the author's main point.

## Interpretive Stance

The interpretive stance is the more microscopic view—the much closer look. This is the view you have when the airplane is landing and specific streets, houses, and individuals can be seen. This is your answer when your friend asks you to detail the opening scene of a movie. When applied to reading, the reader revisits the text and is immersed in the specifics of the text. For example, in contrast to the global stance of a brief summary, the interpretive stance would be orally retelling the story in depth, which most likely requires the reader to revisit the text and include details of the plot, characters, and setting.

### Reading for Literary Experience
- Orally retell the story in depth.
- List the characters in order of importance and explain your ranking.
- Explain the importance of the setting to the story.
- List the steps the main character uses to solve the problem.
- Compare and contrast character X and character Y.
- Write a new ending.

### Reading to Be Informed
- Explain the pro–con relationship.
- Create a graph from the data given in the reading.
- Explain what quotes most clearly express the author's point-of-view.
- Use the facts from the reading to write a fiction story.
- Explain what the expression X means.

### Reading to Perform a Task
- Perform the task.
- Explain this task in detail to your partner.
- Identify any cause-and-effect relationships in this task.
- Describe what would happen if you did not do the steps in the prescribed order.

## Personal Stance

The personal stance is the connection to the reader's own life. It is an authentic reflection when the reader relates his or her personal life experiences and feelings to the reading. The response is a positively egocentric one. It is like telling your friend you would never react to the situation the way the lead actor in a movie reacted. When responding to a reading from this perspective, the reader is the expert because the reaction centers on his or her life experiences.

### Reading for Literary Experience
- Explain how your experiences compare to those of the main character.
- Explain whether you would do the same or something different from character X.
- Explain how the author's message relates to your life.
- Explain how this story would be different if character X lived where you do.

### Reading to Be Informed
- Compare the author's point-of-view to your own.
- List the questions you would ask if you were to interview the author.
- Explain what you would do to remedy the situation presented in this reading.

### Reading to Perform a Task
- Explain under what circumstances you might find it useful to use this information.
- Explain what parts of the directions were difficult for you and what parts were easy for you.
- Complete this application form with your own information.

## Critical Stance

The critical stance is an analysis of and judgment about the author's perspective and craft. Continuing the movie analogy, you analyze how well the cinematography creates suspense or whether you felt the protagonist's accent was convincing. For the reader, it is an analysis of the reading's credibility and what the author does to create meaning.

### Reading for Literary Experience
- Tell what the author did to make you want to continue reading.
- Evaluate the effectiveness of the illustrations.
- Explain whether the sequence of the story was logical.
- Analyze literary techniques (e.g., flashback, symbolism, irony).

### Reading to Be Informed
- Identify the author's bias.
- Determine whether the author presented a complete argument.
- Explain why the author included X.
- Which of the two readings is clearer?

### Reading to Perform a Task
- How clearly is the task explained?
- Identify signal words the author uses to assist you in completing this task.
- Rewrite these directions for someone in a lower grade.
- Discuss whether the title of this reading is appropriate?

As good readers read silently, they intuitively move in and out of the four stances. The Directed Reading Lesson provides opportunities for teachers to ask questions that encourage this recursive movement. The initial Purpose-for-Reading step focuses students primarily on global and interpretive stances for the initial construction of meaning. Rereading questions generated by the teacher may continue to focus students' attention on global and interpretive stances or may encourage students to extend their reading perspectives with personal and critical stance questions.

pp. 18, 22, 27

p. 22

pp. 19, 23, 27

Look again at the anchoring lesson plans in Chapter 2. In each of these lessons, the initial purpose-for-reading questions encourage global and interpretive stances—reading to get the big picture and foundational detail. The English teacher also directs students to pursue a personal stance in the beginning of the Discussion by asking, "Did you like the story? How did you feel about Doodle? What are your feelings toward Brother?"

During Rereading, the English teacher takes students into a critical stance by having the students examine the literary technique of symbolism and critique its effectiveness. The science teacher stays with interpretive stance questions related to specific ways to prevent fires from occurring. The art teacher has students use a global stance and decide why the Native Americans used particular colors and weaving patterns (to create a mood, feeling, etc.), and consider the feelings they are trying to express through their own round weavings.

p. 197
Various stances are used in the Rereading of lessons in Appendix A. For example, a critical stance is taken by the students in the "Healthy Eating for Maximum Performance" lesson as they evaluate their diets by rating them as "good," "adequate," or "inappropriate."

p. 144
In the English lesson "Tales of the Mysterious," students take two different stances: a critical stance to decide whether the author has convinced them that sea serpents exist, and then a personal stance: "How would you feel if you did experience a sea serpent? What would you do? How would your life change if you were to capture the sea serpent?"

Be aware that an activity you write for students may fall into more than one reading stance category. For example, the following instruction requires the responder to take both a critical and a personal stance to respond adequately: "Explain what information in this pamphlet is particularly helpful. Use your own experiences to support how you might use this information." In the next example, the activity requires an interpretive and a personal stance to the reading: "Compare person X to someone you have known. Explain how they are alike and different. Choose one similar personality trait and use examples from the text and from your personal experience to compare these two individuals."

A lesson can be very sound and still not include questions related to each of the four reading stances. Not every lesson lends itself to asking questions related to all four perspectives, and a teacher should not force the four stances. Teachers should always be guided by what is essential to be learned in the content area. What is important is giving students practice over time in thinking about a reading from the various perspectives. Teachers should not overwork a reading selection or disregard the focus of the lesson by including inappropriate stance questions. We recommend that teachers examine the key questions of their lesson plans retrospectively. For example, on a biweekly basis, teachers should systematically analyze if they are neglecting a reading stance. If they are, teachers can be more conscious of including the missing perspective when it can be appropriately incorporated into a lesson.

## SUMMARY

We have a responsibility to help students learn more than the factual detail of the reading. Rereading is an opportunity for students to use and practice higher-level thinking skills, such as inductive reasoning for concept formation and generalizing, and critical thinking and creative thinking as related to content knowledge. Asking students questions during Rereading that engage them in the reading stances—global, interpretive, critical, and personal—is an opportunity to expand the way students relate to reading.

In planning the Rereading step of the Directed Reading Lesson, you should ask yourself the following questions:

**Questions for Planning the Rereading Step of the Directed Reading Lesson**
Students have an initial understanding of the content knowledge in the reading from the Readiness, Silent Reading, and Discussion activities. What should they do with this information?

1. Should students use it as the basis for learning and applying a concept?
2. Is there a content generalization students should be able to make from this information?
3. Should students look at this information with a critical eye and decide what to do or believe?
4. Could students use this information as the basis of thinking creatively and solve an authentic problem?
5. Is there a perspective on this content information—global, interpretive, critical, or personal—that is important to pursue?
6. Would students profit from working with a partner or small group for this activity?

**YOUR TURN**

1. Answer questions 1–5 in the previous section. Then write your Rereading activity or activities. Be sure to include the key questions you will ask students.

2. If you are using this text as part of a course or workshop experience, share the draft of your Rereading plan with another participant. Ask your colleague to decide the following:

   ■ Does the activity appear to be an appropriate outgrowth from the reading and appropriate for the content topic and unit?

   ■ Have you required students to use higher-level thinking skills?

   ■ What type of higher-level thinking is required of students?

   ■ What stances are required by your Purpose-for-Reading and Rereading question(s)?

# CHAPTER TEN

# FOLLOW-UP

*In the end, we retain from our studies only that which we practically apply.*
—*Johann Wolfgang Von Goethe, German playwright*

1. Readiness
   a. Motivation
   b. Tapping and Developing Background of Experience
   c. Concept Development/Vocabulary
   d. Purpose-for-Reading
2. Silent Reading
3. Discussion
4. Rereading
5. **Follow-Up**  ◄ ◄ ◄

You have readied the students to read your content selection, instructed them to read silently with a specific purpose, discussed with them that purpose, and had the students reread and debrief for purposes related to unit goals and higher-level thinking about the topic. You are now ready to plan the final part of the Directed Reading Lesson, the Follow-Up. When you read the anchoring lesson plans in Chapter 2, what did you decide was the purpose of the Follow-Up?

REFLECT

pp. 19, 24, 27

All three lessons in Chapter 2—science, English, and art—had follow-up activities that reinforce—review, rehearse, and use the key content information the students learned. Reinforcement is important in the long-term retention, retrieval, and future use of the content knowledge. For homework, the science teacher has students apply the different causes of fires learned in the lesson to a new situation, this one in their hometown. The English teacher has the students find a symbol in something they had previously read in class or read as a child and explain the use of the symbol. To do this homework assignment, they must use the knowledge learned in the lesson about what a symbol is and how it is used. The art teacher has the students complete their follow-up activity in class by creating a title for their weavings and by explaining how the color schemes and patterns they chose expressed their feelings. The English and science teachers are providing students opportunities to apply the learning to new situations; the art teacher directs an activity that allows students to review the intent of color and pattern in Native American round weavings.

Many of the lessons in Appendix A have reinforcement follow-up activities that are completed in the classroom individually by students or in small groups. For example, in the art lesson, "Photomontage," the students review the steps in this photography process by

p. 129

p. 139

p. 155

creating a photomontage themselves. The family and consumer science teacher has student triads use the facts they learned about SIDS to write dialogue for role-playing scenarios. Look at the English lesson, "The Successful Job Interview," in which students read a theory on job interviews. The follow-up activity has student groups apply this theory by scripting and participating in mock job interviews.

p. 176

p. 202

p. 208

p. 222

p. 230

Other reinforcement follow-up activities are completed by students at home. For example, the follow-up activity of the mathematics lesson, "Line, Bar, and Pie Graphs," reinforces the students' knowledge of the three types of graphs by having them create two graphs for new data as a home assignment. In the science lesson, "Leftovers," the teacher gives the students a homework assignment in which they must use knowledge from the lesson to create a poster warning their neighbors of a meteor entering the atmosphere of their community. In the science lesson, "Relationships in a Habitat," the students use the facts from the lesson for homework to describe their own domestic habitats analogous to the animal habitat. The high school social studies teacher in "The Development of the Supreme Court's Power," instructs students to apply what they learned about judicial review to the Bush–Gore presidential election. The lesson for special needs students on "Reading a Menu" has students review what they have learned about the pizzeria menu and what they have decided to order for lunch by having them explain their decision to their parents that evening to get the money needed for the field trip.

p. 186

Now read the Follow-Up (Closure) of the music lesson, "Traditional Instruments of Africa." The teacher has students write three questions about the topic of this lesson they think will be on the unit test. Students are to base their predictions on the objectives, reading, and class discussions; that is, they review what they learned and write questions reflecting the most important ideas that they believe might appear on a test. In addition to a reinforcement for the students, this assesses student learning for the teacher—what the students think they learned and what they believe is most important.

Notice that another follow-up activity is in this music lesson. Students have a choice of projects, for example, creating a game, learning to play an African instrument, or researching and reporting how traditional African instruments have impacted modern instruments and music (jazz, rock, rap, etc.). The option of creating a game is a reinforcement activity. Students use their knowledge learned in the Directed Reading Lesson as the basis for designing a game that teaches or reviews this information.

The options of learning to play a traditional African instrument and researching are reinforcement in that they ask students to review and use the knowledge learned through the lesson, but they go beyond that knowledge. They enrich the students' knowledge base, broadening their knowledge by learning how to play an instrument or learning how these instruments influenced modern music. These activities add new knowledge; that is, they make new connections for the students.

p. 163

What other lessons in Appendix A included follow-up activities that are enrichment activities? Look at the health lesson, "Eating Disorders." This teacher has planned an enrichment follow-up that has volunteer students visiting websites to research what help is available for the kinds of eating disorders they learned about. In the next day's lesson, these students will report their findings to the class.

p. 197

The follow-up activity of the physical education lesson "Healthy Eating for Maximum Performance" draws students' attention to the fact that the only food listed on their graphic organizer under "Food to Avoid" is "caffeine." The follow-up assignment for the students is to broaden their knowledge of foods that do not contribute to maximum physical performance by using resources, "coaches, the health and fitness magazines . . . and the Internet" and to bring a list of other foods to add to this list.

pp. 226–227

The Spanish lesson "Una Leyenda del Caribe" has enrichment project choices such as reexamining the story to "explain all the elements of sexism," or "search the Internet to find information about the Caribes and Arawaks" and determine whether the version read in class is accurate.

The follow-up activity for the lesson on the novel *Roll of Thunder, Hear My Cry* is also an enrichment activity. Using what they learned in this lesson, students are directed to predict what they believe will happen in Chapter 7 of the novel.

All of these enrichment activities require students to rehearse the knowledge learned in the current Directed Reading Lesson, but the enrichment follow-up extends that knowledge.

**p. 151**

You may have noticed that some of the lesson plans in Appendix A do not have a follow-up activity. The Follow-Up step is, indeed, optional in the sense of being a concluding part of the Directed Reading Lesson. The English lesson, "Nikki-Rosa," for example, ends with the establishment of essential criteria for good biographies during Rereading. The teacher obviously did not believe that an additional activity to reinforce or enrich this knowledge was necessary at that time; however, the teacher will review these criteria when students begin a writing lesson that will lead to a major unit goal: authoring their own biographies of selected individuals.

## SUMMARY

The final step of the Directed Reading Lesson is Follow-Up. It is intended to reinforce, or reinforce and enrich, the content knowledge learned through reading and discussion. The Follow-Up activities can be done in class or as homework. They can be done independently or by groups of students. They may have students use resource or supplementary reading materials. Teachers may even eliminate Follow-Up if they believe the students do not need further supplementary practice or extension.

In planning the Follow-Up step of the Directed Reading Lesson, you should ask yourself the following questions:

**Questions for Planning the Follow-Up Step of the Directed Reading Lesson**
1. Would a follow-up activity help the students' content achievement?
2. Do the students need an activity that only reviews or reinforces the content knowledge? Should it be an activity that reviews but also broadens their knowledge? Should there be more than one activity?
3. Is this an activity students could do at home? Should it be done in class instead; that is, do students need my guidance or that of peers to do this activity successfully? Should it be accomplished by students working independently or with a small group of their peers?
4. If students will be reading new material, is it on an independent level, that is, easy enough for them to read without my directed instruction?

## YOUR TURN

1. Answer the questions in the previous section as you plan your Follow-Up activity or activities.
2. If you are using this text as part of a course or workshop experience, share the draft of your Follow-Up step with another participant. Ask your colleague to decide the following:
   - Does your Follow-Up reinforce the content knowledge of the lesson?
   - If your Follow-Up is an enrichment activity, is it appropriate for the unit and the unit goals?

# CHAPTER ELEVEN

# WRITING WITHIN THE DIRECTED READING LESSON

I write entirely to find out what I'm thinking, what I'm looking at, what I see and what it means.

—*Joan Didion, Contemporary American journalist and novelist*

Read the activities below taken from the Follow-Up of some of the lessons in this text. In addition to being either reinforcement or enrichment activities, what else do they all have in common?

- Find a symbol and in writing explain its use.
- Think of a title for your weaving and in writing explain how your color schemes and patterns express your feelings.
- Write in your journals the key information you learned about space "leftovers."
- Create a poster warning your neighbors about a comet entering their atmosphere.
- Write three questions you believe will be on the test.
- Create a game that helps students learn and review traditional African instruments.
- Write a paper on Josephine Bonaparte's life on Martinique.
- Assume that you have been accepted into the school of your choice and that you have to pay for this school completely on your own. Explain in writing how you would do that using financial aid.
- Look up information on the Paleozoic or Cretaceous period on the Web. Find a known animal that looks like the sea serpents we read about today. In writing, describe its appearance, what it eats, how it breathes, and whether you consider this animal dangerous.
- In your journals, write your predictions for what you believe will happen in Chapter 7 of *Roll of Thunder, Hear My Cry.*

All of these examples involve students in writing to master content. Writing is "language choice on paper" (Mayher, Lester, & Pradl, 1983, p. 1). In secondary classrooms this type of writing can take many forms, from the informal listing of ideas in a journal to the more formal research papers or lab reports. It is different from copying, which does not allow the student choice, and fill-in-the-blank activities, which are minimalist writing because they limit the choices of students.

Using writing in the secondary classroom has many benefits:

- Writing is a process that helps students *discover* what they know, express emerging ideas, and raise questions. It is the expression of concepts and principles the learner constructs. It is learning in the voice of the learner.

- Writing produces a concrete product that indicates to the student and to the teacher whether the student has mastered the content knowledge. Both find out what students know and what they do not know (*assessment*).
- Writing about a topic, as opposed to merely thinking about it, increases the chances that students are *cognitively engaged* in the class. Students need to think to write.
- Writing provides students opportunities to practice and demonstrate *higher-level thinking*—interpreting (What does this mean?), organizing (What comes first? Last?), analyzing (What is important here?), applying ("How does this relate to X?"), reflecting (How is this important to me and my life?).
- Writing improves students' *fluency* and gives them practice in the use of various sentence structures (syntax) and formats (e.g., advertisements, diagrams, summaries, posters, stories, reports, and letters).
- Writing improves the *learning of content* (Langer & Applebee, 1987; Maxwell, 1996). It promotes positive transfer and increases retention of information. Writing requires students to put their reflective thoughts into written words. If students can put their knowledge into their own words, their understanding goes beyond memorization. Writing is a tool whereby students learn a subject (Neubert, 1992; Stover, Neubert, & Lawlor, 1993). Just like reading, writing is a learning tool.

**pp. 15–27**

**REFLECT**

The Follow-Up step is not the only appropriate place in the Directed Reading Lesson where writing can be used as a learning tool. Look back over the anchoring lesson plans in Chapter 2. Your purpose-for-reading is to enumerate, with examples, other parts of the Directed Reading Lesson where writing can be used to facilitate learning.

If the Directed Reading Lesson is written and executed like the lesson plans in Chapter 2, writing as a learning tool will be inherent in the following parts:

- **Concept Development/Vocabulary:** In the vocabulary priming process, students work in pairs and write a draft definition for each word presented.
- **Silent Reading:** As (or after) students silently read, they write responses to the purposes set. If they have successfully comprehended, they will be able to complete the graphic organizer. The very act of writing down—scribing—helps students recall information later and causes them to process the information in more depth (Sorgen, 1998).
- **Discussion:** Students revise their written responses if they work with peers and when they reach consensus during the teacher-led class discussion.
- **Rereading:** Because students are rereading the text and responses to the initial purposes-for-reading to find answers to new purposes, the students usually write their responses, then revise them during the discussion.

Writing is optional during the Motivation and Tapping and Developing Background phases; that is, writing is used at the teacher's discretion. During the Motivation in the art lesson, the teacher has the students write responses to their observations of Navajo rugs. This is followed by an entire-class discussion of student ideas. In their Motivation activities, the science and English teachers do not assign writing; they pose questions, then immediately interact with the students. During Tapping and Developing Background, the English teacher does, however, have the students write about their feelings, but does not have them share their written ideas.

**REFLECT**

What do you think was the basis for the teachers' decision to use or not use writing along with oral discussion? Time constraints? Writing does take more time, if included prior to discussion. Student participation? Writing prior to discussing does encourage more responses per student and more students to participate. The writing produces a concrete record of what students think; therefore, when it is time to discuss, students can listen to others' comments without the fear of forgetting their own contributions. Difficulty of the questions posed? Writing gives students time to process questions that require higher-level thinking. Teachers need to consider these factors when making decisions on the use of writing-to-learn.

## TO EDIT OR NOT TO EDIT

Teachers also need to decide whether the writing assignment should be first draft or edited draft. Writing assignments are often first-draft writings, designed to be used by students as prompts when they share their ideas orally. They may not even be collected and reviewed by the teacher. Generally, these written pieces are not expected to adhere perfectly to the conventions of spelling, punctuation, and grammar because the ideas are the focus, and time is not provided for proofreading.

p. 24

Look at the follow-up homework assignment that the English teacher gives students. They are to locate a symbol used in books, magazines, or newspapers and explain its use. She tells them that they will use their written notes and the symbol artifact they find to present to a small group of their peers. The teacher does not expect an edited product because the student will not transmit this *written* information to the teacher or a classmate.

pp. 19, 27

Other writing assignments do include the expectation that the product be an edited piece of writing. Edited writing eliminates idiosyncratic variations of graphics and syntax so the reader (who is not the writer) can focus on the ideas being presented. Look at the Follow-Up activities in the science and art lessons in Chapter 2. The science teacher asks the students to decide whether they believe "there is a danger of a major city fire happening in Baltimore" and to support their opinion with factors discussed in the day's lesson. She is going to collect and review it; therefore, she has reminded them to edit their work. Doing this as a homework assignment allows students time for both the idea *and* the editing process. The art teacher also tells students to proofread their own work or have someone else help them with proofreading. The writings these students complete will be displayed for all to see with their weavings. Because these writing are going *public,* they need to follow the conventions of standard, written English.

p. 169

Look now at the health lesson plan "AIDS." The students are to demonstrate what they have learned by writing a summary in the form of a speech on AIDS. The teacher gives them a scoring rubric, which draws their attention to the need to organize and edit their writing. The texts of these speeches will be collected and reviewed by the teacher. Selected speeches will be read aloud by their authors in class, and some will be displayed on the bulletin board for students and visitors to peruse, thus, the requirement of edited papers.

## TO GUIDE OR NOT TO GUIDE

The "AIDS" lesson illustrates another important consideration for content teachers in terms of how much guidance students need to successfully complete a writing assignment. This health teacher believes her students, as a result of this Directed Reading Lesson and other previous instruction, can do this writing independently, even as a home assignment. The teacher even cues them to this in the scoring rubric: "Cite examples from the article and graphic organizer in every supporting paragraph." The teacher assumes that the students know what a paragraph is, and how to use introductory, supporting, and summary paragraphs.

Often the reading lesson does not prepare students sufficiently to draft their writing assignment independently. Sometimes the teacher needs to handle the assignment instructionally; that is, the content teacher must ready the students to write through a prewriting process analogous to Readiness in the reading process.

*Prewriting* is the planning stage of the writing process. Read the two lesson plans included in this chapter. Both are Directed Reading Lessons that include phases for prewriting. The first is a high school biology lesson plan; the second is an English plan for middle school students. Your purpose-for-reading is to be informed about the prewriting process. Specifically, you will read the two lesson plans to list the phases of prewriting and explain the purpose of each phase. Record your responses in chart form such as that of Table 11.1.

**TABLE 11.1   Graphic Organizer: Phases of Prewriting**

| PREWRITING PHASE | PURPOSE OF THIS PHASE |
| --- | --- |
| 1. Clarify Assignment | 1. So the student understands the topic and purpose of the writing assignment |
| 2. | 2. |
| 3. | 3. |
| 4. | 4. |
| 5. | 5. |
| 6. | 6. |
| 7. | 7. |

# LOSS OF BIODIVERSITY
## Directed Reading Lesson with Prewriting

**Class Description:** Standard class; high school biology. Students are heterogeneous in achievement. Vocabulary partners are paired with weaker and stronger reader together; pairs change each marking period. In the first part of the unit, the concepts of ecology, habitats, niches, autotrophs, heterotrophs, food chains, the carbon cycle, biomes (aquatic and terrestrial), succession, population growth, and biological diversity were investigated. This lesson will investigate the loss of biodiversity.

**Unit:** Ecology

**Unit Goal:** Students will investigate loss of biological diversity and the importance and methods of maintaining biological diversity in the world.

**HSA Core Learning Goals:** Students will investigate the interdependence of diverse living organisms and the interactions with the components of the biosphere. Students will investigate how natural and man-made changes in environmental conditions will affect individual organisms and the dynamics of populations.

**Lesson Objectives:** Students will be able to:

1. Define *biotic factors* and *abiotic factors*
2. Classify and define four major threats to biodiversity
3. Propose additional threats to biodiversity
4. Argue a solution to the problem of the blue crab, a threatened species

**Performance Assessment**

*Objective     Performance*

1.     Observation of work with partner; class discussion
2.     Graphic organizers collected and reviewed; class discussion
3.     Class discussion
4.     Letters to the editor, collected and reviewed

**Macrostructure Thinking Skills:** Enumeration, classification, problem and solution

**Materials**

- Assigned textbook, *Biology,* Chapter 5, section "Loss of Biodiversity"
- One copy of *A Wrinkle in Time* by Madeleine L'Engle
- *Beautiful Swimmers* by William Warner, Chapter 8, "To Market," p. 185
- Transparencies:
      Steller's sea cow (www.amiq.org/galleries/seacow/seacow.html)
      Prairie vole (http//:campus.murraystate.edu)

Woodland caribou (www.raysweb.net)
Passenger pigeons (www.panda.org)
Leopard frog (www.state.tn.us)
Vocabulary: *abiotic* and *biotic*
Graphic organizers: "Loss of Biodiversity" and "Problem-Solution"
Blue crab

- Steller's sea cow reading from the first chapter of *Global Marine Biological Diversity: A Strategy for Building Conservation into Decision Making,* E. A. Norse, ed., 1993
- News articles: Maryland cuts blue crab quotas a year early, *Environmental News Network,* 12/21/01; Crab pickers decry rules, *The Sun,* 1/18/02; Waterman may continue to feel pinch, *The Sun,* 2/28/02
- Handouts of graphic organizers
- *The Sun* letters to the editor and editorial: Store the vaccine in everyone's arms, 7/7/02; Payment cuts create a crisis for Medicare; 11/17/02; Emerging from the haze, 11/17/02.

## Procedure

### I. Readiness

***a. Motivation (Focus):*** "Yesterday, we studied the concept of *biodiversity.* In your learning log, write what you recall about this concept." Students write. "Now with your vocabulary partners, share your responses for accuracy. Refer back to your vocabulary notebook entries from yesterday to confirm or adjust your understandings."

Students confer. Confirm definition: *the existence of a wide range of different types of organisms in a given place at a given time.*

"I am going to read you a brief passage from a book you might have read in middle school, *A Wrinkle in Time.* What about this reading reminds you of our discussion about biodiversity yesterday?"

*Expected student response:* This is a world where everything and everyone are the same; without biodiversity, the richness of the world would be lost; there would be fewer interactions between and among species; fewer niches would be filled; species would find it more difficult to adapt.

*Transition:* "Unfortunately, this earth of ours has been experiencing the loss of biodiversity for eons."

***b. Tapping and Developing Background of Experience:*** "We all have heard that dinosaurs are *extinct.* [Write word on the board.] What does that mean?"

*Expected student response:* total disappearance of a species

"Look at these pictures. These animals are also extinct. [Show transparencies of prairie vole, passenger pigeons, woodland caribou, and the relic leopard frog.] It is too late for these species, and there are many other species that have been put on the endangered species list because their numbers have become so low that extinction is a possibility if they are not protected." Show transparencies of the manatee, panda, tigers, snow leopard, bald eagle, elephant.

"What is the connection between extinct and endangered species and biodiversity?"

*Expected student response:* increase in loss of species results in loss of biodiversity

"What do you think causes species to become endangered and extinct? Write your hypotheses in your learning log."

*Expected student response:* Students write their hypotheses.

*Transition:* "Our reading today will help you to confirm or expand on your hypotheses to this important question. Before we begin reading, there are two related terms you need to understand."

### c. Concept Development

*Review:* "First, on a piece of scrap paper, write down the definitions of these ecological concepts we have already learned during this unit: species, ecosystem, pollution, and habitat. Then open your vocabulary notebook and confirm what you wrote."

*Initial Learning:* "Now with your partner, look at the overhead, read the statement and then use the examples to draft definitions of *abiotic factors* and *biotic factors.*" Pairs are called on and a class consensus is reached. Students then copy statement, examples, and definitions into their science vocabulary notebooks.

An environment is affected by abiotic and biotic factors. Examine the following examples and define *abiotic factors* and *biotic factors.*

| *Abiotic Factors* | *Biotic Factors* |
|---|---|
| temperature | frogs |
| light | fungi |
| soil | humans |
| moisture (e.g., rainfall, lakes) | grass |
| air currents | flowers |

*Expected student response:* Abiotic factors are nonliving things that affect an environment; biotic factors are the living things that affect or are affected by an environment.

*Transition:* "Now that we understand these two terms, we are ready to pursue the answer to what causes loss of diversity."

### d. Purpose-for-Reading:

Display the purpose-for-reading transparency. "You will be reading today to be informed. You will list and explain four major threats to biodiversity and give examples of each. Use the graphic organizer I am distributing to collect and organize your responses (Figure 11.1). If you find a section confusing to you, put a stick-um on it. That will signal me, as I circulate, to sit down with you and talk you through it. Also, look at the pictures referred to in the text. They will help you image and recall what causes loss of biodiversity (during-reading metacognitive strategies).

## II. Silent Reading:

Circulate and remind students to complete graphic organizers as they finish reading or during reading. At the halfway point, interrupt students and remind them that reading this biology text is often like reading an encyclopedia—it is written very tersely. Encourage them to look back and reread parts, as good readers typically do, when they become aware that they are not comprehending sufficiently to satisfy the purpose-for-reading (during-reading metacognitive strategy).

## III. Discussion:

Two sets of vocabulary pairs will review their responses on the graphic organizer, then an entire class discussion will ensue to reach consensus.

*Note:* When debriefing on "Introduction of Exotic Species," ask students, "What has been in the newspaper recently in Maryland that is an example of this threat to biodiversity?" [*snakehead fish*]

## IV. Rereading:

"Earlier in this lesson, I asked you to hypothesize what causes loss of biodiversity. Look back at the list you made before you read and what we filled in on the graphic organizer. Do your reasons match the four threats in the reading? Did anyone list a threat that was not included in the reading?" If a student volunteers "human exploitation," remind them of the elephant picture. Their endangered species status is due to the ivory trade—slaughtering of elephants for their ivory tusks.

Read to the students the following account of the Steller's sea cows.

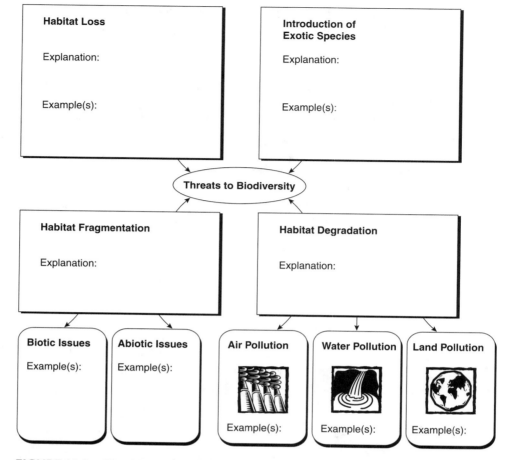

**FIGURE 11.1    Graphic Organizer for Biodiversity Lesson**

*Purpose-for-listening:* "Identify the cause of this extinction. Is it one on your graphic organizer or a different one?"

> In 1741, the crew of a Russian ship stranded on Bering Island in the cold North Pacific discovered huge sea creatures in the surrounding waters. Unlike the seals and whales that the sailors knew, these four-to-ten-ton mammals grazed the abundant seaweed like cattle. The hungry men devised a method of killing the beasts, and found the meat in fact delectable. On reaching safety, they told others of their good fortune. More ships came, taking advantage of this bounteous food source, until in 1768, sailors killed the last Steller's sea cow. From its discovery by Western civilization to its extinction took only 27 years.

> *Expected student response:* humans killing the species; human destruction

Students will be instructed to add "human destruction" as another "threat to biodiversity" on their graphic organizers.

**V.  Follow-Up:**  "Can you think of any other species that are in danger of becoming *endangered* because of human destruction? Any in Maryland?" If needed, use transparency of the blue crab as a hint!

> *Expected student response:*  Maryland blue crab

"The Maryland blue crab is not extinct, yet; it is not yet on the endangered species list, but it is a *threatened species.* Any idea what that means?"

*Expected student response:* its numbers are decreasing so rapidly that it could become endangered

"Why is the future of the blue crab population so important to Marylanders?"

*Expected student response:* food; tourism

Read to students from "To Market," an essay that quotes restaurateurs on the number of crabs they serve each season.

*Transition:* "This problem is so important in this our home state that I am going to ask your assistance in helping to prevent the loss of our blue crab population. Last year, Maryland, Virginia, and the Potomac River Fisheries agreed to a plan that would reduce the crab harvest over three years. This was passed in Maryland, but has caused great controversy with the fisherman, and results to date have not been very effective. I have collected three news articles for you to read so that you can generally understand the situation better. Your purpose-for-reading will be to answer the following:

1. What are the regulations of the laws as they stand today in regard to:
   ■ Size of crab permitted to be caught or harvested?
   ■ Sponge crabs?
   ■ Length of work day for crabbers?
2. What is the position of the crab processors on these regulations?
3. Do these regulations appear to be helping to increase the crab population?

Students read news articles distributed, searching for answers to the purpose-for-reading. Entire class discussion follows.

## Prewriting

**Clarify Assignment:** "What do you think should be done about this problem? I am asking each of you to write a letter to the Baltimore paper, *The Sun,* voicing your concern and giving your recommendation for a solution to the governor and the General Assembly in Annapolis, who must take action on this issue again this year."
Use FAT P transparency and complete with students.

*Expected student response:*  
**F**orm: letter  
**A**udience: governor and General Assembly  
**T**opic: preventing the blue crab from becoming an endangered species  
**P**urpose: persuade them of a solution

**Examine Models and Induce Specifications:** Students will read three sample letters to the editor from the local newspaper to determine what should be included in their letters to the newspaper.

*Expected student response:*  
Statement of problem  
Posing of solution  
Reasons for this solution  
Reasons against other solutions

Specifications are written on the overhead and copied by students for reference.

**Generate/Collect Ideas:** Students will work with their partners to complete the Problem and Solution graphic organizer—"Statement of the Problem" and "Possible Solutions" parts only (see Figure 11.2). Solutions will then be reviewed by the entire class for pros and cons. Reasons against each solution will be refuted. Teacher records oral responses on the overhead projector.

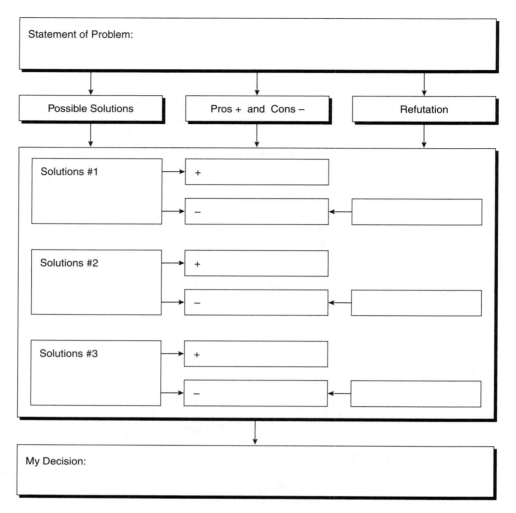

**FIGURE 11.2    Problem and Solution—Biodiversity Lesson**

**Delineate the Topic:** Teacher directs each student to make a choice of solutions.

**Organize/Sequence Ideas:** Students will be directed to decide what order will make the strongest argument.

**Compose Orally:** Using their graphic organizers, students will compose their letter aloud to their partners, beginning with the statement of the problem, their proposed solution, reasons for their solutions, and refutations for alternative solutions.

**Write Draft:** Students will write the first draft of their letters.

The next day, students will reread their letters, make revisions to the content, edit their letters, edit a peer's letter, then word-process their letters for submission to the teacher and for mailing to the newspaper.

**Homework (Follow-Up):** Students will have one week to investigate what threat caused the animals shown earlier in this lesson via transparencies (prairie vole, passenger pigeons, woodland caribou, and the relic leopard frog, manatee, panda, tigers, snow leopard, bald eagle) to be extinct or to be on the endangered species list. Each student will be assigned one animal to classify according to the "Threats to Biodiversity" graphic organizer and to explain its circumstances. Students will be instructed to submit edited papers.

## "THE LADY OR THE TIGER?" WHICH WAS IT?
### Directed Reading Lesson with Prewriting

**Class Description:** English; grade 7; heterogeneous class.

**Lesson Objectives:** The student should be able to:

1. Define *imperious*
2. Complete a story map for the short story "The Lady or the Tiger?"
3. Delineate the specifications for a pro or con writing
4. Justify their chosen ending to the short story based on the pro or con graphic organizer.

### Performance Assessment

| *Objective* | *Performance* |
|---|---|
| 1. | Partner sharing; oral responses to concept attainment activity |
| 2. | Story map completion; oral responses during debriefing |
| 3. | Oral responses during completion of specification sheet |
| 4. | Completion of pro or con graphic organizer; review of compositions |

### Materials

- Transparencies: headline, pictures of medieval dress, feudal chart, pro model, pro or con graphic organizer; specification sheet
- Handouts: "The Lady or the Tiger?" short story by Frank R. Stockton; pro writing model; pro or con graphic organizer; specification sheet
- Overhead projector; LCD projector; screens

## Lesson Procedure

### I. Readiness

*a. Motivation:* Show headline from newspaper, "Plumber Sentenced for Role in Murder," and ask: "What does this headline mean? How does a sentence happen?" [*jury; trial*] "Historically, is this the only way people were judged to determine if they had committed a crime?"

*Transition:* "The story we will read today takes us back in time to the medieval times when trial by jury meant something very different."

*b. Tapping and Developing Background:* Show "Feudal Society" triangle. Explain. Emphasize the line between the nobles and the peasants. Show picture of king, ladies, and lords. "Where might these people fit into the feudal chart?"

Show picture of the amphitheater/arena. "This is where people were often judged as to their guilt or innocence during the feudal times." Describe the design of amphitheaters—where people sat, what they watched, use of animals.

*Transition:* "One of the main characters in our story today is a noble [point to the "Feudal Society" triangle]—a lady—a princess—the king's daughter."

*c. Concept Development:* "At one point in the story, she is described as *imperious*. With your partner, use these clues and define *imperious*:

Clarinda, a teacher, announced to her principal that she would be requesting a transfer for the next academic year. When asked why she wished to leave the school, Clarinda replied, "I can no longer work with Mrs. Rogers, my department chair. She is *imperious*. The principal asked Clarinda to give her some examples of what Mrs. Rogers did to cause Clarinda to conclude that she was *imperious*. Clarinda cited the following:

1. Mrs. Rogers insisted that I use the novel she thought was best for my class, in spite of the fact that the curriculum gives the teacher a choice of three novels.

2. Mrs. Rogers walked into Clarinda's classroom one day and after watching for 3 minutes told Clarinda to sit down in the back of the room, and Mrs. Rogers took over teaching the lesson the way she felt it should proceed.

3. Mrs. Rogers rewrote the district-created unit "Characters in Conflict" and demanded that the English teachers of grade 9 teach it her way.

4. Mrs. Rogers made all the decisions about the new books to be ordered for the tenth grade multicultural unit without consulting the teachers in the department who teach the unit.

5. Mrs. Rogers began the department meeting by pointing out to everyone in the department what she had seen them do incorrectly during her daily stroll through the classrooms.

*Expected definition:* dictatorial; domineering in a hauty way; overbearing

**d. Purpose-for-Reading:** "You will be reading for literary experience. You will identify the narrative elements by creating a story map for Frank Stockton's short story 'The Lady or the Tiger?' Be sure to use the new vocabulary word, *imperious,* on your story map."

**II. Silent Reading:** Stop students halfway and ask them what they are seeing as they read (metacognitive strategy). Circulate and assist with the story map, as needed.

**III. Discussion (Oral Retelling):** "Turn to your partner and using your story map as your notes, summarize the story for your partner. Then have your partner summarize the story for you. Be sure your partner includes all the narrative elements."

After the oral retelling exercise, ask: "What narrative element is missing from this story?" [*solution/outcome*] "Yes. This is an open-ended story: one with no conclusion provided by the author."

### IV. Rereading (Embedding of Prewriting, Pro or Con Decision)

*Clarify the Assignment:* "We are each going to decide how to end this short story. In order to make that decision, we must consider the pros and cons of this decision, that is, why would the Princess give him the sign for the lady (pro life, she is *for* him) and why would she give him the tiger (con to life, she is *against* him). When we do this type of thinking, we should use a pro or con graphic organizer to sort out our reasoning.

*Examine Model and Induce Specifications:* "For example, recently I was asked to share my opinion of whether school systems in this state should continue or discontinue the eighth grade MSPAP for 2002, now that the systems have this option." Show and explain pro or con graphic organizer. "Now let me share with you my written response to this question." Distribute and read it aloud.

**MSPAP TESTING 2002**

The MSPAP testing for 8th grade students *should* take place this year, in spite of the State Department making it optional. There are several valid reasons for this to be the decision of a school system—focus on learning outcomes, focus on authentic and interactive teaching format, and improvement in scoring.

First, and most important, is the continuity of focus on the *learning outcomes* (thinking skills, thinking processes, metacognition, critical and creative thinking applied to content areas) that will be maintained by teachers, students, and administrators if it is decided that the test will be continued this year. If the test is abandoned this year, so will be the appropriate attention given to these crucial learning skills. Teaching and learning will revert to traditional passive instruction instead of progressive interactive instruction using authentic material and tasks. Those who argue to "give teachers a break" will just be "breaking" the focus on essential learning.

Second is the related fact that the new tests, dictated by the new federal law and developed by the State this year, will be closer in *format* to the MSPAP (authentic) than to traditional standardized (multiple-choice) tests. Students in all middle school grades (6, 7, and 8) will be assessed with these new tests; therefore, the instructional focus in middle school should be on teaching and learning that is authentic and interactive.

Finally, the major complaint against the test has been the *scoring* procedure, that is, having Maryland teachers score the test without appropriate reliability of results being assured in the training at some scoring sites. This year, the MSPAP will be scored by scorers hired and trained by a professional, educational testing service; therefore, the school systems should not see the testing as a waste of time because of the potential for unreliable results.

The MSPAP is designed to promote instruction that will prepare students to be successful independent thinkers and learners. This is no time for a holiday from that goal!

"Let's reread it, one paragraph at a time, and decide on the purpose of each paragraph so that we will know what should go into our own decision making. Let's put that into a specification sheet to guide us when doing a pro or con decision writing." Delineate specifications. Write on overhead transparency.

*Expected student responses:*

1. First, state your opinion.
2. Give several reasons (3 or more) for your opinion.
3. Support each reason with details.
4. Counter any opposing opinions.

***Generate/Locate Ideas:*** "Using information from your story map and the story itself, complete the "Pro" and "Con" sections of the graphic organizer with your partner (Figure 11.3)." Debrief as an entire class.

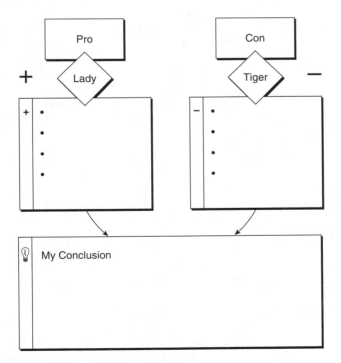

**FIGURE 11.3    Graphic Organizer for "The Lady or the Tiger?"**

*Delineate the Topic:* "Now you must make your individual decision. You decide whether the lady or the tiger came out of the door on the right."

*Sequence Ideas:* "Go back to my opinion piece. How did I order my three supporting ideas? *[most important to least important]* Could it be *least* to *most* important? *[yes, save best for last]* Label or number your reasons going from most important to least important, or least important to most important."

*Compose Orally with a Partner:* "Using your pro or con graphic organizer, tell your decision and reasons to your partner. Begin with your decision, then give your reasons in the order you decided was best. Be sure to elaborate on each reason with support from the story."

*Write Draft:* Students write the first draft of what they decided would be the conclusion of the story.

---

What did you list as the phases of prewriting and the purpose of each phase? Compare your conclusions with Table 11.2.

**TABLE 11.2   Phases of Prewriting**

| PREWRITING PHASE | PURPOSE OF THIS PHASE |
| --- | --- |
| 1. *Clarify the Assignment* | Students understand the form, audience, topic, and purpose of the writing assignment. |
| 2. *Examine Model(s) and Induce Specifications* | Students understand what features must be in their writing. The teacher must select models that are authentic (e.g., actual newspaper letters to the editor) and exemplify the features that students will include in their writing. The writings of previous students can also be effective. |
| 3. *Generate/Locate Ideas* | Students collect information to be included in their writing, guided by a graphic organizer appropriate for the major thought pattern of the writing (pro and/or con, problem and solution, comparison and/or contrast, cause and effect, description, etc.) |
| 4. *Delineate the Topic* | When writing a pro or con or a problem and solution piece, students decide the side or solution they will argue. Sometimes this phase must precede the *Generate/Locate Ideas* phase. For example, if students will be writing a story and describing an animal from the Paleozoic or Cretaceous period, they need to select the animal prior to collecting information. Sometimes the teacher decides the topic; therefore, *Delineate the Topic* is part of *Clarify the Assignment.* For example, after the mock interviews in "The Successful Job Interview" lesson, the students are given the topic for their essays: *summarize the steps in your preparation and analyze your performance.* |
| 5. *Organize/Sequence Ideas* | Students decide on the best internal organization for their facts to ensure coherence and sequencing. Teachers should lead students to reexamine the models for sequencing possibilities. |
| 6. *Compose Orally* | Students use their graphic organizers as notes and talk aloud as if they were writing, thus discovering completeness, omissions, and incongruities of what and how they intend to write as they put voice to their thoughts. |
| 7. *Write Draft* | Students now have something to write—collected ideas in a sequence—for a first draft. Complaints of "I don't know what to write" are avoided. Students experience success in composing a draft. |

Teachers should not assume that students are experienced in revising and editing their first drafts. Content teachers can efficiently and effectively assist novice writers in following their first drafts through to a finished product by doing the following:

1. Allow some time between students writing their first drafts and looking at it again for revision. This allows students to look at it with a fresh perspective.
2. Ask students to reread their first drafts to see if they fulfill the specifications delineated in the prewriting process. Revisions in ideas and organization should be the focus.
3. Ask students to edit.

## SPELLING

Run a spell check if they have word-processed their writing. If the piece has been handwritten, point to each word beginning with their last word and moving through the writing backward to check for spelling errors. This procedure, although tedious, allows students to look at graphics and not focus on meaning. Or have an adult or another student do this and circle misspelled words.

## GRAMMAR AND PUNCTUATION

Run grammar check if they have word-processed their writing. These should be used judiciously, however, because grammar programs do not always offer valid advice. Examine each sentence as a separate entity for errors. Have an adult or another student do this and identify sentences that need scrutiny.

## SUMMARY

Writing fosters discovery, provides an assessment function, triggers cognitive engagement, provides time for higher-level thinking, improves written fluency, and improves the learning of content. In deciding if and how to include writing as a learning tool within the Directed Reading Lesson, you should ask yourself the following questions:

**Questions for Planning the Inclusion of Writing
within the Directed Reading Lesson**
1. Have I included specific directions to the students to write during Concept Development/ Vocabulary, Silent Reading, Discussion, and Rereading?
2. Would students profit from writing during Motivation? Tapping and Developing Background of Experience? Follow-Up? Would it increase participation? Would it improve the quality and increase the quantity of student responses? Is this worth the time I must allocate for writing?
3. If I use writing, should the writing be first draft or edited?
4. If I use writing, do students have the skills and knowledge to complete this assignment independently? If not, have I planned to guide the students through the phases of prewriting and revision?

## YOUR TURN

1. Answer the questions in the previous section. Make revisions in your Directed Reading Lesson plan, as needed, to include your decisions about writing.

2. If you are using this text as part of a course or workshop experience, share your lesson plan with another participant. Ask this colleague to examine the writing activities you have chosen to include and determine the following:
   - Have you used writing appropriately in Concept Development/Vocabulary, Silent Reading, Discussion, and Rereading?
   - If you have planned writing for other parts of the Directed Reading Lesson, how will it contribute to the students' understanding of the content of this lesson?
   - If you have planned writing for other parts of the Directed Reading Lesson, have you decided correctly to employ an independent or instructional approach?

## ONE FINAL CHECK

1. Reread your entire Directed Reading Lesson plan once again to determine whether it is clear and coherent. Use "A Final Check: Specifications for the Directed Reading Lesson in the Content Areas" (Table 11.3) to reflect on your planning. Be sure you have all your materials ready. Rehearse your lesson so that you can teach it with minimal references to your scripted lesson plan. You are now ready to teach this lesson to your students. (If you do not have a class of secondary students at this time, arrange to microteach this lesson with a small group of colleagues in the course or workshop.) If possible, have a colleague observe you teaching this Directed Reading Lesson. Before

---

**TABLE 11.3  A Final Check: Specifications for the Directed Reading Lesson in the Content Areas**

**I. Readiness**
   **a. Motivation\*:** Focus attention on the lesson topic; help connect the topic to the students' lives; generate interest.
   **b. Tapping and Developing Background of Experience\*:** Tap students' background (curricular and life experience); develop background; help students visualize a movie of the mind while reading.
   **c. Concept Development/Vocabulary\*:** Teach essential concepts inductively using contextualized strategies (e.g., concrete representations, guided imagery, concept attainment, and sentence context clues); review previously learned essential concepts.
   **d. Purpose-for-Reading:** Include the generic reading purpose (to inform, to perform a task, or for literary experience), the major thought pattern, and the topic; include during-reading metacognitive strategies you will encourage students to use (e.g., movie of the mind, retelling, and rereading); consider the use of a graphic organizer.

**II. Silent Reading:** Assign silent, independent reading, not oral reading by students.

**III. Discussion\*:** Ensure entire-class consensus on text-based answers.

**IV. Rereading\*:** Develop new purposes-for-reading that reach into higher-level thinking; often relate to unit goals.

**V. Follow-Up\*:** Assign an additional activity for enrichment or reinforcement; optional.

Also Consider:
   1. Reading from a trade book
   2. Use of small group discussion (2–4 students) as scaffolding prior to entire-class debriefing; possible inclusion in parts marked with an asterisk (\*)
   3. Incorporation of a reader response question after silent reading
   4. Use of writing activities

See the observer's checklist for evaluating teacher effectiveness in a directed reading lesson (Table 11.4).

the observation, preview for your colleague "An Observer's Guide to the Directed Reading Lesson" (Table 11.4). Have your colleague use this listing as the criteria for your lesson.

2. After executing the lesson, reflect on the experience and answer the following in writing.

### Reflections on This Lesson
- **Evaluation:** How successful were my students in accomplishing the objectives I established for this learning experience?
- **Praise:** What was successful about my lesson and why?
- **Polish:** What would I change if I were to teach this lesson again? How would I revise this lesson? Why would I make these changes?

### Reflections on Using the Directed Reading Lesson
- **Praise:** What did I like about using the Directed Reading Lesson format?
- **Polish:** What aspects of the Directed Reading Lesson were most difficult for me? Why?

3. Share your reflections with the colleague who observed you teaching this Directed Reading Lesson. Listen to your colleague's reflections about your lesson.

**TABLE 11.4 An Observer's Guide to the Directed Reading Lesson**

**HAS THE TEACHER . . .**

| | |
|---|---|
| Motivation | Tapped student interest by connecting the topic of the upcoming reading to students' lives? |
| Background | Tapped student background so that new information can be connected to previous knowledge?<br>Developed background so students will have a movie of the mind when they read? |
| Concept Development/ Vocabulary | Selected appropriate vocabulary from the upcoming reading for priming?<br>Taught the words in an interactive, inductive manner using contextualized strategies? |
| Purpose-for-Reading | Written the purpose-for-reading questions to include the generic reading purpose, the major thought pattern, and the topic?<br>Included a graphic organizer, if appropriate? |
| Silent Reading | Avoided round robin oral reading by students in order to encourage recursive reading?<br>Encouraged students to use during-reading, metacognitive strategies for silent reading (e.g., imaging, rereading, note-taking, and retelling)? |
| Discussion | Helped students construct the initial meaning of the reading by discussing with the entire class the stated purpose-for-reading?<br>Used small groups for debriefing the purpose-for-reading prior to an entire class discussion, if the content of the reading is difficult? |
| Rereading | Helped students extend understanding of the reading by asking higher-level thinking questions that may require students to revisit the text or their answers to the purpose-for-reading question?<br>Asked additional questions that relate this new learning to unit goals and core learning goals? |
| Follow-Up | Provided an activity for reinforcement or enrichment of the learning from the reading (if necessary or appropriate)? |

# CHAPTER TWELVE

# A VARIATION OF THE DIRECTED READING LESSON: THE DIRECTED READING–THINKING LESSON

If you can look into the seeds of time, and say which grain will grow
and which will not, speak then unto me.

—*William Shakespeare, the Bard of Avon*

The following two lesson plans you are about to read—one for literary experience (narrative) and one for information (expository)—offer a variation to the Directed Reading Lesson. They may initially appear to be standard Directed Reading Lesson plans, but close reading will reveal that the Purpose-for-Reading, Silent Reading, and Discussion are executed in a different manner than in the traditional Directed Reading Lesson. These two lesson plans have a modification, the Directed Reading–Thinking Activity (DRTA), developed by Russell Stauffer in 1969.

Your purpose-for-reading these lesson plans will be to be informed about the variation in format to the Directed Reading Lesson when using a Directed Reading–Thinking approach. You will be contrasting the Purpose-for-Reading, the Silent Reading, and the Discussion components with the approach you learned for the standard Directed Reading Lesson plan.

## ENGLISH LESSON
### Directed Reading–Thinking Lesson

**Class Description:** High School, grade 9; standard class; heterogeneously grouped—below average, average, and slightly above average in achievement. The reading for this lesson is a complex version of the story of Theseus.

**Unit:** Classical Heroes

**Topic:** Theseus and the Minotaur

**Learning Objectives:** Student will:

1. Articulate the plot, characters, and setting of the Theseus myth
2. Define *Minotaur* and *labyrinth*
3. Identify the parents, feats, strengths, and weaknesses of the hero, Theseus
4. Write a first-draft definition of a classical hero, based on the myths of Perseus and Theseus

## Performance Assessment

*Objective*    *Assessment*

1. Responses during discussion
2. Observation of vocabulary partner work; review of students' vocabulary notebooks
3. Completed graphic organizer column; discussion of graphic organizer responses
4. Draft definition and characteristics of a "classical hero"

**Reading Type:**  Reading for literary experience

**Macrostructure Thinking for Reading:** Narrative components—setting, character, problem/conflict, significant events, solution

## Materials

- Transparencies: world map; map of Greece and Crete; picture of Theseus and his father, Aegeus; list of Theseus' previous feats; pictures and transparencies of the Minotaur and mazes; picture of the Minotaur in the labyrinth
- Graphic organizer: matrix of classical heroes (Perseus, Theseus, Jason, Odysseus)
- Students' vocabulary notebooks

# Lesson Procedure

## I. Readiness

*a. Motivation:* "Did you ever forget to do something, and it resulted in negative consequences for you or for someone close to you?" Teacher is prepared with personal example, if needed, to clue students. Students share stories.

*Transition:* "The Greek hero you will meet today is Theseus. He also forgets, and there are grave consequences. Let's meet Theseus now."

*b. Developing Background of Experience:* Show students transparency picture of Theseus and his father, King Aegeus. Identify each character. "Theseus was a very brave and successful warrior. He was responsible for ridding Greece of many evil creatures and men." Show transparency of world map. Ask students to identify where we live in the United States and then find and label Greece (relative location).

Show students the transparency that lists three evil men whom Theseus defeated: Sinus, Procrustus, and Sciron. Briefly, tell the story of each to demonstrate Theseus' bravery and cunning.

"Theseus' greatest challenge, however, occurred on the island of Crete." Show transparency of the map of Greece and Crete. Have students identify Athens (Greece), the island of Crete, and the body of water that separates the two kingdoms (Aegean and Mediterranean Seas).

*Transition:* "Theseus' greatest challenge was in fighting the Minotaur, which lived in the labyrinth on Crete."

*c. Concept Development/Vocabulary:* Show transparencies of the Minotaur. "Look at these pictures, and with your vocabulary partner, draft a definition of the word *Minotaur.*" Call on several pairs for their definitions; reach a class consensus; students copy class definition into vocabulary notebooks; pictures may also be drawn.

> *Expected definition:* a creature or monster with the head and body of a bull, and the torso of a man

Show transparencies of maze games. Call it a two-dimensional labyrinth. Tell students that the Minotaur lives in a three-dimensional labyrinth. Show pictures of hedge and corn mazes. Show transparency of the Minotaur in his labyrinth and ask students what this labyrinth was made of. Instruct students to draft a definition of *labyrinth* as it relates to the Minotaur with their vocabulary partners. Call on several pairs for their definitions; reach a class consensus; students copy class definition into vocabulary notebooks; pictures may also be drawn.

*Expected definition:* a maze carved inside a hill or mountain that housed the Minotaur

**Purpose-for-Reading 1; Silent Reading 1; Discussion 1:**  Read aloud to students the first paragraph of the story, "Theseus and the Minotaur." This paragraph concludes with "and the King issued cruel orders." Ask students to predict what these "cruel orders" might be. Encourage all students to share. Teacher will remain neutral, that is, not reject or confirm any predictions.

Give a copy of the story to each student. Instruct students to read silently the first page and the first paragraph of the second page for the purpose of checking their predictions.

Tell students to reread the section if they cannot find the information to check their predictions.

Discuss student predictions. "What were the "cruel orders?"

*Expected student response:*  The Athenians had to send seven young women and seven men every nine years to be put into the labyrinth where the Minotaur would no doubt find them and devour them. This was repayment for the King of Crete, whose son had been killed while visiting Athens.

"Who volunteers to go to Crete, as one of the sacrifices? [*Theseus*] Does Theseus think he will die?" [No. He believes he will kill the Minotaur and find his companions' way out of the *labyrinth.*] What does he promise his father, King Aegeus?" [*To put up a white sail when he is returning home so that his father will know he has been successful.*] Have students read aloud lines that verify their responses.

**Purpose-for-Reading 2; Silent Reading 2; Discussion 2:**  "Do you think Theseus will be successful? How might he succeed considering the size and nature of the Minotaur and the problem of finding his way out of the labyrinth?" Encourage as many students as possible to make predictions. Have vocabulary pairs talk together first if that produces more predictions. Again, the teacher remains neutral in responding to predictions.

Instruct students to read silently to the last paragraph on the third page of the story to verify their predictions.

Discuss student predictions: "Was Theseus successful? How?"

*Expected student response:*  He caught the Minotaur off-guard/sleeping; he used his fist to stun the Minotaur; he used the spool of thread that Ariadne gave him to find the way out of the labyrinth.

"What promises has Theseus now made?" [*to father—hoist the white sail; marry Ariadne and take her back to Athens with him*]

**Purpose-for-Reading 3; Silent Reading 3; Discussion 3:**  "Do you think he will keep the promise to his father? The promises to Ariadne?" Encourage all students to make predictions. The teacher remains neutral in responding to predictions.

Instruct students to read (silently) to the end of the story to check their predictions.

Discuss student predictions: "Did Theseus keep his promise to his father?" [*No. He forgot to change the sail to white.*] "Did Theseus keep his promise to Ariadne?" [*He tried, but she became ill on the trip back to Athens and died.*] Have students read aloud lines that validate their responses.

*Transition:* "Now that we understand the story of 'Theseus and the Minotaur,' let's summarize the key points by completing the Theseus column on our "Classical Heroes" chart" (see Table 12.1).

**TABLE 12.1** **Classical Hero Chart**

|  | PERSEUS | THESEUS | JASON | HERCULES |
|---|---|---|---|---|
| **Parents** | *Zeus, Danae* | *King Aegeus, Aethra* | | |
| **Feats (foes defeated)** | *The Gorgon Medusa, with snakes for hair; looking at her ugly face was so terrifying that it turned one to stone (petrified); the Gorgon sisters, the three swanlike Graeae, with a single eye among them* | *Sinus, the pine-bender; Procrustus, the innkeeper Sciron, the feet-washer; Minotaur in the labyrinth* | | |
| **Virtues and Strengths** | *Brave, clever, honorable, respectful of gods* | *Brave, strong, chivalrous, honorable, respectful of gods* | | |
| **Flaws and Weakness(es)** | *Boastful* | *Forgetful* | | |

Responses in italics are expected student responses.

**IV. Rereading:** Instruct the students to complete the second column, Theseus, of the "Classical Heroes" chart (Table 12.1). Remind them that they may need to refer back to the reading for some answers. (The first column labeled "Perseus" was completed the previous day when the myth "Perseus and the Gorgon" was read.)

**V. Follow-Up (Extension):** "Now that we have read two stories of Greek heroes, we are going to begin looking for commonalties among them and their adventures to write a definition for the concept *classical hero*. For example, read again silently the information we agreed on in the row about Perseus' and Theseus' feats. What do they have in common? [*Both fought and defeated monsters to rid the country of evil.*] With your vocabulary partner, reexamine the information on your charts, looking for other similarities the two heroes, Perseus and Theseus, and their adventures have in common. Then write a first draft of a definition for *classical hero*. We will reexamine these draft definitions after each of the next two hero stories and revise them after each."

# SOCIAL STUDIES LESSON
## Directed Reading–Thinking Lesson

**Class Description:** Government, grade 9; standard class; below average, average, and slightly above average in achievement; DRP results indicate that half the class reads the text instructionally and half the class reads it on a frustration level.

**Unit:** Political Parties in the United States

**Topic:** Where the Parties Stand Today

**Learning Outcomes:** The student will:

1. Define *platform* and *voucher*
2. Enumerate the stands of the Democrats and Republicans on the issues of role of the government, family values, education, welfare, and spending and taxation
3. State the commonalties between Democratic and Republican beliefs
4. Select a political affiliation and defend the choice

**Performance Assessment**

*Objective    Assessment*

1. Observation of vocabulary partner work; review of students' vocabulary notebooks
2. Completed graphic organizer; class discussion of graphic organizer
3. Observation of responses to rereading questions concerning commonalties between the parties
4. Collection and review of written justifications for choosing a particular political party

**Reading Type:**  To be informed; expository

**Macrostructure Thinking Skill for Reading:**  Enumeration, comparison and contrast

**Materials**

- Transparency of quotes about vouchers
- Copies of the Democratic and Republican platforms available from party websites
- Students' assigned textbook
- Copies of the graphic organizer, "Political Parties—Where They 'Stand' on the Issues."
- Quote from Kyo Yamashiro and Lisa Carlos, "Private School Vouchers" (1995), p. 1, from West Ed website: www.wested.org/policy/pubs/full_text/pb_ft_vouch.htm; December 21, 2001.
- Quote from Anti-Defamation League, p. l, from website: www.adl.org/vouchers_main.html; December 21, 2001.

## Lesson Procedure

### I. Readiness

*a. Motivation:* "In this state, when one registers to vote, the person is asked to register with a political party or to register as an independent. For homework, you were to find two adults (parents, guardians, brothers, sisters, aunts, friends) who were registered. You were to ask them the following:

1. Whether they registered as Democrats, Republicans or Independents
2. Why they chose that affiliation

Let's begin with the Democrats. Let's hear reasons the adults you interviewed chose to register with that party." [List issues on the board.] Repeat for Republicans and Independents.

*b. Tapping Background of Experience:* "Do any of these reasons sound like what the parties stood for historically? Let's first review the origin of the parties and their initial goals. Who were the Federalists and what did they stand for?"

*Expected student responses:* mostly wealthy Northerners who wanted a strong central government; John Adams, Alexander Hamilton, George Washington; government should protect businesses from foreign competition; wanted a national bank and currency

"Who were the Democratic-Republicans (later the Democratic Party) and what did they stand for?"

*Expected student responses:* mostly farmers, artisans, workers; James Madison, Thomas Jefferson; distrusted wealthy eastern aristocrats; wanted all men to vote and participate in government; wanted to be able to buy foreign merchandise if cheaper due to competition

"How did the Republican Party come to be and what did it stand for?" Review the Whig party, the founding of the Republican Party in 1854, and the Republican commitment to northern private big business, tariffs on foreign goods, and so on. "Do you see any parallel in the responses from those adults you interviewed and the original beliefs of the parties?"

*Transition:* "In our reading today, we are going to examine the beliefs of the Democrats and Republicans of *today.* In our next lesson, we will focus on the Independents.

Before we begin reading, there are two vocabulary words we must be sure we understand."

***c. Concept Development/Vocabulary:*** "Each of the political parties currently has a *platform.* You have probably heard the term *platform* used in connection to railroad transportation. [word is written on the board]. What does it mean? [*a place to stand when waiting to board a train*]. I am distributing to you the *platforms* of the Democratic and Republican political parties, which they devised to use at the last presidential convention. Because the platforms are lengthy, I will give each pair of you a part of one of the platforms." Sections are distributed based on reading competence of the members. "Read each platform and then with your vocabulary partner draft a definition of a *political platform.* It really is a figurative use of the definition for a railway *platform.* You are reading your section in order to give a global definition of a *political platform,* not to give the details of what the party's platform is." Several pairs will share their draft definitions with the class; class consensus on a definition will then be reached. Students will copy the word and definition into their government vocabulary notebooks.

> *Expected student response:* a document put out by a political party stating its beliefs or positions on various issues; what a party stands for

"The second word you will need to understand for today's reading is *voucher* [word is written on the board]. On the transparency are two statements taken from publications defending or arguing against the use of *vouchers.* I will read the statements aloud, then with your vocabulary partners, write a draft definition of *voucher.*"

> Private school choice or *voucher* programs allow parents to put tax dollars toward a private education . . . in the form of a subsidy to the chosen school. The dollar value of a voucher is usually equal to, but may be less than, the state average per pupil expenditure, and may cover the partial or full cost of a private school tuition. (Yamashiro & Carlos, 1995, p. 1)

> Most Americans believe that improving our system of education should be a top priority for government at the local, state and Federal levels. Legislators, school boards, education professionals, parent groups and community organizations are attempting to implement innovative ideas to rescue children from failing school systems, particularly in inner-city neighborhoods. Many such groups champion *voucher* programs. The standard program proposed . . . would distribute monetary *vouchers* (typically $2,500–$5,000) to parents of school-age children, usually in troubled inner-city school districts. Parents could then use the vouchers towards the cost of private schools. (Anti-Defamation League, 2001, p. 1)

Several pairs will share their draft definitions with the class; class consensus on a definition will then be reached. Students will copy the word and definition into their government vocabulary notebooks.

> *Expected definition:* money (a paper certificate) given to parents from the government that can be used as tuition to send their children to private schools instead of the local public school.

"You will find that Democrats and Republicans differ in their beliefs about the use of vouchers."

***Purpose-for-Reading; Silent Reading; Discussion (repeated five times, for each row of the graphic organizer):*** "Today we will be examining the Democratic and the Republican platforms. Look at the graphic organizer I am distributing to you (Figure 12.1). Based on what we have read about the historical origin of the parties and what your interviewees have told you, we will be predicting what we believe is the Democratic stand and the Republican stand on the following issues—role and purpose of government, family values, education, welfare, and spending and taxation. We will make predictions about each of these five areas. After each prediction, we will silently read a section of the text to confirm or adjust our predictions. Then we will discuss that area as a class, cite lines from the text to validate our responses, and fill in the graphic organizer with confirmed information."

**IV. Rereading—Generalization:** "Look over your graphic organizer and the reading. In spite of many differences, what do the Democratic and Republican political parties have in common?" (Small groups—two vocabulary pairs; then entire class consensus)

> *Expected student responses:* Both support the Constitution; both want to reduce the national debt; both want some form of welfare; both believe in taxes; both favor human rights.

**V. Follow-up—Extension (Critical Stance):** "You know how your interviewees feel about particular political parties; you also know the historical and current stands of the Democrats and Republicans on major issues. If you were to register tomorrow, which political party would you choose to register with and why?" Students write their responses in their social studies journals.

After students have been given sufficient time to make a decision and write their justification, the teacher will ask, "How many Republicans do we have? Democrats?" Volunteers for each party will then share their reasons for choosing a particular party. Written responses will be collected and reviewed for adequacy of justification.

"Did any of you have a difficult time making a decision? Why? Did any of you find yourself agreeing with some beliefs under the Democrats and other beliefs under the

**FIGURE 12.1  Political Parties: Where They Stand on the Issues**

| | DEMOCRATS | REPUBLICANS |
|---|---|---|
| Role of government | *Look to government to promote the common interests of all American citizens; government is an agent to get things done and make life better for people* | *Emphasize efforts of individual citizens and want government to stay out of the way; tend to distrust government control* |
| Family values | *Promote welfare and other programs that help poor and struggling families; define family broadly to include single parents, nonmarried couples, gay and lesbian couples, etc. as well as the two-parent family* | *Insist that two-parent family is best environment; object to laws that interfere with rights of families; object to laws that support single-parent families over traditional families* |
| Education | *Less in favor of supporting private schools; favor sex education in schools; do not want a voucher system, which they believe would create two quality levels of schools; want education of equal quality for all* | *Believe parents should have a choice in schools for their children; schools should reinforce parental authority, not replace it; support choice of public, private, or parochial schools; object to sex education in schools; favor competition of school types for student attendance; favor vouchers* |
| Welfare | *Support programs to help the unfortunate, e.g., Social Security, food stamps, Medicare* | *Support welfare, but are wary of welfare programs that give aid to people who could support themselves* |
| Spending and taxation | *Believe rich should pay their fair share; therefore, support taxes on luxuries; believe in a higher tax rate for the wealthy.* | *Believe taxes should be kept as low as possible for everyone; taxes should not be higher for the rich so they can spend and help the economy* |

Responses in italics are expected student responses.

Republicans?" Lead students to the understanding that even within a party affiliation, few agree with everything in the party platform. Share the example of Mark Hatfield (R) of Oregon's vote against the Balanced Budget Amendment in 1995. "Tomorrow we will look at these differences within a party."

---

The two lessons have the same parts as other lessons in this book: Readiness (Motivation, Tapping and Developing Background of Experience, Concept Development/Vocabulary, Purpose-for-Reading), Silent Reading, Discussion, Rereading, Follow-Up. Did you notice, however, that the Purpose-for-Reading, Silent Reading, and Discussion parts were done recursively and guided by student predictions? Look at Figure 12.2.

Instead of sending the students into Silent Reading with a purpose-for-reading, both teachers ask students to predict what they think the first part of the reading will include. Students predict the first chunk of the reading, read silently, then discuss it. They then predict the second chunk of the reading, read silently, then discuss it prior to moving on the third part, and so on.

Please note that a *prediction* is an inference, and an inference requires background. The teacher must consider the background information students need in deciding if the Directed Reading–Thinking Activity is a viable alternative. For example, if the social studies students had not previously studied the origins of the Democrats and Republicans and had not interviewed two adults about political preferences, they would not have had sufficient background information to make reasonably valid predictions about how these parties stand on the role of government, family values, education, welfare, and spending and taxation.

To understand how important background is, let's assume you are enrolled in an introductory photography class. Your teacher states that you will be reading about the following types of camera lenses: normal, long, short, fisheye, catadioptric, zoom, soft-focus, and macro lenses. You are then asked to predict when you would use each one. Can you make this prediction? Probably not, unless you have extensive, experiential background in photography. You can predict zoom because you have some life experience (background) with these lenses, but because you probably have no life experience or school experience with the other lens types, predictions are impossible—especially reasonably valid predictions.

If the content teacher cannot ensure adequate background on the part of the students, through life experiences or knowledge from previous lessons or the current lesson, it is better to use the standard Directed Reading Lesson plan format for the reading.

Having considered background information, the teacher must decide how to "chunk" the reading. This depends on the type and difficulty of the reading. Often in an expository

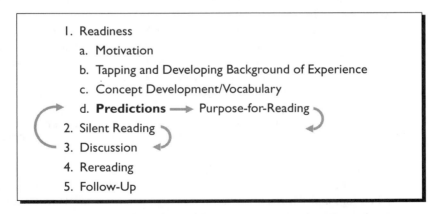

**FIGURE 12.2   Directed Reading–Thinking Approach within the Directed Reading Lesson Format**

piece, sections are clearly delineated by subheads, which make for good prediction points. For example, the social studies reading was divided into sections based on subheads: role of government, family values, education, welfare, spending, and taxation. Each section then appropriately became a chunk for prediction, reading, and discussion. Literary pieces are usually not so clearly delineated. Because the English teacher did not have subheads for guidance, she divided each chunk at cliffhanger points. For example, just before Theseus enters the labyrinth to encounter the Minotaur, the teacher asks the students to predict if and how Theseus will be successful.

In general, the more difficult the reading, the shorter the chunk should be. By difficult, we mean the reading competence of the students (i.e., if the reading selection is at student frustration level) and the conceptual complexity of the information.

The teacher must now determine the stimulus for the initial prediction. This could be a portion of the reading, a subhead in the reading, the title of the reading, or illustrations. The English teacher read the first few paragraphs of the Theseus story, then asked the students to use a line from that paragraph, "the King issued cruel orders," and predict what these "cruel orders" to the Athenians might be. The social studies teacher used the chapter subheads for students to predict the perspective of the Democrats and Republicans on each issue.

Another social studies teacher, preparing a lesson on credit and using an article entitled "What Credit Unions Know About You," transformed this title into the predictive question, "What do you think credit unions know about individuals?" A science teacher had the students examine color pictures and artifacts to predict the various textures of rocks.

Once students have voiced or written their predictions, both teachers instruct them to read silently to confirm or adjust their predictions. This confirmation or adjustment is their purpose-for-reading. After the students have read silently that first reading chunk, they immediately verify the accuracy of the predictions in discussion.

For a relatively short reading that has only one main issue to predict, it is certainly appropriate to have students make only one set of predictions, silently read the entire reading selection, and then discuss the entire reading. For example, a two-page pamphlet on credit bureaus may require just a single prediction: What do you think credit bureaus know about a typical citizen? The class then reads silently to verify and expand on the predictions and then discuss what information the credit bureaus know.

For longer readings, the teacher leads the students to make predictions for the next chunk. For example, the English teacher asks what will occur next in the Theseus story, and the social studies teacher asks what the stand of the parties will be on the issue of family values. After predicting (purpose-setting), students silently read to verify predictions and then discuss the predictions.

The class repeats this recursive process for each chunk. Once the entire reading has been processed, the lesson continues with the standard Directed Reading Lesson's use of Rereading and Follow-Up.

The Directed Reading–Thinking Activity is best used when the reading material will be very difficult for students if they are instructed to read it in its entirety on their own. This approach facilitates comprehension by ensuring that students comprehend each chunk of the reading prior to moving on to the next part. For example, the English teacher knows because of the responses during discussion that her students have understood Theseus' promise before having them read whether he broke it.

A Directed Reading–Thinking approach may be a viable option, too, when students in a particular class have difficulty maintaining attention—self-discipline—during silent reading of content material. We caution teachers in using the Directed Reading–Thinking approach with content reading material that is on students' independent reading level. Independent level reading does not require teacher-guided instruction and support for comprehension, and the relatively slow, directive nature of the Directed Reading–Thinking approach typically causes students to be impatient in the completion of the reading task.

## SUMMARY

The Directed Reading–Thinking Activity is a variation of the Directed Reading Lesson plan. It asks students to make predictions prior to reading all or part of the content selection. Predictions are an important part of cognition. Valid predictions about what the driver in front of us is about to do prevents accidents; invalid predictions or no predictions while watching a movie cause us to be startled with the turn of events.

Good comprehenders constantly interact with the reading; they unconsciously make predictions as they read. The Directed Reading–Thinking approach gives students direct practice in this thinking skill.

## YOUR TURN

1. Look carefully at the reading selection you used for your Directed Reading Lesson. Could this lesson be converted into a Directed Reading–Thinking lesson? Do your students have sufficient background from life, in general, and this lesson or previous lessons to make reasonably valid predictions?

2. Convert your Directed Reading Lesson into a Directed Reading–Thinking Lesson, or if the reading you used does not lend itself to this, find another reading that will. Decide what stimulus you will use to initiate the first prediction. Decide how to chunk the reading. Write the questions you will ask students to generate their predictions.

3. If you are using this textbook as part of a course or workshop experience, teach your lesson to a colleague or small group of colleagues. After teaching the lesson, consider the following with your colleagues:

   ■ Were the students able to make reasonably valid predictions? (that is, was their background sufficient?)
   ■ Were the chunks appropriate in size and placement?
   ■ Was the stimulus used for the initial prediction a good choice?
   ■ Other than the predictive components of the lesson, would you make revisions to any of the other parts of the lesson?

# CHAPTER THIRTEEN

# SELF-REGULATED READING

The greatest sign of success for a teacher . . . is to be able to say "The children are now working as if I did not exist."

—*Maria Montessori, Italian physician and educator*

In Chapter 1, we promised to honor your commitment to teach content. We have fulfilled our promise by sharing a lesson plan model that helps your students learn (become exceptional in) the knowledge and processes of your subject matter. The Directed Reading Lesson combines theoretically sound and research-based reading strategies with subject-specific goals, materials, activities, and assessments.

We now challenge you to assume another commitment: to teach these reading strategies so that your students can become lifelong learners. That does not mean you must abandon your content focus; it means teaching students to assume a more active role in initiating and applying reading strategies. By taking a more active role, they will become more self-reliant than other-reliant when learning through reading. They will be prepared to learn with reading material after you are no longer there as their mediator of learning. This may be in other secondary classrooms where teachers are not schooled in content reading instruction, in postsecondary education where most professors assume (often erroneously) that their students know how to read, in the workplace, and in their personal lives.

In short, we challenge you to teach your students self-regulation. In cognitive psychology, the term *self-regulation* has historically meant the learner's ability to adjust and reestablish equilibrium when cognitive disturbances occur. In relationship to reading to learn content, self-regulation means that students recognize when they do not comprehend and take steps to initiate or restore their understanding of what they are reading. In order to self-regulate, the learner must have the motivation to learn and an arsenal of metacognitive strategies that can be called on to facilitate comprehension and learning. And that is where you come in—motivating them to be independent learners and teaching them the metacognitive strategies for self-regulated reading and learning. Motivating students and teaching them these metacognitive reading strategies means:

- Teaching the strategies explicitly—naming or labeling the strategies, and explaining the rationale and "how to" of the strategies
- Having students practice the strategies with authentic material (your content reading material)
- Having students reflect on their success

As you read in Chapter 7, metacognitive strategies are goal-oriented strategies that facilitate comprehension. Used before, during, and after reading, metacognitive strategies help readers plan, monitor, and evaluate their comprehension.

Before-reading strategies are listed on Table 13.1, "Metacognitive Strategies to Facilitate Reading Comprehension: Before-, During-, and After-Reading Strategies." These

**TABLE 13.1    Metacognitive Strategies to Facilitate Reading Comprehension: Before-, During-, and After-Reading Strategies**

**BEFORE-READING STRATEGIES:  PLANNING FOR COMPREHENSION**

1. Skim the reading for title, boldface print, subheads, charts, diagrams, any focus questions at the beginning or end of the reading, and so on and identify the topic and subtopics. Ask yourself: What is this reading about? What might this reading include?

2. Examine pictures, cartoons, illustrations. Ask yourself: What might I see as I read?

3. Write notes about associations that already occur to you about this topic. Ask yourself: What do I already know about this topic?

4. Skim the reading to determine how the author has written the information. Is it narrative? Should you read for the narrative elements of character, setting, conflict, significant events, and resolution? Is it expository? Do you need to organize your notes for a specific thought pattern—for example, cause and effect, chronological order, pro and con, comparison and/or contrast, classification, description, extended definition? Ask yourself: What type of reading is this? How might it be organized?

5. Write specific questions you might find answers to in this reading. Ask yourself: What might I learn from this reading? Could I use a graphic organizer to collect my notes?

**DURING-READING STRATEGIES:  MONITORING COMPREHENSION**

1. Image while you read. See a movie of the mind while you read. Ask yourself: Can I see what I am reading about? Has the author provided any pictures or other illustrations I should examine again?

2. Check to see if you are learning from the reading. Ask yourself: What were my purpose-for-reading questions? Am I focusing on these? Are there any I need to go back and search for? Am I finding other important information that I should formulate into a question and an answer?

3. Write down answers to your questions. Organize your answers. Ask yourself: Are my answers complete? Can I organize these notes into a graphic organizer to match the structure of this reading? Are there parts of the graphic organizer not yet complete?

4. Stop and retell what you are learning. Ask yourself: Have I paused in my reading, reflected, and retold myself what I have learned so far?

5. Be aware if you do not understand something. Go back and reread the word, sentence, or paragraph before you move on to see if looking back and rereading helps your comprehension. Ask yourself: Am I aware of when I do not understand what I am reading? Should I go back and reread the part that did not make sense to me, or should I read on to see if that clarifies my understanding?

6. Write down questions you have about parts you do not understand. Ask yourself: If after rereading, I still do not understand, do I mark the part in the reading or put a sticky note there to ask the teacher or my group members for clarification?

7. Write down vocabulary that appears to be important to this topic. Write down a definition for each new term. Try to put it into your own words. Ask yourself: Can I explain the words in bold print in my own words? What other words—not in bold print—appear to be important to this topic? Have I recorded the new vocabulary words in my notes with an explanation in my own words? Are there any terms I should ask the teacher or my group members to explain to me?

**AFTER-READING STRATEGIES:  EVALUATING COMPREHENSION**

1. Summarize the major ideas from the reading, if expository. Retell the story if the reading is a narrative. Ask yourself: What is this reading about? Was I able to make a graphic organizer and complete it? What questions do I still have about this reading and this topic? Would it help if I reread certain parts?

*(continued)*

**TABLE 13.1   Continued**

2. Note the key terms introduced in this reading. Record the terms and their definitions in your notes. Ask yourself: What are the important new terms that are introduced? What does each mean? Can I express the meaning in my own words?

3. Personalize the reading. Ask yourself: Why is this reading important to me?

4. Connect the reading to your previous learning in this content area. Ask yourself: How does this new information relate to what I learned in this class yesterday? Last week? In a previous unit?

5. Critically analyze the reading. Ask yourself: Why did the writer write this material? Is this reading believable? Valid? Biased?

6. Conference. Ask yourself: Should I talk to someone about this? What contribution will I make in class about this reading?

 strategies are intended to help the learner make a plan for reading. Are these strategies familiar to you?

The before-reading strategies and the associated questions should remind you of three phases of the Readiness step of the Directed Reading Lesson

- Motivation (1: What is this reading about? What might it include?)
- Tapping background of experience (2: What might I see as I read? and 3: What do I already know about this topic?)
- Purpose-for-reading (4: What type of reading is this? How might it be organized? and 5: What might I learn from this reading?)

In conducting a Directed Reading Lesson, you guide students through the use of these before-reading strategies. They rely on you to ask them the questions or give you the answers that will plan their comprehension approach as they read.

The during-reading metacognitive strategies on Table 13.1 were introduced in Chapter 7: imaging/"movie of the mind," checking for purpose, taking notes/organizing, retelling, rereading/lookbacks, inserts/questions, and noting key vocabulary.

These monitoring strategies support reader comprehension, alert readers when their comprehension is failing, and/or assist readers in "fixing" the comprehension problem. You, no doubt, included one or more of these in your Directed Reading Lesson plan. Which ones did you include?

Now look at the list of after-reading metacognitive strategies Table 13.1. What is the purpose of these strategies?

These strategies are designed to encourage students to evaluate the success of their reading. They should remind you of the discussion, rereading, and follow-up parts of the Directed Reading Lesson. Specifically, students:

- Review and rehearse the learning for future use (1, 4, 6)
- Note, understand, and use new content vocabulary (2)
- Reread (1)
- Take a personal stance to the reading (3)
- Take a critical stance to the reading (5)

If students are to become successful, self-reliant readers of content, they need to learn how to apply independently these before-, during-, and after- (BDA) reading strategies with authentic reading in the content classroom (Butler & Winne, 1995; Garner, 1990). This is where you come in—motivating them to be independent learners and teaching them how to be. Here is a plan for teaching BDA reading strategies and content in your classroom:

**1.** *Give students direct experience.* Give students regular practice learning content knowledge and processes through reading as you guide them through Directed Reading Lesson plans. This gives them direct experience with successful learning of content through reading and employing these strategies. It also models the strategies for them, for example, choosing graphic organizer types based on specific thought patterns, using information from the graphic organizer as the basis for a retelling or a written summary, and using imaging appropriately while one reads.

**2.** *Label and state the purpose of the steps in the Directed Reading Lessons.* Label and briefly state the purpose of each step of the Directed Reading Lesson for students as you initiate it. Have the steps written on a bulletin board, poster, flannel board, transparency or PowerPoint slide, and point to each step at the appropriate time. Your statement of purpose should be brief, such as "We are now ready to tap our backgrounds of experience so that our brains can connect what we are going to read and learn today with what we already know." You would then tap the students' backgrounds as you had planned. After a while, you will be able to ask students "What is the next step in our lesson? Why do we do this step?" And after the step is completed, "How did that step help you to comprehend?" Inquiries like these help students develop an understanding of the process as they experience it directly. It demystifies the reading process. Labeling the steps helps students identify the specific type of thinking they must do in order to facilitate their comprehension. Students begin to recognize that if they perform certain mental operations, they can successfully learn from content text.

Learning to use metacognitive strategies involves understanding the steps and how to apply them, but also depends to a great extent on the motivation of the student. If students realize that the strategies do help them and they understand why they help them, they are more likely to be motivated to exert the significant cognitive energy required to master and internalize the self-regulating behaviors. Belief in the effectiveness of these strategies results in higher levels of motivation and greater effort in their use (Schunk & Swartz, 1991).

**3.** *Teach BDA strategies explicitly.* After repeated practice with explicitly labeled Directed Reading Lessons, explain that you want to help the students use the reading process independently so that they can become independent learners. Ask them to think of times when they will need to learn from content reading and will not have the benefit of a teacher leading them. Remind them of their success using these steps in your class. Inform your students that exceptionally skilled adult readers use these strategies independently to facilitate their comprehension (Pressley & Afflerbach, 1995). Tell them that the steps they have been using with you and the ones they will learn to use on their own have been shown to result in significant improvement in reading comprehension and learning (Haller, Child, & Walberg, 1988).

Next, give students a copy of Table 13.1, "Metacognitive Strategies to Facilitate Reading Comprehension." Explain what *metacognition* is.

Select a text. It should be a "considerate" text in light of its text structure so that students can readily discern the macrostructure for organizing their notes. It should not require development of background and extensive vocabulary priming, because these steps require you to teach directly.

Lead students through the application of the BDA strategies. Do not debrief the content after they apply each, but do answer any questions that arise about the application of the strategy. Lead students through the before- and after-reading strategies, one at a time. For the during-reading strategies, review all of them before the students begin to read silently and encourage them to use these strategies while they read. Circulate while they read silently and encourage individual students to record responses (e.g., creating and completing a graphic organizer and noting key content vocabulary), if they do not appear to be doing so. Coach individual students who are struggling. Remind them of the importance, the purpose, and the how-to of each strategy.

Next, debrief the content of the reading to ensure that lesson objectives were accomplished. Lead a class discussion of text-based, purpose-for-reading questions, then the higher-level, rereading questions you would have asked students if you had been conducting a Directed Reading Lesson with this same reading material. Determine whether students were able to craft an appropriate graphic organizer for organizing their notes. Share appropriate student models or be prepared with one you designed if the students' graphic organizers are inadequate. Also, debrief students on the key vocabulary you would have primed in a traditional Directed Reading Lesson. Prime the words inductively if students do not seem to have learned the terms independently. Remember, you are teaching students to apply effective self-regulating reading strategies, but your first concern is whether they have comprehended the content information.

Finally, ask students to assess their use of the BDA strategies. Which did they find most helpful? Which were most difficult to apply? What will they do differently the next time they use these BDA strategies?

Be prepared to share how you applied a particular strategy using think-alouds. These think-alouds are a type of modeling of the actual use of the strategies. For example, think aloud what clues you used to discern that the reading was expository. Think aloud what thought pattern was the basis of the text structure. Think-aloud what went through your mind as you connected with previously taught content after reading.

Explain to students that mastering these strategies takes time. Reassure them that you will continue to practice these strategies with them in your content classroom. Encourage students to use this reading process in their other subjects when they are not guided through their reading assignments.

**4.** *Continue guided practice.* Because learning to use self-regulatory reading is a long-term process (Anderson, 1992; Anderson & Roit, 1993; Pressley, El-Dinary, Wharton-McDonald, & Brown, 1988), sometimes taking several years before the strategies are used automatically, you should continue to guide student practice throughout the remainder of your course. Continue to use your Directed Reading Lessons regularly and intersperse the BDA approach with your students as described in step 3. Students will need direct reminders and some will need individual coaching to apply these metacognitive reading strategies; otherwise, they will tend to slip back to familiar, less effective reading practices (Garner, 1990; Harris and Pressley, 1991; Woloshyn, Elliott, & Riordon, 1998). Your use of Directed Reading Lessons will continue to model the reading process steps and the specific self-regulatory strategies. As your students practice and debrief the strategies, they will use each more effectively and efficiently.

The more reinforcement your students receive using reading strategies in a variety of content areas, the more efficient and effective their internalization of the strategies will be. Share what you are doing with self-regulatory reading with other team members or faculty in other departments who also teach your students. The added benefit is that the more often you label for your students and colleagues the reading strategies you incorporate into your teaching, the more likely you are to use those particular strategies and the more likely you are to seek out and include additional ones (Fogarty, Perkins, & Barell, 1992)—all to your students' benefit.

## SUMMARY

Using the Directed Reading Lesson format with the direct application of metacognitive reading strategies embedded provides students opportunities for authentic application. Students are not learning an isolated strategy and applying it; instead they are learning that authentic reading in the content area is a process that involves planning, monitoring, and evaluating their comprehension and learning through the often simultaneous and recursive application of proven strategies. It is by internalizing these self-regulating reading strategies that they too can become expert readers.

## Y O U R   T U R N

1. Select a reading from your content area that fits the requirements for introducing students to the independent application of BDA reading strategies. Assume that you have been doing step 2, labeling and stating the purpose of each of the steps of the Directed Reading Lesson with your students. Write and rehearse your introduction of the independent use of the BDA strategies to your students using this content reading selection. Use step 3 to guide your preparation. Be sure to include the following:
   - An explanation to students of what you are about to teach them and why
   - A discussion with them of times they will need to read independently
   - A reminder of the success they have been experiencing with Directed Reading Lessons
   - The distribution to each student of the handout, "Metacognitive Strategies to Facilitate Reading Comprehension: Before-, During-, and After-Reading Strategies"
   - An explanation of what *metacognition* is
   - A lesson procedure for leading students through the reading and application of the BDA strategies
   - A debriefing of the content knowledge (This part requires that you have prepared lesson objectives and purpose-for-reading questions so that you can be sure that students learn the content knowledge through discussion of text-based and higher-level thinking questions.)
   - A debriefing that has students reflect on and assess their use of the BDA strategies
   - The reminder that future practice is necessary

2. Teach your lesson. If possible, have a colleague observe you. After executing the lesson, reflect on the experience:
   - Were the content objectives attained?
   - How successful were students in applying the reading strategies? Which students appeared to need individual coaching? From your observation and from students' self-reports, which strategies were the easiest for students to use? The most difficult?
   - Did the students appear to be convinced of the effectiveness of metacognitive strategies?

# SAMPLE LESSON PLANS

## CONTENT AREA: ART
### PHOTOMONTAGE

**Class Description:** Photography 1; high school, grades 10 through 12; art course; this course satisfies one credit of art for state diploma; prerequisite for course is "Fine and Commercial Art"; achievement range—above average and average

**Unit:** Photo Manipulation

**Topic:** Jerry Uelsmann/Photomontage

### Unit Goals
1. Experience the techniques of photomontage
2. Apply students' knowledge of photomontage to their own work

### Lesson Objectives: The students will:
1. Define *anthropomorphized nature* and *mask*
2. Explain the themes and purpose of Uelsmann's work
3. Explain the steps in creating a photomontage
4. Define *photomontage*
5. Create a photomontage using the techniques employed by Jerry Uelsmann
6. Explain the sources for, feelings from, and obstacles encountered during the creation of students' own photomontages

### Performance Assessment

| Objective | Assessment |
|---|---|
| 1. | Students' oral responses; use of words on handout |
| 2. | Questions on handout collected and reviewed; oral responses |
| 3. | Questions on handout collected and reviewed; oral responses |
| 4. | Questions on handout collected and reviewed; oral responses |
| 5. | Evaluation by peers and teacher of photomontage created |
| 6. | Paragraph reviewed with photomontage |

**Macrostructure Thinking Skills for Reading:** Simple listing and enumeration, chronological order and sequence

### Materials
- *PowerPoint presentation* (teacher created) examples of Uelsmann's works used as motivation
- *Overheads* (teacher created)
  1. Uelsmann's work
  2. Questions for drill

3. Vocabulary handout
4. Steps for entering silent reading
5. Purpose-for-reading handout
■ *Websites:* www.uelsmann.net, www.arts.ufl.edu/ART/creativephotography/faculty/ jerryuelsmann/portfolio.html

# Procedure

## I. Readiness

*a. Motivation:* As students enter the room, they are directed to examine examples of Jerry Uelsmann's work displayed on bulletin boards and PowerPoint slides. They are directed also to complete their drill, displayed on the overhead:

### Drill

1. What type of emotions do you feel when you look at Uelsmann's work? [*an eerie feeling; almost dreamlike*]
2. What subject matter does Uelsmann use in his work? [*clouds, hands, rocks, water, and trees*]
3. Are these pictures fantasy or reality? [*fantasies; none of these pictures actually exists*]

Have the class discuss with the teacher the answers.

"We are continuing our study of photo manipulation; today we will examine the work of Jerry Uelsmann, a pioneer of photomanipulation in the darkroom. We will explore the technique of photomontage and generate an example of our own photomontage in the dark room."

*b. Tapping and Developing Background of Experience:* "Photomontage is an old technique that dates back to the 1920s [Show picture of the fairies]. Has any one seen this picture before?"

*Expected student response:* Yes, it is an example of trick photography that we saw when we studied the history of photography.

"Photomontage has long been used and will continue to fool generations to come. Can any one think of an example today in which photomontage is being used?"

*Expected student response:* In tabloid magazines and the fashion magazines

"In today's world, the technique of photomontage as Uelsmann does it has pretty much disappeared. This type of photography is now created on the computer using programs. Can anyone tell us what programs might be used to recreate these techniques outside of the darkroom?"

*Expected student response:* Adobe Photoshop, Quark Express, and Adobe Illustrator

*Transition:* "Today we are going to explore how the photographer Jerry Uelsmann creates a photomontage in the darkroom."

*c. Concept Development:* "You will be reading some information on Uelsmann, and there are some terms that are probably new to you that you will need to know to understand his work and successfully complete your own photomontage." Distribute the Vocabulary handout for priming vocabulary. "With your vocabulary partner, use the clues on the vocabulary handout and write a draft definition for the words. We will then reach consensus as a class on the definitions, and you will record them in the 'Photography Vocabulary' section of your notebook."

### Vocabulary

1. The following are descriptions of *anthropomorphized nature:*
   ■ a face in the bark of a tree
   ■ a sleeping giant formed from the tops of mountains

- a woman whose dress is actually a waterfall
- talking animals

What does it mean to anthropomorphize nature? [*giving human qualities to things in nature*]

2. Why does one wear a Halloween mask? [*to cover or hide the face; not to be seen*] A photographer would not put a mask on a negative, but he or she might *mask* a part of the negative. What does this mean? How might it be done? [*use paper to cover part of the negative*]

*d.* **Purpose for Reading:** "Keep these words in mind as you read. Your purpose-for-reading today is to be informed about the photographer Jerry N. Uelsmann and his photo techniques. Your reading will be from Uelsmann's website. As you read you will be answering questions about Uelsmann's work and the steps in the process he uses to create a photomontage."

**II. Silent Reading:** "Let's first review how to access the reading online. The steps are on the overhead."

1. Connect to website www.uelsmann.net. Enter this site by clicking on the picture in the center.
2. Go to the link at the bottom of this page to pdnonline; enter the site.
3. Once at this site, enter Q & A (*Question & Answer*); read and write responses on the handout.
4. Next enter Darkroom; read Uelsmann's explanation of each step of the four photomontages he created. Then using your inductive reasoning, summarize the steps he uses each time he creates a photomontage.

"To decide on these steps, you may need to read the steps for each photomontage more than once to see the pattern" (metacognition).

### Photomontage by Jerry N. Uelsmann: Q & A

1. What are some of Uelsmann's themes?

   hands (he's got the whole world in his hands), anthropomorphized nature

2. Why does Uelsmann struggle between wanting to title his works and not titling his works?

   He wants to clue observers in on his feelings when he was creating, but he also wants to allow people to have their own interpretations.

3. What does Uelsmann mean by "Simply stated, my hidden agenda is to amaze myself"?

   He is trying to create images that wow him to help him grow as an artist.

### Creating a Photomontage Darkroom

A. Describe in your own words, the steps Uelsmann would use to create a photomontage.
   1. Put one negative in one enlarger; block or mask the part you want to keep from being exposed; make the exposure.
   2. Put the next negative in another enlarger; mask again everything but the part of the photo to be exposed; make the exposure.
   3. Repeat this for each negative part to be used.
   4. Lower the enlarger to print a very small part.
   5. Block below the enlarger lens to create a soft edge where one image fades into another.

B. Now that you have seen several examples of photomontage by examining the work of Jerry Uelsmann, define *photomontage* in your own words. Later we will record our class definition in our vocabulary notebooks.

   Blending parts of negatives to create a new photograph with a message or a feeling.

**III. Discussion:** Pairs of students review the answers first, then the teacher leads a discussion with the entire class to ensure accuracy and consensus.

**IV. Rereading:** "Reread the steps to creating a photomontage. Do you have a clear understanding of how Uelsmann created his artwork?"

*Expected student response:* by using multiple images and enlargers; masking areas

"Uelsmann is vague about the way he begins a photomontage. Reread his response to the question, 'Do you often have a pre-arranged vision of an image or does a lot of your work start out as one thing and end up as another?' to see what he says. How do you think we would begin to create a photomontage? How might you begin?"

*Expected student response:* by selecting from our negatives some that seem to go together to create some message or show some feeling

"We are now going into the darkroom. I am going to demonstrate how to create a photomontage." Teacher models selecting negatives, trying to create a feeling, and demonstrates making a photomontage using Uelsmann's steps. Teacher also demonstrates "burning-in" and "dodging," light control techniques.

**V. Follow-up (day after the teacher demonstration):** "Today you will create your own photomontage. You will try to amaze yourself! When you finish your photomontage, dry-mount it on an 11 × 14 matte. In a typed paragraph, explain why you chose the pictures you did from your own negative files, what feelings you were trying to express in your photomontage, and the problems you encountered."

Photomontages are displayed around the classroom with statements; students will circulate, observe works, and write one critique. Critique one student's work, include description, interpretation, analysis, and judgment.

Lesson contributed by Cynthia Hendrick, May 2002.

---

## CONTENT AREA: BUSINESS EDUCATION
## STUDENT LOANS FOR HIGHER EDUCATION

**Class Description:** Business education; grades 11 and 12; below, average, and above average students.

**Unit Title:** Loans

**Topic of Lesson:** Possibilities and responsibilities with federal student loans

### Lesson Objectives
1. The students will define the following words: *subsidized, unsubsidized,* and *reneged.*
2. The students will understand the characteristics of the Stafford subsidized and unsubsidized loans and the PLUS loan.
3. The students will understand the responsibilities involved in repaying federal student loans and the consequences of failing to repay loans.
4. The students will apply their knowledge of student financial aid to solve real-life problems.
5. The students will collect data from a table.

### Performance Assessment

| Objective | Assessment |
| --- | --- |
| 1. | Writing defined terms in vocabulary notebook |
| 2. | Graphic organizer collected and reviewed |

3. Graphic organizer collected and reviewed
4. Problem-solving worksheet, homework
5. Problem-solving worksheet

**Macrostructure Thinking Skills:** Comparison and contrast of characteristics of federal student loan options; cause and effect, consequences of failing to repay a loan.

### Materials

- Transparency of article headline (*U.S. News & World Report,* March 1, 1976)
- Handout, "Great Schools at Great Prices," *U.S. News & World Report,* September 18, 2000)
- Overhead transparency for review vocabulary terms
- Overhead transparency for *subsidized* and *unsubsidized*
- Guided imagery reading for *reneged*
- Graphic organizer for silent reading
- Worksheet for rereading
- Unit reading material from www.ed.gov/prog_info/SFA/Student Guide

## Procedure

### I. Readiness

*a. Motivation:* "Today we are going to learn about ways that students can pay for their education after high school. Who plans on attending a university or college?" Students raise their hands. "Who plans on attending some other kind of school, either a vocational school or a trade school?" Students raise their hands. "Good. Now, who has a dear old, rich aunt, grandmother, or other person who's going to pay for your higher education?" Some hands are raised, with the students stating that their parents will be paying for their higher education. "Some students will be relying on parents to pay for higher education, but let's look at some of the costs involved."

*b. Developing Background of Experience:* Show transparency with chart outlining rising costs of a higher education. "As you can see, the rising cost of a higher education has been a hot topic for a long time. This is from a magazine article from 1976. Along with the rising cost of tuition at colleges and other schools comes increased anxiety for parents. Most parents today are starting to save for their children's education before their children are even born."

Pass out handout "Great Schools at Great Prices." "Let's look at some numbers in terms of how much it costs to attend college. The schools listed in this handout are the best bargains, meaning that many schools could cost students even more. Let's look at an example."

"Number 46 in the first column is University of Miami. For students who qualify for a grant, and a grant is money given to students based on financial need, students or their parents still have to pay almost $19,000 per year. Now multiply that times four years of college! Staggering? It's even more if the student doesn't qualify for grants. You can see why parents start saving early."

"Even if your parents have promised to contribute to your education, one or both of you will most likely have to apply for a loan at some time. You may have to apply for a loan to pay for programs your parents won't, like summer programs or if you want to study an extra year abroad. Or for room and board and living costs."

"For those of you who are interested in vocational schools, although the costs may not be as staggering, remember that you may not be making as much as those who go to college. Therefore, the tuition will still mean a great deal in terms of your total income once you graduate."

*Transition:* "Even if you are lucky enough to have resources that will cover the cost of your higher education, the information for student loans applies to other types of loans as well, such as car and house loans. We've already discussed how to buy a car and the basics of banking and investing. Let's review some of the terms you have already learned, since many apply to this area as well."

### c. Concept Development

1. *Review of vocabulary previously learned.* Show transparency with terms from prior lessons: *collateral, guarantor, interest rate, cap, penalty, default, dependent,* and *fixed.* "Please turn to your partner and for the next five minutes review these terms first by discussing what each means with your partners. Then refer to the vocabulary section of your notebook to verify your understanding of each of these terms." Students are seated in two rows arranged in a horseshoe facing the front and have assigned partners who sit next to each other. Seating arrangement is modified regularly and is based on personality and heterogeneous ability. Students review vocabulary with partners.

*Transition:* "Although we have learned much about how to obtain loans from banks, there are some terms that are used mainly when trying to borrow money from the government."

2. *Initial learning of new vocabulary.* "With your partner, define terms *subsidized* and *unsubsidized* using the sentence context clues on the transparency."

1. John wants to buy a stereo for his car. He has some of the money, but not enough to buy the stereo. His parents agree to help him purchase the stereo. They will give him 50% of the total cost. John's purchase of the stereo is *subsidized* by John's parents. John's friend, Peter, will also be buying a new stereo, but his parents will not be *subsidizing* the purchase. Peter's purchase will be *unsubsidized.*

2. People who live in *subsidized* housing have part of their rent paid by the government.

"Who can tell us the difference between subsidized and unsubsidized?"

*Expected student response: Subsidized* is when you get help to pay for something; *unsubsidized* is when you are totally responsible for the costs.

"Now with your partner, define the term *reneged* using the context clues on the transparency."

**Reneged**

You are walking through a mall shopping for some new shoes. In front of you there is a father and a daughter walking as well. The daughter is very excited. The father is telling her that if she can be patient while he buys the books he needs, then he will buy her an ice cream cone. You go into a store to buy your shoes. On the way out of the mall you see the same father and daughter again. This time the little girl is crying and screaming that she was good so she should get her ice cream cone. The father is apologizing but explaining that it is too close to dinner for her to have the ice cream. The father has *reneged* on his promise.

"Who can tell us what *reneged* means?"

*Expected student response:* When a person doesn't do something they have promised to do.

*Transition:* "Now let's learn about some options for financial aid."

### d. Purpose for Reading:

Pass out reading material and graphic organizer. "Today we will be reading to be informed. You will be comparing and contrasting three government loans that are available to pay for higher education and different ways that you can arrange your payments in order to pay these loans back. You will also be using cause and effect—that is, learning what options you have if you have problems repaying a loan and the consequences if you don't repay the loan. Please review the graphic organizer before you begin to read. Since the reading material has been duplicated for you, use your highlighter as you read to mark information that you will then transfer to your graphic organizers" (metacognition).

**II. Silent Reading:** Students read silently and complete the graphic organizer while teacher circulates to answer any questions and monitor progress of completing the graphic organizers (Table A.1).

**III. Discussion:** "Please turn to your partner and compare your answers on the graphic organizer. Resolve any differences." Students compare graphic organizers. Entire-class debriefing follows. Write expected responses on graphic organizer.

"Now let's look at the ugly part, the issue of how to repay student loans. Looking at your graphic organizer, who can tell us the best plan for repayment if you want to keep your total cost as low as possible?"

*Expected student response:* The standard plan is the best option.

**TABLE A.1   Financing Your Higher Education**

### FEDERAL LOAN OPTIONS

| NAME OF LOAN | WHO APPLIES FOR THE LOAN | CURRENT INTEREST RATE INFORMATION | GRACE PERIOD? | TOTAL AMOUNT THAT CAN BE BORROWED |
|---|---|---|---|---|
| Stafford Subsidized Loan | *Student* | *7.59% while in school; 8.19% after school; 8.25% cap* | *6 months* | *$17,125.* |
| Stafford Unsubsidized Loan | *Student* | *same as subsidized* | *6 months* | *$35,125.* |
| PLUS Loan | *Parent* | *8.99%; 9% cap* | *n/a* | *total cost of college less financial aid received.* |

### REPAYMENT PLAN OPTIONS

| NAME OF PLAN | PAYMENT AMOUNT | HOW AMOUNT IS DETERMINED | EFFECT ON TOTAL COST OF LOAN |
|---|---|---|---|
| Standard | *at least $50* | *amount owed* | *least amount of interest; total cost kept to minimum* |
| Graduated | *varies* | *lower, then increases* | *pay more in interest; total cost is more* |
| Income-sensitive | *varies* | *percentage of income* | *increase total interest; increase cost of loan* |
| Loan Consolidation | *varies* | *amount owed* | *interest rate and total interest may be higher; may increase cost of loan* |

### OPTIONS WHEN YOU CANNOT MAKE YOUR PAYMENT

| OPTION | DEFINITION | EFFECT ON LOAN INTEREST | RESPONSIBILITY OF STUDENT | LENGTH OF TIME |
|---|---|---|---|---|
| Deferment | *temporary postponement of loan repayment* | *subsidized—government pays interest; unsubsidized—student pays interest* | *must file paperwork; continue making payments until approved* | *as long as conditions exist* |
| Forbearance | *temporary reduction or postponement of loan payments* | *interest continues to accrue* | *must make request; continue making payments until approved* | *12 month intervals* |

### CONSEQUENCES OF RENEGING ON STUDENT LOANS

1. *tax refund intercepted*
2. *wages garnished*
3. *court action against you*

Expected student responses are in italics.

"Why is the standard plan the best option?"

*Expected student response:* Because you pay the least amount of interest. The total cost of the loan is the amount of the loan plus the interest you pay, so keeping the interest paid low keeps the total cost of the loan down.

"Good. Now, what ways did you find to actually reduce the cost of the loan?"

*Expected student response:* rewards for excellent repayment practices, making payments electronically, repayment incentives, and prepaying part of your loan

"We have discussed the term *guarantor* before when we learned about buying a car by borrowing money. Could someone remind us what that term means?"

*Expected student response:* A guarantor is a person who backs up the person who is borrowing the money. If the borrower doesn't pay the money back, then the guarantor does and then he has to get his money from the borrower.

"Right. Did you notice the term *government guaranteed* in the description of any of these loans?"

*Expected student response:* Yes, they are all government guaranteed.

"This brings us to the next issue. Could someone tell us some of the consequences for not repaying one of these loans?"

*Expected student response:* The government has to collect the money from the student.

"What are some of the ways with which the government can collect unpaid student loans?"

*Expected student response:* garnishing wages, taking tax refund, taking people to collections court

"So when you find that you are having difficulties paying your student loan payments, what should you do?"

*Expected student response:* request a deferment or a forbearance

"What do these do for a student?"

*Expected student response:* The deferment allows students to postpone the payment of their loans; forbearance lets you postpone or reduce the amount of your payments.

"What does a student have to do to for these remedies?"

*Expected student response:* They have to request each of them in writing and must continue to make payments until the request has been granted.

"What do you think is the overall lesson of the reading?"

*Expected student response:* Students and their parents can afford higher education through federal loans, but they should make sure that they plan their budget to pay it back. If they can't, they should not just stop paying the loan payment.

*Transition:* "It seems like you have a good understanding of how these plans work. Let's try to apply this information to some real-life situations."

**IV. Rereading:** Pass out worksheet.

### Financing Your Higher Education—Problem-Solving Worksheet
Show all math work required. Explain your answers using your knowledge of financial aid as well as any information we have learned in the class.

1. You have just been accepted into Some State University and you are elated. It was your first choice of colleges and you worked very hard to get the SAT score

required for admission. Your parents inform you that they are willing to pay your tuition, but since this is an out-of-state school and therefore very expensive, they won't be able to assist with any housing costs. What are your options? Include in your answer why other options are not appropriate.

2. You have just graduated from Some State University with a business degree. Your excellent grades have earned you a job with a high-tech company in their marketing division. Although you are given stock options as part of your employment contract, your actual salary is low, $25,000. This translates to about $850 every other week for your net income. Your student loans are $15,000, borrowed through the Stafford Subsidized Loan program, and you would like to keep interest payments to a minimum. Assuming other fixed costs in your budget (rent, car, insurance, etc.) equal $1,200 each month. You are preparing to meet with your loan advisor to discuss your repayment plan. Discuss each option and why each would or would not be appropriate for your situation.

3. After nine blissful months of employment, the high-tech company you worked for has gone bankrupt and you are out of a job. You have just started making payments on your student loans, but the part-time job you have to pay your living expenses doesn't provide enough money to continue with your payments. What do you do?

"Work in your workgroups (students in front row and students behind them in second row form groups of four students for work groups) to solve the problems. Remember to write out your entire response and the reasons that support your solution." Students work on problem solving.

"Who will share their group's answer to the first question?"

*Expected student response:* Student should apply for a Stafford Loan as a dependent because the parents are still supporting him or her. PLUS loan doesn't apply to the student borrowing money.

"Good. Now who would like to share their group's answer to the second question?"

*Expected student response:* Student could use either the standard plan, since that keeps total interest low and the monthly payments, $174, would be within the budget ($1700 – $1200 = $500 for extra expenses). The student could also use the income-sensitive plan to make allowances for his or her low starting salary. The income-sensitive plan may increase the interest paid, but may pay off loans sooner if the base salary increases. The graduated plan makes you pay more in interest and the loan consolidation doesn't apply since there is only one loan.

"Do any of the options for reducing the total cost of the loan apply to this student?"

*Expected student response:* Yes. The student should ask the loan advisor about these options.

"Who would like to share their group's answer to the third question?"

*Expected student response:* Student should contact the lender to request a deferment or forbearance. Until paperwork is completed, the student should continue to make payments.

*Transition:* "As we can see, financing your higher education can be overwhelming. With some planning and knowledge about how the system works, any student can afford to attend college or a trade school."

**V. Follow-Up:** "For your homework tonight, assume you have been accepted into the school of your choice. Assuming you would have to pay for this school completely on your own, explain how you would do that using financial aid. Second, write a letter to a friend who believes that he or she cannot attend a technical school after high school for financial reasons. Using the knowledge you learned here today, explain why your friend should not see that as a barrier to obtaining a higher education."

Lesson plan contributed by Kelly Throne, June 2001.

## CONTENT AREA: CONSUMER AND FAMILY SCIENCE
## SUDDEN INFANT DEATH SYNDROME (SIDS)

**Class Description:** Family and consumer science; heterogeneous class, grades 10 through 12; reading range in this class is very broad (grade 2 to college); class meets for 78 minutes three times per week

**Unit Title:** Infant Care

**Lesson Topic:** Sudden Infant Death Syndrom (SIDS)

**Unit Goal:** Explain infant care practices that help babies stay healthy

**Lesson Objectives:** After completing the lesson, students will be able to:

1. State the meaning of the acronym SIDS
2. Define: *sudden infant death syndrome, supine, prone,* and *gastroesophageal reflux*
3. Explain the problem (cause; most frequent occurrences, to whom and when)
4. State at least seven ways to reduce a baby's risk of SIDS (solution)
5. Create a rap, song, poem, poster, brochure, children's story, reproducible drawing, or public service announcement related to SIDS

### Performance Assessment

| Objective | Assessment |
|---|---|
| 1. | Student responses during class discussion of SIDS acronym |
| 2. | Vocabulary pair; oral responses; record in vocabulary notebook |
| 3. | Graphic organizer and "SIDS: Facts and Myths" handouts collected and reviewed |
| 4. | Graphic organizer and "SIDS: Facts and Myths" handouts collected and reviewed; use of Baby, Think It Over dolls to role-play different SIDS-related scenarios |
| 5. | Writing-to-learn activity (raps, songs, brochures, posters, poems, children's stories, reproducible drawings, or public service announcements) collected and scored with respective rubrics |

**Macrostructure Thinking Skills:** Problem and solution

### Materials

American Medical Association. (1997). *Family Medical Guide,* p. 663, New York: Random House.

Canfield, Jack. (2001). *Chicken Soup for the Mother's Soul 2,* pp. 314–318. Florida: Health Communications.

Cacciatore, Joanne. (n.d.). "Sibling Grief: Am I Still a Big Brother? The Grief of Children." Retrieved May 7, 2002, from www.missfoundation.org/cherish/sibling.html.

Dunmore, Helen. (1997). *Talking to the Dead.* Boston: Little, Brown.

National Institute of Child Health and Human Development. (2000). *Babies Sleep Safest on Their Backs: A Resource Kit for Reducing the Risk of SIDS in African American Communities.* Silver Spring, MD: National Institutes of Health.

National Institute of Child Health and Human Development. (1999). "Questions and Answers for Professionals on Infant Sleeping Position and SIDS." Retrieved May 3, 2002, from www.nichd.nih.gov/sids/sids_qa.htm; and "Babies Sleep Safest on Their Backs: Reduce the Risk of Sudden Infant Death Syndrome." Retrieved May 3, 2002, from www.nichd.nih.gov/sids/sleep_risk.htm.

National Institute of Child Health and Human Development. (1997). "Sudden Infant Death Syndrome." Retrieved May 4, 2002, from www.nichd.nih.gov/publications/pubs/sidsfact.htm.

Old, Wendie C. (1995). *Stacy Had a Little Sister.* Palatine, IL: Albert Whitman.

SIDS Alliance. (n.d.). *Facts about SIDS.* Baltimore, MD: SIDS Alliance.

Simonowitz, Helen. (1994). "SIDS Response: Family and School Partnership: A Note to Parents." Retrieved May 4, 2002, from http://sids-network.org/famscl.htm.

Smith, Jane Denitz. (1999). *Mary by Myself.* New York: Harper Collins.

Trozzi, Maria. (1999). *Talking with Children about Loss.* New York: Berkley.

Winslow, Joan (as told to Michelle Perry). (n.d.). "A Family's Happiness Destroyed." Retrieved May 4, 2002, from http://sids-network.org/fp/hapdes.htm.

### *Transparencies*

- Brisbane, Holly (2000). *The Developing Child.* New York: Glencoe McGraw-Hill. CT 23, 26–28.
- SIDS Impact (teacher-generated)
- SIDS graphic organizer (teacher-generated; see Figure A.1 for an example)
- "SIDS: Fact or Myth?" handout (teacher-generated)
- SIDS reading vocabulary (teacher-generated)
- Writing-to-learn activity (teacher-generated)

### *Miscellaneous*

- SIDS Directed Reading
- Print collection of SIDS topics (books, poems, web and magazine articles)
- Video: *Sudden Infant Death Syndrome* (NIH/Back to Sleep Resource Kit)
- VCR and television monitor
- Poster board, construction paper, markers, music paper, and other assorted art supplies
- Rubrics
- Baby, Think It Over dolls

## Procedure

### I. Readiness

*a. Motivation:* "Today we will begin by listening to Chapter 1 of *Mary by Myself.* This chapter tells of the death of ten-year-old Mary Vanessa Cole's infant sister, Felicity." Students listen to the story and imagine the feelings and envision the events.

---

**FIGURE A.1    Graphic Organizer for SIDS Lesson**

**Problem: SIDS**

    **S**udden
    **I**nfant
    **D**eath
    **S**yndrome

**In your own words, explain SIDS:** *sudden and unexplained death of a sleeping infant*

**What is the cause of SIDS?** *unknown; some relationship to suffocation*

**SIDS most frequently happens to whom? (age; race; sleeping position)** *2–4 months old; African American infants twice as likely*

**Prevention/Possible Solutions**

1. *Infants should sleep supine (on their backs).*
2. *Use a firm mattress and no fluffy or loose bedding or toys.*
3. *Use no covers that might cover the baby's face while sleeping.*
4. *Do not smoke before or after the birth of the baby.*
5. *Do not let the baby get too warm while sleeping.*
6. *Get good health care—prenatal and after birth.*
7. *Breastfeed, if possible.*

Expected student responses indicated by italics.

"What kinds of feelings did you identify as I was reading? How did you feel as I was reading?"

*Expected student responses:* beginning = happiness, bonding, love, fear, anger, emptiness, helplessness, loneliness, confusion

"What is your prediction as to the cause of Felicity's death?"

*Expected student responses:* choking, smothering, neglect, undetected problems, SIDS

**b. Tapping and Developing Background of Experience:** "Does anyone know what SIDS stands for? Do you know a family that has experienced SIDS? Does anyone know the commonly used term for SIDS?"

*Expected student responses:* Sudden Infant Death Syndrome [written on transparency]; varying student responses; "Crib Death" [cribs do not cause SIDS!]

"The impact of SIDS in the United States is clear and painful. A family has a healthy baby like the ones shown here, then suddenly and quietly, without warning, the baby dies!" Show transparencies of healthy infants. Use transparency of SIDS Impact list as follows.

### SIDS Impact
- SIDS is the leading cause of death in babies between 1 month and 1 year.
- Most SIDS deaths occur when a baby is between 2 and 4 months of age.
- African American babies are twice as likely to die of SIDS.
- More boys die of SIDS than girls.
- There is no way to tell in advance which babies will die.
- A SIDS death happens quickly, with no signs of suffering.
- More SIDS deaths occur in the colder months.

"Does anyone want to comment on this list?"

*Expected student responses:* personal accounts; Why boys and African Americans? Why can't they find out why the babies are dying? Winter issues such as blankets, heavier clothing.

*Transition:* "We now know a few facts about SIDS, the "silent killer" of infants. Please get your vocabulary notebook and sit with your vocabulary partner."

Students work with their vocabulary partners. Weaker and stronger readers are paired together by teacher. Students use the vocabulary section of their notebook for this part of the lesson.

**c. Concept Development/Vocabulary:** During this part of the lesson, the teacher will pronounce each word initially. A visual strategy will be used so that students will be able to find a meaning. Students will first work in vocabulary pairs to create a draft definition for each word. The teacher will write definitions on a transparency. From these definitions the class will develop a class definition. The teacher will also have a preplanned definition for each word, accepting alternative wording as appropriate.

### Vocabulary Words and Preplanned Definitions:
- **SIDS:** (Sudden Infant Death Syndrome): sudden and unexpected death of an infant under one year of age for which no exact cause of death can be determined
- **Supine:** Lying on the back or having face upward (show NIH transparency: place baby face up in crib)
- **Prone:** Lying with the front or face downward (show Brisbane transparency CT 28: place baby face down in crib)
- **Gastroesophageal reflux:** Heartburn, spitting up, burping caused by stomach acid flowing back up to the esophagus

"We will start our vocabulary section with another reading to help with our definition of SIDS. I will be reading a passage from *Chicken Soup for the Mother's Soul 2,* from a selection titled 'A Christmas Memory.' Close your eyes and imagine it is a crisp autumn afternoon." Begin reading on page 314, "The fall weather . . . " and continue until page 316, "He had died sometime during his warm, safe naptime." Students will use the following sentences to develop a definition of *supine*.

> Monisha chose the *supine* position for her baby so she could look at her cute little nose.
> Lying *supine,* Jared could watch the mobile moving above his crib.
> On the colorful quilt, Ashley lay *supine,* looking at the ceiling fan.

Students will use the following sentences to develop a definition of *prone*.

> The baby placed all puzzle pieces in a *prone* position, hiding the bright colorful pictures.
> The nurse found a comfortable *prone* position for the infant before she began massaging his neck.
> As Jack lay *prone,* he looked at his mommy as she prepared dinner.

Students will use the following sentences to develop a definition of *gastroesophageal reflux.*

> While Veronica was pregnant, she suffered from *gastroesophageal reflux* whenever she ate Italian food. She felt a burning sensation in her chest.
> Trina was all dressed for her first night out with her husband since the baby had arrived, when she noticed the stains from *gastroesophageal reflux* on her shoulder.

Also use the soda/burping example too often demonstrated by members of the class! After symptoms are generalized by students, explain the cause of the condition.

*Transition:* "Now that we have learned the vocabulary for today's reading, we will begin!"

**d. Purpose-for-Reading:** "Today you will be reading to be informed. You will each be reading one of two articles published by the Institute of Child Health and Human Development that I downloaded from their website. After you and your partner read your assigned articles and complete your graphic organizers, you will share your information so that you have a more complete understanding of the problem of SIDS and its possible solutions."

**II. Silent Reading:** The better reader in each pair will read "Questions and Answers for Professionals"; the weaker reader in each pair will read "Babies Sleep Safest on Their Backs: Reduce the Risk of Sudden Infant Death Syndrome." Students read silently and complete graphic organizers.

**III. Discussion:** First partners meet to share, confirm, and add information to their graphic organizers. Each reading will provide additional information. Class will engage in a discussion related to SIDS information recorded on the graphic organizers. Reasons for each response will be an important part of the discussion (e.g., "Why is it recommended to use a firm mattress for the baby?").

Teacher records student responses on graphic organizer transparency and class records any additions or corrections to organizers.

*Transition:* "We now know more about SIDS. Let's read the articles again and see if we can distinguish fact from myth regarding SIDS. On the "SIDS: Fact or Myth" handout, write the letter F in the spaces provided if the statement is factual and the letter M if it is a myth. Be prepared to justify your answers during our entire-class discussion."

### SIDS: Fact or Myth?
1. _____ Babies "catch" SIDS.
2. _____ Bed sharing between baby and an adult can result in SIDS.
3. _____ A SIDS death can be prevented.
4. _____ African American babies are twice as likely to die of SIDS.
5. _____ Cribs do not cause SIDS.

6. _____ The chance of a baby dying of SIDS can be greatly reduced by placing the baby in a prone position.
7. _____ SIDS can occur at any age.
8. _____ Doctors have found no increase in choking or other problems in babies sleeping on their backs.
9. _____ Families often feel guilty and responsible for their baby's death.
10. _____ Shots or medicines do not cause SIDS.
11. _____ Babies who sleep supine usually choke on spit up or vomit.
12. _____ "Crib death" is the commonly used term for SIDS.
13. _____ Sleeping in a side position is all right for infants.
14. _____ Supine sleeping causes babies to get flat heads.
15. _____ All babies should be seen for well-baby check-ups.

**IV. Rereading:** Students work in pairs to answer the "SIDS: Fact or Myth?" handout and reread the articles. Both readings will be needed to accurately complete the handout.

"Let's see if we all agree on what is fact and what is myth." Entire class discussion for consensus and reinforcement of information.

*Transition:* "To review some of what we have learned about SIDS, let's watch a short video."

**V. Follow-Up:** Students will watch the SIDS video. Using the Baby, Think It Over dolls, students will be grouped in triads by the teacher and will be asked to create a role-play about SIDS. Students will choose from several different scenarios:

- Parents discussing how to lower SIDS risks
- Physician making new parents aware of SIDS
- Counselor comforting grieving parents who are afraid to have another child
- Group therapy session of SIDS parents
- Friend or family helping SIDS family
- Parents explaining to and reassuring sibling of SIDS child

"Now that we have all this knowledge about SIDS, let's see how we can share it. On the slips of paper in this baby cap I have written several different SIDS scenarios. Please draw one slip per group and create a role-play. You may use the Baby, Think It Over dolls and any other props in the classroom. Each group should create written dialogue between the three individuals and prepare to present the role-play to another group in the class." Students will work together in triads to create the role-play and present to another group.

**Summary:** Students will be asked to choose from several writing-to-learn activity options. A variety of approaches for assessment has been offered to address the different learning styles represented. Students may enjoy the assessment activity because they are allowed to choose an activity geared toward personal strengths. Students should refer to the appropriate rubric provided for assignment criteria.

"You have been identified as an intelligent and creative individual in your community. A group of community leaders has approached you about working on a community-wide effort to increase SIDS awareness. The goal of the committee is to produce items to be used in a public education campaign. They have asked you to create and contribute one of the following:

| | |
|---|---|
| rap | brochure |
| song | children's story |
| poem | reproducible drawing |
| poster | public service announcement |

You should be sure to include information from your graphic organizer and your 'SIDS: Fact or Myth?' handout in your writing-to-learn activity."

Lesson contributed by Nancy Gibson, 2002.

| CONTENT AREA: ENGLISH |
| :---: |
| **TALES OF THE MYSTERIOUS** |

**Class Description:** This English class is a seventh grade class that is heterogeneously mixed. The reading achievement ranges from fourth to tenth grade levels. Most of the time students remain on task and are actively involved in learning.

**Topic of Lesson:** Do Sea Serpents Exist? (Students will be reading "Do Sea Serpents Exist?" by A. Hyatt Verrill)

**High School Core Learning Goal:** The student will demonstrate the ability to respond to a text by employing personal experiences and critical analysis.

**Unit Goal:** Students will compare and contrast the pros and cons that are connected to each of the "Tales of the Mysterious."

**Lesson Objectives**

1. Students will be able to locate and circle Maryland and the general area of the sea serpent sightings.
2. Students will be able to define the terms *carcass, zoologist,* and *affidavit.*
3. Students will be able to list the evidence for and against the question "Do sea serpents exist?"
4. Students will be able to analyze their own personal feelings about experiencing a sea serpent.
5. Students will be able to use the Internet to locate information about a known animal that resembles a sea serpent.
6. Students will be able to write their own story about a sighting of a sea serpent, using the information from the Internet.

**Performance Assessment**

| *Objective* | *Performance* |
| :---: | :--- |
| **1.** | Locate and circle locations on a map |
| **2.** | Vocabulary pairs and oral responses |
| **3.** | Collect and review graphic organizers |
| **4.** | Collect and review journals |
| **5.** | Collect and review Internet exercise handouts |
| **6.** | Collect and review journals |

**Macrostructure Thinking Skill:** Pro and Con

**Materials**

- Transparency of Motivation questions
- Chalk and chalkboard (in classroom)
- Overhead and felt-tip markers (in classroom)
- Map of the United States (found at the website http://nationalgeographic.com)
- Map of the surrounding areas of the Atlantic Ocean (found at the website: http://nationalgeographic.com)
- Map of the World (*Hammond Atlas of the World.* 2nd ed. New Jersey: Hammond, 1998)
- Three pictures of carcasses (the first two pictures were found at the website http://search.corbis.com and the third picture was found at the website www.weirdpics.com)
- Transparency of sentences for defining *affidavit*
- Transparency and copies of graphic organizer (see Figure A.2)
- Thirty copies of the article "Do Sea Serpents Exist?" by A. Hyatt Verrill
- Transparency of the rereading questions
- Thirty copies of handouts for the follow-up exercise

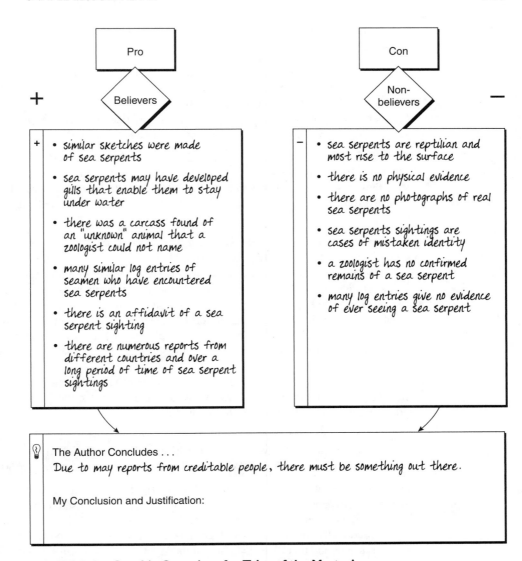

**FIGURE A.2    Graphic Organizer for Tales of the Mysterious**

- Transparency for the summary of the DRA
- Computer lab (at the school)
- Transparency of typed vocabulary words

## Procedure

### I. Readiness

*a. Motivation:* "In your daily journals, respond to the following questions that are displayed on the transparency."

> Have you ever believed in something and other people told you that it was not real?
> What did you believe in?
> Why did you believe in it?
> What were some of the reasons that were expressed to you, concerning why this topic was not real?

Students will write their responses in their journals.

"Who will share with us what you wrote?" Students share their responses. Their answers will vary.

> *Expected student responses:* I believed in the Tooth Fairy because I always found money under my pillow whenever I left my lost tooth under my pillow; I was told that ghosts weren't real because there is no physical proof; I believe in UFOs because of all of the reported sightings. Some people say that only crazy people see UFOs. My older sister told me that Santa did not really exist, but I didn't want to believe her.

*Transition:* "We will be reading an article titled 'Do Sea Serpents Exist?' by A. Hyatt Verrill. This article presents support for both responses to the question: 'Yes, they exist' and 'No, they do not exist.' Ultimately, the article concludes with a choice of one of the responses. Before we read this article, we should discuss our own beliefs about the question being presented."

**b. Tapping and Developing Background of Experience:** "Think about the question 'Do sea serpents exist?' Close your eyes. I would like everyone who believes in the existence of sea serpents to put their thumbs up and for everyone who does not believe in the existence of sea serpents to put their thumbs down." Students physically respond to question. "Everyone open your eyes with your thumbs remaining in their present position. Pair up with someone who does not share your belief. If there are not enough opposing sides, then pair up with someone who shares your belief. Discuss with your partner your reasons for believing or not believing in sea serpents." Students pair up and discuss their responses with their partners.

"As a class, let's discuss our responses and our reasoning. I will make a list of ideas on the chalkboard. On one side I will write the responses of the 'believers' and on the other side I will write the responses of the 'nonbelievers.'"

> *Expected student responses:* I think sea serpents exist because if they weren't real, people would not have seen the LochNess Monster; they don't exist because there isn't physical proof; they exist because real people saw them and reported them.

*Transition:* "Now that we've established who—right now—believes and who does not believe in sea serpents, it's time to learn about where sightings of sea serpents have occurred. "Here is a map of the United States. Who will locate and circle the location of Maryland?" Student locates and circles Maryland on the transparency. "Now, I am going to show you a transparency that displays many of the sighting areas of sea serpents: Florida; Cape Ann, MA; Greenland coast; Orkney Islands; Queenstown, Ireland; Sicily. All of these places are mentioned in the article." Show the class a prelabeled map and point out the locations. Now, let's look at a world map. Who would like to locate and circle the general area of Maryland on the world map? Who would like to locate and circle the general area of the locations that I just pointed out? What do you notice about the sighting locations? [*all within the Atlantic Ocean*] Students locate both areas on the map and circle them.

*Transition:* "Now that we can visualize where these actual sightings are in relation to where we live, we will be able to picture them in our minds as we read. We should become familiar with some vocabulary words that are mentioned in the article."

**c. Concept Development/Vocabulary:** "Please turn your notebooks to your vocabulary section. Write the word *carcass* down as I have displayed it on the transparency." Students copy the word into their notebooks. "I am about to show you three pictures of *carcasses.* The first picture that I am showing you is of a wolf standing over a *carcass,* the second picture is a *carcass* of a beached whale, and the third picture is a *carcass* being pulled out of the sea. From what you have observed in these pictures, think about the definition for the term *carcass.* Now, pair up with your vocabulary partner and draft a definition together." Vocabulary partners are an above average student with an average student or a below average student with an average student. Partners are changed each quarter. Students discuss their responses. Pairs are called on and a class consensus reached on the definition.

*Expected student responses:* It's a rotted dead animal; it shows the bones and flesh of a dead animal; it is when an animal decays; the skeletal structure of a dead animal where flesh and tissue may still remain.

"As I write the definition on the transparency, you should copy the definition into your notebooks."

"The next term that needs to be defined is *zoologist.* Please write this word which I have displayed on the transparency, in your notebooks." Students copy the term into their notebooks. "I will now be taking you through a visual exercise that will help you define the term *zoologist.*"

You are standing on the beach in Ocean City. It is a rainy, cold, fall day. You can hear the waves crashing against the shore. You can smell the dense odor of rotted meat. As you look down at what is in front of you, you want to close your eyes. You are examining the rotting flesh and the large bone structure of the large mass that is right in front of you. You take tedious notes and use gloves to touch the animal. You are stumped about what type of animal is laying right before you. After a long day of scientific examining of an unknown carcass, you return to your cold, cluttered office. All night, you search through your enormous, old bookshelves looking for the answer to your question. What type of animal is this? You know that everyone is expecting you to provide them with the answer, and you can feel the pressure building on your shoulders. Finally you fall asleep at your desk and rest your head on a stack of books.

"You may now open your eyes. You have just experienced an aspect of what a *zoologist* does. Think about what this term means, then with your partner discuss your ideas and draft a definition." Students pair up and discuss their responses. The teacher leads a discussion to reach consensus on a definition.

*Expected student responses:* A person who studies animals; a knowledgeable person who is expected to answer questions about animals; a creditable, knowledgeable person who studies animals.

"As I write the definition on the transparency, you should copy the definition into your notebooks."

"Now it is time to define the last term that is important for our reading assignment. Please copy the word *affidavit,* which I have displayed on the transparency." Students copy the word into their notebooks. "I will read aloud the following sentences that will help you define the term *affidavit.*"

The captain of the ship turned in an *affidavit* to the court stating his sighting of a sea serpent.
The little girl signed an *affidavit* that confirmed her as the witness to a crime.

"Think about your own definition of the term *affidavit.* Now, discuss your responses with your partner." Students pair up and discuss their responses.

*Expected student responses:* It is an important document; it is a document that is used in court; a sworn document that represents the importance and seriousness of an issue.

"As I write the definition on the transparency, you should copy the definition into your notebooks."

*Transition:* "Now that we've defined the necessary vocabulary terms, it is time to look at what our purpose-for-reading will be as we read the article 'Do Sea Serpents Exist?'"

**d. Purpose-for-Reading:** "Your purpose-for-reading is to be informed. You will list the reasons believers think sea serpents exist (the pros) and the reasons nonbelievers think they do not exist (the cons) in the graphic organizer that I am about to distribute. I will read the directions to you. 'Read the article "Do Sea Serpents Exist?" by A. Hyatt Verrill and write down six reasons, given in the article, that support the believers and nonbelievers. Then, write down the conclusion that was made in the article by the author.' " Students listen as teacher reads the directions.

"You should pay particular attention to the pictures of sea serpents provided in this article. This will help you recognize the evidence that supports the believers. Also, as you read, you may want to highlight key information that will help you fill out your graphic organizer" (metacognition).

**II. Silent Reading:** Students silently read the article and fill out their graphic organizers.

*Transition:* "Now that everyone has read the article and filled out the Pro and Con graphic organizer, we will have a group discussion and then a class discussion."

**III. Discussion:** "Please view the displayed transparency to see what group you are in. Meet in these groups and discuss your responses to your graphic organizer. You may add responses to your graphic organizer." Students meet in their reading achievement–based, heterogeneously mixed groups of four and discuss their responses to their graphic organizer, which are based on the article that they just read.

"Let's rejoin as a class and discuss our responses. I will fill out my graphic organizer transparency with student responses." Each group will respond once to each column and to the conclusion section of the graphic organizer.

**IV. Rereading:** "Now you must make a decision. Are you convinced by the pro argument or by the con argument? Make a choice and explain why in the space at the bottom of the graphic organizer. Then we will hear your decisions and justifications." Students write their responses. Entire class vote is taken and justifications for each side are shared.

*Transition:* "Now that we have learned the overall concept of the article, it is time to take a more personal look at the article."

"Read the first column, second full paragraph, on page seven of the article. Before you reread this paragraph, imagine that you are the captain whose experience is being discussed in this paragraph. Respond in your journals to the following questions that are displayed on the transparency and that I will read out loud. 'How would you feel in this situation? What would you do? How would your life change if you were to capture the sea serpent?' " Students will write in their journals.

"Who will share with us their responses to the questions?"

*Expected student responses:* I would be very scared, but I would capture the sea serpent with a net and call for my men from the big ship to help me; if I captured the sea serpent, I would probably become famous and become rich because of what I found.

*Transition:* "Now that we've taken a more personal look at the article, we should examine the knowledge that we have obtained."

**V. Follow-Up:** "We will be moving to the computer lab to look up information on the Internet. I am about to distribute a handout with directions on it. The directions read as follows: 'You are to find a "known" animal on the Internet that looks like the sea serpents described in the article. (*Hint:* You may want to look up information about the Paleozoic or Cretaceous period.) You are also to answer the following questions about your animal. What is your animal named? Describe its appearance. What does the animal eat? How does it breathe? Do you consider this animal to be dangerous?' I have paired you up with the partners that I have displayed on the transparency, and you will work on the handout together." Students enter the computer lab, sit with their partners, and answer the questions to the handout.

"We are going to use the information you gathered from the Internet to write your own story about a sea serpent sighting. First, let's organize your Internet notes. You should include crucial information such as the setting of the story, what the sea serpent looks like, how it acts, and how you deal with the situation. This list of information is displayed on the screen. After you have made notes on these aspects, write your first draft." Students will write their stories in their journals.

Lesson plan contributed by Amanda Reuter-Lancaster, December 1999.

## CONTENT AREA: ENGLISH
## ROLL OF THUNDER, HEAR MY CRY

**Class Description:** English, grade 8, heterogeneous class of below average, average, and above average students.

**Unit:** They Call It Courage

**Unit Goals:** Students will:

1. Understand how authors use authentic historical and geographical background to create historical fiction
2. Recognize that writers instill their fictional characters with qualities such as courage, pride, and determination to help them deal with injustices resulting from prejudice

**Lesson Objectives:** Students will:

1. Define and explain characteristics of the Great Depression, sharecropping, the Ku Klux Klan, Jim Crow laws, and Mississippi in the 1930s
2. Summarize the reading (first six chapters of *Roll of Thunder, Hear My Cry*)
3. Identify the conflicts in the selection
4. Identify traits of major characters
5. Identify specific historical facts in the reading
6. Evaluate the effectiveness of the author's use of setting
7. Predict possible resolutions or courses of action for the conflicts introduced
8. Compare and contrast the views and experiences of the main character with their own views and experiences.

**Performance Assessment**

| Objective | Assessment |
| --- | --- |
| 1. | Jigsaw activity and shared responses |
| 2. | Purpose-for-reading oral and written responses |
| 3. | Purpose-for-reading summaries |
| 4. | Character Web responses |
| 5. | Rereading activity written and oral responses |
| 6. | Rereading activity written and oral responses |
| 7. | Follow-up written and oral responses |
| 8. | "It's Just Not Fair"—personal and character's responses |

**Macrostructure Thinking Skills:** Narrative elements—characters, setting, conflict, and significant events

**Materials**

- Copies of *Roll of Thunder, Hear My Cry* by Mildred D. Taylor
- *Photographs* by Eudora Welty. (1989). Jackson: University of Mississippi Press (excellent collection of photographs of African Americans of Mississippi in the 1930s)
- Handouts:"It's Just Not Fair" and "The Great Depression of the 1930s"
- The Great Depression Visual Aids (*Pictures of a Decade,* 1-30 through 46-30; source: Curmat 973.91 G786)

- *Pictures of a Decade: 1930–1940,* edited from packet of textual descriptions for visual aids (Curmat 973.91 G786)
- Audiotape: *The Great Depression: Music of the 30's* (Public Library 782G)
- "Mississippi" packet with pictures, maps; Microsoft-Encarta, 1994
- "KKK" packet; *The Truth about the Ku Klux Klan,* Milton Meltzer (CCPL 322.42)
- "Sharecropping" packet and pictures; *You Have Seen Their Faces,* Erskine Caldwell and Margaret Bourke-White, 1937 (Q975.04 C147)
- "Jim Crow Laws," in *American History: A Survey, Volume II: Since 1865*
- Students' vocabulary notebooks
- Character Web
- Purpose-for-reading questions handout
- Rereading handout

## Procedure

### Readiness

*a. Motivation and Review:* "In the next few days, we're going to begin a novel entitled *Roll of Thunder, Hear My Cry,* in which the main characters deal with injustices resulting from prejudice. At one time or another, we've all dealt with injustice. For example, as a child I remember thinking how unfair it was to have to sit in the kitchen and eat with my younger brothers and sisters whenever my family had company. All the adults sat in the dining room, and I remember how I could hear them talking and laughing, having a great time while I was stuck in the kitchen with the dirty pots and pans, babysitting my little brothers and sisters. As you can imagine, I was not too pleased with the situation, and I always thought how unfair it was that I was not allowed to eat with the big people, even though I considered myself to be on the same level as them."

"Think about a situation that occurred in your life when you felt that same sense of unfairness. I'm going to pass out a graphic organizer entitled 'It's Just Not Fair.' Take the next few minutes and fill out the organizer. Then we'll share those experiences."

### It's Just Not Fair
It wasn't fair when:

It made me feel:

I reacted by:

Students fill out organizers, then volunteers share their experiences. Ask each student how she or he might have reacted differently, or if there was anything else she or he could have done to correct the situation.

"Based on the experiences we've all shared, how might we define the term *injustice*? [*to be treated unfairly*] Write on the board; have students copy onto vocabulary ditto.

*Transition:* "The characters in *Roll of Thunder* deal with injustice in many ways. The time period and geographical location of the story play a significant role in the plot of the novel. Let's go back in time now to the 1930s, to a time in American history known as the Great Depression."

*b. Concept Development/Background of Experience:* "I'm going to show you some pictures from the 1930s. While I'm doing this, you'll be listening to music from that time period. The first song is entitled 'Brother, Can You Spare a Dime?' As you're listening to the song and looking at the pictures I'll be displaying, I want you to write down on a sheet of paper whatever thoughts or impressions come to mind when you look at the pictures or listen to the music." Play song and display large visuals, sixteen pictures in all. After showing each picture around the class, line them up on the chalkboard and label a number on top of each. When song ends, forward to "We Sure Got Hard Times Now." Play it and the song that follows, "Dark Was the Night, Cold Was the Ground," as background music for the following discussion.

"After listening to the song and looking at the pictures lined up on the board here, what impression do you get of the 1930s?" Discuss each picture separately. Write responses on blackboard.

*Expected student responses:* All men are wearing hats, crowds, sad, lonely, unhappy, depressing, funny clothes, old, lines, selling apples, poor, broken down, no money, tired, no smiles, separate building for blacks, cardboard shacks, run-down old cars, dirty faces

"Now we're going to read the captions written for each picture." Ask volunteers to read aloud caption for each picture.

To summarize, have students work in their cooperative learning (four students to a group, chosen by the teacher to represent a balance of ability, gender, and race) to come up with five words that best capture the essence of the Great Depression. The recorder for each group shares the group's findings with the rest of the class.

*Expected student responses:*

| | | |
|---|---|---|
| unemployment | homeless | desperate |
| beggars | hungry | despair |
| grim | ruin | starving |
| hungry | hopeless | agony |
| suffering | | |

Add this list to the one previously generated on the board. Pass out "The Great Depression" graphic organizer (Figure A.3). Instruct students to record these words under "The Great Depression" section at the top.

**FIGURE A.3   Graphic Organizer for the Great Depression**

**The Great Depression of the 1930s**

**Mississippi in the 1930s**

| LOCATION AND PHYSICAL CHARACTERISTICS | SHARECROPPING | KKK | SEGREGATION AND JIM CROW LAWS |
|---|---|---|---|
| ▪ In the southern United States between Alabama and Louisiana<br><br>▪ Warm, humid climate; long summers with mild winters<br><br>▪ 55% of the land covered with forests<br><br>▪ Soil: clay and sand<br><br>▪ Blacks and whites had separate schools<br><br>▪ Cotton dominated the economy until the 1930s | ▪ Plantation owned by absent landlord<br><br>▪ Land divided and rented to tenants<br><br>▪ Rent paid in cotton<br><br>▪ Credit at local store paid with cotton<br><br>▪ Took children out of school to work the fields<br><br>▪ Emphasis on single cash crops; high interest<br><br>▪ Another form of slavery | ▪ Secret society<br><br>▪ Goal was to maintain white supremacy<br><br>▪ Believed blacks inferior to whites<br><br>▪ Rituals, costumes, secret language<br><br>▪ Created terror in black communities throughout the South - "Midnight Rides"<br><br>▪ Victims beaten and burned<br><br>▪ Members got a sense of importance by belonging<br><br>▪ Against anyone who challenged "traditional American values" | ▪ Separation of races, legally<br><br>▪ Separate but equal<br><br>▪ Literacy tests, poll taxes<br><br>▪ Took away political power from blacks<br><br>▪ Blacks and whites had separate facilities - restaurants, washrooms, etc.<br><br>▪ Blacks could not go to public beaches, parks, etc.<br><br>▪ Lynching - another way to scare blacks |

*Transition:* "We've established the mood of the time period, but before we begin reading it's important for you to know about the way life was in Mississippi in the 1930s. It was very different from life today in Maryland."

Students will be grouped for jigsaw on the following concepts: State of Mississippi in the 1930s, sharecropping, KKK, and Jim Crow laws. Students selected to work in groups according to reading achievement and maturity level. Strongest readers will be assigned the selection on sharecropping, more mature students will be assigned selections on KKK and Jim Crow laws; weaker readers will read the selection on Mississippi—location and physical characteristics.

*Expert Groups:* Students will be instructed to first read their selections and look at the pictures in each packet. They will then write a brief summary of the selection and, as a group, fill out the important characteristics in the "Great Depression" diagram provided.

*Jigsaw:* Students will be regrouped so that one person from each expert group is in the new group. Students will, in turn, summarize the readings and share the information they have listed in their diagrams.

*Entire-Class Activity:* Students will then work with their vocabulary partners to arrive at definitions of the concepts Mississippi, sharecropping, Ku Klux Klan, and Jim Crow Laws. Teacher will note definitions on the board, and ask students to copy into their vocabulary notebooks.

*Expected student responses:*

**Mississippi:** a southern state that has long, humid summers. Main crop in the 1930s was cotton. Over half the state is covered by forest, and the soil is made up of clay and sand. Blacks and whites received separate education in the 1930s.

**Sharecropping:** a system of farming in which tenants paid their rent, fertilizer, food, and other needs with their crops, usually cotton.

**Ku Klux Klan:** a secret society formed to maintain white supremacy in the South and other areas by terrorizing blacks and other groups that seemed "un-American."

**Jim Crow Laws:** laws in the southern states that legalized the separation the races.

**II. Purpose-for-Reading:** "As you read the first six chapters of *Roll of Thunder, Hear My Cry:*

1. In five or six sentences, summarize what has happened so far in the story. Be sure to include the setting, major characters, two significant events, and the major conflict.
2. Fill out the 'Character Web' with the information you get from the reading. This will help you see that each character has distinctive traits. I've already filled in one characteristic of each person to get you started.
3. Complete another 'It's Just Not Fair' chart as it relates to a character in this novel. You might choose Cassie or another character (e.g., Cassie's mother). How was this character's experience and reaction similar to or different from your experience with injustice?

"I have a wonderful book entitled *Photographs,* by Eudora Welty. She took pictures all over Mississippi in the 1930s. The pictures will give you a good idea of what life was like during that era, in that location. Next week, as you're reading the first six chapters, feel free to browse through the book. This will help you to see this book as a movie in your mind as you read" (metacognition).

**III. Silent Reading (1 week):** Students read the first six chapters at home.

**IV. Discussion (45 minutes):** Entire class discusses three purpose-for-reading questions. Teachers writes student responses to Character Web transparency.

**Rereading:** Students will complete the Rereading questions in pairs, based on heterogeneous reading achievement.

1. In Chapter 1, Cassie's father says to her, "Look out there, Cassie, girl. All that belongs to you. You ain't never had to live on nobody's place but your own, and as long as I

live and the family survives, you'll never have to. That's important. You may not understand that now, but one day you will. Then you'll see." Think about the setting and time period of the novel. Think about the many factors that influenced African American life in Mississippi in the 1930s. Why do you think that land was so important to Mr. Logan and his family? Use details from the text to support your statements.

2. List three historical facts found in the novel thus far. Be sure to include the page number for each.

3. Could this story take place if the setting was changed to Maryland today? Why or why not?

Responses will then be shared in a whole class discussion.

### Group Discussion for Consensus

1. Land was important because it meant independence, liberty, freedom from oppression. You worked for no one but yourself. You could not be cheated or taken advantage of. It was a source of pride. Land ownership also indicated a position of power and authority, which the Logans had in their community.

2. Price of cotton dropping, forcing Papa to work for the railroad; KKK burnings; separate schools; sharecropping; condition of books in black schools.

3. The story would have been very different had it been set in a different time and place because circumstances and beliefs vary over time periods and geographical settings. For example, racial discrimination is illegal nationwide, and the KKK is looked on generally as an embarrassment. The growing of cotton would not be possible in Maryland with its climate.

**V. Follow-Up:** "Based on our discussion of the first six chapters of this novel, what do you predict will happen in Chapter 7?" Write your predictions in your journals, then we will share with the entire class." Individual writing, then entire class discussion.

Lesson plan contributed by Deborah Rambo, May 1996.

## CONTENT AREA: ENGLISH (ESL)
### "NIKKI-ROSA"

**Class Description:** ESL/English; Stage III—Speech Emergence; grade 9

**Unit:** Biography (initiatory lesson of the unit)

**Unit Goals:** Students will judge the validity of biographies read.
Students will write a valid biography of someone notable in their lives.

**Lesson Objectives:** At the conclusion of the lesson, students should be able to:

1. Define *biography* and *biographer*
2. Interpret the poem "Nikki-Rosa"
3. Explain the components of a good biography

### Performance Assessment

*Objective   Assessment*

**1.**   Oral responses for definitions

**2.**   Individual interpretations (letters) of the poem collected and reviewed; oral interpretations and written summaries from groups.

**3.**   Oral responses for criteria during Rereading activity

**Materials**

- Biography book examples
- Transparency and handout "Biographies and Biographers"
- Copies of the poem "Nikki-Rossa" by Nikki Giovanni
- Small-group constituency on a transparency

## Procedure

| TEACHER | STUDENT |
|---|---|

**I. Readiness**

*a. Motivation:* Biography books are on display as students enter the room. Students are encouraged to look through them.

Students examine books

*b. Background of Experience and Concept Development*

**1.** Teacher explains that today they will begin a unit on biographies, and distributes the handout listing the titles and authors of the books displayed in the room. This handout is also on the overhead projector.

The teacher shows one book at a time, briefly and enthusiastically relating something about the subject of the biography's claim to fame. To stress the new words, *biography* and *biographer,* the teacher introduces each new book with "This is the *biography* of [subject], and the *biographer* is [author]." Any pictures in the book are shown to students, and a key word or words for each person is written on the transparency next to the title of the biography. For example, "ice hockey" is written next to *Wayne Gretsky* (*Champion Sport Biographies*) by Boughn and Romain. Students repeat the words and copy them onto their handouts.

**2.** Students are instructed to work with their vocabulary partners (one more proficient and one less proficient language user) to write their definition of *biography* based on the examples. Pairs are called on to share their definitions. Initial definition and revisions are written on the board, and a class definition is reached through consensus.

*Expected definition:* A *biography* is a work about a notable person's life, written by someone other than the subject of the biography.

Students are then asked to define *biographer.* First, the teacher reviews with the students what the suffix *-er* often indicates.

*Expected definition:* A *biographer* is the person who writes the biography, the author of the biography.

*c. Tapping Background of Experience:* Teacher invites students to assume that one day a biographer wants to write about them. "List things you would like the biographer to tell about you and your life."

Students volunteer ideas; teacher writes key words on the board.

*Transition:* "Today, you will be reading a poem in which a girl reflects on what a biographer might say about her one day."

*d. Purpose-for-Reading:* "Today, you will be reading for literary experience. Pretend that the girl, Nikki, has written this poem as a letter to you. After you read, you will write back to her and react to her letter. Begin your letter with 'Dear Nikki.' You will be sharing these with your classmates."

Students write notes independently. Teacher facilitates any requests from students for English words to express concepts or ideas they have.

| TEACHER | STUDENT |
|---|---|

**II. Silent Reading (Reader Response):** "Poetry should first be heard, so I will read the poem aloud to you. Then you will read it to yourself. Then you will take turns with your partner reading the poem aloud. Poetry often takes several readings before you get a reaction" (metacognition).

Students listen, read silently, then orally. Students then write their letters to Nikki. The teacher monitors students who need assistance with English words for their letters. Students share letters.

**III. Discussion (Interpretive Community):** Teacher places students in prearranged quad groups (heterogeneous in terms of English language reading and writing proficiency, past opportunities to work together, gender, extravert/introvert) and instructs students to:

1. Read their letters to Nikki aloud, looking for any similarities in the responses.

2. Agree on one to three sentences that summarize what they think the girl is saying in her poem.

Students write summaries.

Teacher instructs the chair of each group to read the group's summary aloud to the class, then leads the students in arriving at a class interpretation of the poem.

**IV. Rereading:** "Based on our discussion and Nikki's advice, what do you think should be essential criteria of good biographies? Read the poem again. Discuss this in your groups."

Teacher leads entire-class debriefing for criteria; teacher writes criteria on the board. "We will use these criteria as we read biographies and eventually write a biography in this unit."

Students reread the poem; groups discuss. *Expected student responses:* accurate description of the events and surroundings in the person's life; accurate description of the person's feelings. Students copy criteria into notes.

### *Biographies and Biographers*

(The teacher selects from a list such as the following, being sure to include an appropriate number of subjects from the students' native countries, some Americans, and an equal representation of genders.)

*Jose Marti: Cuban Patriot and Poet* by David Goodnough

*Ronaldo: Soccer Sensation (Champion Sport Biographies)* by Mark Paddock

*Wayne Gretzky (Champion Sport Biographies)* by Michael Boughn and Joseph Romain

*Mia Hamm (Champion Sport Biographies)* by John Sharkey and Joseph Romain.

*Evelyn Cisneros: Prima Ballerina* by Charnon Simon

*Mark Twain: Legendary Writer and Humorist* by Lynda Pflueger

*Anna Chennault: Informal Diplomacy and Asian Relations* by Catherine Forslund

*The Wright Brothers: Inventors of the Airplane* by Wendie C. Old

*Quanah Parker, Comanche Chief* by William T. Hagan

*Louis Armstrong: King of Jazz* by Wendie C. Old

*Ida B. Wells: Woman of Courage* by Elizabeth Van Steenwyk

*Benjamin Banneker: Astronomer and Mathematician* by Laura Baskes

*Clara Barton: Angel of the Battlefield* by William Bains

*Holocaust Rescuers: Ten Stories of Courage* by Darryl Lyman

*Robert Mugabe of Zimbabwe* by Richard Worth

*Scientist and Astronaut: Sally Ride* by Marian Menzel and Mary Ellen Verheyden-Hilliard

*Madam C. J. Walker: Self-Made Businesswoman* by Della Yannuzzi

*Serena and Venus Williams (Champion Sport Biographies)* by Ken Sparling and Joseph Romain

*Bill Gates: Computer Programmer and Entrepeneur* by Lucia Raatma

*Scientist and Planner, Ru Chih Cheo Huang* by Scarlet Biro and Mary Ellen Verheyden-Hilliard

Lesson plan created by Gloria Neubert.

## CONTENT AREA: ENGLISH
## THE SUCCESSFUL JOB INTERVIEW

**Class:** English grade 12; average ability, most are not college bound. Some students work now, and most will be entering the work force after graduation. The class is lively and co-operative, providing they are actively engaged. Their instructional reading range is grade 8 to college.

**Unit Title:** The Business of English

**Topic:** The Successful Job Interview

### Goals

*High School English Core Learning Goals*

- Students will demonstrate the ability to compose in a variety of modes by developing content, employing specific forms, and selecting language appropriate for a particular audience and purpose.
- Students will demonstrate the ability to control language by applying the conventions of standard English in writing and speaking.

*Unit Goals*

- Students will gain a knowledge of various applications of English in the business world.
- Special emphasis will be placed on students learning the necessary skills to successfully compete for a job, including producing a résumé and cover letter and developing interviewing skills.

**Lesson Objectives:** The students will be able to:

1. Describe and practice the effective use of nonverbal messages and paraphrasing
2. Script and participate in a mock job interview, which will be videotaped, using the steps outlined in the reading
3. Analyze their own performance in the videotaped interview using the criteria from the reading to judge their performance in a short essay (250 words)
4. Identify the two steps to an interview and what each step includes by filling out the graphic organizer handout
5. Explain the reasoning behind each step and how it would benefit the person being interviewed

### Performance Assessment

*Objective*   *Assessment*

1. Concept development of nonverbal messages and paraphrasing; class participation; Rereading questions completed; Follow-Up activity; application of concepts during mock interviews
2. Follow-Up activity; mock interviews
3. Analysis and summary of mock interviews in an essay
4. Purpose-for-reading, filling out graphic organizer; class discussion of reading
5. Rereading questions dealing with rationale completed. Videotaped performance and written essay

**Macrostructure Thinking Skills:** Method analysis: How to interview for employment

### Materials

*Teacher*

- Copies of text for class
- VCR, television, four video camcorders
- Video of nonverbal communication

- An overhead projector, a screen, transparency pens
- Transparencies: Graphic organizer, purpose-for-reading chart, Rereading question
- Handouts: Graphic organizer, purpose-for-reading chart
- Newspaper employment section for each student
- Chalkboard and chalk

### *Student*
- Pen, paper, notebook
- Blank videotape to record interview
- Access to a typewriter or word processor

## Procedure

### I. Readiness

*a. Motivation (15 min):* "Virtually everyone has to work to support himself or herself, and that means a job, which means somewhere along the way everyone must apply for a job and go through the interview process. We have already worked on résumés and cover letters, which are valuable tools in landing a job, but what happens once you are in the door, during the interview, is just as important and will probably decide whether you get the job. This lesson will deal with the employment interview, and we will learn important skills and techniques necessary to have a successful interview. You will begin by looking in the employment section and selecting a job you would like to apply for." The teacher distributes newspapers to class.

"Select a position you feel you might be qualified for now or in the near future. It should be a position you know something about because you will be performing a mock interview for this job. If you have no experience, look for entry-level positions in an area you are interested in. Avoid minimum wage jobs that don't have any chance of advancement." The teacher instructs students to write down at least three potential jobs and any other information contained within the ad. Students look in newspapers and write down prospective job opportunities.

*Transition:* "Many of you have probably gone through this process of looking in the want ads and applying for a job, but you probably haven't examined the process in depth."

*b. Tapping and Developing Background (10 min):* Teacher taps students' background by asking them questions about their work experiences and what the interview process was like for them.

"How many of you work now or have had jobs in the past?" The majority of students respond by raising their hands. "Did any of you have to go to an interview before you got your job?" Many of the students respond by raising their hands.

The teacher calls on a number of students and asks them questions about their employment interviews.

"How did you feel? Were you nervous?"

"What did you wear to the interview?"

"Did you know anything about the company or job before the interview?" "Were there any questions you asked during the interview?"

"Was there anything specific you wanted to know?" Students give a variety of responses.

*Expected student responses:* I wasn't worried because I knew they were desperate for help and I would get the job; my friend, who works there, told me not to worry about what to wear because she had already put in a good word for me.

The teacher points out that these responses indicate a prior knowledge of the company and a personal reference respectively and that they are also important elements to the interview process.

*Transition:* "So we can see from our personal experiences how important prior knowledge of a company and personal references are to getting a job. We also studied the importance of a résumé and cover letter in previous lessons. Next we will examine a couple of communication skills introduced in this reading, which are very important to the interview process."

**c. *Concept Development/Vocabulary (25 min):*** "Let's examine nonverbal messages. We are going to watch a video segment without any sound, and I want you to list as many observations about the characters as you can. Please be prepared to explain your observations." The teacher plays the video with no sound. Students watch video and then in pairs develop a list of observations about the characters and their interactions. The teacher asks for students' observations and writes them on the chalkboard. Students give their observations to the teacher.

The teacher asks the students to give their reasons for their observations. The teacher probes for deeper insight when necessary with questions. "What is the relationship between the two characters? Is there a conflict between them? Is it resolved? What can you tell about the characters from their dress?" Students give their responses.

If the students' responses seem insufficient, the teacher plays the video again, but this time the students have the teacher's questions to guide them. Once a sufficient list is finished, the class develops a definition for *nonverbal messages* and makes a list of ways people communicate nonverbally.

*Expected student response:* Nonverbal messages are the messages you give to other people without using words. Often people are unaware of the nonverbal messages they give and receive. They can be given through dress, body language, facial expressions, or eye contact.

*Transition:* "Of course verbal messages are also important. Now we will examine a technique for improving and confirming your understanding whether you are reading a textbook or listening to an interviewer."

The teacher engages the class as a whole to prime them on *paraphrasing.* The teacher reads a series of three sentences pausing for a minute between each sentence. The students are directed to write what each sentence means in their own words quickly during the time provided. For this exercise the teacher uses the final paragraph of the reading. The teacher asks a few of the students to read what they have written. "We have now completed an exercise in paraphrasing. Can anyone give me a definition of *paraphrasing*?" The teacher writes the definition on the board as the class generates it.

*Expected student response:* To restate or reword the meaning of a sentence or phrase

"Can you think of a situation where paraphrasing could be useful?"

*Expected student response:* on a test, taking notes, on a report, to simplify something complicated

*Transition:* "In just a moment you will read the text. I want you to take note of how nonverbal messages and paraphrasing are used during an interview."

**d. *Purpose-for-Reading:*** "As you read the text 'The Employment Interview,' you are to fill in the chart I'm giving you to record the procedures involved in a positive employment interview. I want you to keep in mind that you will be using these procedures in your own mock interview later" (see Figure A.4).

**II. Silent Reading:** The students read silently and fill in their charts.

**III. Discussion (10 min):** The entire class discusses the chart while the teacher reveals the completed chart on the overhead as each answer is given.

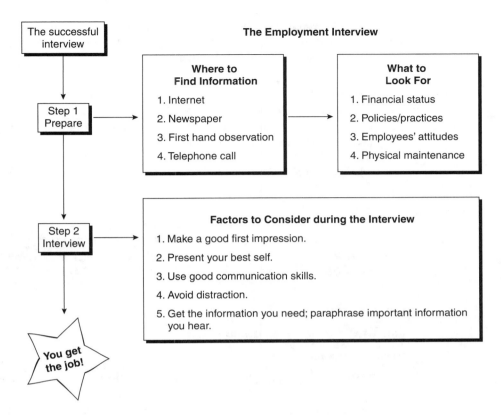

**FIGURE A.4    Chart for Employment Interview Lesson**

*Transition:* "Now that we have covered the basic parts of the interview process, I want you to go back and reexamine the reading and determine the rationale or reason for each part. I also want you to think about how you will apply these steps to your own mock interview."

**IV. Rereading (15 min):** The teacher shows the class a transparency of additional questions dealing with the rationale behind each of the steps (see Figure A.4, which includes student responses). The students are to work in heterogenous groups of three, which the teacher has previously assigned. The students write the answers to the questions in their notebooks and share their answers with the class.

*Transition:* "You should now all have the necessary tools to script your mock interviews. Please keep in mind the techniques we learned in this reading because I will expect you to demonstrate them during the simulation."

**V. Follow-Up (1–2 classes):** The students will script and participate in mock employment interviews. For this activity the students will divide into groups of three based on their selection of prospective jobs from the want ads earlier in the lesson. Students with similar interests will form groups where possible. The students are to apply the techniques they learned in this lesson during their simulated interviews. They should to refer to their résumés and use a cover letter to introduce themselves. The interviews will be videotaped so the students may view their own performances.

During the mock interview one student will operate the camera, another will act as the interviewer, and the third will be the interviewee. Students will take turns being interviewed. The students will script a part for the interviewer, which they will all use; however, the interviewee must perform without a script, although he or she will know what to expect. The teacher will review scripts to make sure they cover the necessary material and are in keeping with the nature of the activity.

*Transition:* Everyone has now participated in all parts of the interview process. I hope you have gained some skills and confidence that will be of use to you outside of school. To finish this lesson you will write a short essay summarizing your experience with the mock interview."

**VI. Summary:** After the mock interviews are finished, the students will write a short essay (250 words) summarizing what they did to prepare for the interview and analyzing their performance based on the criteria from the reading. They should explain each step they took, their reasoning, and the benefits derived from the process.

Lesson plan contributed by Curt Alford, June 1999.

---

## CONTENT AREA: FRENCH
## UNE ESCALE EXOTIQUE À LA MARTINIQUE

**Class Description:** High school, French III class; grades 10, 11, and 12

**Unit Title:** Un Voyage Autour du Monde aux Pays Francophones

**Topic of Lesson:** Martinique

**Unit Goal:** To bring authenticity to the study of French by reading and writing about the culture of Francophone countries

**Lesson Objectives:** By the end of the lesson, students will:

1. Write definitions for the following terms: *une escale, France d'Outremer, la pêche.*
2. Locate and tag Martinique on their Francophone maps
3. Interpret the literal level of the text on Martinique to identify location, climate, industries, government, connection to France, people, and distance from Baltimore
4. Locate information from the text and from www.martinique.org to complete the Francophone country comparison chart
5. Write-to-learn in French their opinions of the author's portrayal of the Martiniquais people

### Performance Assessment

| Objective | Assessment |
|---|---|
| 1. | Student-generated definitions in vocabulary *cahier* |
| 2. | Francophone maps collected and reviewed |
| 3. | Purpose-for-reading questions collected and reviewed |
| 4. | Francophone country comparison charts collected and reviewed |
| 5. | Written opinion paragraphs collected and reviewed |

**Macrostructure Thinking Skill:** Description

### Materials

- Lesson reading "Une escale exotique à la Martinique"
- Class world map
- Overheads: Eastern Caribbean map; cruise ship itinerary; list of Are/Aren't DOM countries; bear fishing from *Bear Shadow* by Frank Asch (New York: Scholastic, 1985)
- Francophone map
- Francophone country comparison chart
- Project list handout

# Procedure

**TEACHER**

## I. Readiness

*a. Motivation:* "To begin I want you to close your eyes as I take you on a guided tour. It is a comfortable 80 degrees, and the sun is brilliant in the sky. A nice breeze is blowing across your face. The birds are singing as you are strolling along a white, sandy beach. To your right is blue, blue water that is calm and inviting. You come across a man selling pineapples. Reggae music is playing in the background. He asks you in French if you would like some and you respond, yes. He cuts open the pineapple and the smell is intense and the flavor even more so as you bite into the pineapple. Now open your eyes and tell us where you imagined you were."

*b. Tapping and Developing Background*

*Transition:* You are in the eastern Caribbean, and this could be a scene from a vacation on Martinique, which will be our next destination on our trip around the world to Francophone countries. Nice change from our last trip to Montréal where it was so cold! Remember that trip?"

Use classroom world map. "Here we are in Baltimore. Who will show us where the Caribbean is in relation to Baltimore?

Martinique is a fairly small island in the Caribbean. Who will locate it for us from this map of the Eastern Caribbean shown on the overhead?

"Who in the class has ever been to the Caribbean or to Martinique?

"And who has ever been on a cruise?"

"Now everyone will have an opportunity to go to the Caribbean by taking a virtual tour of Martinique given by Martinique's tourist office website: www.martinique.org. While some of you are visiting the website, the rest of you should locate and tag Martinique on your Francophone countries map in your folders. Please check where you have marked Martinique with your *voisin*." Teacher circulates room to ensure that all students have correctly located and tagged Martinique on their Francophone country maps.

*c. Concept Development/Vocabulary*

*Transition:* "To understand the reading, we are going to develop a definition for three new words and concepts from the text we will be reading."

"Our first word is *une escale*. On the overhead is an itinerary for a cruise line in the Caribbean. From the itinerary, who will tell us where this ship will be stopping on its cruise?

"Each of these places is *une escale*. With your *voisin* discuss what definition you would give *une escale*.

**STUDENT**

*Expected student responses:* On vacation in Hawaii; in Jamaica; on a French island somewhere; in the Caribbean somewhere

Student volunteers and points the way south to the islands south of Florida.

Student volunteer locates Martinique on overhead map.

Students come up in small groups to sit through virtual tour. Other students work on maps checking it with their partners.

Students know that they are to get out their vocabulary *cahier* and sit with their *voisin* during introduction of new words. Vocabulary partners are one strong language student with one weaker language student.

Students respond: *Freeport, Antigua. . . .*

Students discuss with their partners possible definition in French for word plus translation. *Expected definitions:* port, harbor; place where cruise ships stop

| **TEACHER** | **STUDENT** |
|---|---|

"Exactly, *une escale* is a place where cruise ships stop. In English we refer to this as a 'port of call.' "

*Students write definition in French in* cahier.

Teacher now displays overhead with two lists of countries: La Guadeloupe, La Guyane, La Martinique, La Nouvelle Caledonie are in the right column, and Le Sénégal, Montréal, Le Maroc, and Le Belgique are in the left (concept attainment). "The countries listed in the right hand column are *France d'outremer* while the countries in the left hand column are not. Discuss with your *voisin* a possible definition for *France d'outremer.*" Teacher selects pairs.

*Expected student responses:* all places where French is spoken; all former colonies of France; all part of France

"Yes, these places have all those things in common and are referred to as *France d'Outremer.* Who will give us a definition of France d'Outremer?"

*Expected definition:* countries that are a part of France but are not in Europe

"Correct, the French often refer to these countries as the *DOM—departements outre-mer.* These are countries that are French—they have official *departement* status but are not located on mainland France."

"Our third word is *la pêche.* Now we already know *la pêche* as a fruit that we eat in the summer. Will someone share with us what *une pêche* is?"

*Expected student responses:* pear, peach.

"Yes, peach is one translation of *la pêche.* But it is also something else, and this is the definition that we want to focus on today. I am going to show you a picture with a caption and then you should discuss with your *voisin* a possible definition for *la pêche.*"

Students work in pairs and offer definition: *fishing.* This is agreed-on definition.

"Yes another definition for *la pêche* is fishing. When you *faire la pêche* that means to go fishing. What do you think *un pêcheur* is?" Teacher writes these words on the blackboard.

*Expected student responses:* fisherman

"Yes. Now with your *voisin* make sure you have all the definitions in your *cahiers.*"

Students complete filling in their notebooks with definitions.

### d. Purpose-for-reading

*Transition:* "Today you will be reading to be informed. As you read the following description of Martinique, complete the column for Martinique on your unit chart, 'Un Voyage Autour de Monde aux Pays Francophones.' (see Figure A.5). As you have done for France and Montreal, you will identify the location, climate, main industries, type of government, connection to France, people, and distance from our hometown, Baltimore."

"When you finish reading and completing your chart, write in French your personal response to the following: 'How do I feel about Martinique as a place to vacation? As a place to live permanently?' "

Students complete handout while reading the text.

"Before you start reading, however, take a few minutes to skim the reading and look at the pictures on each page. As you read, look at the pictures on each page and read the captions before you go on. The pictures will help you with some words you don't know and will help you to see what you are reading about"(metacognitive).

**FIGURE A.5   Unit Chart for Martinique Lesson**

Nom _____

### Un Voyage Autour de Monde Aux Pays Francophones Chart

|  | FRANCE | MONTREAL | MARTINIQUE | LA GUYANE |  |
|---|---|---|---|---|---|
| Location |  |  |  |  |  |
| Climate |  |  |  |  |  |
| Main Industries |  |  |  |  |  |
| Type of Government |  |  |  |  |  |
| Connection to France |  |  |  |  |  |
| People |  |  |  |  |  |
| Distance from Baltimore (in miles) |  |  |  |  |  |

**TEACHER**

**II. Silent Reading:** Students read silently in class. Teacher walks around the room and addresses any questions that the students may have. Teacher stops the students when they are about halfway through the reading and asks if they are finding the answers to the purpose-for-reading questions.

**III. Discussion:** Teacher asks several students to read their responses to the personal response question. Then students work with their *voisin,* verify their answers for the chart, and complete or change any responses they may have missed. After the pairs are finished, the class discussion to reach consensus on the chart information will begin. Responses should indicate to the teacher if the students have a literal grasp of the text read.

**IV. Rereading**

**1.** "As you described for your chart box on 'People,' the author paints a vivid description of the people of Martinique.

**STUDENT**

Students read and write their responses.

Students read orally from their journals.

Students complete the comparison chart.

Students work on writing-to-learn activity. Students turn in paragraph at the end of the activity.

**TEACHER**

**STUDENT**

They appear to be all the things that you just mentioned—friendly, happy, generous. But does this description seem to be realistic to you? You are to spend the next ten minutes writing your opinion, in French, of course, which either agrees or disagrees with the author's portrayal of the people of Martinique. You are to state your reasons on why you feel one way or another. You can use the French/English dictionary but try and use words that you know."

### V. Follow-Up

*Transition:* "We've had a great trip to Martinique but its not quite over. I have a list of projects that you can choose from to learn a little bit more about Martinique and its culture. You will have two weeks to complete the project and turn it in before we move on to our next destination: La Guyane."

Students look over list of projects and ask any questions that they may have about it.

*Project List*

1. Make your own *tapisserie* of something typical of Martinique.
2. Create a travel brochure for Martinique explaining why people should come and visit.
3. Create a promotional travel video for Martinique explaining why people should come and visit.
4. Research and write a 2- to 3-page paper on Josephine de Bonaparte's life on Martinique.
5. Cook a dinner containing Martiniquais ingredients and recipes. Serve it to your family. See me for authorization.
6. Write a fictional story about life on Martinique (2 to 3 pages or more).
7. Make up your own project. See me for approval.

*Summary*

To summarize, we're going to go around the room to each person and say in French why we would consider Martinique *une escale exotique*. Now in order for everyone not to use the same reason, I will write the reasons as they are used on the blackboard. We'll use the format: *Martinique est une escale exotique parceque* _____.

Students each give a one sentence reply in French of a reason Martinique is an exotic port of call:

*Il y a des bananes.*
*Il y a des fleurs exotiques.*
*On peut manger des ananas.*

Lesson contributed by Laurie Pham, June 2000.

## CONTENT AREA: HEALTH
## EATING DISORDERS

**Class Description:** Health, grades 10 and 11; heterogeneous in achievement; one half–credit course required for graduation.

**Unit:** Nutrition

**Topic:** Eating Disorders

**Unit Goals:** After completing the unit, students will:

1. Recognize that some people eat for reasons other than hunger
2. Recognize that some eating disorders are serious health problems that require psychological counseling

**Lesson Objectives:** The student will:

1. Define the terms *distorted body image* and *normal body image*
2. List the causes, effects, and characteristics of the three eating disorders
3. List ways to treat eating disorders
4. Explain steps to take if a friend or family member develops an eating disorder

**Performance Assessment**

*Objective    Assessment*

1.    Vocabulary oral responses
2.    Collection and review of graphic organizers; discussion responses
3.    Collection and review of graphic organizers; discussion responses
4.    Follow-up responses

**Macrostructure Thinking Skills:** Comparison and contrast, cause and effect

**Materials**

- One copy of Hautzig's novel, *Second Star to the Right.*
- Transparency: "How do you see yourself?"
- Transparency for vocabulary: *normal body image; distorted body image*
- Graphic organizer: "Eating Disorders"
- Article: "Treating Eating Disorders," *Scientific American,* March 2, 1998

# Procedure

## I. Readiness

*a. Motivation:* Read aloud Chapter 4 from the autobiographical novel, *Second Star to the Right,* by Deborah Hautzig, which describes her first experience with purging/vomiting to rid herself of food that would cause weight gain. At the conclusion, ask students to react orally to the reading.

*b. Tapping Background of Experience:* Ask students if they know of anyone with an eating disorder. Encourage students to share these stories if they wish. Be sure the accounts remain anonymous. Ask students what types of eating disorders they are familiar with (e.g., bulimia, anorexia, binge eating). Ask students what might cause people to develop eating disorders? (Strive for students to recognize the influence of the media on body image.) Ask students whether males or females are more susceptible to developing eating disorders. [*females*] Ask students why females have a greater risk than males.

*c. Developing Background of Experience:* Have students examine the transparency "How Do You See Yourself?" This transparency has a row of people from emaciated to very overweight. "The person who has an eating disorder may look like this [point to emaciated figure], but think that he or she looks like this person [point to very overweight figure]. Some types of eating disorders result from perception problems."

*Transition:* "In a moment, we will read about several types of eating disorders. Before we read, we need to learn a few new terms, so get out your vocabulary notebooks."

*d. Concept Development:* "You will work with your vocabulary partner. [Partners are pairs of one stronger reader with one weaker reader. Partners change each quarter.] I will now show you a list of sentences underneath the term *normal body image.* I will also show a list of sentences underneath the term *distorted body image.* [Show transparency with the list that follows.] Now with your partners, write a draft definition for each of these terms based on the information provided. Now check your definitions in the glossary of your textbook. Copy the glossary definitions into your notebooks."

*Normal Body Image*
I feel good about how I look.
I do not strive for absolute perfection in my appearance.
My self-worth is not based on how I look.

*Distorted Body Image*
I am too fat.
I must live up to other people's standards.

I will never look good enough.

**d.  Purpose-for-Reading:**  "You will be reading to be informed about the causes, effects, characteristics, and treatments for three major types of eating disorders: anorexia nervosa, bulimia, and obesity. You will gather this information on a graphic organizer that we will then use to compare and contrast the eating disorders. If you are reading from your textbook and do not understand some aspect, use one of your yellow sticky notes to mark the place (metacognitive). We will deal with these concerns later, or you may ask me as I circulate."

Teacher distributes the graphic organizer, "Eating Disorders," and displays it on the overhead. Review the labeled parts with the students and tell them to fill in the boxes as they read or after they read (see Table A.5).

**II.  Silent Reading:**  Students read silently and fill out the graphic organizer. Teacher circulates and assists students who have blank areas in their charts. Acknowledge any sticky

**TABLE A.5   Eating Disorders**

| | ANOREXIA NERVOSA | BULIMIA | COMPULSIVE EATING AND OVEREATING—OBESITY |
|---|---|---|---|
| Causes | ■ *emotional problems* | ■ *emotional problems* | ■ *emotional problems* |
| Effects | ■ *dry skin*<br>■ *brittle hair*<br>■ *loss of body fat*<br>■ *wasting away of muscle tissue*<br>■ *dehydration*<br>■ *fainting*<br>■ *irregular heartbeat*<br>■ *loss of menstrual periods*<br>■ *bones become less dense and can fracture easily* | ■ *open sores in mouths*<br>■ *red throats*<br>■ *tooth decay*<br>■ *anemia* | ■ *obesity*<br>■ *other health problems, e.g., heart problems and diabetes* |
| Characteristics | ■ *constant dieting*<br>■ *severe weight loss*<br>■ *illusion of being overweight (distorted body image)*<br>■ *exercise excessively*<br>■ *90% females*<br>■ *insecure*<br>■ *perfectionists* | ■ *eating large amounts of food, then purging through vomiting or use of laxatives*<br>■ *illusion of being overweight (distorted body image)*<br>■ *insecure*<br>■ *perfectionists*<br>■ *eat secretly*<br>■ *mostly females* | ■ *eat huge portions*<br>■ *eat large quantities of sweets and junk food*<br>■ *preoccupied with weight loss or gain* |
| Treatments | ■ *psychological counseling (body image treatment)*<br>■ *drug treatment (e.g., orexin)*<br>■ *Internet intervention* | ■ *psychological counseling (cognitive-behavioral treatment)*<br>■ *Internet intervention* | ■ *psychological counseling (self-help and therapist-led group, cognitive-behavioral treatment)*<br>■ *diet programs*<br>■ *gastric surgery* |

Expected student responses are in italics.

notes and help students to comprehend these sections. Call the attention of the students after ten minutes of reading to remind them to reread to find all the information needed to fill in the chart. Remind them that good comprehenders often have to go back and reread parts that they did not get the first time through (metacognition).

**III. Discussion:** First have students work in triads which the teacher has planned based on heterogeneous grouping by reading achievement level, using the class profile results of the DRP test. Seven triads have one student on an independent level, one student on an instructional level, and one on a frustration level. One triad is composed of three excellent readers who can read the material independently and who read very quickly. They will work together on a separate reading taken from *Scientific American* that deals with the discovery of hormones that might affect the treatment of eating disorders.

Teacher then conducts an entire-class discussion while filling in the responses on a transparency of the graphic organizer. Students who have also read the research article will contribute that information when treatments are discussed.

Conclude by having students note similarities and differences among the three types of eating disorders.

*Expected student responses:*
1. All caused by emotional problems
2. Anorexia and bulimia victims have distorted body images
3. Anorexia and bulimia usually affect woman (media and cultural pressure)
4. All three eating disorders can be helped by psychological counseling

**IV. Rereading:** "Review your graphic organizer charts and the text reading and decide which eating disorder you think is most dangerous. Why? Cite evidence from the reading to support your opinion. Write your response in your journal." Have students make their decisions first independently, then take a class vote. Have various students justify their decisions by citing evidence from the texts.

**V. Follow-Up/Homework/Extension:** "People suffering from these eating disorders usually try to hide what they are doing concerning eating. What do you think might be signals to family members or friends that a person has an eating disorder?"

"If you discover that a friend or relative has an eating disorder, what should you do? Where do you go for help?" Do a search on the classroom computer using Netscape or AOL Health. Show the students the various search results for "Eating Disorder Support Groups" and "Treatment Clinics and Centers for Eating Disorders." Ask for volunteers to visit these sites that evening (at home or at library) and bring back a report the next day to the class members.

---

Lesson plan adapted from the work of Lauren Wilensky, 1999.

## CONTENT AREA: HEALTH
## SEXUALLY TRANSMITTED DISEASES: AIDS

**Class Description:** Health, grades 10 through 12. Class meets for 90 minutes every other day to fulfill the ½ credit that is required for health education. This lesson addresses AIDS, the first topic in the unit, Sexually Transmitted Diseases. Previous units that the class has completed are mental and emotional health, personal hygiene, and nutrition. The lesson is centered around a class reading. The difficulty of the reading for students was established using the cloze procedure, and the results are reported as follows:

- Independent level: 2 students
- Instructional level: 16 students
- Frustration level: 6 students

**Unit Title:** Sexually Transmitted Diseases

**Lesson Topic:** AIDS

**Health Education Learning Outcomes**

*Family Life and Human Sexuality*

- Abstinence from sexual intercourse is a healthy, safe, and responsible decision for adolescents.
- There are sexual behaviors that place individuals at risk for disease.

*Disease Prevention*

- Behaviors and age impact health maintenance and disease prevention.
- Personal health behaviors influence the functioning of the body systems, including the immune system.
- There are ways to prevent, diagnose, and treat HIV/AIDS.

**Unit Goals:** After completion of the unit, students will:

1. Understand the importance of "Just say no"
2. Understand the importance of safe sex

**Lesson Objectives:** The students will be able to:

1. State the meaning of the acronym AIDS
2. Define *semen, vaginal secretions, lymph glands, Kaposi's sarcoma,* and *abstinence*
3. Determine:
   - Four ways in which HIV/AIDS can and cannot be transmitted.
   - Twelve symptoms of HIV
   - Two opportunistic infections associated with HIV/AIDS
   - Two modes of protection against HIV/AIDS
4. Use song lyrics to develop a role-play that incorporates protection skills against HIV
5. Complete a writing-to-learn activity that outlines the causes, symptoms, complications, and protection techniques surrounding HIV/AIDS

**Performance Assessment**

*Objective*   *Assessment*

1. Oral responses of students as we discuss the meaning of the acronym AIDS
2. Vocabulary responses in pairs and in class discussions
3. Completion of graphic organizers
4. Observation of student role-play dialogues
5. Collection and scoring of writing-to-learn activity

**Macrostructure Thinking Skills:** Simple listing, cause and effect, problem and solution, comparison and contrast

**Materials**

- Story of Christopher (Claire Amundsen Schaeffer, http://freegraphic.com/images/downloads/worldaids/index.html)
- Transparency: human immunodeficiency virus (HIV in Your School workshop, Baltimore City Public Schools)
- Reg's story ("World AIDS Day 2001: A local man and woman share daily struggles of living with AIDS," *The Journal of Martinsburg* [WV])
- Transparencies: Kaposi's sarcoma (1995 Cornell University Medical College, http://edcenter.med.cornell.edu/CUMCPathNotes/Dermpath/3604.GIF)
- *EarthShine* by T. Nelson. New York: Orchard Books, 1994.
- Transparency: neck lymph gland drainage (www.24dr.com/reference/pictures/lymphneck.htm)
- AIDS directed reading

- AIDS graphic organizer
- Transparencies: "How is the HIV spread/HIV is not spread by" (HIV in Your School workshop, Baltimore City Public Schools)
- "She Thinks His Name Was John" song lyric handout (written by Sandy Knox and Steve Rosen)
- "She Thinks His Name Was John" CD (performed by Reba McIntyre)
- CD player

# Procedure

## I. Readiness

*a. Motivation:* Begin by reading the story of Christopher, age 32, to the class. This account describes the state of Christopher and his room (once a dining room) in his last days, dying of AIDS. Students listen and envision what the author is describing. "What did you feel as I was reading that passage?"

*Expected student responses:* sadness, anger, fear, confusion, helplessness.

*Transition:* "The disease that was making Christopher so sick was AIDS. There are many feelings and emotions that we can associate with this disease, but I want us to understand AIDS objectively."

*b. Tapping and Developing Background of Experience:* "I know that many of you have learned about AIDS in other classes. Who can tell us what AIDS stands for?"

*Expected student response:* acquired immunodeficiency syndrome (written on board)

"AIDS is caused by HIV, a virus much like the one you get when you catch a cold. HIV is, however, much more serious than a cold, of course. Here is a picture of what HIV looks like. You should remember that the actual virus is so small that it cannot be seen by the naked eye. This picture was made with the use of powerful microscopes." Allow students to view the HIV transparency. This will help to promote their "movie of the mind." Students view the transparency and sketch their own version into their notes.

"It is alarming how quickly the number of AIDS cases is increasing. Look at the chart on the transparency [see Table A.6]. This shows the AIDS case rate per 100,000 population, by state, reported through December 1998."

*Transition:* "Now that we know what HIV actually looks like, we are almost ready to start our reading, which will give us even more information about AIDS and HIV. Let's prepare for our reading by going over some new vocabulary words."

*c. Concept Development/Vocabulary:* During this section of the lesson, the teacher will pronounce each word initially. A strategy will be used so that students can find a meaning to words inductively. Students will pair up with their vocabulary partners and turn to the

**TABLE A.6   Transparency for AIDS Rate of Increase**

| STATE | AIDS CASES | RATE OF INCREASE |
|---|---|---|
| 1. Washington, D.C. | 989 | 189.1 |
| 2. New York | 8,714 | 47.9 |
| 3. Florida | 5,448 | 36.5 |
| 4. Maryland | 1,639 | 31.9 |
| 5. New Jersey | 2,134 | 26.3 |

vocabulary section in their notebooks. Partners consist of a stronger and weaker reader. Students will first work in pairs to develop a draft definition. Then the entire class will discuss and formulate a class definition. The teacher has developed a preplanned definition to ensure accuracy.

### Vocabulary Words and Preplanned Definitions

- **Semen:** Whitish fluid that is discharged from the penis during orgasm that contains sperm, white blood cells, and fluid
- **Vaginal secretions:** Fluid that provides moistness and lubrication to the vagina
- **Lymph glands (lymph nodes):** Small sacs within the human body that are part of the immune system; help destroy all infections that could cause harm to the body.
- **Opportunistic pathogen:** Germs that cause disease in a person with a weakened immune system. These germs do not cause disease in healthy people.
- **Kaposi's sarcoma:** Form of cancer that most often causes purple spots on the skin of AIDS patients; an example of an opportunistic pathogen
- **Abstinence:** choosing not to engage in sexual intercourse.

Students will use the following chart to develop a definition for *semen*.

| *Todd believes that the following are traits that describe* **semen.** *Unfortunately, Todd has the wrong idea about what* **semen** *is.* | *Tamara is correct when she states that the following* are *characteristics of* **semen.** |
| --- | --- |
| Composed of only water | Whitish fluid |
| Contains lots of bacteria | Contains sperm |
| Painful when it is discharged | Is discharged from the penis |
| Discharged at any time | Is discharged during ejaculation |

Students will work with their partners in order to develop a draft definition. Students will use the following chart to develop a definition for *vaginal secretions*.

| *Renee is not correct when she assumes that the following are traits of* **vaginal secretions.** | *Reggie is correct when she says that the following are the right terms to describe* **vaginal secretions.** |
| --- | --- |
| An abnormal fluid | Used to moisten the vagina |
| Used to fight off sperm | Slippery fluid |
| Means that someone has an STD | Is normal in all females |

"For our next word, think back and remember the game, Pac-man. As you remember, I want you to pretend that the actual Pac-man is what we call a *lymph gland,* or *Lymph node.* Can you see in your mind Pac-man moving up and down eating all the little pills as it goes? The little pills can be compared to unhealthy germs and infectons that are in our bodies. When germs enter our bodies, the *lymph glands* act like Pac-man, giving our bodies protection."

Show students the transparency of the *lymph glands*. Allow students to view the transparency to develop a sense of what the *lymph glands* look like. Teacher also shows students the position of *lymph glands* on his or her neck.

Students will work with their partners to develop a draft definition.

Read the following sentence from Reg's Story to begin concept development for the next term: *opportunistic pathogen.* "Reg says *opportunistic pathogens,* which can attack certain systems in his body because of the deterioration of his immune system, are things that he must be careful of because they can become very serious."

Also give students the following examples:

1. Sean has a weakened immune system, due to a disease that he has had for years. He has to be very careful that he does not come into contact with *opportunistic pathogens* that would make him even sicker.

2. Darnel does not have to worry about *opportunistic pathogens* because his immune system is already very healthy.

Students will work with their partners to develop a draft definition.
    Read the following passage from *EarthShine*.

> But now—well the auditions just haven't been coming up like they used to. Nobody's really said it's because he doesn't look the same, but I know that's what it is, I mean, what with all that weight he's lost. Plus, some of the medicine he's had to take has made a lot of his hair fall out, and he's got these brownish red splotches on his face. He calls them beauty marks, but they're really a kind of cancer really—*Kaposi's Sarcoma*—lots of PWA's (patients with AIDS) have them.

Allow students to view the *Kaposi's sarcoma* picture transparencies as a visual. Students will work with their partners to develop a draft definition. Allow students to use the following sentences to develop a definition for *abstinence*.

1. Tina chooses to practice *abstinence* so that she does not get pregnant before she is ready.
2. Molly knows that using condoms is a good way to protect herself from disease, but she believes that *abstinence* is even safer.
3. Winston has a great part-time job and is very busy with school. He believes that having sex right now would just bring too many complications, so he chooses to practice *abstinence*.

Students will work with their partners to develop a draft definition.

*Transition:* "Now that we have learned all the necessary vocabulary words, we will now begin our reading for the day."

d. ***Purpose-for-Reading:*** "Today you will be reading to be informed. After reading the article, you will compare and contrast the ways a person can and cannot acquire HIV. You will also list the symptoms of AIDS, possible diseases that are caused by AIDS, and prevention techniques for AIDS. In essence, you will be dealing with the cause of AIDS, effects of AIDS, and current solutions for AIDS. Use the graphic organizer [see Figure A.6] to record your answers. You will be using your new vocabulary in completing your graphic organizer."

**II. Silent Reading (15 minutes):** Students read silently and fill out graphic organizers. Approximately halfway through the Silent Reading time, the teacher will ask students to stop and turn to their neighbors. Students will retell what they have read so far to their partners. Students will also note the new vocabulary words they have read and how they are incorporated as responses in their graphic organizers.

**III. Discussion (10 minutes):** The class will have a discussion regarding the information on the graphic organizers. Student responses are specified on graphic organizer (Figure A.6).

*Transition:* "Now that we have more knowledge about AIDS and HIV, let's go back and see if we can answer some other questions."

**IV. Rereading (10 minutes):** Students will work with partners to answer the following questions. Groups are formed so that each reader at frustration level is working with readers who are at either independent or instructional level.

1. Your neighbor, Sophia, is starting her new job at the local dentist's office. You know that Sophia has also been having sex with her boyfriend for months now. On the way home from school today, Sophia mentions how nervous she is about working with all the blood and saliva. She is afraid she might get AIDS. What would you say to Sophia? Do you have any advice for her regarding her new job or her relationship with her boyfriend?

    *Expected student responses:* Sophia should be more concerned about acquiring HIV or AIDS through sexual contact with her boyfriend; she can protect herself at work by

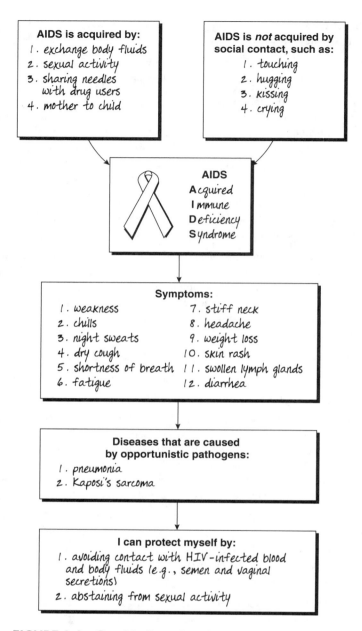

**FIGURE A.6     Graphic Organizer for AIDS Lesson**

wearing gloves and masks; She should treat every patient with caution, since you cannot tell by looking at someone if they are HIV-positive; she should practice abstinence if she if she truly wants to be protected from HIV.

2. You find out that the new teammate on your recreation-league basketball team is HIV-positive. Some of the other players want to quit. What would you do?

*Expected student response:* This question is personal, so there can be no expected response. It is even possible to tell students that they may mark "Do not read" if they want to protect their anonymity. Some students may feel that they will be judged if they answer a certain way. The important task is for students to examine their own values regarding the AIDS issue without being marked for a right or wrong answer.

**3.** List occupations that you think are at high risk for acquiring HIV and how transmission might be possible.

*Expected student responses:*

Doctor or dentist (body fluid contact)
Nurse (body fluid contact)
Phlebotomist (body fluid contact, needle sticks)
Paramedic (body fluid contact, needle sticks)
Any other occupation that comes into contact with the fluids that transmit HIV and AIDS

*Transition:* "We will now listen to a song that has a very real message about AIDS and HIV."

**V. Follow-Up:** Teacher will play the CD recording of "I Think His Name Was John." Students will be asked to create a role-play at the end of the song. This role-play should be a dialogue between the two characters in the song, the AIDS patient and John. Students should address how the woman in the song could have changed her situation to avoid becoming infected with HIV. In other words, what could she have done differently? Encourage creativity! Allow students to address the "real and ugly" issues that are part of the character's situation, that is, alcohol and unprotected sex with a stranger. However, students should use mature language and avoid vulgarity.

Before asking students to begin working on the role-plays, pose the following questions: "Why do you think that the writer of this song titled it 'She thinks his name was John?' What is the significance of the title and how does it relate to the topic of HIV and AIDS?" Students should respond to these questions in their health journals.

*Expected student response:* The writer of the song uses this title to emphasize the importance of protection against HIV/AIDS. It is a powerful disease that can happen to anyone, with one irresponsible act. The character in the song lost her whole life to someone whose name she cannot even remember.

Students will listen to the song. They may also use the written song lyric handout to follow along. Students will then work with their partners from the previous activity to create the role-play. Students will present their role-plays to one other group in the class.

**Summary:** Instruct students to complete the following writing-to-learn activity as a summary of today's lesson. Students should refer to the rubric for assignment criteria.

"Pretend that you are the first American physician to visit Mars. You have been asked by the Martians to give a speech on AIDS and HIV. They are very interested in learning about the disease and how they can protect their public. You can use this opportunity to explain AIDS in your own words and discuss anything that you feel is really important for the Martians to know. Be sure to include information from your graphic organizers."

### Scoring Rubric

#### 5 points
- Includes well-written introduction and summary paragraphs
- Includes four well-developed supporting paragraphs
- Cites examples from the article and graphic organizer in every supporting paragraph
- No grammatical errors
- Incorporates creativity

#### 4 points
- Includes well-written introduction and summary paragraphs
- Includes three well-developed supporting paragraphs
- Cites examples from the article and graphic organizer in most supporting paragraphs
- Few grammatical errors
- Incorporates creativity

*3 points*
- Includes introduction and summary paragraphs
- Includes two supporting paragraphs
- Cites at least two examples from the article and graphic organizer
- Several grammatical errors
- Incorporates some creative aspects

*2 points*
- Includes some attempt at introduction and summary statements
- Includes one supporting paragraph
- Cites at least one example from the article and graphic organizer
- Many grammatical errors
- Little creativity demonstrated

*1 point*
- No evidence of introduction or summary paragraphs
- Little or no evidence of supporting paragraphs
- Does not cite examples from article and graphic organizer
- Excessive grammatical errors
- No creative aspects

*0 points*
- No response to question

---

Lesson plan contributed by Erin Stevens, December 2001.

## CONTENT AREA: MATHEMATICS
## LINE, BAR, AND PIE GRAPHS

**Class Description:** Heterogeneous, general math class, grade 6. The students' reading achievement levels vary from below average to slightly above average. The class is skewed with low-ability students.

**Unit Title:** Graphs, Tables, and Charts

**Topic of Lesson:** Line, Bar, and Pie Graphs

**Core Learning Goal**
1. The student will collect, organize, analyze, and present data

**Unit Goals:** Students will be able to:
1. Form line, bar, and pie graphs from given data
2. Interpret line, bar, and pie graphs

**Lesson Objectives:** After completing the unit, students will:
1. Define the following words: *constant* and *adjacent*
2. Collect and organize various types of data from the class into a table
3. Form a bar, pie, and line graph based on collected data
4. Interpret results of the graphs
5. Explain in writing when it is appropriate to use each type of graph
6. Apply their knowledge of graphs by forming two graphs based on the tiger population worksheet, and by interpreting results in a letter format

## Performance Assessment

*Objective*   *Assessment*

1. Writing defined terms in vocabulary notebooks
2. Graphic organizers collected and reviewed
3. Graph worksheets collected and reviewed
4. Discussion
5. Journals collected
6. Student letters collected

**Macrostructure Thinking Skills:** Definition, comparison and contrast

## Materials

- Bar graph for board
- Sample graphs taken from newspapers, magazines, web sources, and websites
- Overhead paragraph for "constant"
- Graphic organizer for silent reading
- Chart worksheet
- Graph worksheet
- Transparency on tiger population, "Animal Info—Tiger" (www.animalinfo.org/species/carnivor/panttigr.htm)
- Unit material ("Graphs" reading)

# Procedures

## I. Readiness

*a. Motivation:* Have a line graph entitled "Duration of Bus Ride per Mile to School" on the board. Allow the students 1–2 minutes to look at it as they take their seats. "Who rides the bus to school?" Students raise their hands. "Who would like to tell us how long their bus ride is? [*y minutes*] By looking at this chart, we could figure out that you live *x* miles from school." Ask 2–4 students for the time they spend on the bus and determine miles they live from school.

*Transition:* "This is an example of a graph. Graphs can be used to show us different types of data. For example, I could have drawn a line graph showing how long it would take to walk to school, depending on how far away you lived. We could even make a graph based on characteristics of this class, such as the percentage of those with red, brown, and blonde hair."

*b. Tapping and Developing Background of Experience:* "Where else outside of school have you seen a graph like this?"

> *Expected student responses:* newspaper, television, or other classes

Pass around laminated examples of graphs taken from various magazines, newspaper articles, pamphlets, and websites. "As you look at these, try to determine what data they are using and any conclusions you can make." Students examine graphs.

*Transition:* "Today we're going to learn how to form different types of graphs with information that is given to us. Before we start reading, there are two words we need to understand the meaning of. You will need to move next to your vocabulary partner now and have your mathematics vocabulary notebook out on your desk." Vocabulary partners are formed each quarter. Partners are one strong and one weak student based on reading and math achievement, as well as the personality characteristics of diligence and self-discipline.

*c. Concept Development*

*Initial Learning:* Show the following paragraph on an overhead and read the passage to the students.

> It is Saturday morning and your family piles into your red minivan for your yearly trip to Kings Dominion. You cannot control yourself. You lick your lips while dreaming of

all the junk food that you will eat. You can hardly wait to claim your regular seat in the front car of the Anaconda. Your excitement, however, slowly turns to frustration when you realize your father is driving. He drives incredibly slowly. In fact, he drives so slowly that you are sure you could get there faster by running. As you merge onto the highway, you watch your father set the cruise control at 40 miles per hour! Much to your horror, he maintains 40 miles an hour the entire way there. His speed remains *constant*.

"With your partner, draft a definition of *constant*." Call on a pair to report its definition; revise as needed.

*Expected definition:* something that remains the same

"Please write this definition in your vocabulary section of your notebook."

Use concept attainment to define *adjacent*. "The next word we are going to define is *adjacent*. I need a few volunteers to come to the front to help me with this word. Please raise your hand if you would like to volunteer." Students raise their hands. "Okay, Janet, Clelia, Jack, and Tamon, please come up. Janet and Clelia, you stand this way [near one another, almost touching]. Jack and Tamon, you stand this way [at opposite parts of the room]. Janet and Clelia are standing *adjacent* to each other. Jack and Tamon are not. With your partner, define *adjacent*."

*Expected definition:* next to, beside

"Please write this definition in your vocabulary notebook."

*Review:* "Before we read, we need to review two terms we learned several lessons ago: *independent variable* and *dependent variable*. Turn to your partner and explain each. Refer to your vocabulary notebook for the definitions and examples to confirm and adjust your recall."

*Transition:* "Now that we understand these words, we can begin the reading."

**d. Purpose-for-Reading:** Pass out the "Graphs" reading and graphic organizer. "Today, you will read to be informed. You will learn how to make and interpret different graphs, but first you will read to determine characteristics of the three types of graphs. Silently read the selection and complete the graphic organizer."

"Math books can be difficult to read. If you are reading a part and you do not understand it, try rereading. If that fails to help you, put a sticky note on the top of that page. As I circulate, I will look for sticky notes, and stop at your desk to try to help you" (metacognition).

**II. Silent Reading:** Students read silently and complete the organizer while the teacher circulates to help with questions.

**III. Discussion:** "Please turn to your partner and review the characteristics of the different graphs you listed on your graphic organizer [the students are seated in groups of two facing the front, a seating arrangement that is modified on a regular basis based on individual differences and sometimes ability]. Be sure that you and your partner understand each characteristic you wrote on your graphic organizer." Students discuss in groups.

*Line Graph:* "Who can tell us what the characteristics of a line graph are?" Teacher writes students responses on the graphic organizer (see Figure A.7). Pass out worksheets with tables for the students to collect data in and the corresponding worksheet for the students to draw their graphs on.

"Let's do an example of a line graph. We're going to look at the length of time it takes to complete math homework, which depends on the amount of homework given."

| NUMBER OF PROBLEMS ASSIGNED | TIME SPENT |
|---|---|
| 0 | |
| 5 | |
| 10 | |
| 15 | |

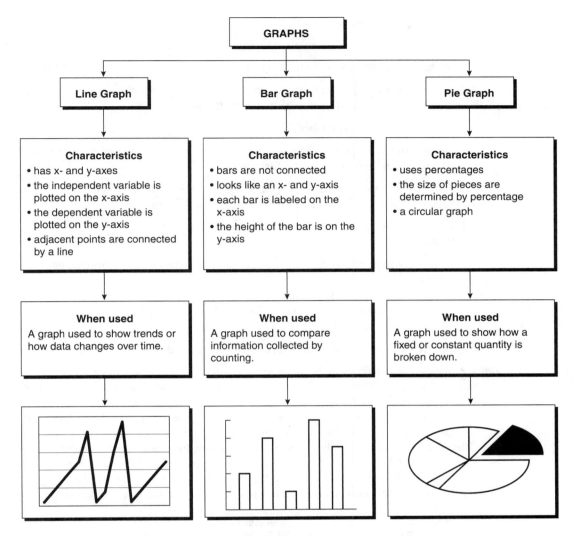

**FIGURE A.7    Graphic Organizer for Line, Bar, and Pie Graphs**

"If you were assigned no homework, how long would it take to complete?"

*Expected student response:* no time

Teacher writes this data on the table on the overhead. "If you were assigned 5 problems (of average difficulty), how long do you think it would take to complete?"

*Expected student response:* 30 minutes

Teacher writes this data on a table on the overhead. "If you were assigned 10 problems (of average difficulty), how long do you think it would take?"

*Expected student response:* 1 hour and 15 minutes

Teacher writes this data on a table on the overhead. "If you were assigned 15 problems (of average difficulty), how long do you think it would take?"

*Expected student response:* 2 hours

Teacher writes this data on a table on the overhead. "Please enter this data on the chart I have given you. When you draw the line graph, what is the dependent variable?"

*Expected student response:* time it takes to do the homework

"What is the independent variable?"

*Expected student response:*  number of problems assigned

"So what goes on the *x*-axis (horizontal line) and what goes on the *y*-axis (vertical line)?"

*Expected student response:*  The amount of homework goes on the horizontal *x*-axis and the time it takes to do homework goes on the vertical *y*-axis.

"Who can tell us how you label the *x*-axis?"

*Expected student response:*  You would label the *x*-axis with the number of homework problems. So 0 would be the first number.

"Right, but 0 is the point at which the *x*-axis and the *y*-axis connect. So your next point would be 5, then 10, then finally 15. Who can tell us how to label the *y*-axis?"

*Expected student response:*  That would also start at 0, but then it would be 30, 90, 120 minutes.

"Please work in pairs and draw the line graph for this data." Teacher circulates to answer questions.

"Which team would like to show us what they came up with?" Team draws its graph on the board. "What does this line chart show us? That is, what can we conclude about homework and time?"

*Expected student response:*  The more homework we get, the longer it takes to complete.

**Bar Graph:**  "The next graph we're going to look at is a bar graph. What are some characteristics of a bar graph?" Teacher writes student responses on graphic organizer. "Let's draw an example of a bar graph. We are going to count all class members and group them into categories based on their hair color. First let's count how many students have blonde hair." Students count the number of students with blonde hair. "Who can tell us how many students have blonde hair?" Students reply. "Please enter this number in your table." Students enter number into their tables. "Now, please work with your partner and do the same for red-, black-, and brown-haired students and enter those numbers in the appropriate places in your table for hair color." Students count the number of students with each type of hair color.

| HAIRCOLOR | NUMBER OF STUDENTS |
|---|---|
| Blonde | |
| Black | |
| Brown | |
| Red | |
| Total number of students | |

"Now that we have this data, we will make a graph to illustrate it. The *x*- and *y*-axis are both numbered the same as in a bar graph, but it is a little different. Who can tell us why it is different?"

*Expected student response:*  The adjacent points in a line graph are connected, but the ones in a bar graph are not.

"Who can tell us what your bar graph should look like?"

*Expected student response:*  There should be bars going up from the *x*-axis.

"Work with your partner to complete the bar graph using the data you just collected." Circulate and answer questions. After five minutes: "Which team will draw its bar chart on the board for us? What does this type of graph show us?"

*Expected student response:*  It compares the number of counted data.

*Pie Graph:* "The next graph we are going to discuss is a pie graph. Who will tell us the characteristics of the pie graph?" Teacher writes student responses on graphic organizer.

"Let's work through an example of a pie graph now. The data we are going to use is clothing. First, anyone who is wearing jeans, raise your hand." Teacher counts the hands and enters them on the table on the overhead. This process is repeated for people wearing skirts, pants, shorts, and other.

| CLOTHING | NUMBER OF STUDENTS | PERCENTAGE |
|---|---|---|
| Pants | | |
| Shorts | | |
| Skirt | | |
| Jeans | | |
| Other | | |
| Total number of students | | |

"Who can tell us how to figure the percentage of people wearing jeans?"

*Expected student response:* You divide the number of people wearing jeans by the total number of students in the class and multiply by 100.

"Please work in pairs to determine the rest of the percentages and enter those numbers in your table." Students work in pairs to figure percentages and they enter the percentages in their table. "Who can tell us what the percentage of students wearing skirts is?" Students reply. This process is repeated until all percentages have been verified as correct.

"What does the shape of a pie graph look like?"

*Expected student response:* It is a circle.

"How does it show how a fixed quantity is broken down?"

*Expected student response:* It is divided into pieces, and the sizes of the pieces are determined by their percentages.

"Good. Now in your teams, complete the pie graph for the data we collected." Students work in pairs to complete the pie graph. Teacher circulates to answer any questions.

"Which team will draw its graph on the board?" Team draws its graph. "Who can tell us what this pie chart shows us?"

*Expected student response:* It shows us the percentage of students who wear certain clothes to school.

"If I was a clothing manufacturer, what might this tell me?"

*Expected student response:* It would tell you that many kids wear jeans, but not as many wear something from the "other" category. Stop producing the "other."

"There are five sets of data described at the end of the chapter you have just read. With your partners, decide what type of graph—line, bar, or pie—would be appropriate to display each set of data."

*Transition:* "As we can see, graphs are used to express a variety of data. We have used them for displaying the number of students with certain characteristics in the class and for showing the impact the number of homework problems has on time needed to complete them."

**IV. Rereading (Generalization):** "Take out your math journal and, using the text information and what you learned from our discussion, write when it is appropriate to use each type of graph—line, bar, pie. Use this sentence starter for each type: 'I would use a _____ graph to show . . .'"

When students have completed their entries, discuss these generalizations and have students record the answers on their graphic organizers. Teacher writes student responses on graphic organizer.

**V. Follow-Up:** Pass out chart on tiger population. "The tiger is an endangered species. Who can tell us what an *endangered species* is?"

>*Expected student response:* It is an animal that is in danger of becoming extinct.

"Good. Does anyone know of any endangered species?"

>*Expected student response:* Elephants, pandas, some bats, are all endangered.

"Good. Does anyone know why these species are becoming endangered?"

>*Expected student response:* People kill them for their body parts. People are destroying their homeland, and this also causes them to die.

"Good. As some of you may know, tigers are also endangered. The primary reason they are endangered is that people kill them for their body parts. This is called *poaching*. The people who kill the tigers are called *poachers*. I am passing out a chart, and as you can see, it lists the tiger population, first by year, then by country. Take a few minutes to look it over. As you can see, the first column lists their population by year. The second column lists their population by country, but each country is subdivided by year. Who can tell us what kind of graphs you could use to express this information?"

>*Expected student response:* You could use all of them.

"Good. For homework, you will design two graphs based on this material. Next, write a letter to a friend or relative discouraging or encouraging them to support a tiger aid charity. Include your graphs and interpret their meaning for support."

---

Lesson contributed by Melissa Brothers, July 2000.

---

## CONTENT AREA: MATHEMATICS
## PROBLEM-SOLVING STRATEGIES

**Class Description:** Algebra I; heterogeneous in achievement; grades 9 and 10. Their reading achievements range from below to slightly above average. The topic is taught in the first quarter of the year. Students sit at desks in rows, and each student is assigned a partner (the student sitting next to them). Partner assignments are based on reading and math achievement (heterogeneous), learning styles, and gender preferences. Pairings are reassigned twice a quarter.

**Unit Title:** Introduction to Algebra I

**Topic of Lesson:** Problem-Solving Strategies

**Core Learning Goal:** The student will apply addition, subtraction, multiplication, and division of algebraic expressions to mathematical and real-world problems.

**Unit Goal:** The student will be able to solve word problems using algebraic models.

**Lesson Objectives:** Students will be able to:
1. Define *reasonable* and *algebraic model*
2. List the steps used to solve specific problems

3. Write algebraic models to find solutions to word problems
4. Use inductive reasoning to list the five steps to problem-solving (word problems)

## Performance Assessment

*Objective*   *Assessment*

1. Oral responses during Concept Development/Vocabulary activities
2. Graphic organizer 1 reviewed; oral responses during discussion
3. Oral responses during discussion; Follow-up homework assignment
4. Graphic organizer 2 reviewed; oral responses during discussion

**Macrostructure Thinking Skills:** Chronological order: list steps used to solve specific problems. Students will use comparison skills (inductive reasoning) and these steps to write a general problem-solving plan.

## Materials

- *Math Curse* by Jon Scieszka and Lane Smith (illustrator).
- Graphic organizer 1 for Silent Reading "A Problem-Solving Plan"
- Graphic organizer 2 for Rereading "Steps to Solving Algebraic Word Problems"
- Transparencies

# Procedure

## I. Readiness

*a. Motivation:* "Today we are going to continue our introduction to algebra by studying how it can be used in real life and how algebra can help you become a better problem solver and decision maker. How many of you earn an allowance from your parents?" Students raise their hands. "How much do you receive each month? [*x dollars*] Does anyone get an amount based on how much work you do?" Some students nod their heads.

"Let's imagine that each of you is given a monthly allowance of $9.95, but for every extra chore you do, you earn an extra $1.67. Next month you want to have $35.00. [Problem is also on a transparency.] Turn to your row partner and discuss different ways you might find the answer. No calculators please; I don't want you to actually find the answer yet. Simply discuss the process or procedures you might use." Students discuss in pairs while the teacher circulates throughout the room to aid with questions."

"It seems like most of you have come up with a couple of ways to figure this out."

*Expected student responses:* Add $1.67 to $10.00 over and over until you get $35.00; subtract $10.00 from $35.00 and then divide by $1.67.

"You probably have figured things out like this before, right? Have you ever realized that you're using algebra?"

*Transition:* "Math is everywhere in real life!"

*b. Background Tapping:* "Let's think about other times that you might use math outside of this class. Any ideas?" If no response, suggest they think about things their parents might do.

*Expected student responses:* Parents calculate interest on loans; calculate speed needed to travel a distance in a certain time; figure out what score you need to earn a particular grade in a class.

"These are all great examples of using math in everyday life. Let me read you part of this story called *The Math Curse*. Listen for the kinds of real-life problems the boy discovers are really math problems."

*Transition:* "Before we get to our reading, we need to learn two new terms. Please take out your vocabulary notebooks, date today's entry, and label it "Problem Solving.""

*c. Concept Development/Vocabulary:* "The first term we need to define is *reasonable.* Who can give us some examples of how you have heard this word used? Please give a synonym for *reasonable* with your answer.

> *Expected student responses:* Mom shops for clothes that are a reasonable price [*reasonable* means cheap or inexpensive]; Dad and Mom make compromises that are reasonable [*reasonable* means fair]; My sister doesn't make reasonable decisions [*reasonable* means smart or rational].

"All of these are correct definitions for *reasonable,* but let's look at how we use *reasonable* in the mathematics sense. Look at these sentences containing the word *reasonable* and draft a definition of *reasonable* with your partner." Show transparency.

> If you are asked for a number between 1 and 10, 7 is a *reasonable* answer.
> Julie is a high school student. It is *reasonable* to say her age is between 14 and 18.
> Sebastian has 13 quarters. It is not *reasonable* to say that he can buy something that costs $5.00.

"Let's come up with a definition to write in our vocabulary notebooks." Call on pairs and reach consensus with the class.

> *Expected definition:* The answer you arrive at is accurate, logical, makes sense, fits the specifications in the problem.

"The other term we need to define is *algebraic model.* You're actually already familiar with what this is, but we've never given it an official name. Look at these two examples of algebraic models and with your partner draft a definition of *algebraic model.*" Show transparency.

> You want to calculate how long it will take to burn 100 calories on a stair stepper if you burn 2.5 calories per minute. An *algebraic model* for this problem would be $2.5x = 100$
> If you want to buy the same amount of 2-cent candies and 3-cent candies, and you have $8.10, an *algebraic model* you can use is: $.03x + .02x = 8.1$

Teacher calls on pairs to share definitions, and reaches class consensus.

> *Expected definition:* a number equation that is used to solve a word problem

*d. Purpose-for-Reading:* "Today we will be reading to be informed. We will be listing the steps [chronological order] used in solving the three problems in the text reading and then generalizing these steps to fit a broad range of problems. Please use the graphic organizer to record the steps of each example." Distribute graphic organizer 1: A Problem-Solving Plan (see Figure A.8). "Please remember that reading a math book often requires careful reading, and you often have to reread parts more than once to comprehend the information" (metacognitive reminder).

**II. Silent Reading:** Students read and complete their first graphic organizer independently. Teacher circulates among the students to answer questions.

**III. Discussion:** "It seems like everyone has had time to complete the graphic organizer. Please turn to your partner and discuss the steps used in each of the three example problems. If you disagree on any step, please discuss it thoroughly and come to an agreement."

"What is the first step in example 1?" Repeat for all steps of the three examples, calling on different pairs for each answer. Refer to the completed graphic organizer for expected answers. If there is significant disparity in steps, have students on opposing viewpoints discuss and reach a conclusion.

"Thumbs up if you understand how to solve these specific problems; thumbs down if you are still confused." If any students are thumbs down, take time to address questions before moving on.

**FIGURE A.8  Graphic Organizer I for Problem-Solving Lesson**

**GRAPHIC ORGANIZER I: A PROBLEM-SOLVING PLAN—REAL-LIFE PROBLEMS**

**Example I: Law Enforcement**

1. Understand the Problem
   Need to Know?  How fast was John driving?
   Given?  John's ticket was $180; speed limit is 45 miles/hour; fine is $15 for each mile/hour over the speed limit.

2. Verbal Model?  Amount of speeding ticket equals $15 times miles/hour over speed limit

3. Labels for Verbal Model?  Amount of speeding ticket = $180
   Miles/hour over speed limit = $x$

4. Algebraic Model:
   Equation?  $\$180 = 15x$
   Solution?  $x = 12$
   John was driving 12 + 45 miles/hour; therefore, John was driving 57 miles/hour

5. Check Result:  45 miles/hour = 0 fine; 46 miles/hour = $15 fine; 47 miles/hour = $30 fine

**Example 2: Air Traffic Control**

1. Understand the Problem
   Need to Know?  What speed must the aircraft travel for two hours?
   Is that speed reasonable?
   Given?  Aircraft must maintain 350 miles per hour to avoid stalling
   Aircraft is traveling 500 miles/hour
   Aircraft is 360 miles from destination
   Aircraft must wait 2 hours to land

2. Verbal Model?  Speed of airplane times flight time equals distance to travel

3. Labels for Verbal Model?  speed of airplane = $x$ (miles per hour)
   flight time = 2 (hours)
   distance to travel = 360 (miles)

4. Algebraic Model
   Equation?  $2x = 360$
   Solution?  $x = 180$

5. Check Result:  $2 \times 180 = 360$; not reasonable since aircraft must maintain 350 miles/hour to avoid stalling; aircraft will need to circle in a holding pattern

**Example 3: Class Grade**

1. Understand the Problem
   Need to Know?  Can I get an A in this class?
   Given?  There are five 100-point tests given in this class.
   There is a final test worth 200 points.
   90% and above is an A.
   My scores on the first five tests are 88, 92, 87, 98, and 81.

2. Verbal Model?  Sum of previous tests plus score on final test equals 90% of total test points.

3. Labels for Verbal Model?
   Sum of previous scores = 88 + 92 + 87 + 98 + 81 = 446
   Score on final test = $x$
   90% of total test points = 0.9[5(100) + 200] = 630

4. Algebraic Model:
   Equation?  $446 + x \geq 630$
   Solution?  $x \geq 630 - 446$
   $x \geq 184$

5. Check Result:  Since there are 200 points possible on the final test, if I get 184 or more, I can get an A for the class.

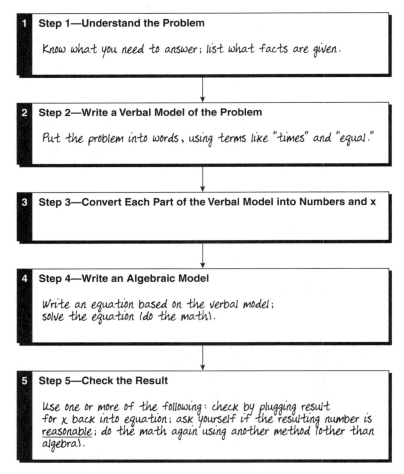

**1** **Step 1—Understand the Problem**

Know what you need to answer; list what facts are given.

**2** **Step 2—Write a Verbal Model of the Problem**

Put the problem into words, using terms like "times" and "equal."

**3** **Step 3—Convert Each Part of the Verbal Model into Numbers and x**

**4** **Step 4—Write an Algebraic Model**

Write an equation based on the verbal model; solve the equation (do the math).

**5** **Step 5—Check the Result**

Use one or more of the following: check by plugging result for x back into equation; ask yourself if the resulting number is reasonable; do the math again using another method (other than algebra).

**FIGURE A.9    Graphic Organizer 2 for Problem-Solving Lesson**

**IV. Rereading (Generalization):** "To apply our new knowledge of using algebra to solve everyday problems, we need to write some general instructions. Our goal is to fill out this graphic organizer with five steps that can be used for all of the problems demonstrated today and problems we will do in the future." Distribute graphic organizer 2: Steps to Solving Algebraic Word Problems (see Figure A.9). "Let's do the first step together. Look at Step 1 for all three problems. Look at what all three have in common. Then write down with your partner what a general rule for the first step of solving algebraic word problems would be." Students write and discuss. Teacher then leads entire-class discussion to reach consensus on Step 1. See graphic organizer (Figure A.9) for acceptable responses.

"We will do the remaining four steps using the "Think, Pair, Share" method. First use paper from your notebook and write down your ideas about what the four steps are. Then turn to your partner and discuss your steps to see if you agree. If you don't agree, listen to each other's reasoning and make a decision for the step."

Students write and discuss. Teacher then leads entire-class discussion to reach consensus on Steps 2 through 5. See graphic organizer (Figure A.9) for acceptable responses.

**V. Follow-Up (Application and Reinforcement):** "Tonight in your math journal, write your own real-life, algebraic word problem. Be sure to include a variable that must be solved. On the back of the page, follow the steps to solve your problem. Tomorrow you will trade them with your partner before handing them in to me."

Adapted from a lesson plan contributed by Christine Jankowski, November 2000.

## CONTENT AREA: MUSIC
### TRADITIONAL INSTRUMENTS OF AFRICA

**Class Description:** General music, grade 8; heterogeneous in achievement

**Unit Title:** Afro-American Music

**Lesson Topic:** Traditional Instruments of Africa

**Unit Goals:** Students will:

1. Experience traditional and popular music through listening, critiquing, and performing
2. Describe the elements, styles, and uses of music in various cultures using appropriate terminology
3. Compare musical performances, creations, and products through listening and discussion
4. Apply acquired knowledge to create and demonstrate musically artistic products

**Lesson Objectives:** Students will:

1. Determine components of sound production through listening, observation, and discussion
2. Identify instrument families by determining common attributes of examples
3. Derive meanings of *gourd* and *resonator/resonating chamber* through context clues and discussion
4. Classify examples of traditional African instruments through written response to a reading assignment
5. Create a list of common materials used to make traditional African instruments; identify the function of each material in relation to sound production
6. Define the elements of sound: pitch, duration, and timbre
7. Apply knowledge of traditional African instruments by creating and presenting a student-directed project

### Performance Assessment

| Objective | Assessment |
|---|---|
| 1. | Oral and written responses to drill (Day 1) and oral and written responses from group consensus (Day 2) |
| 2. | Oral responses (Day 1) and review of responses on graphic organizer |
| 3. | Vocabulary pair oral responses |
| 4. | Review of responses on graphic organizer 1 |
| 5. | Oral responses from group consensus (Day 2) and written responses on homework (graphic organizer 2) |
| 6. | Oral responses from group consensus (Day 2) |
| 7. | Creation and presentation of extension project |

**Macrostructure Thinking Skills:** Classification and examples, comparison and contrast

### Materials

- Video from media center: B. McFerrin (1996). *Bobby McFerrin: Spontaneous Inventions.* (available from Clearvue/eav, Chicago)
- Personal and school instruments grouped as follows:
  **a.** Mbira, conga, bongos, maracas, washboard
  **b.** Guitar, violin, ukulele
  **c.** Trumpet, fife, recorder
- Overheads: (1) sentences for *resonate;* (2) sentences for *gourds;* (3) graphic organizer 1, "Traditional Instruments of Africa"; graphic organizer 2, "Materials and Functions" to be used for vocabulary priming; graphic organizer 3, "Three Things Necessary to Make Sound on an Instrument"

- Handouts: graphic organizer 1, "Traditional Instruments of Africa"; graphic organizer 2, "Materials and Functions"; graphic organizer 3, "Three Things Necessary to Make Sound on an Instrument"; "Traditional Instruments of Africa—Extension Project"
- Authentic gourds
- Text for reading assignment

## Procedure

### I. Readiness

*a. Motivation/Tapping Background of Experience:* Teacher shows a portion of the video that demonstrates body percussion while students think about and respond to the following questions in the "Drill" section of their notebooks: "Is this man using an instrument while he performs? Why or why not?"

Teacher surveys the class to determine the numbers who agree, disagree, or are unsure. Students respond by raising hands. Teacher asks for volunteers to support their decision.

> *Expected student responses:* He isn't using any because you have to have a separate instrument, if it makes a sound it can be an instrument.

"Today we will be reading an article that will help you better determine the answers to these questions."

*b. Developing Background of Experience:* "When we learned about the music of Latin America, we discussed the importance of rhythm and percussion instruments in the listening examples we heard. Today we will be taking a look at some traditional African instruments. Here are some instruments from a number of different cultures. What do they have in common?" Teacher displays instrument groups, plays each briefly, and asks students to identify three commonalities within each group. Students respond by writing answers independently and a consensus is then reached with a partner. Teacher directs class discussion to determine that the three main families are *string, percussion,* and *wind* and the way sound is produced for each group of instruments is also decided.

*c. Concept Development/Vocabulary:* "You will need to think about these three categories of instruments while you read today.

There are also some other words that will help you understand the reading. Take out your music vocabulary notebooks. Sit with your vocabulary partner." Partners are paired each quarter based on behavior, interest, and personality as well as reading and class achievement. Teacher proceeds with vocabulary priming using overhead with the following sentences.

> *Overhead 1*
> Jim was surprised at the way his voice *resonated* in the cave when he spoke. His echo seemed to go on forever.
> Because Erin's electric guitar is solid wood, she needs to use an amp to create a loud sound. Bryan's acoustic guitar is hollow; it has a "built-in" *resonating chamber.*
> Jeff needs a new muffler for his car. The one he has now acts more like a *resonator.* You can hear his car coming a mile away!
> What does a *resonator or resonating chamber* do?

Students use "Think, Pair, Share" drill to derive the meanings of *resonator* and *resonating chamber* as "something that creates an echo or makes a sound louder." Students enter the definitions in the "Vocabulary" section of their notebooks.

Teacher passes *gourds* around the class and indicates that they are often used as decorations in the fall. Teacher shares this sentence written on the overhead transparency:

> *Overhead 2*
> Jenna decorated the Thanksgiving table with little pumpkins, *gourds,* and other squashes. She hoped her guests would know that they were not to be eaten.

Students use "Think, Pair, Share" drill to derive the meaning of a *gourd* as "a squash-like vegetable that is usually not eaten." Students enter the definitions in the vocabulary section of their notebooks.

**d. *Purpose-for-Reading:*** "Keep these words in mind as you read today's assignment. You will be reading to be informed about traditional African instruments. As you read you will be classifying and giving examples of these instruments. You should complete graphic organizer 1, 'Traditional Instruments of Africa' [see Figure A.10] while you read. Be sure to look at the pictures in the text of the instruments described."

**II. Silent Reading:** Students read and write responses on graphic organizer. Teacher circulates to assist students.

**III. Discussion (5 min):** Teacher and students go over graphic organizer 1 together to ensure accuracy and consensus. Considering the background of experience and readability of the article, small-group discussion first is not necessary.

*Closure for Day 1:* "Think back to the video we were watching at the beginning of class." Teacher surveys the class again to see whether consensus has been reached regarding answers to the drill questions. Teacher also asks students to classify the "instrument" the performer used. Students respond that Bobby McFerrin is using body percussion, which is considered an instrument. "Tomorrow we will discuss the materials used to make traditional African instruments. We will also compare the instruments and find out what is needed to make sound. Your homework is to reread the article and complete graphic organizer 2, 'Materials' [see Figure A.11]."

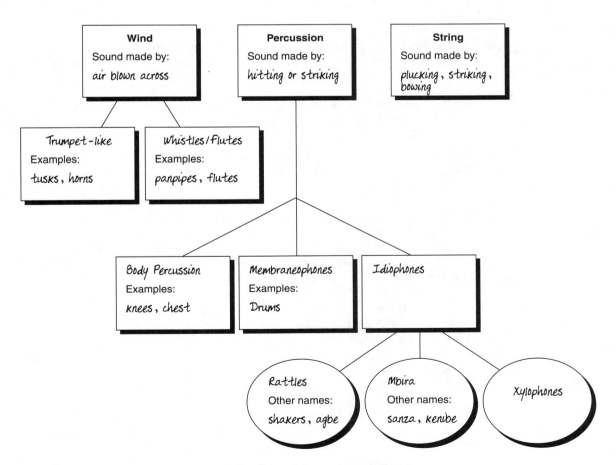

**FIGURE A.10   Graphic Organizer 1: Traditional Instruments of Africa**

**FIGURE A.11     Graphic Organizer 2: Materials**

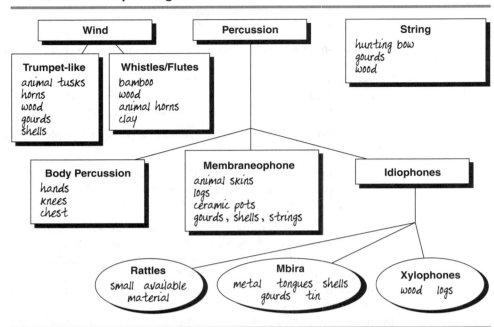

## IV. Rereading (Day 2)

*Activity 1:* Students are put into triads to review their graphic organizers. Triads are heterogeneous in terms of gender, behavior, and achievement. Teacher then reviews the graphic organizer with the entire class.

*Activity 2:* Students respond in notebooks to the following question: "Based on what you read yesterday and last night, decide which family of instruments is most important to musicians in the African culture. Support your decision with two solid reasons."

> *Expected student responses:* Percussion, because there are so many more percussion instruments. Also it said that rhythm is the heart of African music, and percussion plays the rhythms.

*Activity 3:* "Now you will work in your groups to determine the three things necessary to make sound on an instrument. You will reread the section on percussion instruments to make an inference about the purpose for each material you listed. Decide with your group members why that material is needed on the instrument. Discuss how that material changes or affects the sound. As you work, compare the information you discover about the different percussion instruments. Three common themes should emerge. Complete graphic organizer 3 first [see Figure A.12]. Use clues from the pictures to help you. When you have finished all of the percussion instruments, go back and highlight the three most common reasons." Summary of directions is placed on overhead.

Teacher guides the whole class through the "membraneophones" to model appropriate responses and thus further ensure success in small groups.

***Entire-Class Debriefing:*** Teacher calls on a representative of Group 1. Representative responds with reasons for each material. Teacher asks one representative from each of the remaining groups if they want to agree, disagree, or add to the list. Teacher indicates points of agreement on the overhead and directs answers to the three most common responses. "What three things keep coming up?"

**FIGURE A.12   Graphic Organizer 3:   Rereading:   Three Things Necessary to Make Sound on an Instrument**

| INSTRUMENT | WHY THE MATERIAL IS NEEDED ON THE INSTRUMENT |
| --- | --- |
| **MEMBRANEOPHONES** | |
| *animal skins* | *vibrates* |
| *logs* | *echoes; gives sound* |
| *ceramic pots* | *changes the quality of the sound* |
| *gourds, shells, strings* | *resonates* |
| **IDIOPHONES** | |
| **Rattles** | |
| *available materials* | *changes sounds; different materials would sound different* |
| **Mbira** | |
| *metal tongues* | *vibrates—changes pitch* |
| *shells* | *echoes* |
| *gourd* | *echoes* |
| *tin* | *changes sound* |
| **Xylophones** | |
| *wood* | *vibrates; gives sound* |
| *logs* | *echoes* |

**Conclusion:** *something vibrates or makes a pitch; something echoes or resonates; something gives each instrument a special sound.*

(Expected student responses are in italics.)

*Expected student responses:* On every instrument something vibrates or makes a pitch, something echoes or resonates, and something gives each instrument a special sound.

Teacher introduces the elements of sound by labeling "pitch," "duration," and "timbre or tone color." Students record terms and definitions in their vocabulary section.

**V. Follow-Up:** Teacher explains that as an extension activity, students will choose a project that uses the knowledge they have gained about traditional African instruments. Some time will be given in class, but some of the project must be completed as homework. Students must complete the project and make a presentation to the class. Students read assignment sheet. Teacher entertains questions.

## Traditional Instruments of Africa—Extension Project

**Purpose:** Students will apply knowledge of African instruments by creating and presenting a project that reflects their understanding of the *classification, examples, materials, and functions* of traditional African instruments. Students may also apply knowledge of the elements of sound production: *pitch, duration,* and *timbre.*

**Guidelines:** Students may work alone or in groups of two. Two half-periods will be available for students to work on the project in school. If additional time is needed, projects must be completed for homework. Completed projects and presentations will be due _____. Teacher will provide scoring rubric once project is chosen.

**Project Ideas:** Other ideas are welcome. Please discuss your idea with the teacher, however, before you proceed.

- Invent a new instrument based on a combination of at least two traditional African instruments. Draw your instrument and label and describe the elements of sound production.
- Based on your knowledge of the materials that are used in these instruments, design and construct a working instrument that reflects or resembles a traditional African instrument. Be prepared to perform on the instrument. MATERIALS MUST BE APPROVED BY A PARENT/GUARDIAN!
- Create a game that could be used to teach younger children about the different classifications and examples of traditional African instruments. Include rules and all necessary materials to play.
- Learn to play one of the traditional African instruments. Perform a short piece for the class and demonstrate the elements of sound production.
- Research the ways traditional African instruments have impacted modern instruments and music (jazz, rock, rap, etc.). Summarize your findings for the class.
- Create a short story that tells of the legend of one or more of the instruments. Be sure to incorporate the elements of sound production and materials used for traditional African instruments.

**Closure:** Students respond to the following question in their journal section. "Write three questions from this lesson (yesterday and today) that you think will be on the test for this unit, 'Afro-American Music.' Base your predictions on the objectives [on the board], what you read, and our class discussions."

Lesson contributed by Cathie Wheeler Yeagle, 1999.

---

## CONTENT AREA: MUSIC
## CIVIL WAR MUSIC: "BATTLE HYMN OF THE REPUBLIC"

**Class Description:** High school, grades 9 through 12; mixed chorus (soprano, alto, tenor, bass). Students are of heterogeneous musical ability and reading achievement. We have already studied songs associated with WWI and WWII, Vietnam, and September 11. This lesson will introduce a well-known song from the Civil War era entitled "Battle Hymn of the Republic."

**Unit:** Historical Events: The Role Music Has Played

**Unit Goal:** Students will understand the relationships between major nineteenth- and twentieth-century historical events and the patriotic music that emerged.

**Lesson Objectives:** Students will:

1. Write definitions for the following terms: *vintage, wrath, watch-fires,* and *transfigure*
2. Identify measure numbers of lyrics, dynamic and style markings, and interpretation of lyrics
3. Write and discuss the overall meaning of "Battle Hymn of the Republic"
4. Select another song that connotes meaning through the poetic quality of the lyrics

### Performance Assessment

| Objective | Assessment |
| --- | --- |
| 1. | Observation of vocabulary partner work; review of students' vocabulary notebooks |
| 2. | Completed graphic organizers; class discussion of graphic organizer |
| 3. | Partner and class discussion of the song's overall meaning |
| 4. | Written explanation (2–3 paragraphs) describing the lyric meaning of another song |

**Reading Type:** Reading to be informed

**Macrostructure Thinking Skills for Reading:** Description

**Materials**

- "Battle Hymn of the Republic" (SATB) Arranged by Roy Ringwald (Fred Waring choral arrangement)
- Religion in the Civil War website (www.nhc.rtp.nc.us:8080/tserve/nineteen/nkeyinfo/cwnorth.htm)
- Transparency containing the sentences for *vintage* and *transfigures*
- Picture of camp scene containing *watch-fires*
- Graphic organizer handout
- Graphic organizer transparency

## Procedure

### I. Readiness

*a. Motivation and Developing Background of Experience:* "During the past month, we have been studying the relationship between songs and historical events that reveal common thoughts and emotions people have during those times. Name several songs that we have studied that represent historical events during the twentieth century."

*Expected student responses:* "God Bless the USA," "God Bless America," "Yankee Doodle Dandy," "Caissons Go Rolling Along," "Stars and Stripes Forever,"

"Today, we will begin our study of music from the nineteenth century starting with a Civil War song entitled 'Battle Hymn of the Republic.' What I am about to show you are several pictures from the Civil War [show pictures from the website Religion in the Civil War: The Northern Side]. Imagine how soldiers, other military personnel, husbands, wives, children, and other family members may have felt during this time while I read aloud the following story."

In 1861, along with Massachusetts Governor Andrews and a Unitarian Church Pastor, Julia and her husband, Dr. Samuel Ward, were invited to watch a military review of federal troops. Following the inspection, as the Howes were returning to the city of Washington, the streets were filled with soldiers singing "John Brown's Body," a song named for one who had been hung for his efforts to free the slaves. A clergyman in the party, James Freeman Clarke, who knew of Julia's published poems, urged her to write a new song for the war effort to replace "John Brown's Body." Here's her account of what happened next:

"I replied that I had often wished to do so. . . . In spite of the excitement of the day I went to bed and slept as usual, but awoke the next morning in the gray of the early dawn, and to my astonishment found that the wished-for lines were arranging themselves in my brain. I lay quite still until the last verse had completed itself in my thoughts, then hastily arose, saying to myself, I shall lose this if I don't write it down immediately. I searched for an old sheet of paper and an old stub of a pen which I had had the night before, and began to scrawl the lines almost without looking, as I learned to do by often scratching down verses in the darkened room when my little children were sleeping. Having completed this, I lay down again and fell asleep, but not before feeling that something of importance had happened to me."

The words for this hymn were first published in the "The Atlanta Monthly" (February 1862) as the "Civil War Battle Song of the Republic"; she was paid $5 for her contribution. Julia Ward Howe's religious conviction showed in the way that Old and New Testament Biblical images were used to urge that people implement, in this life and this world, the principles that they adhered to. "As he died to make men holy, let us die to make men free." Turning from the idea that the war was revenge for the death of a martyr, Howe hoped that the song would keep the war focused on the principle of ending slavery. At the start of the war, the aim of the Northern policy was to save the Union, not to free the slaves; but mixed results on the battlefield prompted a reassessment of their goals. The conviction grew that God would continue to chastise the North and would not allow it to win the war until it took steps to end slavery. Churches made what had started as a war for the preservation of the Union into a war of liberation. This transformation was also paralleled in the Lincoln administration. By 1862, Lincoln announced his intention to free slaves in areas still in rebellion against the government by the start of 1863.

"I will now play a CD recording of Julia Ward Howe's poem that we know as the 'Battle Hymn of the Republic.' We'll then write and talk about what you saw in your mind as you listened and how you felt."

**b. Tapping Background of Experience:** "How many of you have family members who served in WWI, WWII, Vietnam, or Desert Storm?" Students share examples of family members. "How many of you have family members that currently serve in the military?" Students share examples of family members. "What are some reasons why people serve in the military?"

*Expected student responses:* preserving our freedom; showing national support; believing in an important cause, and so on.

"Take out your journals and for the next five minutes, let's write about how you felt while you listened to the recording of 'Battle Hymn of the Republic.' What images came to your mind?"

*Transition:* "Before we begin reading the words to the 'Battle Hymn of the Republic,' there are some new vocabulary words we need to learn in order to better understand the lyrics and meaning of the song. Move to your vocabulary pairs and take out your notebooks now."

**c. Concept Development/Vocabulary:** "The first new concept is *vintage* [write the word on the chalkboard]. Read the following sentences on the transparency, then with your vocabulary partner draft a definition of *vintage.*"

1. The waiter asked the restaurant customer what *vintage* wine he preferred.
2. The highest priced bottle of wine at the auction was a *vintage* 1961 merlot.

*Expected definition:* a particular type or year of wine

Call on one vocabulary pair to give its draft definition. Instruct the other pairs to listen to determine whether they agree. Ask for any revisions, and decide on a class definition. Students copy word and definition into their vocabulary notebooks.

"The next word is *wrath* [write the word on the chalkboard]. Listen to the following sentence: In 1999, the state of Maryland felt the *wrath* of Hurricane Floyd as it hit shore. In your vocabulary pairs, define the word *wrath.*"

*Expected definition:* any action carried out in intense anger, rage, fury

Call on one vocabulary pair to give their definition. Instruct the other pairs to listen to determine whether they agree. Ask for any revisions, and decide on a class definition. Students copy the word and definition into their vocabulary notebooks.

"Next we will examine the word *watch-fires* [write the word on the chalkboard]. Look at this Civil War picture. Notice the tents in the background and the men sitting around the *watch-fires.* Discuss with your partner a draft definition for *watch-fires.*"

*Expected definition:* a fire kept burning at night for those staying awake to watch or guard

Call on one vocabulary pair to give their definition. Instruct the other pairs to listen to determine whether they agree. Ask for any revisions, and decide on a class definition. Students copy the word and definition into their vocabulary notebooks.

"The last word we'll examine is *transfigures* [write the word on the chalkboard]. Read the following sentences on the transparency, then with your vocabulary partner draft a definition of *transfigures.*"

3. His will was *transfigured* by association with the will of others.
4. The great cliffs and domes were *transfigured* in the hazy golden air.

*Expected definition:* to transform; to pass or be seen in

Call on one vocabulary pair to give their definition. Instruct the other pairs to listen to determine if they agree. Ask for any revisions, and decide on a class definition. Students copy the word and definition into their vocabulary notebooks.

*Transition:* "Now that we have an understanding of these new key vocabulary words, we are ready to interpret the lyrics of the song."

d. **Purpose-for-Reading:** "Today you will be reading the lyrics from 'Battle Hymn of the Republic' to be informed. As you read through the lyrics, look at the dynamic and tempo markings. Either while you read or after you read, complete the graphic organizer." Distribute the graphic organizer (see Table A.7) and review the format of what is to be completed.

**TABLE A.7**   **Graphic Organizer for "Battle Hymn of the Republic" Lesson**

| MEASURE NUMBERS | LYRICS | DYNAMICS AND STYLE MARKINGS | INTERPRETATION OF LYRICS |
|---|---|---|---|
| Measures 7–22 | Mine eyes have seen the glory of the coming of the Lord; <br> He is trampling out the vintage where the grapes of wrath are stored; <br> He hath loosed the fateful lightning of His terrible swift sword; <br> His truth is marching on | *mp: mezzo piano; crescendo to forte* | *The presence of the Lord was felt by those who believed in the cause, and His "truth" would be made known to all.* |
| Measures 23–30 | Glory, glory, hallelujah! <br> Glory, glory, hallelujah! <br> Glory, glory, hallelujah! <br> His truth is marching on | *Forte: loud* | *Celebrate and rejoice in the Lord's presence and the truth of His promise.* |
| Measures 31–40 | I have seen Him in the watch-fires of a hundred circling camps; <br> They have builded Him an altar in the evening dews and damps; <br> I can read His righteous sentence by the dim and flaring lamps, <br> His day is marching on | *mf: mezzo forte marcato* | *Reading the word of the Lord took place regularly at night while in camp. This kept His "truth" alive.* |
| Measures 43–48 | Glory, glory, hallelujah! <br> Glory, glory, hallelujah! <br> Glory, glory, hallelujah! <br> His truth is marching on | *p: piano* | *Celebrate and rejoice in the Lord's presence and the truth of His promise.* |
| Measures 53–60 | In the beauty of the lilies Christ was born across the sea, <br> With a glory in His bosom that transfigures you and me; <br> As He died to make men holy, let us die to make men free, <br> While God is marching on. | *p: piano; Slowly— expressively crescendo to forte* | *The purpose of the war was to end slavery (even through death). Christ did the same by dying to make men spiritually free.* |
| Measures 61–68 | Glory, glory, hallelujah! <br> Glory, glory, hallelujah! <br> Glory, glory, hallelujah! <br> His truth is marching on. <br> Amen. | *Maestoso ff: fortissimo mf—f—ff* | *Celebrate and rejoice in the Lord's presence and the truth of His promise.* |

Students are to complete the third and fourth columns—Dynamics and Style Markings and Interpretation of Lyrics

**II. Silent Reading:** The students read the lyrics in the soprano, alto, tenor, and bass arrangements and complete their graphic organizers. Teacher circulates to assist students who might be having difficulty with the graphic organizer.

**III. Discussion:** Place transparency of blank graphic organizer on overhead projector. Ask for student responses and record on the graphic organizer. Ask students for elaboration, as necessary. Instruct students to add any information or revise their own graphic organizers, if needed. Point out the new vocabulary words learned as students contribute responses using these terms. Ask students to elaborate on how the dynamics and style markings accentuate the meaning of the lyrics (see expected student responses in italics on the graphic organizer).

**IV. Rereading:** "Reread the lyrics to the song while I play the CD recording again. Afterward, think about the overall meaning of the lyrics. What was the purpose of Julia Ward Howe's poem? How would the words have inspired those fighting on the side of the North and family members who supported the cause?" Students reread the lyrics while listening to the recording. During this time, teacher writes the discussion questions on the board. Provide time for students to individually write down their thoughts.

"First, share what you wrote down with your partner." Provide time for students to share. "Next, share your ideas with the class." A discussion is facilitated by calling on pairs throughout the class in response to the two questions.

*Expected student responses:* The purpose of the poem was to keep the message clear about the major reason for fighting the war—the end of slavery. The words would have inspired those in the military and family members because of emphasis on the Lord and the belief He would help them succeed in reaching their goal.

**V. Follow-Up (Reinforcement):** "Tomorrow, we will learn to sing the 'Battle Hymn of the Republic,' using what we learned today about its meaning to give it the appropriate musical interpretation.

"For homework tonight, find an example of a song that connotes a message. Bring in the lyrics and write a 2- to 3-paragraph description as to what the words mean and the overall message of the song. Notice how the words to songs are really poems set to music."

Lesson plan created by Elizabeth Wilkins.

---

## CONTENT AREA: PHYSICAL EDUCATION
## AQUATICS SAFETY

**Class Description:** Physical education, aquatics; ninth through twelfth grades; level V special education—learning disabled (LD), emotionally disturbed (ED), pervasive developmental disorder (PDD), and traumatic brain injury (TBI)

**Unit:** Water Safety

**Unit Goal:** Students will have the knowledge to pursue a variety of aquatic activities in a safe and appropriate environment.

**Lesson Objectives:** The students will be able to:
1. Discuss and list safety precautions that they have taken or that they know should be taken in a variety of aquatic environments.
2. Accurately identify pictures depicting safe and unsafe behavior in and around an aquatic environment.
3. Define *safe behavior* and *unsafe behavior* in and around an aquatic environment.
4. List and explain the reason for swimming safety rules.

5. Identify the safety rule for swimming that students consider to be the most important.
6. Create a brochure with a partner to promote safety in all aquatic environments.

## Performance Assessment

*Objective   Assessment*

1.   Written and oral responses during Tapping Background of Experience
2.   Oral responses during Concept Development/Vocabulary
3.   Oral responses during Concept Development/Vocabulary
4.   Graphic organizer responses and oral responses during Discussion.
5.   Responses during Rereading activity.
6.   Brochures collected and reviewed.

## Macrostructure Thinking Skill: Enumeration

## Materials

- Cart with an overhead projector, whiteboard, dry erase markers.
- Books
  *Safety in the Water* by Joanne Martin, ABDO, Edina, MN, 1999.
  *Safety in Water* by K. Carter, Rourke Press, Vero Beach, FL, 1994.
  *Water Safety* by Nancy Loewen, Child's World, Chanhassen, NJ, 1997.
  *Superguides Swimming* by Rick Cross, Dorling Kindersley, New York, 1997.
  *Swimming* by Bernie Blackball, Heinemann Library, Des Plaines, IL, 1999.
  *Swimming and Aquatics Safety* by Red Cross, National American Red Cross,
    Washington, D.C., 1981.
- Transparencies: Blank; variety of aquatic environment samples; developing questions
- Pictures of safe and unsafe behaviors
- Handout of graphic organizer for reading
- Sample brochure

## Procedure

### I. Readiness

*a. Motivation:* "We have gone through our daily class routine, discussed the rules for our pool, and have taken a tour of our pool. Now we are ready to talk about safety in other aquatic environments. Where else can you go swimming other than in our pool?" Write answers on white board as generated by students.

*Expected student responses:* ocean; lake; river; quarry; outdoor pool; bay

"Those are all great answers. All of these are fun places to swim, but they can also be dangerous places to swim." Students listen and observe transparencies of a variety of aquatic environments.

*b. Tapping Background of Experience:* "How many of you have been swimming at any of the places shown on the transparencies?" Students share personal experiences about swimming in different aquatic environments. The teacher leads a discussion using guide questions to facilitate student reflection about past swimming experiences. Questions are preprinted on transparencies, and student answers should be recorded under each question. Students will answer the questions on a preprinted handout.

"Close your eyes and think back to when you went swimming. Feel the cool water all around you and hear the splashes of people as they swim by you."

1. What things did you do when you went swimming to make sure you had fun but didn't get hurt?
2. How did you play with your friends in the water to make sure neither you or your friends got hurt?
3. If you went swimming outside, how did you protect yourself from the weather?

4. Did any of you swim in a place where you shared the water with fish or other animals?
5. Was there a lifeguard or other person there to make sure you were safe while you were swimming?
6. Did any of you swim in deep water? How did you know it was deep?

Students write their answers on preprinted handout and discuss each question after taking a minute to answer it in writing.

*Transition:* "Now we are going to look at some pictures of people in aquatics environments. We have to decide as a class whether we think these pictures show safe or unsafe behavior."

**c. *Concept Development/Vocabulary:*** Pair students for "Think, Pair, Share" activity. Pairs will decide and record their answers after observing each picture. Pictures are numbered to correspond with the answer sheet. Students should be paired so that weaker readers are paired with stronger readers.

Students work together to decide and record answers. Teacher then leads discussion about each picture: Is it safe or unsafe behavior? Why? "With your partner, draft definitions of *safe behavior* and *unsafe behavior* in and around an aquatic environment." Students work together on definitions, and then an entire-class discussion is conducted to reach a decision on definitions.

> *Expected definitions:* Safe behavior in and around an aquatic environment does not result in injury to a person. Unsafe behavior in and around an aquatic environment causes or could cause injury or even death to a person.

Students record this definition in their PE vocabulary notebooks.

*Transition:* "We are ready to read some facts about water safety. As I hand out the reading assignments, take a minute to look at the pictures. Think about what each picture is showing and whether the picture shows safe or unsafe behavior" (metacognitive prereading strategy: looking at graphics).

**d. *Purpose-for-Reading:*** "Today we are reading to be informed. As you read the book or packet about water safety that I have handed out, mark an X on your graphic organizer next to each of the safety rules the book explains [see Figure A.13]. Then on the back of the graphic organizer sheet, explain the reason for each rule your book explains. That is, why should you follow the rule? What could happen if you did not follow the rule?" Books are distributed according to reading abilities of students. Very low readers and nonreaders can be given a book on tape that has been cued by number so that they can utilize the graphic organizer.

**II. Silent Reading:** Students read the book or packet they receive and record responses on the graphic organizer provided. (metacognitive during-reading strategy: notetaking and checking for purpose)

**III. Discussion:** The teacher leads a discussion about what each student found in his or her assigned reading. "Let's talk about the safety rules you found in your reading assignment. Whose book discussed the first rule, 'Learn to swim?' What is the reason for that rule?"

Each of the twelve rules will be discussed in this manner and relating each rule to the concept of *safe behavior* in and around aquatic environments.

**IV. Rereading:** "Can you think of any aquatic rules that we have not read about and discussed, but should be on our list?" Discuss any additions offered by the students.

"With a partner who has read a different book, answer the following questions; one person can be the recorder, or you can take turns writing the answers."

1. What was the book or packet you read about? (global)
2. What do you think is the most dangerous thing about swimming? Why? (critical)
3. If you and a friend are going swimming outside, which safety rule is the most important to remind your friend about? Why? (Interpretive)

Entire-class debriefing of questions follows.

# Safety Rules for Swimming

*Below are 12 rules for safe behavior in and around aquatic environments. Put an X next to each rule your book explains. On the back of this sheet, explain the reason for each rule your book discusses.*

____ 1. Learn to swim.

____ 2. Swim with a buddy.

____ 3. Follow rules on signs.

____ 4. Swim with an adult or with lifeguard supervision.

____ 5. No running.

____ 6. Use flotation devices if you cannot swim.

____ 7. Check for deep water.

____ 8. Be aware of animals.

____ 9. Look for hidden dangers under the water.

____10. Watch for storms.

____11. Call for help when needed.

____12. Do not swim near boats.

**FIGURE A.13   Graphic Organizer for Aquatics Safety Lesson**

**V. Follow-Up:** "Water safety is important for everyone. We are going to spread the word about what we have learned about water safety. Using the computers in the computer lab, we are going to create a water safety brochure. We will work in pairs to create a brochure that tells everyone about safe and unsafe behaviors in aquatic environments. Choose a partner who has read a different book than you read about water safety. I am passing around an example of what your brochure will look like. You will also receive a list of brochure specifications."

*Brochure Specifications*
1. The front must have a title and one graphic.
2. The inside should have a list of safe behaviors, a list of unsafe behaviors, and at least one graphic.
3. At the bottom of one of the inside pages, type one sentence about why you think a person should know about water safety before going swimming (personal).

Lesson contributed by Heather Semies, May 2001.

## CONTENT AREA: PHYSICAL EDUCATION
### HEALTHY EATING FOR MAXIMUM PERFORMANCE

**Class Description:** Physical education, grades 10 and 11; heterogeneous in academic and psychomotor ability class; elective, ½-credit course

**Unit Title:** Physical Fitness

*High School Core Learning Goals*

1. Maintain a self-monitored personal fitness program designed to improve targeted health-related fitness components.
2. Construct, evaluate, and modify as needed a personal fitness program aimed at minimizing preventable health risks.
3. Set realistic long-range fitness and activity goals consistent with personal skill potential.
4. Choose to participate regularly in self-directed recreational and leisure activities.

**Unit Goal:** Students should have an understanding of proper eating habits needed by athletes to attain maximal performance.

**Lesson Objectives:** Students will be able to:

1. Categorize and define *glucose, carbohydrates,* and *glycogen*
2. Identify six negative effects of improper eating
3. List foods that are good for helping to generate energy
4. List foods to be avoided by young athletes
5. Evaluate their own diets for appropriate energy foods

**Performance Assessment**

| Objective | Performance |
|---|---|
| 1. | Oral responses during entire-class discussion; categorization graphic organizers collected and reviewed |
| 2. | Oral responses during discussion; cause-and-effect graphic organizers collected and reviewed |
| 3. | Oral responses during discussion; cause-and-effect graphic organizers collected and reviewed |
| 4. | Oral responses during discussion; cause-and-effect graphic organizers collected and reviewed |
| 5. | Oral responses during Rereading discussion |

**Macrostructure Thinking Skills:** Cause and effect, enumeration

**Materials**

- Magazine article: Manore, M. M. (May/June 2000). "Fueling Exercise," *ACSM's Health & Fitness Journal,* vol. 4, pp. 34–35.
- Two graphic organizers (categorization and cause and effect)—handouts and a transparency of each.

## Procedure

### I. Readiness

*a. Motivation:* "For the last few weeks we have been working on muscular and cardiovascular endurance. What types of movements and exercises have we been doing in the class to achieve these goals?"

> *Expected student responses:* weight lifting, running, plyometrics, cross training, team games

"What does the body need to perform these activities successfully?"

> *Expected student responses:* muscle, power, flexibility, endurance, speed

"All of those answers are correct, yes, but what do the muscles require to do these movements?"

> *Expected student responses:* energy, fuel, food

"Eating before vigorous activity is important for the body to store up energy to ensure that it doesn't run out during an activity. It is similar to the thought that you will not start off on a long car ride on an empty tank of gas. Eating and drinking before activity can help ensure maximal performance by storing energy and helping to prevent dehydration. It is best to do this at least 15 minutes to a half an hour before activity to allow for digestion."

**b. Tapping Background of Experience:** "How many of you compete in sports or vigorous activity outside of this class?" Student raise hands. "How many of you eat a pregame meal? What does it consist of?" Call on students who have raised their hands and ask what they eat and write down some of the answers on the board. For later reference, have all students write down what they had to eat before they came to class today and what they had for dinner last night.

"What are some possible problems that could occur from not eating or hydrating before vigorous activity? You are allowed to guess." Expect a variety of correct and incorrect answers; record all responses on the board.

**c. Concept Development/Vocabulary:** "We begin today a series of lessons that deal with nutrition and physical fitness. We will use a chart during these lessons to help us distinguish nutritional elements. [Distribute categorization chart.] You will use the information on the overhead to help you place the following three terms in the correct place on your chart and to define each: *carbohydrates, glucose,* and *glycogen.*"

"Work with your vocabulary partners to categorize and define these three terms." Vocabulary partners are paired heterogeneously based on reading achievement results and athletic experience of each student.

Show overhead transparency:

> The night before the big game, our coaches ordered wheat pasta with tomato sauce, thick slices of wheat bread, and lots of green vegetables and fruits for us. They told us that this menu was high in *carbohydrates,* our bodies' major source of energy. *Carbohydrates* are sugars (simple carbohydrates) and starches (complex carbohydrates) found in food. The sugars are easy for the body to process. One type of sugar is *glucose.* Many accident victims and patients who need surgery are given *glucose* intravenously to help maintain their energy levels while their bodies are in any crisis. *Glucose* goes directly into the bloodstream and gives us instant energy. In fact all the cells use *glucose* as their primary source of energy. Any *glucose* that is not needed immediately for energy is stored in the muscles and liver in the form of a starch for later use. This is called *glycogen.*

Pairs complete the activity; entire-class discussion for consensus is conducted.

Expected student responses are on the categorization graphic organizer (see Figure A.14).

**d. Purpose for Reading:** "Read the article that I have given you to be informed. You will be identifying the six possible effects of not eating properly before, during, and after exercising (see Figure A.15). Then you will list foods to avoid and foods to use to maximize your athletic performance (see Figure A.16). I am distributing a graphic organizer for you to use to record your responses."

**II. Silent Reading:** Students read the article silently and record responses on the worksheet provided by the teacher. During the reading time, the teacher circulates and encourages students to record answers on their graphic organizers.

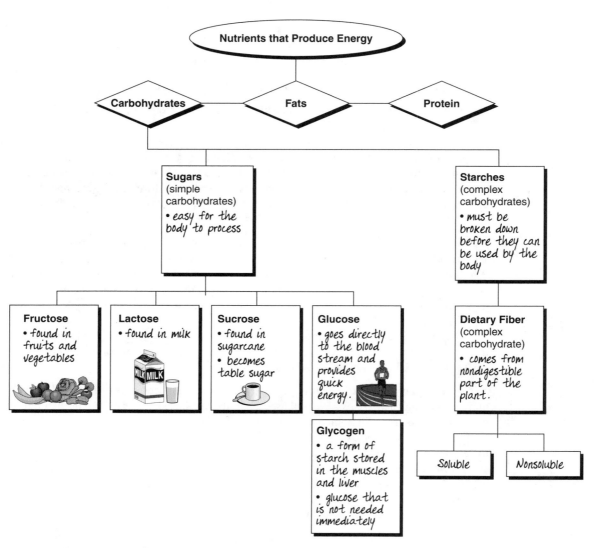

**FIGURE A.14  Categorization Graphic Organizer**

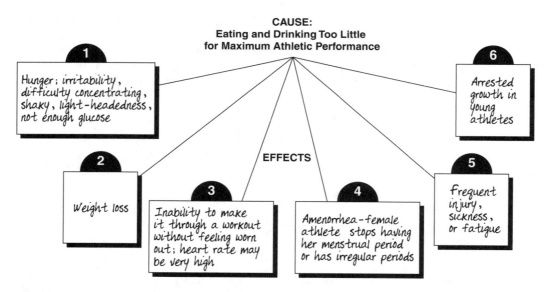

**FIGURE A.15  Cause-and-Effect Graphic Organizer**

| Energy Foods for Athletes | Foods to Avoid |
|---|---|
| 1. Carbohydrates the night before exercise | 1. Caffeine products (sodas and coffee)—serious side effects |
| 2. A sport drink before, during, and after workouts | 2. |
| 3. A glycogen replacement beverage after workouts | 3. |
| 4. Fruit (fresh and dried) | |
| 5. Energy bars | |
| 6. Yogurt | |
| 7. Low-sugar, high-fiber cereals | |
| 8. Low-fat milk | |
| 9. Bagel, bread, crackers | |
| 10. Lots of water! | |

**FIGURE A.16    Energy Foods and Foods to Avoid**

**III. Discussion:** Teacher leads discussion of answers and records correct responses on a transparency of the chart. Expected student responses are on the graphic organizer. During the discussion of "Energy Foods for Athletes," have students relate each food to the "Nutrients That Produce Energy—Carbohydrates" on the categorization graphic organizer. For example, energy bars are on the list of foods to eat because they provide dietary fiber for energy; fruit is on the list because it provides fructose (sugar) for energy; milk provides a source of lactose (sugar) for energy.

**IV. Rereading:** "Early in this lesson, I asked you to record what you had for dinner last night and what you had to eat before this class. With your partners, share your responses, then evaluate if your diet would be appropriate if we had been exercising during this class. Refer back to the article and your graphic organizers to remind you of what the author was saying about appropriate food and drink. I will be asking you to share with us whether your diet was 'good,' 'adequate' or 'inappropriate.'" Pairs judge, then individuals are asked to give their ratings and explanations.

**V. Follow-Up:** "You probably noticed that the article gives quite a few suggestions for appropriate foods for athletes, but the list of foods to avoid is quite limited. Do you think that an athlete should avoid only caffeine beverages? For our next session, use your resources— your coaches, the health and fitness magazines you read, and the Internet—to make a list of other foods you should avoid to maximize your athletic performance. Be sure you can also explain the reason for avoiding the foods."

Lesson adapted from the work of Matthew Redmond.

## CONTENT AREA: SCIENCE
### "LEFTOVERS"

**Class Description:** Science, grade 9; general/earth science class. The students in this class are labeled standard ability; thus the class includes below average, average, and above average students. They are studying a unit on the solar system. In a previous lesson, they have learned about the formation of the planets and their moons and have viewed a film concerning this phenomenon. In this lesson, they will discover what became of the "leftover" material that was not used in the formation of the planets or moons.

**Unit Title:** The Solar System

**Core Learning Goal:** The students will demonstrate the ability to use scientific skills and processes to explain the physical behavior of the environment, earth, and the universe.

**Unit Goals:** The students will demonstrate an understanding of the formation and behavior of the components of our solar system, including the planets, moons, asteroids, comets, and meteors.

**Lesson Objectives:** The student will be able to:

1. Write definitions for the following new terms: *erosion, gravity,* and *nucleus*
2. Classify and describe the "leftover" objects in the solar system: asteroids, comets, and meteors
3. Predict the possible results of one of these objects coming in contact with the Earth
4. Propose a solution to a hypothetical problem based on new knowledge of asteroids, comets, and meteors

**Performance Assessment**

*Objective*     *Assessment*

1.     Work with vocabulary partner; class discussions of definitions; writing of definition into notebooks
2.     Completion of graphic organizers; discussion; journal entries
3.     Poster advertisements
4.     Letters to the commissioner

**Macrostructure Thinking Skills:** Classification, comparison and contrast

**Materials**

- Text reading, "Leftovers"
- Reading: "Eyewitness Accounts" (mstrong@vignette.com, aduniven@htcomp.net, Ekko47@aol.com)
- Transparencies: asteroids, comet, and meteor shower (*Secrets of Space: Asteroids, Comets, and Meteors,* Carole Marsh, Twenty-First Century Books, 1996)
- Red balloon filled with helium and a blue balloon filled with air
- Nucleus (*Biology: The World of Life,* 7th ed., Robert Wallace, Addison-Wesley Longman, 1997)
- Transparency: Grand Canyon (*Grand Canyon,* Jan Mell, Crestwood House, 1998)
- Graphic organizer "Classifying the Leftovers"

## Procedure

### I. Readiness

*a. Motivation and Tapping Background of Experience:* We begin with a brief review of the components of the solar system that we are familiar with. "Thinking back to yesterday's lesson, can we name some of the objects in our solar system?"

> *Expected student responses:* the sun, the Earth, Mars, Mercury, Venus, Jupiter, Saturn, Uranus, Neptune, Pluto, and moons

"Based on what you already know, are these the only objects in our solar system?" Student answers may vary. Because of the popularity of "space movies," the general class consensus will probably be "No." "If the sun, planets, and moons are not alone in our solar system, what other kinds of objects might we suggest occupy this space with them?"

> *Expected student responses:* comets, asteroids, meteors, satellites, and space probes

"All of those answers are correct; however, can anyone tell us where space probes and satellites come from?"

> *Expected student responses:* They are human-made; we send them into space with our shuttle; engineers from NASA make them.

"Can anyone tell us where meteors, asteroids, and comets come from?" Students will be unsure of the answer to this question.

> *Expected student responses:* Stars blow up and their pieces float around; they come from outside of our solar system.

Teacher should avoid suggesting that these predictions are either correct or incorrect. "Today, by reading to be informed, we will discover where these objects come from and how they behave in space. Before we go on, has anyone ever seen one of these objects?" Students' reactions will vary depending on experiences.

> *Expected student responses:* Yes, my dad and I saw the comet a couple of years ago when we went camping; no, I have only seen these objects in movies.

"How do you think you might feel if you saw one of these objects?"

> *Expected student responses:* I would be scared that it might hit us! I would be fascinated! I would feel excited!

Conclude this phase of the Readiness section with a few readings of eyewitness accounts of the meteor shower of 1966 (Leonids). "All of those emotions are quite possible. Let's hear what some people have had to say about these phenomena who have actually seen them! Did you know that in 1966 there was a spectacular meteor shower? Perhaps your parents or grandparents saw it. I am going to read for you three actual eyewitness accounts from people who really saw it happen. Listen for their reactions and how they describe what they saw. How did these eyewitnesses describe the meteor shower?"

> *Expected student responses:* Thousands of cat scratches covering the sky; like sparklers on the 4th of July; a hundred shooting stars in one hour.

*Transition:* "Before we begin our reading assignment on asteroids, comets, and meteors, there are a few vocabulary words I would like to go over with you so that you will understand your reading better. Please pair up with your vocabulary partner, and turn to the vocabulary section of your science notebook." Partners are composed of one better reader and one weaker reader based on a reading achievement test given at the beginning of the year.

**b. Concept Development/Vocabulary:** Place a list of the new vocabulary words on the overhead, and uncover only the first word. "The first word we will develop a definition for today is *erosion.*" Put up a color transparency of the Colorado River running through the Grand Canyon. "This is a photograph of the Colorado River running through the Grand Canyon. The Grand Canyon was formed by the process of *erosion.* With your partner, discuss and draft a possible definition for *erosion.*" Students work in pairs to draft a definition while viewing the transparency. "_____, would you tell the class what you and your partner have decided for a draft definition of erosion?"

> *Expected definitions:* A process by which water wears down or cuts through rock; erosion occurs when water removes layers of rock over time.

Teacher records all appropriate definitions that the students provide. "Now, let's copy the best definition into our notebook." Students will copy definition.

Uncover the next vocabulary word. "The next word we will examine is *gravity.* To help you define this word, I will make a demonstration for you. To complete this demonstration, I will need two balloons." Prior to class, teacher will have filled a red balloon with helium and a blue balloon with air. Teacher shows them to the class. "I have two balloons in my hands. Please observe what happens to these balloons when I let them go." Students view the demonstration.

The red balloon will float to the ceiling while the blue balloon will fall to the floor. "The blue balloon acts the way it does because of *gravity*. The red balloon is not affected by gravity. With your partner, draft a definition for *gravity*."

*Expected definition:* a force that pulls things to the ground.

Teacher writes the appropriate definition on the transparency. Students copy the best definition in their notebooks.

Uncover the third and final word: *nucleus*. "Lastly, we will discuss the word *nucleus*. The word *nucleus* has generally the same meaning, but it can be used in a variety of contexts. Thinking back to your studies last year in biology, who can tell us what *nucleus* meant in biology?" Teacher shows students the diagram of the cells to spark memory of previous learning.

*Expected definitions:* a cell's brain; the part of the cell that controls its other parts

"That is correct; however *nucleus* can have a more general definition. Let's look at it in this context." Uncover the following statements:

My father, mother, brother, and I make up the *nucleus* of my family.
The eye of the hurricane is the *nucleus* of the storm.

"Now, by using the biology-related definition that you already know, and examining the word in these contexts, draft a general definition for *nucleus* with your partner." Students work together to generate a definition. Teacher asks several groups for their definitions.

*Expected definitions:* the *nucleus* is the center of something; it is the strongest, most powerful part.

Teacher records appropriate definitions on the transparency. "Now record the best definition in your notebooks." Students copy definition into their notebooks.

*Transition:* "Now that we have defined several important key words in our reading, we are ready to begin reading. I hope that after completing our Readiness activities, you feel prepared to begin this reading assignment. Are there any questions before we discuss our purpose-for-reading?"

*c. Purpose-for-Reading:* Teacher instructs students to locate in their textbooks the chapter "Leftovers," using their table of contents. Teacher distributes the graphic organizer, "Classifying the Leftovers" (see Table A.8).

"You now have the reading and a graphic organizer, which is in the form of a chart. You will fill in the graphic organizer as you read or after you read to ensure you understand the important concepts. The general purpose for reading is to be informed. You will be reading to classify the 'leftover' objects in space. Specifically, you will be able to classify these objects as asteroids, comets, or meteors and describe each so that we can compare and contrast them. Be sure you look at the pictures that are included near each of the reading sections. Seeing the asteroids, comets, and meteors in your mind as you read will help your comprehension and recall of the important information" (metacognitive reminder).

**II. Silent Reading:** The students read silently while filling out their graphic organizers.

**III. Discussion:** Bring the class together for debriefing. Because of the straightforward nature of the reading and the linear nature of the graphic organizer the students will probably not need to debrief in small groups before a whole-class discussion. Teacher places a blank graphic organizer on the overhead. Teacher and students work together to fill in the graphic organizer. Students offer answers to complete the chart. They will fill in any gaps in their own chart, and correct any errors. Expected student responses are in italics on the graphic organizer.

**TABLE A.8    Classifying the "Leftovers"**

| "LEFTOVER" CHARACTERISTICS | ASTEROIDS | COMETS | METEORS AND METEORITES |
|---|---|---|---|
| Size | ½ mile to several hundred miles in diameter | 1–10 kilometers in diameter; very long tails | a grain of sand to the size of a house |
| Composition | large chunks of rock and metal; inner belt = metals; outer belt = rocky | "dirty ice balls"; made of dust, gas, and water | bits of space debris; metals, rocks |
| Physical features | oblong shape; many craters on the surface; resembles a potato | hard icy region—nucleus; gas and dust around the nucleus—coma; coma is blown by solar wind, creating a tail | round shape; crystal structure |
| Location in our solar system | the asteroid belt; a region between the planets Mars and Jupiter | throughout the solar system; likely created between Uranus and Saturn | throughout the solar system; pulled to Earth's atmosphere by the Earth's gravity |
| Examples of famous "leftovers" | Gaspa—studied up close in 1991 by the Galileo spacecraft | Haley's comet—75-year orbit around the sun; collision in 1908 in Siberia | November 12, 1833, meteor shower; house-sized meteorite that fell in Arizona 25,000 years ago |
| **My Drawings:** | **Asteroid** | **Comet** | **Meteor** |

Expected student responses are in italics.

*Transition:* "Now that we have a clear understanding of the characteristics of these "left-over" space objects, let's apply that knowledge to a possible real-world situation."

**IV. Rereading:** "Please keep the reading and chart on your desktop, and take out a clean sheet of paper. For this activity, you will be writing a letter. Your purpose will be to propose a solution to a problem and to support it with evidence in the reading. Let's listen to the scenario."

> It is the year 2050 and you are an astronomer working for NASA. Unfortunately, the Earth is in trouble. Because of overpopulation, the needs of the people on Earth have exceeded the resources available. The environment has been damaged severely. The Earth has been depleted of essential metals and has very little clean, pure water left. In your research, you have come up with a possible solution to the world's dilemma. Your purpose is to propose a solution to the world's dilemma. You will propose this solution in a letter to your commissioner. In the letter, be sure to support your solution with concrete evidence from your research (reading). Use the appropriate form for a letter."

Students write a letter offering a possible solution. They revisit the text to find evidence. Examine the possible solutions with the class. Students share their letters.

> *Expected student responses:* obtaining metals from asteroids in the inner belt; getting water from comets

**V. Follow-Up:** "Tonight, you will create an advertisement on a small poster, the size you might see on a telephone pole. A small meteor, approximately 5 yards in diameter, is going to enter our atmosphere. The meteor is expected to impact the Earth somewhere within the bounds of your small rural town. You predict that this event will have serious effects on the people in the community and the environment. Keeping your predictions in mind, create an advertisement to warn the town of the arrival of the meteorite. Be sure it is informative and promotes the safety of the people in your town."

**Summary:** "Before we end class today, take out your science journals. In your journal, write a personal reflection. Respond to the questions displayed on the overhead."

What new information have you gained about asteroids, comets, and meteors?

Was any of this information particularly interesting to you?

If you had the opportunity, would you like to see a passing comet or a meteor shower? Why or why not?

Lesson contrubuted by Kelly Dison, June 1999.

---

## CONTENT AREA: SCIENCE
## RELATIONSHIPS IN A HABITAT

**Class Description:** Biology, grade 9; heterogeneous, standard class. In the first part of this unit, the concepts of ecology, biosphere, abiotic factors, and biotic factors were investigated, and we will now be investigating relationships in a habitat.

**Unit Title:** Ecology

**Core Learning Goals:** Students will investigate the interdependence of diverse living organisms and their interactions with the components of the biosphere.

**Unit Goals:** Students will investigate the relationships of a habitat, focusing on various relationships and on the organization of these relationships with respect to the habitat.

### Lesson Objectives

1. Given pictures, examples, and a story, the students, working in pairs, will be able to "discover" working definitions for: *species, interaction, relationship,* and *predator–prey relationship.*
2. Given a graphic organizer, the students will be able to classify in hierarchical order various relationships in a habitat.
3. Given the same graphic organizer, the students will be able to use critical thinking skills and apply their knowledge by describing their own habitat and their relationships in that habitat.
4. Without the use of any aids, the students will create and fill in, completely, a KWL chart by the end of class.
5. From their own knowledge base, the students will hypothesize how humans affect habitats and relationships in habitats.

### Performance Assessment

| Objective | Assessment |
|---|---|
| 1. | Discovery vocabulary; partner discussion; written definitions in notebook |
| 2. | Filling in graphic organizers; discussion in small groups and as whole class |
| 3. | Filling in the graphic organizers |
| 4. | Creation of KWL charts; filling in K and W before reading; filling in L as a summary |
| 5. | Journaling; discussion in small groups and as a whole class |

**Macrostructure Thinking Skill:** Classification

**Materials**

- Textbook chapter, "Organisms in Ecosystems," reading
- "Relationships in Habitats" graphic organizer
- Transparency of "Relationships in Habitats"
- Species transparency
- Interaction transparency
- Relationship transparency
- Vocabulary transparency
- Flow chart of hierarchy of organization
- Transparencies: desert; forest; Chesapeake Bay; a yard

## Procedure

**TEACHER**                                                                 **STUDENT**

### I. Readiness

*a. Motivation and Tapping Background of Experience*

**1.** "Last class we talked about abiotic and biotic factors. The class before that, we talked about the biosphere and the ecosystem. Today we are going to put these pieces together so we can see the big picture. Then we are going to investigate another piece of the big picture we have put together."

**2.** Show the flow chart of hierarchical organization transparency (Figure A.17). "Let's fill in the details on this flow chart together to review what we have already learned. We have been going backward through this flow

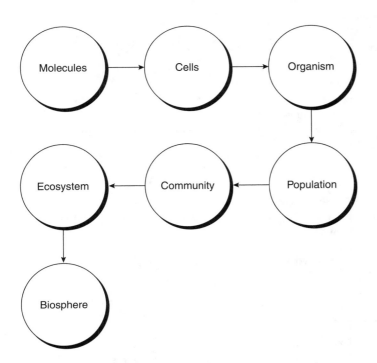

**FIGURE A.17    Hierarchy of Organization Flow Chart**

**TEACHER**

chart. We started with the largest element, a biosphere. Who can tell us what the biosphere is? Does it include living and nonliving things? Is the atmosphere part of the biosphere?" Write the students' definition on the transparency.

3. "Now, what is an ecosystem? What is the scientific way of saying living things? What is another name for non-living things?" Write the definition of ecosystem using the terms abiotic factors and biotic factors.

*Transition:* "Looking at our flow chart, what do you think we are going to investigate today?"

4. "What communities do you live in? What other communities do you belong to?

   Just as you belong to and live in communities, animals and plants also live and belong to communities. Where do you think you would find communities of plants and animals? Let's take a look at some of the areas where communities of plants and animals live."

5. Put up the transparency of a desert. "This is a picture of a desert community. Has anyone ever been to a desert?"

6. Put up the transparency of a forest. "As you can guess, this is a forest. Has anyone ever been in a forest? What kinds of things did you see living in the forest?"

7. Put up a transparency of the Chesapeake Bay. "This is a picture of something quite close to us. Does anyone know what it is? The Chesapeake Bay. Who has been boating or fishing around here? Who has been to the Inner Harbor? The Chesapeake Bay has many different communities in it just as there are many communities around here."

8. Put up a transparency of a yard. "This is something even closer to you. Within your communities there are other communities. How many of you have seen birds, squirrels, trees, and bugs in your own yard? In your own yard and your neighbors' yards live communities of plants and animals."

9. "Take out a sheet of paper and fold it lengthwise into three. Label the first column with a K (for *know*), the second with a W (for *want* to know), and the third column label with an L (for *learned*). Fill in what you already know about communities, habitats, and relationships in habitats. Take a few more minutes to fill in what you would like to know at the end of this lesson."

*b. Concept Development/Vocabulary*

"Open your notebooks to your vocabulary section."

1. Put up the vocabulary transparency. Only uncover the first word, *species*.

**STUDENT**

Individual students answer: "The Earth."
"Yes, it includes everything living and nonliving."
"The atmosphere is included."

"All the nonliving and living things in an area."
"The non-living things are abiotic factors."
"The living things are biotic factors."
"Communities."

Students name the housing developments they live in. Students tell what groups and organizations they are in. Some possible answers: "school, church, youth group."

Students answer:
"Yes."
"No."

Possible answers:
"Yes."
"Trees, bushes, squirrels, birds."

Responses:
"A bay."
"The Chesapeake Bay"
Students raise their hands in acknowledgment.

Students raise their hands in acknowledgment.

Students make and fill in KWL charts.

**TEACHER**

     "First we are going to work with the word *species.*"

     Put up the first page of the *species* transparencies. Uncover only the birds. "These are all different *species* of birds." Uncover the cacti. "These are all different *species* of cacti."

     Put up the second page of the *species* transparencies. Uncover only the dogs. "These are all different *species* of dogs." Uncover the daffodils. "These are different *species* of daffodils. *All* of these are different *species.* Now with your partner write a draft definition for the word *species.*"

     "What definitions have you come up with?" Write the correct definitions on the overhead next to the word.

     "Make sure you write down the definition we agree on in your notebooks."

**2.** Put the vocabulary transparency back up, and uncover the second word, *interaction.* "Our next word is *interaction.* In science, there are many words that have prefixes that give you clues to the meaning of the word. *Interaction* is one of these words. The prefix is *inter-.*

     Think of words that have the prefix *inter-* like *interstate,* which means between states; *interlock,* which means to fit together; *intermingle,* which means to talk among each other; and *intermission,* which means between acts of a play or performance." Put up a transparency with these words and their definitions. "Given these examples, talk with your partner to figure out a definition for the prefix *inter-.*"

     "Using the prefix *inter-* as a clue for the definition and this story, discuss with your partner possible definitions for *interaction.*"

     From the same transparency as the word with their definitions, uncover the following:

> When I was at the zoo, I saw the *interactions* of a mother and baby gorilla. The baby was playful and used its mother as a jungle gym. The mother sat there patiently letting the baby play. The mother would play with the baby a little, and it would every once in a while try to hold the baby to clean it, but the baby would resist getting cleaned. The baby just wanted to play.

     As a class discuss and write the definition on the transparency.

**3.** Put the vocabulary transparency back up and uncover the third word, *relationship.* "The third word we are going to look at is *relationship.* There are many kinds of *relationships.* Take a look at these *relationships* I have written on the transparency and with your partner try to find a common link, or something that all of these

**STUDENT**

Students talk over definitions with their partners while still looking at the species transparencies.

Students answer:
"Different types of one kind of animal or plant."
"Different plants and animals."
"Plants and animals that have different features from each other."

Students talk and figure out possible definitions for the prefix *inter-:*
"Between things."
"Among many things."

While looking at the excerpt and the definition of the prefix *inter-,* the students discuss possible definitions for the word *interaction.*

Possible answers include:
"How two animals get along."
"Actions and connections between things."
"Two or more things acting on each other and affecting each other."

The students talk among themselves to find the common link. Some of the answers given:
"Two people connected by something."
"Things or people that have to be around each other."

*relationships* share." Put up a transparency with the following pairs (Relationship transparency):

> Mother and child
> Teacher and student
> Boyfriend and girlfriend
> Boss and employee
> Friend and friend

Write the definition on the overhead.

**4.** "The last concept you need to understand before beginning your reading is *predator–prey relationship*." Put the vocabulary transparency back up and uncover the last vocabulary concept, *predator–prey relationship*. "Examples of *predators* are animals like lions and wolves. Examples of *prey* are animals like zebra and rabbits. Given these examples and using the definition we came up with for relationship, as well as some of the other definitions we discovered, what do you think a *predator–prey relationship* is?"

> Briefly discuss as a class and write the definition on the overhead.

Students discuss with their partners. Possible student responses are:
"A connection between two animals in which one eats the other."
"Two types of animals that live around each other because one eats the other one."
"Interactions between two species in which one animal kills and eats another . . . don't have a good relationship with each other."

*Transition:* "Now that we have found working definitions for the terms *species, interaction, relationship,* and *predator–prey relationship,* you are just about ready to read."

### c. Purpose-for-Reading

Hand out textbooks and have students locate the chapter "Organisms in Ecosystems." Distribute the graphic organizer "Relationships in Habitats" (see Figure A.18).

> "Today you will be reading to be informed. You will classify and define various relationships in a habitat. The graphic organizer will help you collect and classify the information from your reading."

Students receive the reading and the graphic organizer.

**II. Silent Reading:** At this time the students are given 25–30 minutes to read "Organisms in Ecosystems" and to fill out their "Relationships in Habitats" graphic organizers. Students are reminded to check their completed graphic organizers to see whether they used each of the four new vocabulary concepts in their responses (metacognitive and vocabulary reinforcement).

### III. Discussion

**1.** "In small groups at your tables, take five minutes to discuss the answers you wrote on your graphic organizer." Groups change weekly. They are usually triads or dyads of students grouped together because of varying achievement in science and reading.

Students discuss their answers at their tables.

**2.** Put up a transparency of the graphic organizer on the overhead. "I would like one student from each group to come up and write one answer on the overhead. Then explain how and why you chose that answer."

Students get up one at a time to write answers on the overhead. Students should check their answers and fill in any missing answers at this time.

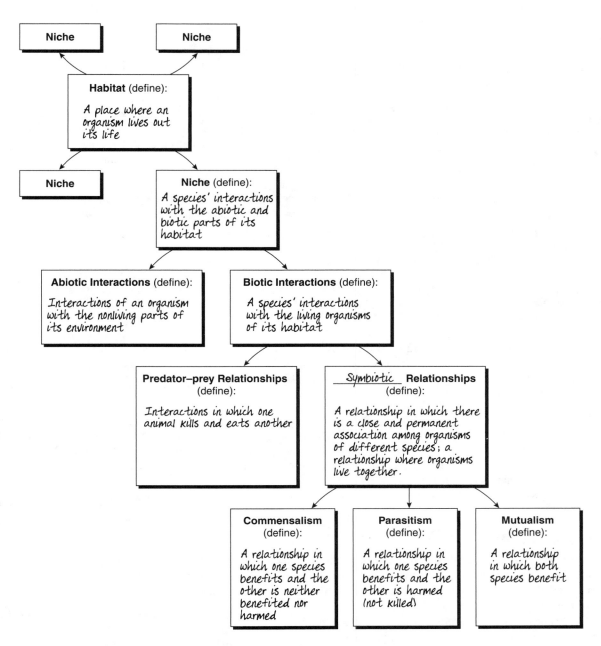

**FIGURE A.18** **"Relationships in Habitats" Graphic Organizer**

**TEACHER**

**STUDENT**

"Please check your answers and fill in any blanks on your web as we go through the web together."

## IV. Rereading

1. "At the beginning of class I asked what communities you live in, and you told me the housing developments and apartment complexes you live in. Then I asked what communities you belong to, and you said things like school and church. Which of these two communities

**TEACHER**

you belong to would you call your habitat? Which would you call your niche?" Ask each student to explain his or her answer.

"Your web should be completely filled in with all the words and their definitions."

**2.** "Before you reread, think about humans' roles in a community. Do humans affect different habitats and the relationships in them? How do you think humans affect the habitats and these relationships? Open your science journals and write down your ideas on this topic."

**3.** "Now go back and reread your passage to help you give examples of how humans could affect habitats and relationships within a habitat. The text does not cover human effects, but it gives you examples of the relationships. As you are rereading, also think about how all of the levels of relationships are affected by a change in the habitat or a change in just one relationship. Take notes of your thoughts and examples on the same page in your journal."

**4.** "In your groups, share your thoughts and ideas on how humans affect their habitats and the relationships in those habitats. Use reasoning, logic, and the text to support your thoughts and ideas."

"Who would like to share their examples and ideas with the class?"

**V. Follow-Up**

*Summary:* "To wrap up this lesson on communities and relationships in habitats take out your KWL chart that we started at the beginning of the lesson. It is time to fill in the last column of the chart. What did you learn today? Did all of your questions get answered? Take the next five minutes to write down as many things you learned as possible. As you leave, I want you to turn in these charts in the box for your class."

*Homework:* "Tonight for homework, you are going to put yourself into our graphic organizer. You will describe your habitat and your niche. Then you will explain two abiotic interactions and two general biotic interactions. From there include one predator–prey relationship you have, and list one of each of the symbiotic relationships you have. I am giving you another graphic organizer for you to do this assignment on. Be creative! Explain all your answers. What questions do you have?"

**STUDENT**

Students respond:
"The developments we live in are our habitats."
"School, church, and other organizations are like a niche." "A habitat is the physical place where something or someone lives, and a niche is the roles, interactions, and relationships that something or someone has in its habitat."

Students write their answers, ideas, and notes on a separate piece of paper in their journals.

Students discuss in their groups. Students then give examples of how humans could affect habitats and the relationships in those habitats.

Students volunteer their responses.

Students fill out the last column of the KWL charts. Students will turn in the KWL charts as they leave the classroom.

The students will be graded on validity and completeness of information in the L column.

Students receive another "Relationships in Habitats" graphic organizer.

Lesson contributed by Susy Miller, December 2000.

## CONTENT AREA: SOCIAL STUDIES
## HISTORY OF MARYLAND

**Class Description:** Social studies, grade 7; standard, heterogeneous achievement; inclusive class with four students with learning disabilities (receptive/reading)

**Unit Title:** The Thirteen Colonies

### Core Learning Goals for Social Studies

1. Students will demonstrate an understanding of the history, diversity, and commonality of the peoples of the nation and world, the reality of human interdependence, and the need for global cooperation, through a perspective that is both historical and multicultural.
2. Students will demonstrate an understanding of geographic concepts and processes to examine the role of culture, technology, and the environment in the location and distribution of human activities throughout history.

**Unit Objectives:** Students will be able to:

1. Recognize all thirteen colonies on a map
2. For each colony, retell who founded the colony, when it was established, and the reasons it was established, then induce the concepts of *commercial* and *proprietary* charters
3. Realize the importance of each individual colony
4. Understand the relationship between colonists and the people already living in America.
5. Understand the relationship between colonists and England.

**Lesson Objectives:** Students will:

1. Define the terms *prosperous* and *inherited*
2. List the reason that George Calvert wanted to leave England and found a colony
3. Explain the origin of the name of Maryland
4. Write a draft of a persuasive letter citing pro and con evidence for the establishment of a colony south of Virginia as opposed to in Newfoundland

### Performance Assessment

*Objective*     *Assessment*

1.     Vocabulary oral responses.
2.     Oral responses during discussion of timeline.
3.     Oral responses during discussion of timeline.
4.     Drafts of letters collected and reviewed.

**Macrostructure Thinking Skills:** chronological order, cause and effect

### Materials

- Transparencies: Maryland; George Calvert; vocabulary sentences; purpose-for-reading statement; timeline graphic organizer; unit graphic organizer—map of the colonies; maps of Maryland/Potomac area and Canada
- Overhead projector
- Videotape
- Picture of St. Mary's, Maryland
- Text reading on the history of Maryland
- Graphic organizers: timeline and map of the colonies
- Picture worksheet with four questions

# Procedure

## I. Readiness

***a. Motivation:*** "Are there any sports fans here? [*Yes*] Specifically, are there any basketball fans in here? [*Yes*] Tell us who you believe is the best basketball player ever." Teacher calls on students raising their hands.

> *Expected student responses:* Michael Jordan, Larry Bird, Magic Johnson, and so on.

"What if I told you that I am even better than those players you believe are the best? I believe I'm even better than Jordan. I average 70 points per game, 20 rebounds, and my hang-time is at least 2 minutes." Students laugh. "I also think that you all should think and tell everyone that I am the best basketball player ever. In fact, for you to pass my class, you must believe that I am the best player ever. How many of you think you're going to change your mind and believe that I am now the best basketball player?" A couple of students raise their hands. "Those of you who just raised your hand, why did you change your mind?"

> *Expected student response:* because we want to pass the class

"Those of you who didn't raise your hand, why? Do you not want to pass this class?"

> *Expected student response:* No, Michael Jordan is my favorite player, and I still think he is the best.

"So just because I say that you should believe that I am the best doesn't mean you actually will, right?

*Transition:* "This is exactly what some of the people thought in England during the 1600s. Instead of who the greatest basketball player was they were being told they had to believe in the same religion that the King did, the Church of England."

***b. Tapping Background of Experience:*** "Now we have already looked at how Virginia and Massachusetts were established. Who remembers the key motives for the creation of these colonies?"

> *Expected student response:* Virginia was established for economic motives and Massachusetts was established as a Puritan community.

"Good. We are now going to talk about how Maryland was established. For homework last night I asked you to find a picture of a place you may have visited in Maryland. Take out your pictures now." Students place pictures on their desk.

Teacher distributes worksheet. "On this page you will see a space for your picture. Underneath the space are four questions that I would like you to answer about your picture. I will place a roll of tape on each table so that you can put your picture in the space provided. Begin working on that now." Students silently work on the picture project.

### Questions
1. Where is this picture taken?
2. Describe the scenery.
3. What was the weather like?
4. If you lived in this area, what might you do for your occupation?

"Now you are going to share your picture and the information you wrote about it with the other students in your table group." Students share information with members of their group. Desks are arranged in clusters of four. Members of each cluster are grouped according to a mixture of gender, ethnicity, and reading achievement levels.

Teacher goes around to each group and makes notes of different places students have been. "I would like for some of you to share your pictures with the whole class." Teacher calls on students selectively so that various areas of Maryland are represented. Teacher uses map of Maryland to illustrate where these places are located. Students present information to the class. "Now I would like to share my picture with you. This is St. Mary's City and this is where I went to college. It's located on the Potomac River that leads out to the Chesapeake Bay [show transparency of the map of Maryland]. It has many wooded areas. It is usually warmer than other parts of Maryland because it is located in the most southern part of Maryland. There are many tobacco farms in the area. It is also where the first capital of Maryland was located."

"From all of our pictures we have learned what about Maryland?" Teacher writes on the board the following and has students draw the italicized conclusions:

Climate: *Usually warm; can have cold winters, etc.*
Farms: *Yes, especially on Eastern Shore*
Fishing: *Yes, especially on Chesapeake Bay*
Waterways: *Chesapeake Bay; Atlantic Ocean; many rivers and streams*

*Transition:* "Today we are going to see how all these qualities of Maryland attracted George Calvert to the area and made him want to settle here, but first there are two important words we must be sure we understand for the reading."

**c. *Concept Development/Vocabulary:*** "Imagine what I am describing. I have an uncle. He dresses in Ralph Lauren suits. He drives a red, convertible Porsche. He lives in a very large house along the Eastern Shore. He has three maids and a butler. In his house he has an indoor swimming pool and a tennis court. Sometimes when he gets bored he likes to fly his jet to his house in California. My uncle is a *prosperous* man. Now with your group, draft a definition of *prosperous.*

Teacher calls on various groups to tell their draft definition, then writes the final definition on the board. Students copy the definition into the vocabulary section of their notebooks.

*Expected definition:* successful financially; rich; wealthy

Teacher shows the following sentence on a transparency:

On my wedding day, I *inherited* from my mother a gold necklace that had been in my family for many generations. When my grandmother died, I *inherited* all of her china that was hers and now would be mine.

"With your group, draft a definition of *inherited.*" Teacher calls on various groups to tell their draft definition, then writes final definition on the board. Students copy the definition into the vocabulary section of their notebooks.

*Expected definition:* to receive something that has belonged to someone else when they die or no longer need it

*Transition:* "Good. Now that we have prepared ourselves with the vocabulary, we are ready to tackle the reading selection. Your purpose-for-reading is on the overhead transparency."

**d. *Purpose-for-Reading:*** "Today we will be reading to be informed. We will be reading the selection on Maryland, in particular, about George Calvert. Here is George Calvert, our first Lord Baltimore [show transparency of a picture of Calvert]. You will be reading to fill in the timeline. There are a series of events that you will put on the timeline in chronological order." Students will complete the graphic organizer (see Figure A.19). Teacher reviews the graphic organizer with students. "Please remember if you don't understand something it is helpful to reread the passage."

Students with learning disabilities have a textbook at home. The teacher tells them what they will be reading in class the next day so that they can do a first reading at home. These first readings often take these students longer than the other students in the class. In this way, the students with learning disabilities can be doing a second reading in class, a reading that is usually faster than their first attempt.

**II. Silent Reading:** Students read silently the article "Maryland" and complete the graphic organizer in the packet.

**History of Maryland**

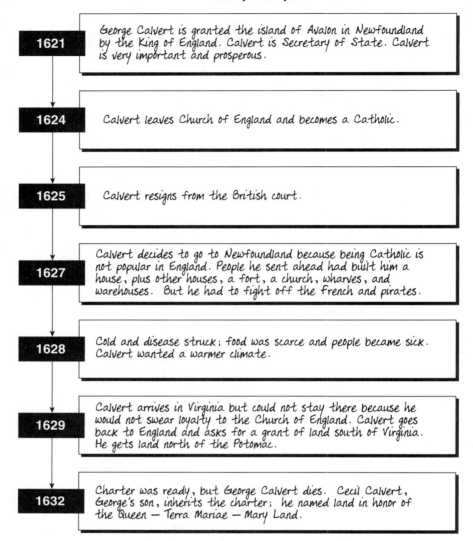

**1621** — George Calvert is granted the island of Avalon in Newfoundland by the King of England. Calvert is Secretary of State. Calvert is very important and prosperous.

**1624** — Calvert leaves Church of England and becomes a Catholic.

**1625** — Calvert resigns from the British court.

**1627** — Calvert decides to go to Newfoundland because being Catholic is not popular in England. People he sent ahead had built him a house, plus other houses, a fort, a church, wharves, and warehouses. But he had to fight off the French and pirates.

**1628** — Cold and disease struck; food was scarce and people became sick. Calvert wanted a warmer climate.

**1629** — Calvert arrives in Virginia but could not stay there because he would not swear loyalty to the Church of England. Calvert goes back to England and asks for a grant of land south of Virginia. He gets land north of the Potomac.

**1632** — Charter was ready, but George Calvert dies. Cecil Calvert, George's son, inherits the charter; he named land in honor of the Queen — Terra Mariae — Mary Land.

**FIGURE A.19    Graphic Organizer for History of Maryland Lesson**

**III. Discussion:** Teacher goes through the graphic organizer with students, recording key events on a transparency of the timeline. "Who is the main person we are talking about in this article?"

*Expected student response:* George Calvert

"Let's look at our first date, 1621." Each date and the important events are reviewed.

Teacher shows maps—world map and map of Canada to show where Newfoundland is located and map of the Atlantic colonies to show Virginia and the Potomac area when they are discussed. Information about previously learned concepts of "charters" and Church of England vs. Catholicism are reviewed as the associated events are discussed.

"Now within your table groups, you will form two pairs and using your timelines you will orally retell the story of George Calvert and the founding of Maryland. One member will start with the first event in the story, 1621, and the next person will tell about the next, 1624, and so forth. Remember that the reading is in chronological order so make sure you start your retelling with the year 1621, when George Calvert was given the island of Avalon in Newfoundland by King James I."

**IV. Rereading:** "You will need to revisit the text and your timeline for this next assignment. You are going to pretend you are George Calvert and you are on your way back to England to ask for a charter for the new land. Write a letter to the King asking for this charter. Be sure to include your reasons for wanting a colony (pro) and why it wouldn't work in Newfoundland (con). You will need to persuade him! Before you begin writing, list your reasons for not wanting to stay in Newfoundland, then list your reasons why you want a charter in this new land." Students read text silently, make lists, and write letters. Teacher calls on some students to read their letters.

**V. Follow-Up and Summary:** "Let's now go back to our unit graphic organizer. For our map, we can now label Maryland, when it was established (1632), by whom (George and Cecil Calvert), and why (religious purposes)." Teacher asks for responses from students.

---

Lesson contributed by Tina Wasowicz, December 2000.

## CONTENT AREA: SOCIAL STUDIES
## THE DEVELOPMENT OF THE SUPREME COURT'S POWER

**Class Description:** Social studies, grade 11; U.S. history; all students are academically gifted; text is college level; most students will take the Advanced Placement history examination for college placement and credit

**Unit Title:** The Judiciary's Role under the Constitution

**High School Core Learning and Unit Goals:** The following are selected from relevant Maryland High School Core Learning Goals:

I. Political Systems: "The student will demonstrate an understanding of the historical development and current status of principals, institutions, and processes of political systems."
   a. Indicators of Learning: "The student will analyze the origins and development of the United States political system from the late 18th Century to the present."
   b. Content. To achieve these indicators, appropriate content includes the following:
      1. "Supreme Court cases that significantly reflect or influenced change in society: *Marbury v. Madison, Dred Scott v. Stanford, Plessy v. Ferguson, Brown v. Board of Education, Miranda v. Arizona*"
      2. "Issues of states' rights vs. federal power during specific periods in United States history."
      3. "Emancipation and Civil War amendments to the Constitution."
      4. "Relationship of the three branches."

*Source: Maryland High School Assessment Social Studies Core Learning Goals.* (2000). Retrieved from the World Wide Web: www.mcps.k12.md.us/curriculum/socialstd/MSPAP/HAS_US.html.

**Lesson Objectives:** Following the reading of "Developing Supreme Court Power," class discussion, and related activities, the students will be able to:

1. Define the terms: *unconstitutional, immunities, police, due process,* and *regulatory*
2. Explain the basic processes of the judicial branch of government (will receive enrichment through additional later lessons)
3. Define *judicial review* (requires mention and knowledge of *Marbury v. Madison*)
4. Explain the Supreme Court's articulation and expansion of its power *over time* and across various important legal issues, such as states' rights (requires knowledge of decisions in key cases, with emphasis on *Marbury v. Madison*)

5. Recall and evaluate the role of the Supreme Court in shaping civil liberties during different periods of American history (requires knowledge of relevant key cases; regulatory power will be revisited in a later unit for greater in-depth analysis)

## Performance Assessment

*Objective*   *Assessment*

1.   Oral responses during Concept Development/Vocabulary
2.   Graphic organizer 1 collected and reviewed; individual and group oral responses
3.   Graphic organizer 2 collected and reviewed; oral responses
4.   Graphic organizer 2 collected and reviewed; oral responses
5.   Graphic organizer 3 collected and reviewed; oral responses

**Macrostructure Thinking Skills:**  Sequence, chronological order, cause and effect

## Materials

- Overhead projector with computer display capabilities, especially for the Web
- Text reading: "Developing Supreme Court Power"
- Transparency of "Separation of Powers and Checks and Balances" taken from organizational chart from *"We the People . . ."* (Calabasas, CA: Center for Civic Education, 1987), 53
- Graphic organizers: sequence chain; cause and effect; comparison and contrast
- *Virtual Tour of Supreme Court.* (2000). http://oyez.nwu.edu/tour/index.html. Includes pictures and information on current and important past Justices and the Supreme Court building in Washington
- Lesson day's newspaper headlines taken from www.nytimes.com and www.cnn.com
- Copies of "Court Systems of the United States"; organizational chart from *"We the People . . ."* (Calabasas, CA: Center for Civic Education, 1987), 71.
- The *New York Times*. 1/26/00. "Tracking the Legal Challenges." Retrieved November 28, 2000 from the World Wide Web: www.nytimes.com
- Copies of Associated Press article. "Bush and Gore Make Pleas to Supreme Court." Retrieved November 28, 2000 from World Wide Web: www.nytimes.com/aponline/politics/AP-Scotus-Recount.html

# Procedure

## I. Readiness

*a. Motivation and Tapping of Background:*  Use current events to get students interested and tap their background knowledge by showing how history shapes their lives. "As you may remember, we have been studying the origins and development of the Constitution. In fact, we finished our unit on the presidency. Unsurprisingly, in light of current events, we focused a considerable amount of attention on how the president is selected." Teacher will use overhead projector to display visual cues in the form of that day's newspaper headlines and photos to remind students of previous lessons' material, especially the electoral college. Teacher will read headlines and captions aloud to help further this preliminary tapping of background knowledge and stimulation of motivation.

"How many of you discussed, or heard discussed, such issues with family friends during the weekend? Stirred some pretty strong feelings, didn't it? What were some of the opinions or statements that you heard?" Some or all students raise hands or nod heads.

> *Expected student responses:*  My dad says that if it isn't cleared up soon as to who won the electoral college, the House of Representatives will decide who is president; I heard on the news last night that despite Bush being certified in Florida there is no way of telling for sure who is president yet because of all the ongoing lawsuits.

"We know that the struggle over the presidency is still evoking strong feelings, but as your comments remind us, it is only one part of the government. That fact sometimes gets lost. Let's review briefly the system that the Constitution sets up to govern the country at the federal level. [Teacher puts up transparency of separation of powers and checks and balances.] How many branches are there? And what are they?"

*Expected student response:* three—the executive, the legislative, and the judicial

"Good. What do we call this arrangement of dividing power among three branches?"

*Expected student response:* the separation of powers

"Good. What is the system by which one branch is prevented from gaining too much power and stepping out of its proper bounds?"

*Expected student response:* checks and balances.

Students explain some of the checks, such as impeachment. "Right. Now, as you may recall, we have had units about the presidency and the Congress. In particular, as [student X] just touched on, we learned about the House of Representatives' potential role in selecting the President."

*Transition:* "So far, we have largely overlooked the last branch, which has come into prominence recently as both Bush and Gore campaigns have increasingly turned to it to help them win. [Student Y] just mentioned it, and it's the last one on the chart we haven't discussed. What is it?"

*Expected student response:* the Supreme Court or judicial branch

Teacher pulls up *New York Times* article "Bush and Gore Make Pleas to Supreme Court." Teacher also hands out hard copies of the article to students. "Yes! As you can see from this article, the Supreme Court is now going to play a central role. Who will read the headline for the class?" A student reads headline aloud.

### b. Development of Background of Experience

*Transition:* "So now the Supreme Court is involved! How did that happen? And what is it about the judicial branch that made the candidates think that they could secure what they wanted with a court decision? To understand these specific issues about our present day and age, we first need to use our analytic skills as historians to learn more about the larger history of the Court and its power in our constitutional system. This task will help us put present-day events in context. This task will also start us on our next unit on the judicial branch, which is part of the core learning goals we laid out for ourselves at the beginning of the year. We will start today by reading 'Developing Supreme Court Power' in your texts." Teacher directs students to chapter and page. "Skim over the title, boldface, and pictures, and ask yourself what the piece might convey about the history of the Supreme Court's power? Ask yourself, what type of writing is this?"

> ### Metacognitive Previewing Strategy (skimming, studying pictures, activating textual knowledge, and setting purpose-for-reading and key questions):
> 1. Students look over piece and ask, "What might this piece include?" *Expected answer:* Discussion of court cases and concepts, such as judicial review and due process.
> 2. Students ask, "What might I see?" *Expected answer:* Court proceedings and decisions.
> 3. Students ask, "What type of selection is this?" *Expected answer:* Expository text on a historical subject. Historical content will cue them to expect sequence, cause and effect, and comparison.

Teacher checks for these answers after giving students a minute or two.

"Good. Just as we did last week to help us read articles about county election officials deciding when a dimple is not a dimple, let's picture in our minds what happens in courts before we get into this piece. To begin, let's ask what we already know about the legal process. To help you with this question, think about an episode of a lawyer and police show like *Law and Order.* What do you see in your mind?"

***Metacognitive Previewing Strategy (movie of the mind and tapping of background):***
Teacher here helps students tap their background with a prereading movie of the mind for purpose-for-reading and key questions as well as building on an earlier visual preview of the piece. Both activities are part of the overall process of scaffolding.

> *Expected student response:* Students begin to visualize a prototypical sequence of courtroom scenes, such as cross-examination and arraignment. Once they are done, they raise hands and describe the adversary system of justice, laws, and procedures for both sides to follow, and the role of judges. (Students may not know, and will not be required to know during the first lesson, the technical terms or organization of what they are conveying about the judicial system. Again, the goal is to refresh or tap background knowledge to help students comprehend the meaning of the reading selection that will begin to introduce them to such information.)

"Good. You all know more than you may have at first thought. Now, to help you visualize your knowledge with regard to the Supreme Court in particular, take a look at this virtual tour." Teacher runs virtual tour of Supreme Court building and current justices from *Oyez, Oyez, Oyez* website to help prepare students for the reading with a second prereading movie of the mind. Students will see pictures of various chambers and offices as well as pictures and facts about present and past justices.

"Now, as you go through this court, imagine that you are a historian there this Friday and are looking at the justices who are sitting behind that big bench and are listening to both campaign's lawyers arguing that the law and the Constitution support their respective candidates. What are some questions that might run through your mind if this were your first time there and you knew only what you do right now but wanted to learn more as a historian about how and why the court works? What are some subtitles, so to speak, in your movie of the mind?"

> *Expected student response:* How did this case get to the Court? What power does the Court have over the matter? Why?

### c. Concept Development/Vocabulary

*Transition:* "Good questions. Our reading will help us understand these matters and other important ones. However, as with some of our other readings this year on constitutional and legal affairs, there are some difficult and unfamiliar words and concepts that we need to know before we start reading. So take out your notebooks and open them to your vocabulary section. Also, please make sure that you are in the groups to which I assigned you last week."

*Grouping Criteria:* Students are grouped (four students per group) for each two-week cycle according to personality to avoid either domineering or passive behavior as well as stigmatization. Academic ability is usually a heterogeneous mix, but given the selectivity of the school most students are above average; thus, this is usually dependent on A versus B students.

"Define the word *unconstitutional* by using hints or clues in the following sentence" (written on board and read aloud).

> A law passed by Congress mandating that everyone become a Catholic would be *unconstitutional* because it violates the provision for separation of church and state.

> *Expected definition:* a law or action in conflict with the Constitution

With some elaboration on the meaning of the prefix un-, this definition will be entered into students' notebooks.

"I know you all just finished a unit in biology on the immune system. As you may recall, your immune system provides protection against disease. Now *immunity* can also have a similar meaning in regard to the law. Imagine that you are being threatened by government officials or private citizens in the way germs threaten your body. Imagine also that you have a symbolic shield provided by the Constitution to ward off these people in much the same way your skin prevents germs from getting into your body. On the shield is the phrase *legal immunities*. Who can tell us what *immunities* might mean here?"

*Expected definition:* a form of legal protection against unfair or cruel treatment

This definition will be put in students' notebooks.

"I know you think the *police* are law enforcement officers, but this definition of the word is actually derived from an older meaning, which is what we want here. See if you can discern this particular meaning from this sentence" (written on board and read aloud).

Detectives, health inspectors, and fire fighters all exercise the government's *police* power for the sake of individuals' and the overall community's well being.

*Expected definition:* government power to ensure order and safety

This definition will be put in students' notebooks.

"*Due process* is tricky at first, but imagine you've been arrested simply for wearing blue. Your lawyer says to the police that the related law is unfair and unreasonable. At your trial, the judge will not let you or your lawyer speak in your defense. You scream out, 'All of this violates my right to *due process*.' What does it mean?"

*Expected definition:* The law and the means of enforcing it should both be fair and reasonable.

This definition will be put in the students' notebooks.

"I have here the student handbook [taken out of desk]. In here is a section entitled 'Dress Code Regulations.' Now if it said that the headmistress had regulatory power to decide how you will and will not dress, what would you say *regulatory* means? Look at the root of the word as a clue."

*Expected definition:* the ability to make a rule to control a group of people for specific purpose

This definition will be put in students' notebooks.

*Transition:* "Now that we have a grasp of these key terms and have focused our minds on the new unit's issue for today and drawn on what we already know, we can now proceed with the reading selection."

*d. Purpose-for-Reading:* "We will be reading this chapter to be informed about the Supreme Court's power. To help analyze it, we will need to employ our thinking skills of cause and effect, chronological order, and sequence. We will also use a few graphic organizers to help process the information we gain. I'm going to put several key questions up on the board. Please keep them in mind while you are silently reading." Teacher places the following on a transparency for the board.

*Purpose-for-reading:* to be informed about the development of the Supreme Court's Power

### Key Questions
1. Explain the basic principles and process(es) by which the judicial branch operates. Use graphic organizer 1, the sequence chain, to chart this process (see Figure A.20).
2. What is judicial review? Explain how the Supreme Court has gained and expanded this power. Use graphic organizer 2—the establishment of judicial review—cause and effect (see Figure A.21).

**II. Silent Reading:** "In answering all questions except 1, make sure to consider key court cases. Legal reading is not something to be read quickly. Please read slowly and carefully and reread important and complex passages. We need to self-monitor our reading processes to make sure that we are ascertaining what information and meaning we can. Make sure to check to see whether you are finding the answers to the purpose-for-reading by completing your graphic organizers."

**Sequence Chain: Process and Procedures of the Judicial Branch**

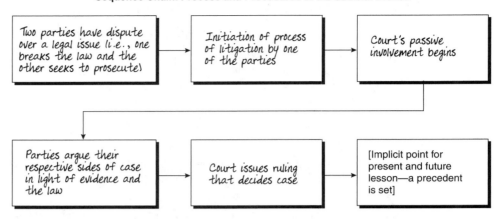

Two parties have dispute over a legal issue (i.e., one breaks the law and the other seeks to prosecute) → Initiation of process of litigation by one of the parties → Court's passive involvement begins

Parties argue their respective sides of case in light of evidence and the law → Court issues ruling that decides case → [Implicit point for present and future lesson—a precedent is set]

**FIGURE A.20    Graphic Organizer 1 for Supreme Court Lesson**

**Cause and Effect**

Case of *Marbury v. Madison*,
Establishment of Judicial Review

**Influences and causes . . .**

1. President Adams makes last-minute appointment
2. Jefferson tries to have some withdrawn
3. Marbury files suit

**Leading to the event . . .**

1. Marshall accepts case
2. Both sides argue in court
3. Court issues ruling

**Outcomes and effect of events . . .**

1. Marbury loses
2. The Supreme Court establishes ability to review the constitutionality and unconstitutionality of laws and government actions

**FIGURE A.21    Graphic Organizer 2 for Supreme Court Lesson**

Students read selection and fill out graphic organizers. Time has been allotted by giving students two-and-half times what it took the instructor to perform the same tasks.

After announcement, the teacher circulates to ask questions and ensure that students are self-monitoring by completion of organizers.

***Retelling (about 10 minutes into the reading):*** "I see that you are reading and taking notes on the section about *Plessy v. Ferguson.* Understanding this case is important to your purpose-for-reading. What can you tell me about this case from what you can recall? Use your notes if you need to."

> *Expected student response:* This case declared that state segregation laws were constitutional. It represented an example of the Court not using the Reconstruction amendments to ensure equally the due process rights of all individuals, especially African Americans.

Students then continue to work individually.

**III. Discussion:** "Now that we have had a chance to do the reading individually, let's use our conference skills by building a consensus on the questions in our groups."

***After-Reading Metacognitive and Evaluating Strategies (conferencing, retelling, and listening):*** Teacher circulates around class to guide discussion as students engage in interpersonal monitoring through conferencing. In particular, this process will enable students to check what they have read (implicitly including listing to varying extents). Teacher then shifts to whole-class discussion. During this stage, the teacher will also complete appropriate graphic organizers on transparencies and overheads. At all points, teacher will assess the quality of students' performance through their oral responses.

> *Question 1* (see expected responses on graphic organizer 1).
> *Question 2* (see expected responses on graphic organizer 2). The case was called *Marbury v. Madison,* and occurred around 1800. In it, Mr. Marbury and Mr. Adams disagreed with Mr. Jefferson over commissions for an office. Next, Mr. Marbury filed a case with the Supreme Court, and Mr. Marshall accepted it. The Court, it should be stressed, had to wait for Mr. Marbury to take action. Finally, the court ruled. In doing so, it successfully asserted the power of judicial review, but Mr. Marbury ironically did not get his commission.

"How has the Court expanded its authority over time? Make sure to use examples of cases to illustrate." Teacher has students elaborate on cause and effect in relation to chronology and sequence as well as implicitly phasing into some preliminary summarization.

> *Expected student response:* Using judicial review as established in *Marbury v. Madison,* the Court proceeded to rule on matters of constitutionality in a widening array of legal issues; these included states' rights and laws (as it did, for example, in *Dartmouth College v. Woodward),* due process and regulatory power (as it did, for example, in *United States v. E. C. Knight Co.* and *Debs v. United States),* and civil liberties (as it did, for example, in *Brown v. Board of Education of Topeka).* In all these instances, the Court reaffirmed and expanded its role as the arbiter of the Constitution.

*Note:* The concept of *precedent,* which is used implicitly here, will be examined explicitly and in-depth in the next lesson in the unit on the judiciary.

**IV. Rereading**

*Transition:* "Now that we have a good grasp of judicial review and how it has been used and expanded, let's use our skills of not only sequence, chronological order, and cause and effect, but also comparison to analyze how the Supreme Court has used its power in different ways over time. We can approach this issue by comparing the status of individual civil liberties, especially of African Americans in different periods and the basis on which the Court has ruled. This will require a closer examination of the text, so it will help if we reread carefully on this matter." Teacher cues students to use higher-level thinking skills to construct answers to questions.

"But first let me say that while we will be concentrating here on civil liberties, we could also do it with the issue of economic regulation. However, please hold onto your notes on regulatory power, as we will return to it next week when we start our unit on the market revolution. This transforming burst of economic growth started during Jefferson's presidency and created tremendous political conflicts between the two major political parties, between the states and federal government, and among the three branches of government over what the law and economic policy should be as the United States became increasingly capitalist, expansionary, and industrialized. Court decisions, such as that in the *Dartmouth College* case, played huge roles that we will need to explore in more depth."

*Note:* I decided to make this lesson plan decision as it enables students to better understand *regulatory* power more thoroughly and in a better context that also fits with the class's course of study and textbook layout.

"As noted, to help think through and prepare before you answer this tough question on civil liberties, we are going to reread the appropriate sections. However, let's first take a moment to go back over what we mean by due process and police power. Who can tell us? Be sure to illustrate with an example." Students offer definition from Concept Development/ Vocabulary phase with the addition of listing examples of the cases about which they have read.

"Now, as we have said so far all of this year, we need to make sure that we learn how the past affects our lives. Of course, this requires that we first understand what role our subject plays in our own lives. For instance, do we have civil liberties? Do the courts protect them? Let's confer over these questions within our groups. It may help to think about current issues that are in the media such as the right to vote or events in your lives such as who can attend this school today and who was once unable to or what your rights were when some of you got your first speeding ticket and had to go to court!" This will immediately get the attention and tap the experience of many sixteen- or seventeen-year-old juniors.

Students confer in groups for several minutes. Teacher circulates around class to ensure students are engaged in self-monitoring using the same skills as in previous group-work sessions. Teacher then shifts discussion out of groups to whole class.

> *Expected student response:* Students discuss among other things the role that civil liberties play in the integration of the school, their right to have attorneys present at trials, and their right to go to court to make sure one can vote. Some mention the role of the courts in hearing civil liberties cases on voting in Florida. They agree that they enjoy the many benefits of civil liberties and that the courts generally protect them.

*Transition:* "Okay, good, we have a decent grasp of civil liberties in our lives, let's compare the present and the past and try to explain what we discern. Put more precisely, we need to reread carefully to compare and contrast the Supreme Court's approach to individual civil liberties (especially those of African Americans) over time and, in particular, to consider what changes, if any, have occurred and on what different grounds the Court has justified its decisions. This organizer should help you. After you reread the appropriate parts of the reading, please fill it out. As always, check to see if you are self-monitoring your progress." Teacher puts key question transparency on the board and hands out organizer (see Figure A.22).

**During-Rereading Metacognitive Strategies (rereading, checking for purpose, and taking notes/organizing):** Students reread and use skills of comparison to fill out organizer while teacher floats around class to ensure student self-monitoring. Teacher then shifts to whole-class discussion of question to construct meaning and draw conclusions.

"Okay, based on what you know from the rest of the lesson as well as this particular reading, what are differences that you note and why are there differences, that is to say, how did the court justify its actions?"

> *Expected student response:* Students emphasize that the court did not use the Reconstruction amendments, especially the due process clauses, in conjunction with the Bill of Rights to increase the civil liberties of individuals before the 1950s whereas since then it has. In particular, they assert that the Court used states' rights and police doctrines to uphold their earlier restrictive rulings but no longer do so as a result of in-

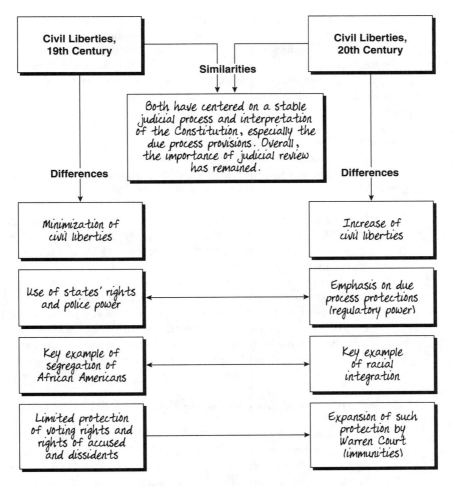

**FIGURE A.22   Graphic Organizer 3 for Supreme Court Lesson**

creased application of due process. Moreover, as a point of emphasis, they concentrate their examples on the segregation of African Americans (noting the "separate but equal" doctrine as a result of *Plessy*), but they observe that today due to *Brown*, integration is the norm. Through hints from the teacher, they in turn make note of the rulings of the Warren Court and infer that previously voting rights and the rights of the accused and dissidents were less protected as in the *Debs* case. They conclude that the Court has shifted in its use and interpretation of the Constitution over time and, in doing do, has played a major role in shaping and ultimately advancing individual civil liberties after earlier stifling of them. In regard to similarities, the students observe that the process through which the Court receives cases and exerts its power has remained the same. Along these lines, they also note that, while interpretation and use of doctrine has changed, the Constitution, particularly the due process clauses, has remained the same and has been the axis around which struggles over the meaning and extent of civil liberties have taken place in the judiciary.

Teacher fills out organizer on transparency in response to students' conclusions.

## V.  Follow-Up

### a.  Summary

*Note:* I have my students write regular journal entries that require them to perform the overlapping tasks of personalizing and critically analyzing the reading and thereby connect it to their lives. This performance-based assessment has set criteria of being a thesis-driven argument in the form of a several-paragraph essay in which the students utilize evidence drawn from the reading and offer their opinions. Such assignments are used for students to demonstrate mastery over content through judiciously selecting the most important themes and facts of a piece and organizing them into a coherent summary while offering an interpretation as to their historical significance, especially in regard to (1) their impact on students' lives and (2) their relation to other material they have studied.

*Transition:* "You all have done an excellent job today and yesterday of covering some very difficult material. For the rest of the period today, I want you reflect on what we have learned by writing a journal entry on the following issue." Teacher writes assignment on board. It is an elaboration on key question number four.

> *Journal assignment:* One of the central principles of democratic government is that the will of the majority as expressed through their elected representative, the Congress and president, must prevail. The practice of judicial review seemingly contradicts this principle. Examine how you might be affected by such an argument in relation to your life (i.e., your civil liberties or a regulation that impacts your parents' business) and conclude how you might draw up a defense of judicial review. Be sure to consider how judicial review has been used in various ways over time since what may be a valid defense of this power in one period or case may not be valid in another. Also be sure to incorporate what else you have learned so far about the Constitution, especially the system of checks and balances as judicial review exists and can be justified only within this context.

Students spend rest of period writing in journals that will later be collected for assessment.

> *Expected student response:* The essays will vary from one student to another. In addition to a thoughtful reflection on how the Court impacts their life, a good essay will include implicit or explicit mention of what judicial review is, how the court system works, several of the areas the Court has shaped (such as states' rights and due process), shifts in the Court's position, specific relevant cases, and the relationship of the courts to the other branches. Such a response is realistic for students who are preparing for AP exams.

***b. Homework:*** "Okay, at the beginning of class yesterday we began by introducing the subject of the Supreme Court's power by way of the judiciary's role in settling the election fiasco in Florida. Although we have not touched on it directly today, implicit in our lesson, notably in many of the cases you have read about, was the fact that there are several layers to the judiciary in this country. The vast majority of cases the Supreme Court examines do not start there, but rather in one of several lower courts as you can see from this chart I'm handing out [hands out chart laying out the structure of the judiciary]. Tonight or tomorrow during study hall in the library, take this chart, the article I handed out yesterday on the Bush and Gore campaigns turning to the Supreme Court, and additional related articles you find in the newspaper or the Internet, and:

1. Trace the steps by which the two candidates' respective cases worked their way through the levels of the judiciary.
2. Discern the issue(s) the Supreme Court is considering using its power of judicial review. To do this assignment, create a sequence chart or timeline. As with similar assignments, I have blank sequence charts you can use or feel free to create your own on your computers.

Lesson contributed by Justin Hill, December 2000.

## CONTENT AREA: SPANISH
### *UNA LEYENDA DEL CARIBE*

*Note:* This lesson is *conducted* in Spanish and the reading is in Spanish. However, this lesson plan is *written* here in English so that all readers of this text can access it.

**Class Description:** Spanish III; grades 10 through 12

**Unit Title:** Legends from the Caribbean

**Unit Goal:** Students will demonstrate an understanding of Spanish-speaking, primitive island cultures

**Lesson Topic:** The Tainos' beliefs about their origins

**Lesson Objectives**

1. Students will write definitions for the following terms: *aldea, oscuridad,* and *soportar.*
2. Students will interpret *Una Leyenda del Caribe* for the narrative elements of setting, characters, problem, significant events, and solution.
3. The student will write a summary of the legend in Spanish.

**Performance Assessment**

| Objectives | Assessment |
|---|---|
| 1. | Vocabulary pair work; oral responses |
| 2. | Story map graphic organizers collected and reviewed |
| 3. | Summaries collected and reviewed |

**Macrostructure Thinking Skill:** Narrative elements

**Materials**

- Map of the world
- Transparencies: map of the Caribbean, comparison-and-contrast graphic organizer; story map graphic organizer
- *Una Leyenda del Caribe* reading; comparison-and-contrast graphic organizer; story map graphic organizer
- "Discovery of the Caribbean," pp. 404–406, in *Lands and People* (Danbury, CT: Grolier, 1992), one copy for teacher

## Procedure

**TEACHER**

**STUDENT**

### I. Readiness

*a. Motivation:* "Close your eyes. Travel back to a time when there is no electricity, go back further. Candles haven't been invented yet. It is nighttime. You are not alone. You are sitting cross-legged in an open meadow of tall grass surrounded by forests. A stream gurgles by somewhere behind you at the edge of the forest. You look up at a waxing quarter moon. You see stars that stretch from horizon to horizon. You feel a sweeping breeze rush past you, the night is full of sound. Murmured conversation and soft laughter mix with the wild sounds of the forest. As your tribe settles into the customary circle, the elder begins his story. What kind of story is about to be told?"

Students respond:
"A fable, a tribal story, a story about nature."

| **TEACHER** | **STUDENT** |
|---|---|
| ***b. Tapping and Developing Background of Experience*** | |
| **1.** "Has anyone ever heard any stories about the origins of primitive peoples?" | Students respond:<br>"Native American stories;<br>"Greek, Roman, and Norse myths." |
| **2.** "Why do people create these tales?" | "To explain the world around them; to ease their fears of the unknown; to entertain or to teach their children." |
| **3.** Use the world map. "Our story takes place in the Caribbean. Who will show us how to get there from our hometown? Has anyone ever been to the Caribbean?" Overview the islands, especially Windward and Leeward islands, using a transparency of the area. | Student comes to front and shows the relative locations.<br>Students share any travel experiences. |
| **4.** "Has anyone every heard of the Caribs or the Arawaks, sometimes called the Tainos? These are both indigenous Caribbean tribes. Listen while I read you a short segment that compares and contrasts these two tribes." Read from *Lands and People.* Distribute comparison-and-contrast graphic organizer (see Figure A.23) and have students complete it while teacher reads the segment again. Discuss with entire class. Record responses on transparency of the graphic organizer. Stress the contrast between the two tribes (physical appearance, personality, disposition) as background for the upcoming reading of the legend. | Students share any background.<br><br><br>Students complete graphic organizers and then participate in the entire-class discussion. Expected student responses are on the graphic organizer. |

**Caribes**
- tall and brown
- long, shiny black hair
- altered shape of their heads by placing boards on the forehead and the back of the head, so that their heads came to have a boxlike look
- scarred cheeks with deep incisions, which they painted black
- bracelets were made from the bones of dead enemies
- perforated their noses and inserted fish bones or pieces of tortoiseshell
- cannibals—boiled humans to make a stew
- belligerent
- waged bitter and relentless wars against Europeans

**Both Indigenous Tribes of the Caribbean**

**Arawaks (Tainos)**
- tall; moved gracefully
- dark eyes and friendly smiles
- depressed skulls in childhood with a wooden frame
- loved to play games with balls for fun
- ate primarily root vegetables and corn
- lovable, peaceful dispositions
- loved their neighbors

**FIGURE A.23    Indigenous Tribes of the Caribbean Graphic Organizer**

**TEACHER**

*c. Concept Development/Vocabulary:* To understand the reading better we are going to develop definitions for three new words.

1. "Read the following sentence, and with your partner draft a definition of *aldea."*

    There were not many homes or even shops in the cozy, little aldea in which she lived.

    "That's correct. *Aldea* can mean town, but it usually refers to a village."

2. "What kind of word do we call one that sounds the same in English and Spanish?"

    "That's right. The word *oscuridad* is a cognate. Who remembers what 'dad' at the end of a Spanish word means? See if you can get it from these sentences."

    The actress did not get any more parts and soon she faded into *oscuridad.*

    The spaceship floated off, deep into space, around the far side of the moon into *oscuridad.*

3. "Our last word is yet another cognate. Can anyone guess just from the sound of it what *soportar* might mean? Take a minute and talk it over with your partner.

    "Yes, that is the general meaning. In the context you will be seeing it, however, it is used in a negative sense. For example, 'I cannot *support* or tolerate even one more book in my backpack.' "

*d. Purpose-for-Reading:* "Today we will be reading for literary experience. While you silently read *Una Leyenda del Caribe,* you will identify the narrative elements of setting, characters, conflict or problem, significant events, and solution. Be sure to note the words and translations provided at the bottom of the sheet." Teacher distributes story map graphic organizer (see Figure A.24).

**II. Silent Reading:** Students read silently in class. Teacher circulates through class and addresses any needs students may have. Teacher stops class about halfway through reading and asks if students are finding answers to purpose-for-reading questions.

**III. Discussion:** Teacher reviews the graphic organizer to ensure students comprehend the basics of the story. Teacher fills in overhead as students provide answers.

"Using the legend and your story map organizer, write a summary of the legend (in Spanish) in your Spanish journals."

**STUDENT**

Students go to vocabulary section of their notebooks and sit with their vocabulary partner. Partners are reassigned each quarter based on class achievement. Pairs are heterogeneous in terms of achievement to encourage tutoring.

Students discuss various meanings for *aldea.*

Students add definition to their vocabulary sections.

Students reply, "It's a cognate."

Expected word: *obscurity*—not to be seen anymore.

Students record sentences and definition in their vocabulary notebooks.

Students guess *support.*

Students write definition.

Students fill out charts as they read silently.

Students break into small groups to discuss what they have written on their graphic organizers. Groups consist of four members—two vocabulary pairings. A facilitator is appointed for each group. Students are encouraged to speak only Spanish during discussion.
Facilitators respond with group answers.
Students write summaries.

**FIGURE A.24    Story Map Graphic Organizer**

**Title:** Una Legenda del Caribe-La Creacion

**Setting**

**When:** Before the world began, then later on earth in tribal villages (aldea), as the world developed.

**Where:** In the Caribbean Islands

**Characters**

1. Atabei
2. Yucaju
3. Guacar (Jurucán)
4. Locuo
5. Guaguyona
6. Yaya
7. Caribes
8. Tainos

**Problem/Major Conflict**

Jurucán causes trouble for the people and animals which his brother, Yucaju, has created. The Tainos grow to believe that Yucaju protects them from the Caribes and Jurucán.

**Significant Events**

1. Atabei creates the world, then has two sons
2. Yucaju creates man and living things.
3. Guacar is jealous and becomes Jurucán.
4. Jurucán terrorizes Taino. (soportar)
5. Yucaju sends protection and Locuo populates the world. (oscuridad)

**Solution**

The Tainos believe when Columbus lands that he has been sent to save and protect them from the Caribes.

---

**TEACHER**

"Now exchange with your vocabulary partner, read what your partner wrote, and check that all the narrative elements are included."

**IV. Rereading:** "With your partner, answer the two questions (in Spanish) displayed on the overhead."

What was the author's purpose in telling this story?

What is the author's message?

Teacher leads entire-class discussion

**STUDENT**

Students read and note any omissions for their partners.

*Expected student responses:* "The author tells this story to give background on the Tainos. This background helps to understand why the Tainos thought Yucaju sent the Spaniards to help protect them from the Caribes."

"The author's message is that our culture can shape our decisions."

**V. Follow-Up:** Students may choose a project from the following list.

1. Write in Spanish a story of origin. It may be in the form of a poem, a song, or a story.
2. Create a map showing the areas in which the Tainos or Arawaks lived.
3. Compare and contrast Jurucan and Yucaju.

4. Search the Internet to find information about the Arawaks and the Caribes, then decide whether the story version read in class is accurate.
5. Create a map of the areas in which the Caribes were active.
6. List and explain all elements of sexism found in this story.
7. Find out the population of Tainos and Caribes around the year 1492 and again around the year 1692.
8. Choose a recipe from the handout (available from the teacher) and prepare it.

Lesson contributed by Emmy Furbish, December 2000.

## CONTENT AREA: SPECIAL EDUCATION
### READING A MENU

**Class Description:** Special education daily skills class of six students. This group of students has a variety of disabilities that include Down syndrome, autism, social/emotional disorder, ADD, and ODD. The grade level ranges from 9 to 12, and the students range in age from 14 to 20 years old.

**Unit Title:** Eating in a public establishment

**Topic of this Lesson:** Reading a menu to order lunch

**Unit Goal:** Students will follow procedures to eat in a public restaurant by selecting food items, estimating costs, ordering, and paying for the meal.

**Lesson objectives:** The students will:

1. Define *stromboli, pasta,* and *submarine*
2. Read a menu from a local restaurant
3. Identify their lunch choices from a menu
4. Add up how much their lunch should cost
5. Bring the appropriate amount of money with them for the field trip

### Performance Assessment

| Objective | Assesment |
|-----------|-----------|
| 1. | Definition—students' oral responses during Concept Development/Vocabulary |
| 2. | Completion of a handout that requires them to identify the categories of food on the menu and specific varieties within a category |
| 3. | Recording their lunch choices on a handout |
| 4. | Adding the cost of the items they will order and recording this information on a handout |
| 5. | Sharing their lunch choices with parents and bringing the required amount of money from home |

**Macrostructure Thinking Skill:** Simple listing from categories

### Materials

- Copies of the menu from the restaurant for the upcoming field trip—includes pictures needed for vocabulary study
- Picture of a submarine (water vessel)
- Vocabulary sheets for notebooks
- Worksheet for locating information on a menu
- Worksheet to record lunch choices
- Transparencies of worksheets

# Procedure

## I. Readiness

*a. Motivation:* "On Wednesday, this class will be walking to Patrick's Pizzeria for lunch. When we go to the restaurant, you will be ordering your own lunch. Today, I will be giving you a practice menu to read and to choose from."

*b. Tapping Background of Experience:* "I know that all of you have eaten out in restaurants. Think about one of your favorite restaurants. What is its name and why was it your favorite?" Students volunteer their experiences.

"Think about a time you have gone out to dinner with your family. The hostess hands you a menu. Your parents tell you to look at the menu to see what you want to eat. What did you do to make the choice?"

*Expected student responses:* asked parents for help; looked at pictures

"After you made your choice of what you wanted to eat, how did you let the restaurant know what you wanted to eat?"

*Expected student responses:* told the waiter or cashier

"Today we will be looking at the menu from Patrick's Pizzeria [hand out copies of the menu]. This is the restaurant we will be walking to on Wednesday for lunch."

*c. Concept Development/Vocabulary:* "I have placed a menu in front of you. We will take some time to look at the different areas of the menu. What are some of the different sections you see? How can you tell what are the headings for different sections of the menu?"

*Expected student responses:* Pizza, Stromboli, Hot Submarines, Salads, and Pasta; larger, red print indicates different kinds of food.

"Look at the picture I am pointing to on the menu. This is a picture of a *stromboli.* [Write word on the board.] Work in pairs to come up with a description of this picture." Students look at the picture of the Stromboli. They will construct a definition for this food.

*Expected definition:* A Stromboli is an enclosed sandwich of cheese and pepperoni wrapped in pizza dough.

"Let's look again at the menu. Look at this picture. It is a picture of pasta. Again work in pairs to come up with a description for the picture." Students will study the picture of pasta and construct a meaning.

*Expected definition:* a variety of noodles made of dough; spaghetti

"Now look at the menu again. Look at this picture. It is a picture of a *submarine.* From the picture, what kind of food is it?"

*Expected student response:* a long roll with meat, cheese, and salad in it

"Have you ever heard the word *submarine* used a different way, that is, not as something to eat?" Show students picture of a *submarine* (water vessel). Let students discuss *submarine* as a water vessel and how the sandwich is shaped like a water *submarine.*

"I have prepared a handout with the definitions of our three new vocabulary words on it. Let's read each of these together. Now draw a picture of each next to the definition to help you remember" (see Figure A.25).

*d. Purpose-for-Reading:* "You will be reading to be informed. You will need to read this menu to answer the questions on the worksheet and to decide what you will like to order for lunch later this week."

**FIGURE A.25 Reading a Menu Graphic Organizer**

Name: _____ Date: _____

### READING A MENU

**Look at the *Stromboli* section of the menu.**

A. What are three different kinds of stromboli?
1. _chicken_
2. _steak_
3. _Italian_

**Look at the *Pasta* section of the menu.**

A. What kinds of pasta could you order?
1. _spaghetti with 4 meatballs_
2. _spaghetti with hot Italian sausage_
3. _lasagna_

B. What else is served with pasta?
1. _garlic bread_
2. _fresh green salad_

**Look at the *Submarine* section of the menu.**

A. A submarine can be ___hot___ or cold.

B. List three kinds of cold submarines:
1. _Italian_
2. _tuna_
3. _roast beef_

C. List three kinds of hot submarines:
1. _cheese steak_
2. _cheeseburger_
3. _pizza steak with cheese_

**Look at the *Pizza* section of the menu.**

A. How many slices of pizza are in a medium (12") pizza? ___six___

B. List five toppings you can have on a pizza:
1. _meat_
2. _cheese_
3. _mushrooms_
4. _pepperoni_
5. _sausage_

**II. Silent Reading:** The students read the menu silently and complete their worksheets. The master tutor and the teacher will circulate to assist the students who might be experiencing difficulty and to encourage them to look for answers for the worksheet.

**III. Discussion:** "You have had time to read the menu and locate the information to answer the questions on your worksheet. With your partner, please share your answers you wrote on you worksheet." Students work in pairs to check each other's answers. After time has

**FIGURE A.26    What's for Lunch?**

Name: _____     Date: _____

**WHAT'S FOR LUNCH?**

**What I want to order:**                    **Cost:**

(food) _____     _____

(drink) _____     _____

Total of lunch  =  _____

I need to bring _____ in order to have enough money for lunch.

been given for sharing, the class gives answers to be placed on the transparency. Students come up to write their answers on the transparency and locate the information on the menu.

**IV. Rereading:** "You will now go back and reread the menu. This time you will be making a decision on what you would like to order for lunch. Look at the worksheet in front of you. On this worksheet you will write down what you want to order for lunch on Wednesday when we go to Patrick's for lunch. You will also write down the price for your food and drink. When you have this completed, you will add up the prices to find out how much money you need to bring for lunch." Students reread menu and complete the worksheet (see Figure A.26).

**V. Follow-Up (homework):** The students use their worksheets and explain their lunch choices to their parents to get the needed money prior to the field trip.

Lesson contributed by Betsy Turner, May 2002.

# THE CLOZE PROCEDURE FOR PLACEMENT IN READING MATERIAL

The cloze procedure was originally designed by Wilson Taylor (1953) as an efficient means for determining how students will be able to interact with particular textual material. The cloze procedure is based on the psychological premise of *closure,* which is the human tendency to bring closure—to complete—a perception.

In the cloze procedure, students are given a typical passage from the textual material they will read in future lessons, and are instructed to fill in blanks where words from the text have been systematically deleted the way the author would write the text. The degree to which the student can do this closure activity reflects how successfully students can use their decoding skills, and background, semantic, syntactic, and text structure knowledge to comprehend the reading and thus fill in the blanks correctly. The results from the cloze procedure will indicate whether a student can handle a particular reading selection independently (without teacher-guided instruction), instructionally (with directed reading instruction), or whether the student will find the reading frustrating (thus requiring maximum teacher-guided, directed reading instruction and adaptation, or the selection of alternative reading material).

### Constructing the Cloze

1. Select a passage from the reading or text you are considering using with your students. The passage needs to be representative of the full text. It should be at or near the beginning of the textual material to avoid absence of student background that would be developed if the students read the text sequentially. Avoid introductions or forewords if they are not representative of the way the rest of the text is written.
2. Type the passage just as the author has written it. Leave the first sentence intact, but beginning with the second sentence, delete every fifth word (if science or math, you may choose to delete every seventh word). Where a word has been deleted, type a space for the word. Use fifteen spaces for each deletion so that you do not clue students to the length of the missing word. Continue typing with deletions until you have fifty deletions. Type the next sentence, which will be the last sentence of the cloze, without any deletions.

### Administration of the Cloze

1. Use class time to administer the cloze. One-half hour is usually sufficient time for all students, but use your own judgment. The cloze is not a timed test, and students with special needs may need more time.
2. Explain to the class that you are planning their next unit of study and are making decisions about the materials they will read; therefore, you need their assistance. Tell students that this is not a graded exercise, but that they must try to do their best so that the reading materials you select will help them to learn the content information of the next unit of study.

3. If students have little or no experience with the cloze procedure, show the class a sample cloze passage (possibly on the overhead projector) different from the one they will do. Explain the procedure and practice doing some of the cloze together.

4. With the sample cloze, and again just prior to distributing the cloze they will complete for text placement, tell students:

   ■ First read through the entire passage without filling in any blanks to get a sense of the content and writing style.

   ■ Then begin to fill in the blanks the way you believe the author would complete each blank. This is not a Mad Lib, a game you may have played at home that encourages creating funny stories.

   ■ Complete each blank with only one word.

   ■ Spelling does not count, but you should try to be as accurate as possible so that when these are scored, I will not misinterpret the words you choose.

   ■ No one gets all the words correct, so do not be anxious; even 50 percent correct is a good score.

5. Have the class complete the cloze silently and individually, not with a partner or group.

### Scoring the Cloze

1. Only *exact* word replacements are counted as correct in the placement cloze procedure. This has been shown to be the most valid scoring system for placement purposes (Bormuth, 1966, 1968; Miller & Coleman, 1967; Ruddell, 1964). Accepting synonyms will not change the scores appreciably, but will result in much less efficient scoring on your part.

2. Multiply the total number of correct responses by 2 to determine each student's final cloze score.

### Interpreting the Cloze Results

Use the following percentages to determine how each student can handle reading the material tested:

■ *Independent reading*—58 percent to 100 percent. These students can be assigned to read this material on their own without Directed Reading Lessons. Consider using enrichment materials within Directed Reading Lessons for these students to challenge them appropriately.

■ *Instructional reading*—44 percent to 57 percent. These students will need this reading to be couched within Directed Reading Lessons.

■ *Frustration reading*—below 44 percent. These students may need simpler reading or alternative learning materials. If these are not available, use Directed Reading Lessons with maximum adaptations for comprehension. Consider using a Directed-Reading-Thinking approach.

*Note:* We recommend the use of the cloze procedure as a means of determining how a student will be able to work with particular textual material. Unlike other approaches, (e.g., readability formula tests on the material paired to survey reading achievement scores of students), the cloze has the advantage of being an inclusive procedure that involves the students interacting with the actual content reading, engaging all their operative cueing systems, and coping with all the reader- and text-related variables that affect comprehension. Thus, it is an authentic diagnostic procedure.

**aesthetic stance**  A reader response approach; a reader's subjective reactions to a reading

**BDA strategies**  Metacognitive strategies used before, during, and after reading to help readers plan, monitor, and evaluate their comprehension

**cause and effect**  A text structure; an analysis of conditions and outcomes of an event

**chronological order/sequence**  A text structure; ordered steps in a process; stages in development; events according to time

**classification/categorization**  A text structure; dividing a group of items into smaller groups that share common characteristics

**cloze procedure**  An authentic diagnostic procedure for determining how (independent, instructional, frustration) a student can interact with a particular reading selection

**cognitive structure**  Information stored in the long-term memory to which learners must connect new information in order to learn

**collaborative learning**  Groups of students (e.g., pairs, triads, or quads) sharing ideas; a scaffolding strategy to facilitate learning

**comparison and/or contrast**  A text structure; explicating similarities (comparison) and/or differences (contrast) between or among people, places, processes, objects, events, and so on, usually involving a list of traits as the basis of the comparison and contrast

**concept**  The idea we have of something by understanding its observable characteristics or essential attributes; words are labels for concepts

**concept attainment**  An inductive approach; for vocabulary, the teacher presents examples and nonexamples of the word whose meaning is to be learned and asks students to use these clues to define the word

**Concept Development/Vocabulary**  The third phase in the Readiness step; the purpose of this phase is to ready the students with an initial understanding of key vocabulary they will need in order to understand the content selection

**concept formation**  A form of inductive reasoning; a thinking process for organizing information about an entity and associating that information with a label (a vocabulary word)

**concrete representation**  A direct experience, the real artifact, or a picture of the vocabulary word

**creative thinking**  An inventive thinking process in which data are used in unique combinations

**critical stance**  The reader is asked to analyze and judge the author's perspective and craft; requires use of critical thinking

**critical thinking**  A reflective thinking process that focuses on making judgments (e.g., fact or opinion? authentic? credible?)

**decode**  Making sense of graphics; the printed representation of speech sound or spoken words

**decontextualized approach**  A list-of-words-in-isolation approach; includes having the teacher present selected vocabulary words and asking for volunteers to tell what the words mean; no clues are provided to assist students in inducing a definition

**description**  A text structure; concrete details that give the reader a mental picture of the object, person, scene, and so on

**developing background of experience**  Adding to cognitive structure

**Directed Reading Lesson**  A lesson plan format that helps the content teacher focus on teaching content knowledge and processes while at the same time incorporating reading strategies as learning tools

**Directed Reading–Thinking Lesson**  A lesson plan that is similar in format to the Directed Reading Lesson except students are asked to predict what they think will be included in the reading; a recursive process of predictions for purpose-setting, silent reading, and discussion that is repeated for each section of text that is read

**during-reading metacognitive strategies**  Used during Silent Reading to assist students in making meaning from the content text (e.g., movie of the mind, checking for purpose, taking notes/organizing, retelling, rereading/lookbacks, inserts/questions, elaborating, and noting key content vocabulary)

**editing**  Proofreading to correct grammar, punctuation, and spelling errors

**efferent stance**  The reader carries away information from the reading

**elaborating**  A metacognitive strategy that involves pausing in Silent Reading to reflect on how new information relates to previous content knowledge learned in the current unit of study or course, or how it connects with one's personal life

**enrichment activity**  A follow-up activity that broadens the learner's knowledge

**enumeration/simple listing**  A text structure; a list of factors that does not require a specific order

**experiential background cueing system**  Comprehension is facilitated or hindered based on one's past experience

**expository text structure**  A text written to inform, explain, show, and tell. The most common expository text structures employed in secondary textbooks are based on the thought patterns of categorization/

classification, cause and effect, chronological order/sequence, comparison and/or contrast, definition, description, enumeration/simple listing, pro and/or con, and problem and solution

**extended definition** A text structure; not a brief dictionary definition, but a more lengthy explanation of characteristics of a concept

**Follow-Up** An optional fifth step in the Directed Reading Lesson; used to reinforce or enrich information the students learned through reading and discussion

**frustration reading level** A level at which the reader comprehends less than 50 percent of information

**generalizing** Inferring general statements from facts or examples

**general vocabulary** Words whose definitions remain constant and are used in all disciplines

**global stance** A general overview of the reading

**graphic cueing system** Printed representation of speech sounds

**graphic organizer** A visual representation of a thought pattern to show relationships among key bits of information

**guided imagery** A contextual strategy in which the teacher describes a scene in detail to help students create a picture of the vocabulary word in their minds

**imaging** Using one's background of experience, as well as pictures, illustrations or other visuals provided in the reading or by the teacher to visualize what is being read

**independent level** A level at which the reader comprehends better than 90 percent without teacher-guided instruction and support

**inductive approach** An approach in which the teacher presents specific facts or examples; then guided by the teacher's eliciting questions, the students infer and state a generalization

**initial learning of vocabulary** Constructing meaning of a word

**inserts/questions** A metacognitive strategy that involves writing a question in the margin of the reading or on a sticky note to ask for clarification from the class or teacher when the discussion begins

**instructional conversations** Discussions designed to promote learning; using eliciting questions, restatements, and pauses to extend student contributions; building on and extending previous responses

**instructional level** A level at which the reader comprehends 75 percent or more of the content

**interpretive stance** Requires the reader to detail the specifics of the text, such as plot, characters, and setting

**key** The purpose for reading questions and the acceptable and expected student responses

**learning-to-read stage** Initial stages of learning to read; usually places emphasis on word recognition skills (e.g., phonics and structural analysis) along with comprehension

**look-backs** Looking back to what has already been read—a word, group of words, a sentence, a group of sentences, a paragraph or several paragraphs—and rereading to understand

**macrostructure** How the text is organized; the overall thought pattern of a reading

**matrix** A type of a graphic organizer that uses columns and rows for collecting information for the thought pattern of compare and contrast

**metacognitive strategies** Strategies that allow readers to plan, monitor, and regulate comprehension; BDA strategies

**Motivation** The first step in getting the students ready to comprehend the selected reading material; the purpose of this step is to help students focus their attention on the content topic for the session, to arouse their curiosity and interest, and to help the students connect the topic with their personal lives

**movie of the mind** Readers create mental images and scenes in their minds as they read

**multitext approach** An approach that uses more than one text in a particular lesson in an attempt to allow each student to read at his or her instructional reading level

**narrative text structure** Requires the reader to process a "story grammar"—setting, characters, plot, conflict, significant events, and outcome or solution

**nonspecific vocabulary** Words that change meaning, often from discipline to discipline

**noting key content vocabulary** A metacognitive strategy that involves stopping to pay particular attention to understanding words primed by the teacher prior to Silent Reading and to note any other vocabulary that seems crucial to the topic and purpose-for-reading

**oral retelling** A reflective tool that requires readers to organize information from the text and to provide a personalized summary to a peer

**personal stance** When the reader relates personal experiences and feelings to the reading

**prediction** Foretelling what will happen or what information will be included

**pro and/or con** A text structure; a presentation of one or both sides of an issue in an attempt to persuade; sometimes making a judgment about which is best; sometimes presenting errors in arguments to prove one side as correct or best

**problem and solution** A text structure; clarifying the problem, posing solutions, and sometimes consequences of solutions

**productive vocabulary** Vocabulary the students use in discussion or in writing; generative vocabulary

**Purpose-for-Reading** The fourth and final phase of the Readiness step; helps focus the learner on the goal of the reading experience and gives them parameters for monitoring the successful completion of the reading task; should include three parts: (1) the generic purpose for reading, (2) the primary thought pattern that will be used for comprehension, and (3) the main topic of the reading

**purpose-for-reading questions**  Usually text-based questions that require readers to recognize and record factual information from text

**reader response approach**  A reader's subjective reactions to a reading; an aesthetic stance; in this approach, there is no right or wrong answer, assuming the reaction is rationally defensible

**Readiness**  The first step in the Directed Reading Lesson; designed to move students up to the reading

**reading**  Using graphic, semantic, syntactic, background, and text structure clues in a recursive manner to construct meaning with text

**reading stances**  Different vantage points from which a reader can gain ideas and build well-rounded, thoughtful understanding of a text

**reading to learn**  Learning content information using reading materials; learning with text

**receptive vocabulary**  Words understood when reading or listening

**reciprocal teaching**  A comprehension strategy in which a student acts as the leader or "teacher" by orally summarizing the information, asking questions to identify the important information in the reading, identifying confusing issues, asking the group for clarification on those issues, and asking the group members to make predictions

**reinforcement activity**  A follow-up activity in which students review the information learned in the lesson

**Rereading**  The fourth step in the Directed Reading Lesson designed to have students attend to reading for new purposes, different from those given in the Readiness step; the goal is to have students extend their understanding of the content

**rereading/lookbacks**  A metacognitive strategy that involves looking back to what has already been read—a word, group of words, a sentence, a group of sentences, a paragraph or several paragraphs—and rereading to understand

**retelling**  A metacognitive strategy used at various points in the reading; checking comprehension by stopping to articulate silently to oneself what has been learned or by sharing this retelling orally with a peer who is also reading the content material

**review of vocabulary**  Reinforcement of meanings after initial teaching; not to be used before initial learning

**self-regulatory strategies**  Metacognitive reading strategies students use to assess and further their own understanding of the text

**semantic feature analysis chart**  A graphic representation for variables that can be described with a "Yes" or "No" form of response; either the variable exists or does not exist

**semantics**  A cueing system readers use to make meaning of print material; the meaning of individual words or concepts

**Silent Reading**  The second step in the Directed Reading Lesson; independent reading to answer the purpose-for-reading established during the Readiness section using the multiple-clueing systems of graphics, semantics/vocabulary, syntax, background, and text structure

**stances**  Ways readers recursively interact with the reading material and develop their interpretations; the four reading stances are global, interpretive, critical and personal

**structural analysis**  Finding the meaning of a word based on an understanding of its structure, for example, its affixes

**syntactic complexity**  The number and placement of embedded clauses and phrases that contribute to the difficulty of comprehension

**syntax**  The order of words in sentences, clauses, and phrases; patterns of language help determine meaning

**taking notes/organizing**  A metacognitive strategy that involves writing out answers to the purpose-for-reading, filling in a graphic organizer provided by the teacher, or constructing one's own graphic organizer to organize the information

**Tapping Background of Experience**  The second phase of the Readiness step; accessing students' curricular and life experiences relevant to the upcoming reading; mobilizing cognitive connections for the new learning

**T-chart**  A type of graphic organizer in linear form used for the thought pattern of comparison and contrast

**technical vocabulary**  Words that have only one definition, usually unique to a particular content area

**text structure**  The organization of a particular genre of writing; can be categorized according to the major thought patterns required for reading (e.g., comparison and/or contrast, cause and effect, chronological order/sequence, problem and solution)

**trade books**  Nontextbook reading material (e.g., novel, biography) available to the general public; can be used to bring "voice" to a content area topic

**Venn diagram**  A type of graphic organizer using overlapping circles for comparing and contrasting

**visualization**  *See* **guided imagery**

**vocabulary**  A stock of concepts represented by oral or written words

**vocabulary priming process**  The process of teaching essential vocabulary words inductively in the Readiness part of the Directed Reading Lesson

Abbott, E. A. (1952). *Flatland*. London: Penguin.

Achebe, C. (1959). *Things fall apart*. New York: Astor-Honor, Inc.

Alvermann, D. E. (1986). Graphic organizers: Cueing devices for comprehending and remembering main ideas. In J. F. Baumann (Ed.), *Teaching main idea comprehension* (pp. 210–226). Newark, DE: International Reading Association.

Alvermann, D. E. (2000). Classroom talk about texts: Is it dear, cheap, or a bargain at any price? In B. M. Taylor, M. G. Graves, & P. VanDenBroek (Eds.), *Reading for meaning: Fostering comprehension in the middle grades* (pp. 136–151). Newark, DE: International Reading Association.

Alvermann, D. E., & Moore, W. W. (1996). Secondary school reading. In R. Barr, M. L. Kamil, P. B. Mosenthal, & P. D. Pearson (Eds.). *Handbook of reading research* (Vol. 2, pp. 951–983). New York: Longman.

Alvermann, D. E., Weaver, D., Hinchman, K. A., Moore, D. W., Phelps, S. F., Thrash, E. C., & Zalewski, P. (1996). Middle and high school students' perceptions of how they experience text-based discussions: A multi-case study. *Reading Research Quarterly, 31,* 244–267.

Anderson, R. C., Hiebert, E. H., Scott, J. A., & Wilkinson, A. G. (1985). *Becoming a nation of readers: The report of the Commission on Reading*. Champaign-Urbana, IL: Center for the Study of Reading.

Anderson, V. (1992). A teacher development project in transactional strategy instruction for teachers of severely reading disabled adolescents. *Teaching & Teacher Education, 8,* 391–403.

Anderson, V., & Roit, M. (1993). Planning and implementing collaborative strategy instruction for delayed readers in grades 6–10. *Elementary School Journal, 94,* 121–137.

Andrade, H. G. (1999). *Student self-assessment: At the intersection of metacognition and authentic assessment*. Paper presented at the annual meeting of the American Educational Research Conference, Montreal, Canada. (ERIC Document Reproduction Service No. ED431030).

Anno, M., & and Anno, M. (1983). *Anno's Mysterious Multiplying Jar*. New York: Penguin Putnam Books.

Anti-Defamation League. (2001). School vouchers: The wrong choice for public education. Available: www.adl.org/vouchers_main.html

Appleman, D. (2001, Summer). Quoted in R. Allen. English teachers fight back. *Curriculum Update, 1–3,* 6–8.

Armbruster, B. B., Anderson, T. H., & Ostertag, J. (1987). Does text structure/summarization instruction facilitate learning from expository text? *Reading Research Quarterly, 22,* 331–346.

Aronson, E., Blaney, N., Sikes, J., Steohan, G., & Snapp, M. (1978). *The jigsaw classroom*. Beverly Hills, CA: Sage.

Au, K. H. (2002). Multicultural factors and the effective instruction of students of diverse backgrounds. In A. E. Farstrup & S. J. Samuels (Eds.). *What research has to say about reading instruction* (pp. 392–413). Newark, DE: International Reading Association.

Baker, L., & Brown, A. L. (1984). Metacognitive skills and reading. In P. D. Pearson (Ed.), *Handbook of reading research* (pp. 353–394). White Plains, NY: Longman.

Barnett, J. E., & Seefeldt, R. W. (1989). Repetitive reading and recall. *Journal of Reading Behavior, 21,* 351–361.

Barr, R., Blachowicz, C. L. Z., & Wogman-Sadow, M. (1995). *Reading Diagnosis for Teachers* (3rd ed.). White Plains, NY: Longman.

Baumann, J. F., & Kameenui, E. J. (1991). Research on vocabulary instruction: Ode to Voltaire. In J. Flood, J. M. Jensen, D. Lapp, & J. R. Squire (Eds.), *Handbook of research on teaching the English language arts* (pp. 604–632). New York: Macmillan.

Beake, L. (1993). *Song of Be*. New York: Holt.

Beck, I. L., & McKeown, M. G. (1996). Conditions of vocabulary acquisition. In R. Barr, M. L. Kail, P. Mosenthal, & P. D. Pearson (Eds.), *Handbook of reading research:* (Vol. 2). (pp. 789–814). White Plains, NY: Longman.

Beck, I. L., Perfetti, C. A., & McKeown, M. G. (1982). The effects of long-term vocabulary instruction on lexical access and reading comprehension. *Journal of Educational Psychology, 74,* 506–521.

Beers, G. K. (1996a). No time, no interest, no way! The 3 voices of aliteracy. Part 1. *School Library Journal. 42,* 30–33.

Beers, G. K. (1996b). No time, no interest, no way! The 3 voices of aliteracy. Part 2. *School Library Journal, 42,* 110–113.

Betts, E. A. (1946). *Foundations of reading instruction*. New York: American Book.

Beyer, B. K. (1987). *Practical strategies for the teaching of thinking*. Boston: Allyn & Bacon.

Billingsley, B. S., & Wildman, T. M. (1990). Facilitating reading comprehension in learning disabled students: Metacognitive goals and instructional strategies. *Remedial and Special Education, 11,* 18–31.

Biracree, T. (1989). *Althea Gibson*. New York: Chelsea House.

Blair-Larson, S. M., & Williams, K. A. (Eds.). (1999). *The balanced reading program: Helping all students achieve success.* Newark, DE: International Reading Association.

Bormuth, J. R. (1966). Readability: A new approach. *Reading Research Quarterly, 1,* 79–132.

Bormuth, J. R. (1968). Cloze test reliability: Criterion reference scores. *Journal of Educational Measurement, 5,* 189–196.

Bos, C. S., & Anders, P. A. (1990). Effects of interactive vocabulary instruction on the vocabulary learning and reading comprehension of junior high learning-disabled students. *Learning Disability Quarterly, 13,* 31–42.

Broadwater, J. C. (2001, November 11). Learning to read with ears, eyes. *The Baltimore Sun,* p. 2B.

Bromley, K., Irwin-DeVitis, L., & Modlo, M. (1995). *Graphic organizers: Visual activities for active learning.* New York: Scholastic Professional Books.

Brown, A. L., & Day, J. D. (1983). Macrorules for summarizing texts: The development of expertise. *Journal of Verbal Learning and Verbal Behavior, 22,* 1–14.

Bunting, E. (1980). *Terrible things: An allegory of the Holocaust.* Philadelphia: Harper & Row.

Bunting, E. (1991). *Fly away home.* New York: Clarion.

Burger, D. (1965). *Sphereland: A fantasy about curved spaces and an expanding universe.* New York: Thomas Y. Crowell.

Butler, D. L., & Winne, P. H. (1995). Feedback and self-regulated learning: A theoretical synthesis. *Review of Educational Research, 65,* 245–281.

Carle, E. (1987). *The very hungry caterpillar.* New York: Philomel.

Cawelti, G. (Ed.). (1999). *Handbook of research on improving student achievement.* (2nd ed.). Arlington, VA: Educational Research Service.

Clarke, J. H. (1990). *Patterns of thinking: Integrating learning skills in content teaching.* Boston: Allyn & Bacon.

Cleary, B. (1983). *Dear Mr. Henshaw.* New York: Morrow.

Cochran, T. (1997). *Roughnecks.* New York: Harcourt Brace.

Crane, S. (1968). *Maggie and other stories.* New York: Airmont.

Davey, B. (1983). Think aloud—Modeling the cognitive processes of reading comprehension. *Journal of Reading, 27,* 44–47.

Davidson, N. (1985). Small group cooperative learning in mathematics: A selective view of the research. In R. Slavin (Ed.), *Learning to cooperate: Cooperating to learn* (pp. 211–230). New York: Plenum.

Dewdney, A. K. (1984). *Planiverse: Computer contact with a two-dimensional world.* New York: Copernicus Books.

Dicaire, D. L. (2000). *Biography of 50 legendary artists of the early 20th century.* Jefferson, NC: McFarland.

Dicaire, D. L. (2001). *More blues singers: Biographies of 50 artists from the later 20th century.* Jefferson, NC: McFarland.

Dickson, S. V., Simmons, D. C. & Kameenui, E. J. (1998). Text organization: Research bases. In D. C. Simmons & E. J. Kameenui (Eds.), *What reading research tells us about children with diverse learning needs: Bases and basics* (pp. 239–277). Mahwah, NJ: Lawrence Erlbaum Associates.

Dixon, R., Carnine, D., & Kameenui, E. J. (1992). Curriculum guidelines for diverse learners. *Monograph for the national center to improve the tools of educators.* Eugene: University of Oregon.

Duke, N. K., & Pearson, P. D. (2002). In A. E. Farstrup & S. J. Samuels (Eds.). *What research has to say about reading instruction* (pp. 205–242). Newark, DE: International Reading Association.

Dygard, T. J. (1979). *Outside shooter.* New York: William Morrow.

Englert, C. S., & Thomas, C. C. (1987). Sensitivity to text structure in reading and writing: A comparison between learning disabled and non-learning disabled students. *Learning Disability Quarterly, 10,* 93–105.

Ennis, R. H. (1985a). Goals for a critical thinking curriculum. In A. L. Costa (Ed.), *Developing minds: A resource book for teaching thinking* (pp. 54–57). Alexandria, VA: Association for Supervision and Curriculum Development.

Ennis, R. H. (1985b). A logical basis for measuring critical thinking skills. *Educational Leadership, 43,* 44–48.

Exline, J. D., Pasachoff, J. M., Simons, B. B., Vogel, C. G., & Wellnitz, T. R. (2001). *Earth science.* Needham, MA: Prentice-Hall.

Fillion, B., & Brause, R. S. (1987). Research into classroom practices: What have we learned and where are we going? In J. R. Squire (Ed.), *The dynamics of language learning: Research in reading and English* (pp. 201–225). Urbana, IL: ERIC/RCS. (ERIC Document Reproduction Service No. ED280080).

Fitzgerald, J., & Spiegel, D. L. (1983). Enhancing children's reading comprehension through instruction in narrative structure. *Journal of Reading Behavior, 15,* 1–17.

Flavell, J. H. (1976). Metacognitive aspects of problem solving. In L. B. Resnick (Ed.), *The nature of intelligence* (pp. 231–236). Hillsdale, NJ: Erlbaum.

Flood, J., Lapp, D., Flood, S., & Nagel, G. (1992). Am I allowed to group? Using flexible patterns for effective instruction. *The Reading Teacher, 45,* 608–616.

Fogarty, R., Perkins, D., & Barell, J. (1992). *The mindful school: How to teach for transfer.* Palatine, IL: IRI/Skylight Publishing.

Fournier, D. N. E., & Graves, M. F. (2002). Scaffolding adolescents' comprehension of short stories. *Journal of Adolescent & Adult Literacy, 46,* 30–38.

Fox, M. (1985). *Wilfrid Gordon McDonald Partridge.* Brooklyn, NY: Kane/Miller.

Fox, P. (1991). *Monkey Island.* New York: Orchard.

Friend, M., & Bursuck, W. (1999). *Including students with special needs: A practical guide for classroom teachers.* Boston: Allyn & Bacon.

Frayer, D. A., Frederick, W. C., & Klausmeier, H. J. (1969). *A schema for testing the level of concept mastery* (Tech. Rep. No. 16). Madison: University of Wisconsin Research and Development Center for Cognitive Learning.

Freiberg, H. J., & Driscoll, A. (2000). *Universal teaching strategies.* (3rd ed.). Boston: Allyn & Bacon.

Gambrell L., & Jawitz, P. (1993). Mental imagery, text illustrations, and children's story comprehension and recall. *Reading Research Quarterly, 28,* 265–276.

Garner, R. (1990). When children and adults do not use learning strategies: Toward a theory of settings. *Review of Educational Research, 60,* 517–529.

Garner, R., & Reis, R. (1981). Monitoring and resolving comprehension obstacles: An investigation of spontaneous lookbacks among upper-grade good and poor comprehenders. *Reading Research Quarterly, 16,* 569–582.

Glasser, W. (1986). *Control theory in the classroom.* New York: Harper and Row.

Goldman, S. R., & Rakestraw, J. A. (2000). Structural aspects of constructing meaning from text. In M. L. Kamil, P. B. Mosenthal, P. D. Pearson, & R. Barr. (Eds.), *Handbook of reading research* (Vol. 3, pp. 311–335). Mahwah, NJ: Lawrence Erlbaum Associates.

Goleman, D. (1995). *Emotional intelligence.* New York: Bantam.

Gomi, T. (1993). *Everyone poops.* New York: Kane/Miller.

Gonyea, J. C. (2002). Ten in-demand job skills. *AOL: Careers and Work.* Retrieved January 4, 2002, from http://content.workplace.aol.monster.com/career changers/articles/self_assessment/skills

Grouws, D. A., & Cebulla, K. J. (2000). Improving student achievement in mathematics (Part I: Research findings). *Digest.* Columbus, OH: ERIC/SME. (ERIC Document Reproduction Service No. ED445925).

Guzzetti, B., Snyder, T., & Glass, G. (1992). Promoting conceptual change in science: Can texts be used effectively? *Journal of Reading, 35,* 642–649.

Haller, E. P., Child, D. A., & Walberg, H. J. (1998). Can comprehension be taught? A quantitative synthesis of "metacognitive" studies. *Educational Researcher, 17,* 5–8.

Hamaker, C. (1986). The effects of adjunct questions on prose learning. *Review of Educational Research, 56,* 212–242.

Hare, V., & Borchardt, K. M. (1984). Direct instruction of summarization skills. *Reading Research Quarterly, 21,* 62–78.

Harris, A. J., & Sipay, E. R. (1990). *How to increase reading ability: A guide to developmental & remedial methods* (9th ed.). White Plains, NY: Longman.

Harris, K., & Pressley, M. (1991). The nature of cognitive strategy instruction: Interactive strategy construction. *Exceptional Children, 28,* 392–403.

Harris, T. L., & Hodges, R. E. (Eds.). (1995). *The literacy dictionary: The vocabulary of reading and writing.* Newark: International Reading Association.

Hautzig, D. (1999). *Second star to the right.* New York: Greenwillow Books.

Herman, P. A., Anderson, R. C., Pearson, P. D., & Nagy, W. E. (1987). Incidental acquisition of word meaning from expositions with varied text features. *Reading Research Quarterly, 22,* 263–284.

Hesse, K. (1997). *Out of the dust.* New York: Scholastic.

Hootstein, H. (1995). Motivational strategies of middle school social studies teachers. *Social Education, 59,* 23–26.

Horowitz, R. (1985). Text patterns: Part II. *Journal of Reading, 28,* 534–541.

Hoyt, L. (1999). *Revise, reflect, retell: Strategies for improving reading comprehension.* Portsmouth, NH: Heinemann.

International Reading Association. (2001, August). Fact and fiction. *Chronicle,* 13.

Jenkins, J. R., Stein, M. L., & Wysocki, K. (1984). Learning vocabulary through reading. *American Educational Research Journal, 21*(4), 767–787.

Johnson, D., Johnson, R., Holubed, E., & Roy, P. (1991). *Cooperation in the classroom.* Edina, MN: Interaction Book Company.

Jordan, C. (1985). Translating culture: From ethnographic information to educational program. *Anthropology and Education Quarterly, 16,* 104–123.

Jordan, M. (1998). *For love of the game: My story.* New York: Crown.

Juster, N. (2001). *The dot and the line: A romance in lower mathematics.* New York: Sea Star.

Kimmell, S., & MacGinitie, W. H. (1985). Helping students revise hypotheses while reading. *The Reading Teacher, 37,* 768–771.

King, A. (1992). Comparison of self-questioning, summarizing, and note taking review as strategies for learning from lectures. *American Educational Research Journal, 29,* 303–323.

Langer, J. A. (1992). Rethinking literature instruction. In J. A. Langer (Ed.), *Literature instruction: A focus on student response* (pp. 35–53). Urbana, IL: National Council of Teachers of English.

Langer, J. A. (1995). *Envisioning literature: Literary understanding and literature instruction.* New York: Teachers College Press.

Langer, J. A., & Applebee, A. N. (1987). *How writing shapes thinking: A study of teaching and learning.* (Research Report No. 22). Urbana, IL: National Council of Teachers of English.

Ladson-Billings, G. (1994). *The dreamkeepers: Successful teachers of African American children.* San Francisco: Jossey-Bass.

Lasky, K. (1994). *The librarian who measured the earth.* NY: Little, Brown & Co.

Lauber, P. (1986). *Volcano.* New York: Bradbury.

Lehigh, S. (1999, September 22). The age of ignorance. *The Baltimore Sun,* p. 10F.

Lesesne, T. S. (1996). Reading aloud to build success in reading. In G. K. Beers and B. G. Samuels (Eds.), *Into focus: Understanding and creating middle school readers* (pp. 245–260). New York: Christopher-Gordon.

Levin, J. R., & Pressley, M. (1981). Improving childrens' prose comprehension: Selected strategies that seem to succeed. In C. M. Santa & B. L. Hayes (Eds.). *Children's prose comprehension: Research and practice* (pp. 44–71). Newark, DE: International Reading Association.

Lewin, T. (1995). *Sacred river.* New York: Houghton Mifflin.

Lifford, J., Byron, G., Eckblad, J., & Ziemian, C. (2000). Reading, responding, reflecting. *English Journal, 89,* 46–57.

Lou, Y. Abrami, P. C., Spence, J. C., Paulsen, C., Chambers, B., & d'Appollonio, S. (1996). Within-class grouping: A meta-analysis. *Review of Educational Research, 66,* 423–458.

MacLachlan, P. (1991). *Journey.* New York: Doubleday.

Martinez, A. (1989). *A meta-analysis of reading aloud.* Presentation at Phi Delta Kappa seminar, Houston, TX.

Maruki, T. (1982). *Hiroshima no pika.* New York: Lee & Shepard Books.

Maryland State Department of Education. (1998–1999). *Maryland High School Assessment Prototype: Algebra.* Baltimore, MD: Maryland State Department of Education.

Maryland State Department of Education. (1998–1999). *Maryland High School Assessment Prototype: English I.* Baltimore, MD: Maryland State Department of Education.

Maryland State Department of Education (2002). *School improvement in Maryland: Promising practices.* Retrieved January 4, 2002, from http://mdk12.org/practices

Marzano, R. J., Brandt, R. S., Hughes, C. S., Jones, B. F., Presseisen, B. Z., Rankin, S. C., & Suhor, C. (1988). *Dimensions of thinking: A framework for curriculum and instruction.* Alexandria, VA: Association for Supervision and Curriculum Development.

Marzano, R. J., Pickering, D. J., & Pollock, J. E. (2001). *Classroom instruction that works: Research-based strategies for increasing student achievement.* Alexandria, VA: Association for Supervision and Curriculum Development.

Maxwell, R. (1996). *Writing across the curriculum in middle and high schools.* Boston: Allyn & Bacon.

Mayher, J. S., Lester, N., & Pradl, G. M. (1983). *Learning to write/Writing to learn.* Upper Montclair, NJ: Boynton/Cook.

McGee, L. M. (1982). The influence of metacognitive knowledge of expository text structure on discourse recall. In J. Niles & L. A. Harris (Eds.), *New inquiries in reading: Research and instruction* (pp. 64–70). Rochester, NY: National Reading Conference.

McKeown, M. G. (1991). Effects of graphic organizers and levels of text difficulty on less-proficient fifth-grade readers' comprehension of expository text. *Dissertation Abstracts International, 51,*(09), 3028A.

McKeown, M. G., Beck, I. L., Omanson, R. C., & Pople, M. T. (1985). Some effects of the nature and frequency of vocabulary instruction on the knowledge and use of words. *Reading Research Quarterly, 20,* 522–533.

McKeown, M. G., & Curtis, M. E. (Eds.). (1987). *The nature of vocabulary acquisition.* Hillsdale, NJ: Erlbaum.

Meyer, B. J. F., Brandt, D. M., & Bluth, G. J. (1980). Use of top-level structure in text: Key for reading comprehension of ninth-grade students. *Reading Research Quarterly, 16,* 72–103.

Mfume, K. (1997). *No free ride: From the mean streets to the mainstream.* New York: Ballantine.

Michener, J. A. (1978). *Chesapeake.* New York: Random House.

Miller, G. R., & Coleman, E. G. (1967). A set of 36 prose passages calibrated for complexity. *Journal of Verbal Learning and Verbal Behavior, 6,* 851–854.

Milner, J. O., & Milner, L. F. (1999). *Bridging English* (2nd ed.). Upper Saddle River, NJ: Merrill.

Mochizuki, K. (1995). *Baseball saved us.* New York: Lee & Low.

Montgomery County Public Schools. (2001). Vocabulary instruction. Handout to teachers.

Morrow, L. (1986). *Literary centers.* York, ME: Stenhouse.

Murray, J., & McGlone, C. (1997). Topic overview and the processing of topic structure. *Journal of Educational Psychology, 89,* 251–261.

Myers, W. D. (1988). *Fallen angels.* New York: Scholastic.

Myers, W. D. (1992). *Somewhere in the darkness.* New York: Scholastic.

Nagy, W. E., Herman P. A., & Anderson, R. C. (1985). Learning words from context. *Reading Research Quarterly, 20,* 233–253.

National Council for the Social Studies. (1994). *Expectations of excellence: Curriculum standards for social studies.* (Bulletin 89). Washington, DC: National Council for the Social Studies.

National Council of Teachers of English Language and Learning Across the Curriculum Committee. (2002). *Learning through language: A call for action in all disciplines.* Urbana, IL: NCTE.

National Council of Teachers of Mathematics. (2000). *Principles and standards for school mathematics.* Alexandria, VA: National Council of Teachers of Mathematics.

Nelson-Herber, J. (1986). Expanding and refining vocabulary in the content areas. *Journal of Reading, 29,* 626–633.

Neubert, G. A. (1992). Using writing to learn mathematics. *Virginia Mathematics Teacher, 18,* 10–12.

Neubert, G. A., & Binko, J. B. (1992). *Inductive reasoning in the secondary classroom.* Washington, DC: National Education Association.

Neuschwander, C., & Geehan, W. (1997). *Sir Cumference and the first round table: A math adventure.* Watertown, MA: Charlesbridge.

Nuthall, G. (1999). The way students learn. Acquiring knowledge from an integrated science and social studies unit. *Elementary School Journal, 99,* 303–341.

Nuthall, G., & Alton-Lee, A. (1995). Assessing classroom learning: How students use their knowledge and experience to answer classroom achievement test questions in science and social studies. *American Educational Research Journal, 32,* 185–223.

O'Donnell, A. M., & Dansereau, D. F. (1992). Scripted cooperation in student dyads: A method for analyzing and enhancing academic learning and performance. In R. Hertz-Lazarowitz & N. Miller (Eds.), *Interaction in cooperative groups: The theoretical anatomy of group learning* (pp. 120–141). New York: Cambridge University Press.

Palinscar, A. S., & Brown, A. L. (1983). *Reciprocal teaching of comprehension-monitoring activities* (Tech. Rep. No. 269). Champaign, IL: Center for the Study of Reading, University of Illinois.

Palinscar, A. S., & Brown, A. L. (1984). Reciprocal teaching of comprehension-fostering and comprehension-monitoring activities. *Cognition and Instruction, 2,* 117–175.

Palinscar, A. S., & Brown, A. L. (1985). Reciprocal teaching: Activities to promote reading with your mind. In T. L. Harris & E. J. Cooper (Eds.), *Reading, thinking and concept development: Strategies for the classroom* (pp. 147–159). New York: The College Board.

Palinscar, A. S., & Brown, A. L. (1986). Interactive teaching to promote independent learning from text. *The Reading Teacher, 39,* 771–777.

Palinscar, A. S., David, Y. M., Winn, J. A., & Stevens, D. D. (1991). Examining the context of strategy instruction. *Remedial and Special Education, 12,* 43–53.

Paris, S. G., Wasik, B. A., & Turner, J. C. (1991). The development of reading strategies. In J. Flood, J. M. Jensen, D. Lapp, & J. Squire (Eds.), *Handbook of research in the English language arts* (pp. 609–635). NY: Macmillan.

Paterson, K. (1979). *The great Gilly Hopkins.* New York: Avon.

Paulis, C. (1998). *Resource guide for improving MSPAP reading performance schoolwide.* Howard County, MD: Howard County Public School System.

Pearson, P. D., & Fielding, L. (1991). Comprehension instruction. In R. Barr, M. L. Kamil, P. Mosenthatl, & P. D. Pearson (Eds.), *Handbook of reading research* (Vol. 2, pp. 815–860). White Plains, NJ: Longman.

Pearson, P. D., & Spiro, R. (1982). The new buzz word: Schema. *Instructor, 91,* 46–48.

Perfetti, C. A., Britt, M. A., & Georgi, M. C. (1995). *Text-based learning and reasoning studies in history.* Hillsdale, NJ: Erlbaum.

Powell, G. (1980, December). *A meta-analysis of the effects of 'imposed' and'induced' imagery upon word recall.* Paper presented at the annual meeting of the National Reading Conference, San Diego, CA. (ERIC Document Reproduction Service No. ED199644).

Presseisen, B. Z. (1985). Thinking skills: Meanings and models. In A. L. Costa. (Ed.), *Developing minds: A resource book for teaching thinking* (pp. 43–48). Alexandria, VA: Association of Supervision and Curriculum Development.

Pressley, M., & Afflerbach, P. (1995). *Verbal protocols of reading: The nature of constructively responsive reading.* Hillsdale, NJ: Erlbaum.

Pressley, M., El-Dinary, P. B., Wharton-McDonald, R., & Brown, R. (1998). Transactional instruction of comprehension strategies in the elementary grades. In D. Schunk & B. J. Zimmerman (Eds.), *Self-regulated learning: From teaching to self-reflective practice* (pp. 42–56). New York: Guilford Press.

Pressley, M., Gaskins, I. W., Wile, D., Cunicelli, E. A., & Sheridan, J. (1991). Teaching strategy instruction across the curriculum: A case study at Benchmark School. In S. McCormick & J. Zutell (Eds.), *40th yearbook of the National Reading Conference.* Chicago: National Reading Conference.

Pressley, M., Goodchild, F., Fleet, J., Zajchowski, R., & Evans, E. D. (1989). The challenges of strategy instruction. *Elementary School Journal, 89,* 301–342.

Pressley, M., Johnson, C. J., Symons, S., McGoldrick, J., & Kurita, J. (1989). Strategies that improve children's memory and comprehension of text. *Elementary School Journal, 90,* 3–32.

Pressley, M., Levin, J. R., & McDaniel, M. A. (1987). Remembering versus inferring what a word means: Mnemonic and contextual approaches. In M. G. McKeown & M. C. Curtis (Eds.), *The nature of vocabulary acquisition* (pp. 107–127). Hillsdale, NJ: Erlbaum.

Pressley, M., Schuder, T., & Bergman, J. (1992). A researcher-educator collaborative interview study of transactional comprehension strategies instruction. *Journal of Educational Psychology, 84,* 231–246.

Richardson, J. S., & Morgan, R. F. (2000). *Reading to learn in the content areas* (4th ed.). Belmont, CA: Wadsworth/Thomson Learning.

Routman, R. (1998). Selected reading-writing strategies for L. D. and other at-risk students. In C. Weaver (Ed.), *Practicing what we know: Informed reading instruction* (pp. 377–393). Urbana, IL: NCTE.

Rosenblatt, L. (1978). *The reader, the text, the poem: The transactional theory of the literary work.* Carbondale, IL: Southern Illinois University Press.

Rovee-Collier, C. (1995). Time windows in cognitive development. *Developmental Psychology, 31,* 147–169.

Ruddell, R. B. (1964). A study of cloze comprehension technique in relation to structurally controlled reading material. *Proceedings of the International Reading Association, 9,* 298–303.

Ruddell, M. R. (1994). Vocabulary knowledge and Comprehension: A comprehension-process view of complex literacy relationships. In R. B. Ruddell, M. R. Ruddell, & H. Singer (Eds.), *Theoretical Models and Processes of Reading* (4th ed., pp. 414–447). Newark, DE: International Reading Association.

Ryan, E. B., Ledger, G. W., Short, E. J., & Weed, K. A. (1982). Promoting the use of active comprehension strategies by poor readers. *Topics in Learning and Learning Disabilities, 2,* 53–60.

Ryder, R. J., & Medo, M. A. (1993). The effects of vocabulary instruction on readers' ability to make causal connections. *Reading Research and Instruction, 33,* 119–134.

Rylant, C. (1993). *Missing May.* New York: Orchard.

Sadoski, M. (1999). Comprehending comprehension. *Reading Research Quarterly, 34,* 493–500.

Schatz, E. K., & Baldwin, R. S. (1986). Context clues are unreliable predictors of word meanings. *Reading Research Quarterly, 21,* 439–453.

Schoenfeld, A. H. (1987). What's all the fuss about metacognition? In A. Schoenfeld (Ed.), *Cognitive science and mathematics education* (pp. 189–215). Hillsdale, NJ: Erlbaum.

Schunk, D. H., & Swartz, C. W. (1991, April). *Process goals and feedback: Effects on children's self-efficacy and skills.* Paper presented at the annual meeting of the American Educational Research Association, Chicago.

Schwartz, R. M. (1988). Learning to learn vocabulary in content area textbooks. *Journal of Reading, 32,* 108–117.

Schwartz, R. M., & Raphael, T. (1985). Concept definition: A key to improving students' vocabulary. *The Reading Teacher, 39,* 676–682.

Scriven, M. (1976). *Reasoning.* New York: McGraw-Hill.

Sharan, Y., & Sharan, S. (1992). *Expanding cooperative learning through group investigation.* New York: Teachers College Press.

Short, E. J., & Ryan, E. B. (1984). Metacognitive differences between skilled and less skilled readers: Remediating deficits through story grammar and attribution training. *Journal of Educational Psychology, 76,* 225–235.

Silverstein, S. (1996). *Falling up.* New York: HarperCollins.

Simon, S. (1997). *Strange mysteries from around the world.* Madison, WI: Turtleback Books.

Sinclair, U. (1981). *The jungle.* New York: Bantam.

Slavin, R. E. (1995). *Cooperative learning.* (2nd ed.). Boston: Allyn & Bacon.

Smagorinsky, P. (2002). *Teaching English through principled practice.* Upper Saddle River, NJ: Merrill-Prentice-Hall.

Smith, J. D. (1999). *Mary by myself.* New York: HarperCollins.

Sorgen, M. (1998, October 2). *Brain research: Implications for teaching and learning.* Handout from the Maryland ASCD State Conference.

Sousa, D. A. (2001). *How the brain learns.* Thousand Oaks, CA: Corwin Press.

Spivey, N. N., & King, J. R. (1998). Readers as writers composing from sources. In R. B. Ruddell, M. R. Ruddell, & H. Singer (Eds.), *Theoretical models and processes of reading* (4th ed.). (pp. 668–694). Newark, DE: International Reading Association.

Stahl, S. A., & Fairbanks, M. M. (1986). The effects of vocabulary instruction: A model–based meta-analysis. *Review of Educational Research, 56,* 72–110.

Stahl, S. A., Hynd, C. R., Britton, B. K., McNish, M. M., & Bosquet, D. (1996). What happens when students read multiple source documents in history? *Reading Research Quarterly, 31,* 430–456.

Staples, S. F. (1989). *Shabanu: Daughter of the wind.* New York: Alfred A. Knopf.

Stauffer, R. G. (1969). *Directing reading maturity as a cognitive process.* New York: Harper & Row.

Steinbeck, J. (1939). *The grapes of wrath.* New York: Viking Press.

Sternberg, R. J. (1987). Most vocabulary is learned in context. In M. G. McKeown & M. E. Curtis (Eds.), *The nature of vocabulary acquisition* (pp. 89–105). Hillsdale, NJ: Erlbaum.

Stewart, I. (2001). *Flatterland: Like Flatland only more so.* Cambridge, MA: Perseus Publishing.

Stover, L. T, Neubert, G. A. & Lawlor, J. C. (1993). *Creating interactive environments in the secondary school.* Washington, DC: National Education Association.

Stover, L. T. (1996). *Young adult literature: The heart of the middle school curriculum.* Portsmouth, NH: Boynton/Cook.

Taylor, M. D. (1976). *Roll of thunder, hear my cry.* New York: Bantam.

Taylor, W. S. (1953). Cloze procedure: A new tool for measuring readability. *Journalism Quarterly, 30,* 415–433.

Tomlinson, C. A., & Kalbfleisch, M. L. (1998). Teach me, teach my brain: A call for differentiated classrooms. *Educational Leadership, 56,* 52–55.

Tompkins, G. E. (1997). *Literacy for the 21st century: A balanced approach.* Upper Saddle River, NJ: Merrill-Prentice-Hall.

Touchstone Applied Science Associates, Inc. DRP book link [Computer software]. (2002). Brewster, NY: Touchstone Applied Science Associates, Inc.

Vacca, R. T. (2002). Making a difference in adolescents' school lives: Visible and invisible aspects of content area reading. In A. E. Farstrup & S. J. Samuels (Eds.). *What research has to say about reading instruction* (pp. 184–204). Newark, DE: International Reading Association.

Vacca R. T., & Vacca, J. L. (2002). *Content area reading: Literacy and learning across the curriculum* (7th ed.). Boston: Allyn and Bacon.

Van Allsburg, C. (1984). *Mysteries of Harris Burdick.* Boston: Houghton Mifflin.

Van Allsburg, C. (1987). *The z was zapped.* Boston: Houghton Mifflin.

Vygotsky, L. (1978). *Mind in society: The development of higher psychological processes.* Cambridge, MA: Harvard University Press.

Wagner, R. K., & Sternberg, R. J. (1987). Executive control in reading comprehension. In B. K. Britton & S. M. Glynn (Eds.), *Executive control processes in reading* (pp. 1–21). Hillsdale, NJ: Erlbaum.

Walberg, H. J. (1999). Generic practices: Cooperative learning. In G. Cawelti (Ed.), *Handbook of research on improving student achievement* (2nd ed., p. 19). Arlington, VA: Educational Research Service.

Webb, N. M. (1991). Task-related verbal interaction and mathematics learning in small groups. *Journal for Research in Mathematics Education, 22,* 366–389.

Webb, N. M., & Palincsar, A. (1996). Group processes in the classroom. In D. C. Berliner & R. C. Calfee (Eds.), *Handbook of educational psychology* (pp. 841–876). New York: Macmillan.

Webb, N. M., Troper, J. D., & Fall, R. (1995). Constructive activity and learning in collaborative small groups. *Journal of Educational Psychology, 87,* 406–423.

Weinstein, C. (1994). Learning/Strategic teaching: Flip sides of a coin. In P. Pintrich, D. Brown, & C. Weinstein (Eds.), *Student motivation, cognition, and learning: Essays in honor of Wilbert J. McKeachie* (pp. 257–273). Hillsdale, NJ: Erlbaum.

Weisberg, R. (1988). 1980s: A change in focus of reading comprehension research: A review of reading/learning disabilities research based on an interactive model of reading. *Learning Disability Quarterly, 11,* 149–159.

Weisberg, R., & Balajthy, E. (1989). Transfer effects of instructing poor readers to recognize expository text structure. In S. McCormick, & J. Zutell (Eds.), *Cognitive and social perspectives for literacy research and instruction: Thirty-eighth yearbook of the National Reading Conference* (pp. 279–285). Chicago: National Reading Conference.

West, W. C., O'Rourke, T. B., & Holcomb, P. J. (1998). Event-related brain potentials and language comprehension: A cognitive neuroscience approach to the study of intellectual functioning. In S. Soraci & W. J. McIlvane (Eds.), *Perspectives on fundamental processes in intellectual functioning* (pp. 131–168). Stamford, CT: Ablex.

Wittrock, M. C. (1990). Generative processes of comprehension. *Educational Psychology, 24,* 345–376.

Woloshyn, V. E., Elliott, A. E., & Riordon, M. (1998). Seven teachers' experiences using explicit strategy instruction in the classroom. *Journal of Professional Studies, 5,* 18–28.

Woolfolk, A. E. (1998). *Educational psychology.* (7th ed.). Boston: Allyn & Bacon.

Yamashiro, K., & Carlos, L. (1995). Private school vouchers. Available: www.wested.org/policy/pubs/full_text/pb_ft_vouch.htm

Ysteboe, P. (2001, Spring). Literature and geography (grades 6–8). *North Carolina Geographic Alliance Newsletter 12,* 12–13.

Zabrucky, K., & Ratner, H. H. (1992). Effects of passage type on comprehension monitoring and recall in good and poor readers. *Journal of Reading Behavior, 24,* 373–391.

Zahorik, J. (1996). Elementary and secondary teachers' reports of how they make learning interesting. *Elementary School Journal, 96,* 551–564.

Zemelman, S., Daniels, H., & Hyde, A. (1998). *Best practice: New standards for teaching and learning in America's schools* (2nd ed.). Portsmouth, NH: Heinemann.